D0049559

ROMANS AND ALIENS

J.P.V.D. BALSDON

The University of North Carolina Press
Chapel Hill

Published in 1979 by
Gerald Duckworth & Co. Ltd.
The Old Piano Factory
43 Gloucester Crescent, London NW1

ISBN 0–8078–1383–4

Library of Congress Cataloging in Publication Data

Balsdon, John Percy Vyvian Dacre, 1901-
Romans and aliens.

Includes bibliographies and index.
1. Rome – Civlization – Foreign influences.
2. Rome – Foreign population. 3. Acculturation.
4. Assimilation (Sociology). 5. Citizenship – Rome.
6. Culture conflict. 7. Aliens (Roman law).
I. Title.
DG78.B26   1979   937   79–14471
ISBN 0–8078–1383–4

Photoset in Great Britain by
Specialised Offset Services Limited, Liverpool
and printed by
Unwin Brothers Limited
Old Woking

CONTENTS

PREFACE

I dedicate this book to the memory of E.A. Barber, L.R. Farnell, R.R. Marett and B.W. Henderson who were my Oxford tutors more than half a century ago, men for whom I entertain even more grateful admiration today than I did then, for in the interval I have discovered for myself something of the difficulties of teaching and scholarship. This book has been written – in intervals of gardening and cooking – in the seven years since I retired from active teaching in the Oxford College in which I was once an undergraduate and those tutors of mine were Fellows (and, indeed, three of them Rectors). In these seven years, and for many years before that, I have enjoyed the stimulating encouragement of Colin Haycraft, himself a classical scholar of whom those tutors of mine would have thought highly, who is now my publisher. I am grateful, too, to many Oxford friends, in particular to Peter Parsons, who has allowed me to pick his brain on papyrological matters, to Michael Reeve, who has vetted – and improved – two chapters of the book and to Peter Brunt who has helped me by his trenchant criticism of several other chapters. Oxford tutors and professors are busy people, and help of this sort is a real self-sacrificing kindness. I am more than grateful; as I am also to my old Greats pupil John Weale who, not for the first time, has sacrificed a great deal of his leisure time, lynx-eyed, to reading my proofs.

And I must express my appreciation of the inestimable privilege of access to the Bodleian and the Haverfield libraries in Oxford; it is because of proximity to them that I live where I do.

The purpose of the book is to enquire how Romans regarded other peoples and indeed how they regarded themselves, and how other peoples regarded the Romans; how they communicated and how they infected one another, given the marked differences in their background and customs. The title is not a perfect title, but the best that we could devise. For a similar book about Greeks and other peoples, 'Greeks and Aliens' would be a perfect title, because the Greeks divided humanity sharply into two classes, Greeks and Barbarians. The Romans, on the other hand, did not divide people sharply into 'Romans' and 'Peregrini', though in Rome the praetor who dealt with cases in which non-Romans were involved was called the Praetor Peregrinus. Some *peregrini* were Roman subjects, politely known as 'allies', *socii*; others were foreigners, living outside the Empire. A reason why the distinction was not as sharp as in Greece was that in the Roman world people were changing from one category to the other all the time. The bulk of recruits to the auxiliary army, for instance, were *peregrini*; after completing their set terms of service, they enjoyed a metamorphosis and became Romans.

Because the book covers such a wide field of different topics, I have thought it best to have a separate bibliography for each chapter, and this bibliography is printed at the start of the notes on each chapter. A learned friend of mine expressed surprise at the antiquity of some of the books which I quote; these are in the main doctorate dissertations of the nineteenth century, the sort of work which, with its close concentration of interest on the subject in hand, never seems to me to lose its value. Scholars have grown no cleverer in the last hundred years; it is simply that they have more (particularly in the way of inscriptions and papyri) to be clever about.

J.P.V.D.B.

Publishers' note

The author died soon after finishing this book. The publishers are grateful to Messrs F.A. Lepper and J. Weale for seeing the book through the press.

CHAPTER ONE

Romans, the Gods' Own People;
Rome, Capital of the World[1]

(i) Romans in Italy

Within the two extremes, the frozen North and the torrid South, was the temperate zone; and in this Italy had the finest position of any country in the world, 'for the land juts out in the direction which is most advantageous, between the East and the West'. Thus the elder Pliny; Strabo adds the geographical advantage of having Greece and Africa at its doorstep.[2]

Spain came second, with all the mineral wealth that Italy lacked – or, the elder Pliny would have said, refused to exploit. The minerals were there in abundance, he claimed, but mining was forbidden by law. It was because of all these unexploited minerals that wine and fruit in Italy had their delicious flavour.[3]

After Spain came Gaul.

The far East, like many other parts of the world, was out of the picture because its highly valued and expensive products were inessential for the good life, proved agents of corruption.

The most costly product of the sea is the pearl; of the earth's surface, rock-crystal; of the earth's interior, diamonds, emeralds, gemstones and vessels of fluorspar; of the earth's increase, the scarlet kermes-insect and silphium with spikenard and silks from leaves, citrus wood from trees, cinnamon, cassia and amomum from shrubs and costus from roots. As for those animals which are equipped to breathe, the most costly product found on land is the elephant's tusk and on sea the turtle's shell; of the coats and hides of animals, the most costly are the pelts dyed in China and the Arabian she-goat's tufted beard, which we call 'ladanum'. Of creatures that belong to both land and sea, the most costly products are scarlet and purple dyes made from shell-fish.[4]

Things that you did not find in Italy.

Still, East, West – from the Ganges to Cadiz, from the wealth and servility of the Orient to the warlike Spaniards and Germans – Italy was best.

This, a favourite theme of Augustan poetry,[5] was fit matter for the encyclopedia also, and the elder Pliny was breathless in trumpeting the virtues of Italy and its inhabitants.

Italy had abundant supply of water, healthy forests, mountains penetrated by passes, fertile soil, rich pasture and harmless wild creatures. There were wolves and bears, of course; but Pliny was thinking of lions, tigers, panthers, large and venomous snakes.[6]

The necessities of life were present in abundance: crops, wine, olive oil, wool, flax, young cattle, horses. The grain of Italy was praised even by Sophocles; its reeds made the best arrows; if mining was not forbidden, Italy would be even more productive than Spain.[7]

And what a people! In virtue, all the world over, Rome had no rival. She had produced more outstanding men in every branch of achievement than the rest of the world put together. Cicero had already stated that, by comparison with Roman, all other civil law was ridiculously amateur, because no other people had ever possessed *prudentia* as the Romans possessed it; the Roman talent (*ingenium*) was incomparable. Italy, according to the paean with which the elder Pliny closed his work, possessed outstanding men, outstanding women, outstanding generals, outstanding soldiers – even outstanding slaves.[8]

Roman success was proof enough of her enjoyment of divine favour. Opening up the world with all its bountiful resources, Rome was a second sun, 'Heaven's representative among mankind'. In a letter to the island of Teos in 193 BC it was stated that 'our piety is evident from the favour of the gods which we enjoy'.[9] The Romans were the gods' own people, in fact. 'Spaniards had the advantage over them in point of numbers, Gauls in physical strength, Carthaginians in sharpness, Greeks in culture, native Latins and Italians in shrewd common sense; yet Rome had conquered them all and acquired her vast empire because in piety, religion and appreciation of the omnipotence of the gods, Rome was a *nonpareil*.'[10] So Cicero. Other imperial peoples, including the British, have recaptured this particular form of smugness: 'Land of hope and glory, home of God's elect.'

Romans were the master-race, *populus victor gentium*.[11]

Partly under constraint, partly of their own free will, kings and peoples of the earth became Rome's imperial subjects, overcome by the strength and generosity of the Roman people.[12]

(ii) Romans on their own history

Rome had no rich and colourful mythology like that possessed by every city of ancient Greece. There was the Arcadian Evander from Pallantion (hence the name of the Palatine);[13] and Hercules had been in Italy on his way back from the far West, but – until, in the second century BC, Roman aristocrats set about constructing divine genealogies for themselves – that was all. There was no time when divinities had been about the place, as in Greece, leaving fairy-story romances as well as colourful records of fornication, murder, and other outrages,[14] nothing really before the arrival of survivors from Troy; and the Trojan war was not myth but history. If Mars fathered

Romulus and if the Dioscuri appeared in Rome with the news of the battle of Lake Regillus, these were miraculous features of real history, mytho-historical.

Though the Aeneas story, by which the best Roman aristocrats were Trojan, *Troiugenae*,[15] was heroic and glorious (if the treatment of Dido raised any doubts, it had to be remembered that Africans were notoriously sexy [see p.69]), the second, the Romulus and Remus, foundation-story – virgin birth (*she* said it was a god), wolf-blood, murder, the asylum, a home for down-and-outs, fratricide and rape – had little in it that was idyllic. Unfriendly foreigners might mock (see p.180, but the Romans themselves accepted the story uncritically and with sentimental pride, to show from what small beginnings they had risen in the world. Whatever the methods, nobody could doubt the subsequent success of the Foundation.

The motherly she-wolf was '*our* she-wolf', a lesson in gentleness to other beasts; she was 'the best of nurses'.[16]

The defeat of the fledgling Republic by Lars Porsena was converted into a Roman success-story with the limelight turned on the super-human courage of Romans, men and women alike, Horatius at the bridge, Mucius with his charred stump of an arm and Cloelia.

There was the sack of Rome by the Gauls, a humiliating episode to which spiteful Greeks, conscious of their own success in repelling the Gauls, were pleased to allude scornfully.[17] But, again, in the Roman history books glory outshone dishonour: the aged senators sitting with their staves in the temples, waiting patiently to be slaughtered; Camillus to the rescue.

In Virgil's *Aeneid* the highlights of Roman history prophetically portrayed by Vulcan on Aeneas' shield[18] were, for a start, the she-wolf and the twins and after that the rape of the Sabine women and the subsequent reconciliation of the two peoples. Then came the horrifying dismembering of the treacherous Alban Mettius Fufetius on the orders of king Tullus Hostilius and Porsena's siege, with its hero and heroine, Horatius Cocles and Cloelia. Next, the Capitol saved from the Gauls by the geese and Manlius. After that, a big jump to Catiline in hell, paying fit penalty for his crime, and Cato in a very different kind of after-life, regulating affairs for the pious. Finally, and in great detail, Actium with its heroes, Octavian and Agrippa, and its villains, Antony and the Egyptian queen.

Roman historians saw Roman history through the same distorting mirror.* When 'outrageous Carthaginian cunning', *infamis calliditas*, met its match in Roman deceitfulness, this was not cunning but prudence (*prudentia*).[19] In the steady course of expansion through

---

* Salvador de Madariaga, *Memoirs*, 1974, 118, 'The sincerity with which Americans believe that the history of their country is one of peaceful progress is only equalled by the profound conviction Britons hold of having always fought for the freedom of every European nation as well as for the freedom of the seas.' The Romans' attitude to the history of their own country was by no means unique.

incessant war, first in the Italian peninsula, then outside it, Rome was never the aggressor. All her wars were 'just wars', and that fact was exemplified, as long as expansion was limited to the Italian peninsula, by the Fetial procedure. Before a state was attacked, it was invited to 'hand back' its aggressive depradations, whether it had taken anything or not. Only in the event of its refusing to meet this reasonable request, was it attacked. Outside Italy, when Rome conquered a foreign people, it did it for that people's own good – the Gauls, for instance, so that they might be saved from the Germans.[20]

A remarkable feature of Roman history was its shamelessly pragmatic character. In a speech which Livy put into the mouth of the Samnite Pontius,[21] dishonourably cheated over the surrender terms at the Caudine Forks in 321 BC, the Romans were told, 'You constantly practise deception under the specious pretext of legality; 'Semper aliquam fraudi speciem iuris imponitis'.[22] From any standpoint except the Roman, nothing could be more true. Pontius instanced the Roman heroising of Cloelia and the other girls who escaped from Porsena's camp and swam the Tiber; what had they done in fact but break their sworn oath when they escaped?[23] What of Rome's salvation from the Gauls – the payment of a stipulated sum of money which the great hero Camillus, once Rome was relieved, recovered by slaughtering the Gauls as the money was being paid over?[24] Far earlier there was the utterly amoral conduct of Rome's third king, Tullus Hostilius, in ensuring that responsibility should rest with Alba and not with Rome for the outbreak of war. Both cities had sent Fetial envoys to demand restitution;[25] at Rome the Alban envoys were richly entertained and denied the opportunity of presenting their ultimatum until the news arrived that the Roman ultimatum had already been delivered and rejected by Alba. So, in the eyes of the gods, Rome was not the aggressor. The whole story of events following the Roman surrender at the Caudine Forks, with Postumius as a Roman hero, is a masterpiece of disingenuousness; when, after being surrendered to the Samnites (and so, theoretically, ceasing to be a Roman and becoming a Samnite himself) Postumius kicked the Roman Fetial, so as – in the eyes of the gods – to put Rome morally in the right when war was resumed, the Samnite Pontius reasonably asked whether this was some children's game that they were playing.[26]

Yet all this is in Livy; indeed, Pontius' speech is presumably a piece of Roman historical fiction-writing. There is a smug, uncritical self-assurance in it all, because, in due course, the Romans always won through. The girls won Porsena's admiration and he and the Romans reached an accommodation. Tullus Hostilius and the Romans emerged victorious over Alba. The Romans survived the Gallic siege and were not out of pocket. The Caudine Forks were avenged. Pragmatically, Roman history was one great success-story. And, ethically, the conduct of Rome could not be faulted – as long as you followed the peculiarly Roman code of ethics.

Success, anyhow, was indisputable evidence of divine favour. It was achieved in the only way in which true *felicitas* could be achieved, under the joint patronage of Virtue and Fortune.[27]

So that it was an outrageous slap in the face to honest Roman convictions when in 155 BC the Greek philosopher Carneades in Rome shamelessly propounded the doctrine that Roman success was not the result of honest behaviour at all, but of the pursuit of self-interest accompanied by injustice to gods and men alike.[28]

It was beyond dispute that private life in the early days of Rome attested the rule of *sanctitas* – *vetus sanctitas*.[29] The members of the ruling families were honourable men, unquestioning patriots, public obedience to the state matching the private obedience of a family and household to its master's *patria potestas*. There was no luxury, no trade. The greatest men in the state farmed their small-holdings with no more than a single slave apiece; all the food that Manius Curius required was a baked turnip.[30]

Then in private life at some time during the second century BC the rot set in, the consequence, some said, of the rich loot acquired from Rome's first conquests in Asia Minor, by L. Scipio and then by Manlius Vulso. Polybius dated the decline from the third Macedonian war; the historian Calpurnius Piso considered 154 BC to be the vital date; and Posidonius, followed by Sallust, thought the destruction of Carthage in 146 to have been the decisive moment.[31] The door was opened to avarice and *superbia*, to material extravagance and self-indulgence.

In public life there was a similar degeneration. Philippus negotiated with Perseus in 172 BC like a clever trickster, not as an old-fashioned honest Roman diplomat; this was *nova sapientia*, and did not please the older generation. And in domestic politics there was the start of a century of revolution, the senate at arms with the populace and the popular leaders, a new and sinister chapter in Roman history. Was this the blood of Remus calling out for vengeance? Given these awful consequences of success, had Rome's imperial conquests been worth while? Florus was to ask the question.[32]

Just as the conservative Briton today speaks nostalgically of the Dunkirk spirit, the lesson of Roman history seemed to be that Romans were at their best when seemingly beaten to their knees in time of war. The last century of the Republic was a century of declining morals, declining standards. After which came 'the long peace' of the early Empire, which was no less effective in destroying the Roman fibre. 'Now we suffer the evils of long peace,' Juvenal moaned; 'extravagance, a fiercer enemy than any armed foe, has taken us by assault, exacting vengeance for a conquered world.'[33]

The acceleration of private extravagance was beyond question. But this view of a moral decline in public life did not agree at all points with the records. What of the violent confrontations of Senate and populace in the fifth and fourth centuries BC during the long period of plebeian emancipation? And, as for trickery, it would be hard to beat the knavery of king Tullus Hostilius in the deception by which he fooled the gods and the Roman envoys alike and turned his aggressive designs against Alba into a holy war (p.4 above).[34]

The Greek Strabo took a different view of Roman history. At the start, he wrote, the Romans were simple fighters, as barbaric and uncultured as the Boeotians, but once they came into contact with civilised peoples, 'they devoted themselves to cultural pursuits as well as to the art of war and so established world dominion'.[35]

In viewing the past, emotion was more important than fact. The tyrannicide Brutus had to have more than the spirit of his namesake who expelled the Tarquins; he must be in direct line of descent from the first great 'liberator'. The first Brutus, however, had two sons and killed them both for their unhealthy political views when they were little more than boys and unmarried.[36] But why make difficulties?

And early Roman history was made to serve above all as a storehouse of edifying models of good conduct, *exempla*, for which purpose fiction might sometimes take the place of fact.

St Augustine listed some of the most conspicuous:[37] Lucius Brutus for a start; Manlius Torquatus, who executed his (brave) son for disobedience on campaign; Furius Camillus, who from banishment saved Rome; Marcus Curtius and the Decii, father and son, who sacrificed their lives in *devotio* for Rome; M. Horatius Pulvillus, who thought that his priestly duties took priority over the death of his son; P. Valerius Poplicola, consul in 509, 508 and 504 BC, who received a pauper's funeral; Quinctius Cincinnatus, who was fetched from his plough to save Rome; Fabricius, who was deaf to all Pyrrhus' temptations.

And M. Regulus, consul in 256 BC, who perished at Carthage a year later.

Regulus supplied two *exampla*, the second utterly fictional. First, when the slave who ran his less than five-acre farm died, he asked to be allowed to resign his military command so as to return home and manage it. Instead, the State assumed responsibility for the farm, so that his wife and children should not starve.[38]

Secondly, after capture by the Carthaginians in Africa in 255 BC, he was sent to Rome to advocate an exchange of prisoners. Instead, once in Rome, he spoke successfully against the exchange as not being in Rome's interest and then, true to his word, returned to Carthage and death in the agony of indescribable torture. His eyelids were slit and stitched, so that he could not close his eyes. Then, after periods in darkness, he was exposed to the full glare of the dazzling sun. Horace was not the only Roman to be moved by the pathos of the story to a transport of patriotic admiration. Yet Polybius, writing in the second century BC, evidently knew nothing of it. Somebody invented it more than a century after Regulus' death.*[39]

Roman history was full of heroes and heroines: Cornelius Scipio Nasica, chosen for his unblemished character to receive the image of the Great Mother on her arrival in Rome at the end of the second Punic war; a Lepidus sent to be tutor to a young Egyptian king; the consuls of 278 BC, one of them Fabricius, who warned their enemy Pyrrhus that his doctor was out to kill him; Virginius, the father of Virginia. Virginia and Lucretia were *exempla*, women to whom virtue was more precious than life, cases to be quoted in the rhetorical schools in defence of a young soldier who killed an officer rather than submit to his corrupt advances.[41]

There were the stock villains, Spurius Cassius, Spurius Maelius and Marcus Manlius, but their examples were edifying because they met with their due desert.[42] On the other hand there were the great killers who killed for Rome's good: Servilius Ahala, another ancestor of Brutus the tyrannicide, who killed Maelius; Scipio Nasica Serapio, who killed Tiberius Gracchus, and L. Opimius who killed Tiberius Gracchus' brother – to say nothing of Cicero, who dealt with Catiline and his fellows in 63 BC.[43]

That the value of history lay in its usefulness was a truism brayed by everybody in antiquity who wrote history, and Cicero thought that there were more and better *exempla* in the history of Rome than in that of any other state.[44] You appealed to the examples of history when they suited your situation and your argument,†[45] as in the course of your education in rhetoric you had been taught to do. Of this, perhaps as an imaginative *jeu d'esprit*, Tacitus has, in two successive chapters, given an extremely comic travesty.

In AD 62 the anti-hero Caesennius Paetus and his spiritless army were under siege by the Parthian king Vologeses at Rhandeia in Armenia. The Roman army had no appetite for a fight. They appealed to the *exempla* of the ignominious surrenders of the Roman armies to the Samnites at the Caudine Forks and in 137 BC at Numantia in Spain, 'and the Samnites were only an Italian people, while the Parthians are Rome's imperial rivals. Rome in the old days was powerful and people speak of it with praise; yet, when things turned ugly, the first thought of the Romans of those days was to save their own skins'.[46]

Soldiers on the far eastern boundary of the Empire who

---

* Perhaps we can guess the circumstances of its invention. A pro-Carthaginian history[40] of the first Punic war contained, unlike the Roman history books, a hideous account of the sadistic treatment of two Carthaginian prisoners by Regulus' widow in Rome. Her behaviour might almost be excused if her husband had suffered even more agonising torture at the hands of the Carthaginians.

† Unless you were an Epicurean, for there were no edifying *exempla* of men in pursuit of pleasure or the absence of pain, and this was a stick with which to beat the Epicureans, Cic., *De fin.* 2,67.

remembered the wrong lessons in the history which they had read at school.

So Paetus had to go, cap in hand, to Vologeses, to get the best terms that he could. Vologeses sent an emissary, to whom Paetus made a speech recalling the exploits of Lucullus and Pompey and he listed the achievements of Roman emperors in securing Armenia and appointing its kings. Nothing could have been more inept. 'You may have these fancy ideas,' the Parthian told him; '*we* happen to have the power.'

Under Augustus, Dionysius of Halicarnassus wrote his Greek history of early Rome for a Greek-reading public (see p.199), and the thesis which the book was meant to emphasise was that in their origins the Romans were not barbarians at all, but Greeks.[47] How, one wonders, did the Romans accept that thesis? According to their own tradition, they were not Greeks but Trojans.

Dionysius was a friendly Greek. Other Greeks, who were not friendly at all, had fun in pillorying the stories of Rome's foundation and early history (see pp. 180f.).

Laudatores temporis acti. Vetera extollimus, recentium incuriosi. Not only was history the better for being remote; a historian was the better for being dead. This obsession with Rome's distant past riled the historians who wrote about recent history and they protested. Modern Roman history had its *exempla* too, 'hearts just as pure and fair' as in antiquity. Anxious, like all historians, to attract readers, Tacitus hammers the point home, and so does Velleius Paterculus.[48]

Yet, in another mood, Tacitus, as a 'modern historian', indulges in self-pity. First he envies the ancient historian of Rome his subject, Armageddon writ large, while for Tacitus himself there was nothing better to do as a historian than to rake over the muck-heap of law suits and suicides under the most despotic of the early emperors. More than this, the historian of recent events had to watch his step, for there were a thousand ways in which what he wrote could cause offence. While, as for the distant past, who minded whether it was Carthage or Rome that the historian praised?[49]

Still, whatever Tacitus might write in order to attract readers, his general outlook was nostalgic; nothing was as good as it had been in the past. Courage, patriotism, public and private morals, self-discipline – all were on the decline. Oratory reached its peak in the Ciceronian age and since then there had been a sad decline: that is the note on which the elder Seneca introduced his *Controversiae* and Tacitus his *Dialogus*.

Our present age, unconcerned by its spiritual and moral degeneration, finds excitement in the technological advances of science and industry, thanks to which it enjoys delights – sanitation, artificial light and heat, mechanical transport, television, washing machines – which earlier generations lacked. Materialism is all-important, and by the criteria of materialism the standards of living are rising all the time. In Rome when the basic standards ceased to be spiritual and became materialistic, the new materialism affected all classes up to a point – the public baths, gladiatorial fighting and chariot-racing – but it was a stable and not an advancing materialism, little different at the end of the second century AD from what it had been two hundred years earlier. And the extravagant features of the new materialism were enjoyed only by the upper crust: the scents and tastes and silks imported from the East.

In the days of the Empire there were those who, looking back over the long history of Rome, thought of different stages in human life – infancy, childhood, adolescence, youth, approaching old age, senility – and, when the comparison was made, it was hard to escape the conclusion that the dynamic period of Rome's growth was over and old age had set in when Republicanism ('Freedom') ended and the rule of the Caesars began. Rome's infancy was in the time of the kings; adolescence (independence) dated from the start of the Republic and Rome's youth was the period of the great wars of conquest. After that, she showed signs of failing; this was the period of the civil wars, of the advent of old age. So far, so good, but what after that? How was a historian who wished for imperial favour to represent the age of the Caesars?

The elder Seneca, in a fragment of whose history we first encounter this notion of bodily growth, boldly called the Empire a second childhood, or rather a second infancy. Once more Rome needed guidance and there were emperors to control the body politic as in the early days there had been kings. Florus, a friend of the emperor Hadrian, reckoned the early Empire a period of enfeebled old age, but then allowed the cycle to start again and described Rome's 'second youth' in the time of Trajan. Ammianus Marcellinus in the fourth century found a neat way of avoiding offence. Old men in the evening of life, sensible men, good parents who have brought up their sons well, delegate the management of their affairs to those sons. And that was what Rome in its old age had done; it had delegated control to the emperors.[50]

What, if you took a long view and cast your eyes back over the centuries, was the Roman achievement? Until the latter part of the second century AD there was a simple and not unconvincing answer to the question: the whole civilised world at peace.[51]

(iii) The city of Rome

In Italy Rome had the finest situation that a city, in particular, a capital city, could have – near the sea and connected with the sea, but

with none of the strategic weakness of a maritime city which was in
constant danger of attack by sea.

Moreover, 'maritime cities are prone to a certain moral
degeneration, for they receive a mixture of strange languages and
customs, and import foreign ways as well as foreign merchandise; so
that none of their ancestral institutions could possibly remain
unchanged ... Many things, too, that cause ruin to states as being
incitements to luxury are imported by sea'.

So the younger Scipio in Cicero's *De republica*, expressing a view
which had the authority of Plato, Aristotle and others.[52]

Carthage, for instance. 'Geography, not race, explains the
fraudulence and mendacity of the Carthaginians. Thanks to their
harbours, they were involved in a wide variety of intercourse with
merchants and foreigners; and so, with their minds set on profit, here
was an open invitation to skilful deception.'

Cicero again.[53]

The same argument had been used in an elaborate speech given by
Appian as made by the consul Censorinus in 149 BC to Carthaginian
envoys as they recoiled under the final Roman ultimatum that they
should abandon Carthage and found a new city eight miles inland
from the sea. The history of naval powers like Athens and Carthage,
he assured them, was a history which inevitably culminated in
disaster. They should console themselves by reflecting on the
unbroken success of Rome, a city set ten miles inland from the sea.[54]

Stability was all-important, and stability was the quality of an
agricultural as opposed to a seafaring people, as Censorinus stressed.
The Romans were an agricultural people; if the Carthaginians turned
to agriculture, they might become stable too. The attempt to cure
pirates by turning them into farmers was made on the Illyrian coast in
the second century BC without success. Pompey tried again; instead of
executing or enslaving the 20,000 pirates whom he took prisoner, he
sought to make them good citizens by turning them into farmers.[55]

The selection of the site of Rome by Romulus was, therefore, an act
of genius; 'he must have had an inkling that Rome would in time be
capital of the greatest of Empires, for in no other situation in Italy
could a city have supported our present far-flung dominion'. Rome
was the home of empire and of glory, *domicilium imperii et gloriae*; it was
'the light of the world, the citadel of humanity'.[56]

In 390 BC, after the sack of Rome by the Gauls, there had been a
proposal that the citizens should migrate and make Veii their capital.
According to the tradition, an act of chance following on a powerful
speech of Camillus had killed the project, a speech in which – in Livy's
composition – the geographical advantages of the site of Rome,
stressed by Cicero and by the elder Pliny, were emphasised and, more
important, the deep religious traditions – Juppiter, Vesta, the
palladium – which it would be disaster to uproot.[57]

All over the city there were the vestiges of ancient history, vestiges in particular of Romulus and Numa, which, one may suppose, were pointed out to open-mouthed country-cousins when they visited their friends and relatives in the city. On the Palatine, carefully preserved as an Ancient Monument, there was the tiny wattle hut in which the Founder himself (or, perhaps, his foster-father Faustulus) lived, the *casa Romuli*.* You had only to refer to 'the hut', and everybody knew what you were talking about. Near the hut was the cornel tree which had sprouted from a spear thrown by Romulus from the Aventine, a superhuman feat on any reckoning. And, still on the Palatine, there was the Lupercal cave where the she-wolf had retired after suckling the babes and beside it a statue-group of the she-wolf and the twins.[58]

Down in the city there was the Regia, now the High Priest's Chancellery, but where Numa once lived. And here, in a shrine, were the twelve figure-of-eight shields which the Salii took out once a year in the spring and capered about with and which, with more capering, they returned in the autumn, one (nobody knew which) genuine, a historically attested flying saucer which descended from the heavens in Numa's time, the other eleven indistinguishable copies which he had had made.

There was all the mystique of the Vestal Virgins' little College and their temple, where was housed the palladium which Aeneas brought from Troy. In the Forum there was the *lacus Curtius* (not in fact a lake at all), about which there was one legend after another. Was this the place where the earth once yawned and only closed when the brave Marcus Curtius (and his innocent steed) leapt into it? Or was it the site of the swamp into which the Sabine Mettius Curtius rode and so escaped? Or what?

Not far from the Rostra, from which the orators spoke (the ship-beaks captured from Antium in 388 BC), was the *puteal*, the place of the 'black stone' which is to be seen today, the place where Romulus was buried or perhaps (if Romulus levitated and became a god) Faustulus – or Hostius Hostilius, grandfather of king Tullus Hostilius, perhaps. And nearby in the Comitium was the *ficus Ruminalis*, flourishing vigorously and carefully attended to, the sacred fig under which the twins were suckled; it had flown down here from the Capitol where it once grew, under the influence of Attus Navius, that master of augury and miracle, back in the time of king Tarquinius Priscus.

On the Capitol was the walled enclosure, the place between the two groves, 'intra duos lucos' (rather small for its purpose, it must have seemed), where the fugitives sought asylum at Romulus' invitation. And there was the temple of Juppiter Feretrius, repaired by Augustus, where Romulus deposited the first ever *spolia opima*.

All over central Rome one chapter after another could be dredged up from Rome's colourful past, even without all the resources of

* There was, indeed, a second on the Capitol.

today's *Son et Lumière* in the Forum.

Not unnaturally, therefore, the thought of moving the capital from the Seven Hills sent a shiver down every patriot's back, particularly the thought of moving it to the East, to Alexandria or to a rebuilt Troy. This, people muttered, was something which Cleopatra might have persuaded Julius Caesar to do and what, under her influence a victorious Antony would certainly have done, something which the emperor Gaius was thought to have contemplated. Where Troy was concerned, Horace made Juno issue a dire warning in her own name and Juppiter's.[59] And the city of Rome kept its unchallenged status as long as Juppiter reigned supreme. It was the first Christian emperor who founded a second (eastern) capital.

Polyglot and cosmopolitan, Rome was not only the secular capital of the Empire; it came also to be the centre of many of the Empire's religious cults. Nobody had ever doubted that the temple of Juppiter on the Capitol was the focus of the Roman state religion. By the second century AD Rome was also the centre of the cult of the Great Mother, which had been introduced at the end of the second Punic war and even of the cult of Isis, which the State accepted far later; it was to Rome that the hero of the Golden Ass came for his final initiations into the innermost circle of devotees. Fostered by Julia Domna, the Syrian cult of Juppiter Heliopolitanus on the Janiculum made headway until it was killed by the antics of the emperor Elagabalus. Yet it was from Syria that Sun-worship came to Rome, to reach its apogee in the third century with Aurelian's temple of Sol Invictus. And, finally, Christianity itself. Sanctified by the blood of the two greatest martyrs, Peter and Paul, this 'Babylon', a Babylon no longer, was the seat of the senior bishop of the Christian Church – a Church centred in Rome and a Church whose structure, with its degrees of subordination in authority, preserved the Roman imperial spirit of discipline and good order.[60]

(iv) The city populace

Rome was the greatest of cities, *princeps urbium*.[61]

Scholarly calculations of the size of the resident population of the city at the end of the Republic and beginning of the Empire vary from a quarter of a million at one extreme to nearly two millions at the other, with a preponderant view in favour of a figure between three-quarters of a million and a million. The slave element is generally estimated as having been in the region of 200,000 to 250,000.[62]

Except for the occasional rich freedman, there was no middle class in Rome. The number of the domiciled upper-class was very small, perhaps six hundred senators and two thousand equites.[63] It was this small section's disparagement of freedmen and of the city mob of which a satirist like Juvenal was the mouthpiece. This smug, self-satisfied aristocracy persisted, however rapidly its membership may have changed; still in the fourth century AD it existed, treating the rest of the world with a disdain at which others besides Ammianus Marcellinus chafed.

Rome was a vast cosmopolitan city, the same kind of magnet as any great modern capital city; for Seneca's account of Rome could be applied with little alteration to London or New York:

Look at the crowds for whom, vast as Rome is, there is hardly sufficient housing accommodation; the majority of them are aliens in a sense (*patria caret*). They have flooded in from the country towns of Italy, in fact from all over the world. And their motives for coming? A hope to get on in the world in some cases, the necessary condition of some public or diplomatic post in others; in others, self-indulgence in search of a good, rich opportunity for vicious living. Some come to Rome for education, others for the games; some to be near their friends, others – workers – because Rome gives them greater scope for displaying their skill. Or they have brought something to sell, a beautiful body or, perhaps, a beautiful voice. Rome offers high rewards for good qualities and bad alike; and so every sort of being has come here. Call them up and ask them one by one where they come from. Most of them, you will find, have left home and come to Rome, the greatest and loveliest city in the world – *but not theirs*.[64]

Whether from Italy, the provinces or from outside the Empire, some of these 'outsiders' were visitors, staying for a shorter or a longer period and then going home again. Others had settled, or had the intention of settling, in Rome. The first large influx had been of peasants from the Italian countryside in the agricultural depression of the second century BC, families which within a generation or two had become hardened – or softened – townees with no desire to return to the countryside;[65] after which, the invasion increased in size and variety.

The foreigners (*peregrini*) were likely to remain foreigners, for Roman citizenship was not to be acquired by such people except by decree of the Senate under the Republic or by individual grant of the Emperor later. They included, in the jaundiced satirist's abuse, tricksters of all kinds: priests of foreign cults, fortune-tellers, astrologers, creatures who delved into magic.[66] They came from Greece, Asia Minor, Syria, Egypt or even from further east, perhaps from India.

In the modern world the French are xenophobic and so, to an even greater degree, are the English.

Mrs Thrale, reporting on Dr Johnson:[67]

What would you expect, says he, of Fellows that eat Frogs? He was indeed willing enough at all Times to express his hatred and Contempt of our Rival Nation, and one day when a person mentioned them as agreeable from their Gaiety – I never yet, says Johnson, saw a Frenchman's Gaiety as good as an Englishman's Drunkenness ... We all know how well he loved to abuse the Scotch ... To one of them who commended the Town of Glasgow, he replied – Sir, I presume you have never yet seen Brentford.

In the city of Rome, slaves apart, there were the resident Roman citizens, some immigrants or persons descended from immigrants, some freeborn, some freedmen or of freedman-stock, mostly of eastern Mediterranean origin. These, with *peregrini* from the East, were the target of Juvenal's abuse: 'I hate a Greek city'; 'the Syrian Orontes is now a tributary of the Tiber'. Like Tacitus, Juvenal was an unrepentant xenophobe; Greeks, Syrians, Egyptians, Jews – he hated them all.* More than half a century earlier Lucan expressed the same cynicism. 'If the battlefield of Pharsalus demanded a soaking of Roman blood, let it at least spare Galatians, Syrians, Cappadocians, Galli, the outlandish Hiberi, Armenians and Cilicians; these, once the civil wars were over, would make up the Roman populace.'[68]

Sociological historians, working on the evidence of surviving epitaphs, are driven to accept Juvenal's general picture of the population of Rome and to believe that by the first century of the Empire only a small portion of the city-residents of Rome were of genuine Italian-Roman stock.

It has been estimated that of the city populace of 70 BC there were 40,000 adult males of free birth[69] and that in 44 BC, before Caesar unloaded 70,000 men from Rome on to his new colonies,[70] there were 70,000 men of free birth, together with about 150,000 fully enfranchised freemen and 100,000 who were informally manumitted (the later *Latini Iuniani*);† so that freedmen and their families – people of foreign ancestry – constituted some three-quarters of the city populace.[71]

It may well seem surprising that it was easier in Rome for a foreigner to acquire Roman citizenship through slavery than if he were free and independent. Indeed a character in Petronius' *Satyricon* states that, as a provincial subject, he sold himself into slavery, this being the easiest avenue to Roman citizenship.[72]

Cicero states, in a highly rhetorical context, that hard-working and meritorious slaves might earn their freedom after a mere six years of servitude, but this must have been exceptional and the case only with good household slaves.[73]

Even if the fact of their being freedmen or of freedman stock is not stated explicitly in their epitaphs, freedmen – usually of eastern Mediterranean origin – can be identified with some confidence by their third names, for instance Hilarus, Januarius, Primus, Felix, names which were either Greek or which freeborn Romans avoided (see p.154).[74]

It has been claimed that an examination of plebeian epitaphs from

---

* Martial (7,30) introduces us to a lady of easy virtue whose tastes were the opposite of Juvenal's: 'Caelia, you give your favours to Parthians, Germans, Dacians, Cilicians, Cappadocians. To you comes sailing the randy Egyptian from Memphis, the dark Indian from the Red Sea. Circumcised Jews, Alan horsemen – you will sleep with anybody except a Roman. Why, my young Roman lady, is that?'

† On whom see p.87.

Rome in the early Empire shows between 80 per cent and 90 per cent of freedmen, predominantly eastern; but it is reasonably objected first that the sample (the totality of surviving inscriptions) is far too small to warrant any firm conclusion and secondly that this does not reflect the proportion of freedmen in the city population because freedmen were more likely to be commemorated in epitaphs (because of their own or their family's pride in their achievement) than were poor freeborn Romans, for whom the erection of a tombstone could be a crippling expense. Even so, it may well be true that by the end of the first century AD 'most of the Roman populace had the blood of slaves in their veins'.[75]

This view receives some support from the evidence of the recently excavated tombs below the Vatican. Of 105 individuals named in the inscriptions (67 male, 38 female), 55 have Greek *cognomina* (Berenice, Chelidon, Chryseros, Ganymedes) and 50 Latin; 22 are freedmen or freedwomen, and the great majority of the rest are evidently of freedman stock.[76]

The city *plebs* was the bilgewater (*sentina urbis*), the dregs (*faex Romuli*),[77] in the language of the upper-class Roman, people living on the dole (free corn) and living for the games and public entertainments.

Nothing could be lower than the mob, but it had its gradations, and the 'Cockney' plebs (*plebs ingenua*) whose number was decreasing every day under the Empire was to be prized against the foreign slave households, Syrians, Paphlagonians, Galatians and the like, slaves today, Roman citizens tomorrow.[78]

Yet even the true-bred Roman of the city mob was a pitiable object in the eyes of his or her betters; Juvenal's woman wondering whether to throw over an inn-keeper and marry a man who kept a second-hand clothes shop is a good example.[79]

Even in the days when the city-mob was only beginning to change its character the younger Africanus abused it – when it tried to howl him down – reviling its members as 'step-children of Italy', people whom he had once taken as prisoners and sold into slavery.[80]

A more charitable, as well as a more sensible, view would have been that these were the people without whom there would have been nothing to eat, no shops, no public services.

Dionysius of Halicarnassus, a Greek whose approach should have been reasonably objective, was as horrified as anybody by the quality of many of those who secured enfranchisement and swelled the Roman mob. Officials of some sort – censors or consuls – should conduct a rigid scrutiny, he declared, and expel the discreditable characters *en masse*, send them off somewhere to establish a colony.[81] Not, of course, that, in whatever corner of the Empire they were planted, they would be a particularly good advertisement for the Roman name.

(v) Life in Rome

A generation and more ago the glamour of London was not diminished by the incidence of its notorious pea-soup fogs; nor, however loudly people complained, was that of Rome in antiquity by its noisiness, smoke and risk of fire.[82] Apartment blocks were tall, with several stories, up to seventy feet high in accordance with Augustus' regulations. Tyre, indeed, was the only city in the world to resemble Rome in the height of its domestic buildings, the result in both cases of the need to house a large population in a limited space. Remarkable, too, to the foreigner was the fact that so many houses in Rome had water laid on.[83]

As is universally the case, foreign nationals tended to cluster together for comfort and security and often, as was particularly the case with the Jews, for the sake of having near-by shops which stocked their exotic foodstuffs. The Jewish settlements were in Trastevere and also – thirteen synagogues have been identified – in other parts of the city.[84] There were settlements of Syrians on the Aventine (where the temple of Juppiter Dolichenus was built in the second century AD) and on the Janiculum, where the temple of Juppiter Heliopolitanus was built at the end of the first century AD. Egyptians lived largely in the Campus Martius, in the neighbourhood of the Pantheon. Trastevere was a low quarter and a smelly one; tanneries, for instance, had to be sited on that bank of the river.[85]

Like such modern capitals as London, Paris and New York, Rome was a shopper's paradise, a mart with the produce of the whole world on sale – to anybody who had the money, for living and shopping in Rome was an expensive business. You shopped in the Velabrum for food, in the via Sacra for jewels and in the Saepta as you would in Bond Street or in the Burlington Arcade in London today. There you could buy every kind of luxury article, even pricey slaves.[86]

There were no outstanding ancient buildings such as you would find in Greece, but, apart from remarkable public utilities (water supply and sewerage), in the way of modern building (from the early Empire onwards) Rome was the architectural capital of the world. There was the succession of imperial *fora* and of imperial baths, Vespasian's Temple of Peace, the Colosseum, Hadrian's Temple of Venus and Rome. The elder Pliny thought the Republican Basilica Aemilia, the Forum of Augustus and the Temple of Peace the three most beautiful buildings extant. Pausanias chiefly admired Trajan's Forum, particularly its great basilica, whose bronze roof he considered one of the wonders of the world. In the fourth century Constantius was particularly impressed by Pompey's Theatre, Domitian's Odeum and

Stadium (the Piazza Navona), the Pantheon and the Temple of Venus and Rome.[87]

All the world over, Rome had the kind of reputation which Paris enjoyed at the end of the nineteenth century as a home of extravagance and fast living. This was Dio Chrysostom's picture of Rome, and it was Lucian's[88] and, with pious abhorrence, it was the picture formed by the Jews and Christians: Rome was Babylon, the Great Whore. Indeed, apart from the whole Christian tradition, the nearest thing to evidence for the fact that St Peter was ever in Rome is the statement in his first epistle that 'he sent greetings from the Church in Babylon'.[89]

Life in Rome for the affluent was one thing, for the needy it was another. For them, as long as they succeeded in getting on to the list of officially registered residents, the greatest attraction of Rome lay in the fact that the government guaranteed a monthly ration of grain, at first (when Gaius Gracchus introduced the scheme) at below market price, from the end of the Republic at no cost at all.

For all Juvenal's vituperation and for all the nostalgia of Horace and Martial for the tranquillity of the countryside, none of them would have chosen to live for long spells away from the city. How could any educated man live – hide himself – in the provinces when he might be living in Rome? As Dr Johnson said of another great capital city, 'When a man is tired of London, he is tired of life'.[90]

CHAPTER TWO

Snobbery Begins at Rome[1]

Roman society was built on the idea of deference (*obsequium*) in the family as in the State. Whatever their age, sons and daughters owed deference to their father, who had the sanction of power over them (*patria potestas*); their wholehearted and sincere submission was an exaltation of *obsequium*; it was *pietas*. Freedmen and clients owed deference to their patrons. More than deference, the soldier owed unquestioning obedience to his officers, citizens to the magistrates of the State. In a class-ridden society all owed deference to those above them. Any other behaviour was contumacious, *contumacia*.

At the top were senators, 'Right Honourables', *viri clarissimi*, as they were eventually to be called.

Senators were moved by upper-class pride and self-assurance, *dignitas*. It was for the sake of his *dignitas* that Julius Caesar plunged the whole world into war in 49 BC. His *dignitas*, he said, was more precious to him than life itself; he could not have looked himself in the face if he had acted differently.[2] *Dignitas* was static; *auctoritas* was the same quality, become dynamic. And the senator had his influence, his *gratia*. He had a position to keep up, a position to live up to.

Loss of position, *infamia*, disgrace in the eyes of the world, was the worst blow that could hit him – to be the victim (however uninnocent) of criminal proceedings and to be banished from Rome and Italy (see pp. 104f.) or, in some ways worse, to live on in Rome under a cloud. Under the Republic a man who had been a senator lost his public reputation, suffered *infamia*, if, when – normally at five-year intervals – the censors published the official list of senators, his name was missing from the list. He knew the reason well enough, though he may not have been cited in the courts and certainly was not cited by the censors and given any opportunity of defending himself on a specific charge. His *dignitas* was shattered, and his social embarrassment must have been considerable. Was his post full of embarrassed letters from sympathetic friends? Did he suffer the hypocritical sympathy of his political opponents, his *inimici*, to whose number one or both of the censors may have belonged? Were there fewer invitations to dinner? Was it hard to explain himself when, at a time when the Senate was meeting, some ignorant fellow asked why he was not there? He could make a show of bravado, and threaten, as Metellus Numidicus the censor was threatened in 102 BC and Metellus Macedonicus the censor in 131, when the tribune Atinius Labeo, excluded from the Senate not for misconduct but on a legal technicality, was all for throwing him off the Tarpeian rock.[3] Or he could hit back by prosecuting the censor in the courts, as an expelled tribune prosecuted M. Antonius for *ambitus* in 97 and in 184 Lucius Quinctius Flamininus, a guilty man if there ever was, expelled with six others from the Senate by Cato, secured the cooperation of his distinguished brother, who was offended by the insult offered to the family's *dignitas*, in seeking to invalidate all the contracts which Cato as censor had let out. However in this case there was some comfort to the criminal's pride. When he was seen to shrink into a back seat at the theatre, the audience rose to its feet and protested, until Lucius resumed his place among the consulars, the place due to his *dignitas*. But popular applause could not restore him his seat in the Senate. What was the reaction of Manlius, another senator expelled by Cato on the ground that he had kissed his wife in the sight of his daughter, we are not told.[4]

Or he could shrug off such disgrace philosophically, recognising Roman political life for the snakes and ladders game that it was; he could go back and start again. So Lentulus, one of the senators expelled in 70, made a second career and had reached the praetorship in 63, when he was expelled as a Catilinarian and had his neck broken by the public executioner. C. Antonius, another of those expelled in 70, was luckier. He had climbed to the top and was consul in 63. But his luck did not last; he was soon to be exiled.

The senatorial order was no more united than were the gods on Olympus; there was the same in-fighting. A man had his political friends (*amici*) and his political enemies (*inimici*), and this in-fighting no more affected senatorial prestige than did the same well-attested in-fighting affect the prestige of the Olympian gods. Ares and Aphrodite were humiliated by Hephaestus, caught in bed together, and this gave the gods a good laugh; but nobody's godhead was affected.

The bluer a man's blood, the better – membership of a patrician rather than of a plebeian family. His ancestry was unassailable, if the founder of his family had come over with the Conqueror (Aeneas), if he had Trojan roots and was *Troiugena*. Better still, after the aristocratic family-tree-culture of the second century BC, many aristocrats could assert divine ancestry. 'My aunt Julia,' as Julius Caesar said at her funeral, 'was on her father's side (my own family) descended from Venus.' The last patrician aristocrat to be Roman emperor, Servius Sulpicius Galba, went back to Juppiter on his father's side and, on his mother's, to Pasiphae, wife of Minos.[5] At human level, a man should have consuls among his ancestry and so, in

Roman language, belong to the nobility, be *nobilis*.

The rest of the world was not allowed to forget a man's distinguished ancestry. There was the picture gallery, the *tablinum*, off the hall of a distinguished man's Roman house with the family tree on the wall and the death-masks of his ancestors, all of which were paraded at the public funeral of a member of the family, at first of male members and later even of female. And when at the start of his public career a young sprig of a notable family was a moneyer, free to select a subject for the design of public coins, he looked first into his own family history to find a subject worth illustrating.

All this background the 'new man', the 'man with no father' (like Cicero or, later, Augustus' friend and adviser M. Agrippa) lacked, and he was not allowed to forget the fact. There were no traditions in his own family: how could he make a good senator?

To attack an aristocrat on the ground of his ancestry was to attack him on a very sensitive spot. But, if enough research was done on his mother's side of the family, this was sometimes possible. Cicero's taunting of Piso Caesoninus, the consul who helped to exile him in 58 BC, illustrates the technique of such defamation. Piso's maternal grandfather was a businessman in Milan called Calventius (evidently in itself a comic-sounding name, like Bambalio – 'Stutterer' – the third name of Antony's third father-in-law). The man was an Insuber – indeed (why bother about a little obstacle like the Alps?) a Transalpine, a Gaul, 'Gallus', which was also the Latin for a cockerel and the opportunity for the crudest of Ciceronian wit.[6]

Antony discovered (or invented) a maternal great-grandfather for Octavian, a man who was African, ran a scent-shop and then was a baker at Aricia in Italy. Enemies of Vitellius put out that his family was founded by a freedman whose son married a prostitute, the daughter of a baker. And, nearer reality, Piso, the *bête noire* of Germanicus, is said to have despised the emperor Tiberius' children as being lower in the social scale than himself because of their partly equestrian blood (Atticus having been their great-grandfather).[7]

The emperor Gaius was so much repelled by the thought of Agrippa as an ancestor that he preferred to believe that his mother was born out of wedlock, from Augustus' incest with his daughter Julia.[8]

The 'new man' came from a family which had never taken any part, or any outstanding part, in Roman politics; even though it might be old, respected and wealthy, it was described by the aristocrat as 'sordid, contemptible and obscure'. But when the aristocrat declared that the new man lacked *virtus*, he exposed himself to attack because one of the most irritating qualities of the *parvenu* – like the elder Cato, Marius and Cicero – was that he was always comparing his own *virtus* with the *virtus* of the aristocrat's remote ancestors and contrasting it with the aristocrat's own degeneracy.[9]

So with a certain bravado the 'new man', launched successfully on a public career or having achieved a measure of political success, could boast about his newness, particularly in public speeches, because the Roman public naturally approved of a self-made man, in his origins one of themselves. Velleius Paterculus, who was such a man, gave examples of such success, using the (when he wrote, triumphant) career of Sejanus as a peg to hang them on. He wrote with attractive modesty: 'mediocritas mea', 'an ordinary man like myself'. But more often success went to the new man's head. A *parvenu* of very different temperament from Velleius Paterculus, the historian Tacitus, a man who achieved the greatest success in his public career, was a social snob of the first order; he could compete with the aristocrats on their own ground.[10]

So much for senators, who constituted an order (*ordo*) of their own; for the Roman social system knew only two orders, Senators and People – the official title of the Roman state was 'Senatus Populusque Romanus'. It was not until the late second century BC that a new section of the upper class – by definition distinct from the senatorial order – took shape, largely as a result of the legislation of C. Gracchus, and required a name. These were men with a certain wealth qualification (400,000 sesterces), whom Gracchus pressed into public service, to be jurymen in the public criminal courts if they lived in Rome, and to manage the vast imperial business of organising the collection of indirect taxes and custom duties. These last were known as 'Publicani', the jurors as 'Judices'. But for the class as a whole a more honourable name won currency: they became known as the Knights – the *Equites* – doubtless because they were the non-senatorial element in the eighteen centuries of *Equites equo publico*, in which at one time all wealthy young men had served as cavalry in war.

So, with Gracchus' legislation, the state – in Varro's expression – became two-headed. You had always been able to tell a senator by sight from his broad purple stripe and from his shoes with their crescent-shaped buckles. Now the Equites could be identified on sight, and this was widely resented. In the theatre fourteen rows (behind the seats for senators) were reserved for them, an honour perhaps devised by Gracchus and abolished by Sulla, but reintroduced by the tribune Roscius in 67 BC, and the cause of great popular indignation which on one occasion in the theatre four years later Cicero's oratory was called on to quell. Moreover the Eques wore, and often brandished, a gold ring on his left hand. In the Empire when imperial favour conferred the knighthood on some very strange people indeed, ex-slaves even, this was greatly resented, as we know from the elder Pliny, an Eques himself. It was a splendid sight when one of these upstarts was crucified publicly during the civil war of AD 69, gold ring and all. Believe Tacitus.[11]

Nobody loved Equites when they were Publicani, because nobody in history has ever loved a tax-collector. In their other business activities, as bankers and financial advisers, they were indispensible to senators (Atticus, for instance, to Cicero) as to all other rich people.

Equites might be blue-blooded, as truly patrician as any senator; indeed they might be close relations of senators. They might be as rich or richer. And they might lead the most creditable of existences, estate-owners, good and successful farmers, dabbling perhaps in local politics and assets to their communities, *domi nobiles*. They might be men of the highest culture.

Julius Caesar reduced their tax-collecting activities, but Augustus gave them public duties comparable with those performed out of Rome by senators: army commands (of auxiliary units, and of the Praetorian Guard, while senators commanded legions) and certain provincial governorships (Egypt, too important and sensitive to entrust to a senator, and the smaller frontier provinces).

But still, as long as they kept out of politics, their rise in prominence was acceptable to senators. Criticism was provoked by the man who threw tradition to the winds, remaining an Eques and eclipsing his betters (senators) by achieving the highest political power (and wealth) without responsibility. This was *ambitio praepostera*.[12] The bad Eques was the man who grew too big for his boots, Sejanus and, before Sejanus, Maecenas. Maecenas might be the descendant of kings, but he was sloppy, *mollis*. He didn't even dress decently, not bothering to put a belt on when he gave the watchword to the Guards;[13] yet, Agrippa apart, he had greater influence over Augustus than any senator. And what of the blatant conceit of Cornelius Gallus, recording his successes as Prefect all over Egypt, even on the pyramids, in language which might suggest that he was emperor and not merely an emperor's equestrian underling?[14]

Equites, of course, had their *dignitas*, like senators; and it was an important moment in social history when at the end of the first century AD they consented to work in direct subordination to emperors as heads of the great imperial bureaux which in the early Empire had been controlled by freedmen. In the third century they were to oust senators from all the major posts in imperial administration, command of the legions and of the most important provinces.

They acquired titles like senators. When senators became Right Honourables, *Viri Clarissimi*, Equites were *Viri Eminentissimi*, 'Their Excellencies', if they commanded the Praetorian Guard, *Viri Perfectissimi*, if they were members of the imperial secretariat, *Viri Egregii* and *Viri Splendidi*, in that order.

On a sordid plane, if they were in public service, they were graded and spoken of in terms of their annual income, as *ducenarii*, if they drew two hundred thousand sesterces a year, *centenarii* if they were paid half that sum, and *sexagenarii* if their annual salary was sixty thousand sesterces.

A beneficiary was under a lasting debt to his benefactor who, as long as this indebtedness continued to be recognised, was himself bound in return to offer protective services. In a continuing relationship which the Romans called *clientela* the benefactor was 'patron' (*patronus*) and his beneficiaries his 'clients', and as between Roman families the relationship continued from generation to generation. This had once been a valuable relationship in days when a patrician could count on the votes of his plebeian clients and in return protected their interests at law. This 'special relationship' existed too between a distinguished Roman family and the inhabitants of a province whose absorption into the Roman empire was largely the work of a member of that family (a conquering Roman general, for instance), or perhaps a member of the family had successfully championed their interest as a barrister in the courts at Rome. This was the relationship too of a former master to slaves whom he had freed, whose first two names were normally his own (see p.154).

By the end of the Republic this relationship as between freeborn Romans had lost its practical value. It was now chiefly for the sake of ostentation that the ambitious politician acquired what clients he could, obsequious attendants swarming round him as he went each morning from his house to the Forum in Rome, supposed evidence of his influence and popularity. In the Empire it was the function of such clients to queue up to greet their patron at his morning reception (*salutatio*), often in his bedroom. They endured discomfort (rising early, walking long distances through muddy streets, trying to keep their togas clean) and they were subjected to a variety of insults from their patron's contemptuous slaves and, indeed, often from their patron himself. And their reward? A small tip, a little food to eat off the premises (*sportula*), an occasional invitation to return for dinner, when once again they would be treated with every mark of contempt. In a Roman context, the insensitive vulgarity of the patron is understandable; but who were the clients who at so high a cost to their own dignity achieved so little material benefit? Were they decayed gentry, happy (like a Victorian governess) to boast of their association with the prosperous rich?

The freedman's relationship to his patron will have differed in different circumstances, sometimes close and friendly as between Cicero and Tiro and Cicero's brother and Statius, sometimes unfriendly, with the patron wondering whether to invoke his legal right to insist on his freedman's removing himself to the distance of a hundred miles from Rome (see p.102). All turned on the freedman's continuing usefulness to his patron, and on his deference (*obsequium*), which a cynic might have pronounced to be the only virtue that a freedman could possess. Once a slave, always a slave. When a slave was freed, he was released into a hostile world. If he asserted himself, he was 'uppish' in the eyes of his betters – arrogant, contumacious. Cicero was horrified by the airs which his brother's freedman Statius gave himself, and in the Empire there was worse to come when freedmen were admitted to the knighthood by emperors, given honorary magisterial insignia, when they made fortunes which put them in the top millionaire bracket and were even praised publicly, as Pallas was praised by Claudius, before the Senate; the disgrace of it all was enough after half a century to make the younger Pliny blush. There was the awful story of the bounder Callistus, sold in a job lot as an unsatisfactory slave by his master, then emerging as a powerful imperial minister and banning his former master from his receptions.[15]

Freedmen should clearly be left to enjoy their own society, as they did very happily in Trimalchio's circle of friends at Puteoli (Pozzuoli), a society reproduced with nice but by no means cruel mockery by Petronius, men and women who judged life by purely materialistic standards which some might say were refreshingly modern.

People were respectable or common, *honesti* or *vulgares*, generally a matter of birth; you were *honeste natus* or *ignobilis*. 'Drink up,' says Trimalchio in Petronius' *Satyricon*; 'my guests yesterday were more classy (*honestiores*), and I gave them less good wine than this.' The young roué Encolpius struggled to avoid making a gaffe when he dined with Trimalchio; he wanted to show that he was accustomed to dining in respectable company, 'inter honestos'.[16] And society at large was destined to crystallise into two broad classes, the *honestiores* (outside Rome, largely the town-councillors, *decuriones*) and the *humiliores*. In AD 368 or thereabouts the City Prefect Ampelius ordered that no *honestus* should be seen chewing food in public.[17] As between the two classes there were different penalties for the same offence – deportation, for instance, if you were *honestior* where, if you were *humilior*, you might be crucified or thrown to the beasts in the arena.[18]

There were a number of ways in which men might earn the disdain of their self-styled betters: by the clothes which they wore (see pp.219f), by the kind of Latin that they spoke – uncertain aspirates, an Italian or provincial accent or vocabulary (see pp. 128f) – or by their comic foreign-sounding names, evidence, it was to be assumed, of slave origin or slave parentage (see pp.154f).

In the judgment of smart Roman society, people sank in the social scale, the further they lived from Rome. A Roman municipal big-wig might be 'domi nobilis', a man of standing at home, but he was something of a rustic, unfamiliar with the modes of the capital. Or if he adopted those modes, it was just as bad. Sejanus' seduction of the princess Julia Livilla made Tacitus shudder; he was not an *adulter* merely, but a *municipalis adulter*.[19] Worse still was a *provincialis*, a Roman from the provinces, whether he was the descendant of a family which had emigrated from Rome or Italy or a man of barbarian stock who had received or inherited Roman citizenship.

The horror of the run-up to the civil war of 49 BC and of the civil war itself was accentuated by the fact that the closest and most confidential associate of each of the antagonists was a recently enfranchised *provincialis*. The attempt to put an end to Cornelius Balbus' Roman citizenship in 56 BC misfired and for Cicero eleven years later, humiliatingly enough, there was no other approach than through him to the absent dictator. On the other side was Theophanes, the only man who could interpret (and some said, guide) Pompey's tortuous mind, a nasty character, a Mytilenean Greek who had adopted Balbus, which doubled the horror of it all. A creature from Cadiz adopted by a creature from Mytilene, 'Gaditanum a Mytilenaeo'. And, as if all this was not enough, with typical Greek sycophancy, the Mytilenean was made a god of by his compatriots.[20]

'I was born a provincial and an equestrian and have risen to be one of the top people of the State', Seneca told Nero, and that was why he had the political enemies that he had. Successive admissions of Gauls to the Senate caused a series of nightmares to the best Romans. Cicero and his contemporaries were horrified by Julius Caesar's new Gallic senators who came, in the main, from south of the Alps. Nearly a century later the senators whom Claudius consulted were shocked by his proposal to introduce senators from northern Gaul. Was it not enough that Gauls from north Italy had battered their way into the Senate already? 'An parum est quod Veneti et Insubres curiam inruperint?'[21]

Yet these were Tacitus' own people, for as likely as not he came from southern Gaul. So he dropped the Roman aristocratic mask for once and reflected on the revivifying effect of the new blood transfusions, under the Flavians, of Italian townsmen, even provincials, into the Senate: Tacitus himself and others like him, good men and rich, no doubt (as the emperor Claudius would have said approvingly), but men who retained a peasant mentality, careful with their money and reluctant to squander it. 'Domesticam parsimoniam intulere.'[22]

At the bottom of the social scale, below even the provincial, was the *rusticus*, the country bumpkin whom, universally, the city-dweller despised. 'Uncultured rustic clots like you,' Apuleius shouted at his prosecutor; 'uti tu es, inculti et agrestes.' Were such people men, or were they animals, Cicero asked?[23]

Beyond the frontiers were foreigners, objects of scorn. Whatever Tacitus might choose to write in his *Germania* in praise of the great blonde-haired palefaces beyond the Rhine, they were men who wilted in normal Mediterranean conditions, unable to face the sun, drinking too much and going flabby (see pp.214f). Orientals were softies (as, within the empire, were Greeks). Foreigners tended to be governed by

kings, and a Roman senator, a *vir clarissimus*, betrayed his Roman
dignity if he did not address a king as his inferior: the young
Coruncanius lecturing queen Teuta in 229 BC; the young M. Lepidus
abusing Philip V of Macedon, whose royal breeding taught him to
behave politely in face of such rudeness; Popillius Laenas putting
Antiochus Epiphanes in his place, drawing a ring round him in the
sand and telling him not to step out of it until he had returned a
proper answer.[24]

Poverty was reprehensible if reprehensibly incurred, by dissipated
living; even so, a gentleman should respect the *dignitas* of the class into
which he was born; if driven to be a gladiator, for instance, he should
avoid fighting as a *retiarius*, bare-faced, recognisable, an
embarrassment to his acquaintances.[25] Senators whose fortunes fell
below the million mark (the lowest sum to qualify for membership of
the Senate) were to be commended if they retired gracefully from the
Senate of their own accord with as little fuss as possible. On the other
hand, if they belonged to old families and had children to guarantee
the continuance of those families, they should automatically be placed
on public assistance, subsidised from the emperor's private purse.
Witness the case of Marcus Hortalus and the emperor Tiberius who,
reasonably enough, did not believe in this kind of open-ended
subsidy.[26]

In the schoolboy's rhetorical exercises, interestingly, no social
barrier seems to have existed between rich and poor. 'A pauper and a
rich man were friends'; this is a not uncommon background to a
rhetorical problem in that world of educational fantasy. Or, if the rich
man and the pauper were enemies, their sons were friends.[27]

For a professional philosopher it was wrong not to be poor; how
indeed, it was asked, could Seneca be a philosopher and a millionaire
in one? Were not the heroes of early Roman history advertisements for
the virtue of poverty? Poverty existed in terms of material wealth, and
who was the real pauper? The man who was never satisfied with what
he had but aspired to greater wealth still, the *avarus*.* So philosophers
argued.

The squandering of their resources by the wealthy, as Lucullus
squandered his wealth, was generally criticised. On the other hand, a
man should live like a gentleman and entertain with a certain
assurance and style. Here is Cicero's disparaging account of Piso
Caesoninus as a host:[28] 'There was nothing in Piso's house to reflect
refinement, elegance or good taste – nothing, in fact, except for his
sex-life, to stretch his purse. There was no embossed plate. You drank
from enormous cups made in Placentia (in honour of his origins). As
for the menu, there was no shell-fish, no fish at all, only a lot of meat
and that not as fresh as it might have been. The waiters at table were

---

* 'The greedy man is always poor', 'Semper inops quicunque petit', Claudian, *In Rufinum* 1, 200.

dirty, some too old for the job. The same man doubled the parts of house-porter and cook. There was no baker in the house, no wine-cellar. Bread was brought in from a shop, wine from the wood. There were Greeks, packed five to a couch.' And there is Horace's extremely displeasing account of Nasidienus' dinner: good food, a bad cook, bad waiting and a vulgarly ostentatious host. But the most disagreeable feature of the dinner lay in the ill-manners of the two guests, *umbrae*, who were brought by Maecenas who, perhaps, to judge from this and from his unpleasant dig at Agrippa's undistinguished origins at a recitation described by the elder Seneca, whatever you may think about his dress, was not a particularly pleasant man.[29]

Culture-snobbery, on the other hand, anyhow from the early Empire onwards, except in Petronius' *Satyricon*, came not from above but from below. Vulgar ostentation of culture and the lack of it in great Roman households is attacked by people like Juvenal and, of course, by Greeks like Lucian (see p.186) and, later, Libanius. And Ammianus Marcellinus in the fourth century criticised a Prefect of the City for being less cultured than a *nobilis* should be, and recorded his horror that the reading of the Roman aristocracy was limited to the satires of Juvenal and the biographies of Marius Maximus.[30]

There is a nice account in a letter of the younger Pliny which, as told, is not snobbish at all, of going to dinner with a retired soldier living in the country, preparing himself with agricultural know-how in anticipation of earthy conversation and discovering to his surprise that the man was a cultured scholar, speaking Greek as fluently as he spoke Latin.[31]

At commercial level, cultural pretensions were laughable, in the circle of Trimalchio and his well-heeled (*succosi*) friends. The *Aeneid* was jumbled up with Atellan verse and Trimalchio's pretentious knowledge was in fact ignorant clap-trap.[32]

Moral snobbery too. Philosophers were people who, like Diogenes to Alexander, talked even to emperors as if they were dirt. And if we seek a parallel to the jingle about the Lowells and the Cabots – 'The Lowells talk only to Cabots and the Cabots talk only to God' – we find it in the sophist Polemo, who 'spoke to cities as a superior, to rulers without submission and to gods as equals'.[33]

The question 'What does your father do for a living?' could hardly arise in correct circles, because in correct circles his living came, respectably enough, from the slave-labour on his estates, which he farmed, as likely as not, by bailiffs, and from rented property, even including brothels.* Cicero's disparagement in the *De officiis* of all

---

* *Dig.* 5, 3, 27, 1, 'In multorum honestorum virorum praediis lupanaria exercentur.' English readers of a certain age will remember the question of Church of England property in Paddington.

occupations which enabled men to live, to say nothing of living well, is notorious;* he would have agreed with Bacon: 'The ways to enrich are many, and all of them foul.' There were grades in disrepute, with tax-collectors, brothel-keepers, actors and slave-dealers at the bottom. Auctioneers, too, had a bad name always. Dio Chrysostom disparaged occupations which were unhealthy, inactive and sedentary, luxury occupations which pandered to the rich, beauty-parlour attendants, interior decorators, actors, musicians, auctioneers, shyster lawyers and brothel-keepers. When Valerius Maximus recorded an act of pious generosity on the part of undertakers in Rome (they charged nothing for the public funeral of the consuls Hirtius and Pansa in 43 BC, because they had died heroes' deaths in war), he apologised to his readers for mentioning people so sordid, people whose only pursuit in life was filthy lucre.[34]

The attitude of high-class gentry to money-lending was not altogether inconsistent. Much depended on the part of the world in which your operations were conducted. Big lending operations in the provinces, even if they broke the law, could be countenanced; Cicero might be shocked by the scandalous loan made by the virtuous Marcus Brutus to Salamis in Cyprus, but that monumentally virtuous man Marcus Cato, Brutus' uncle, presumably approved. And Seneca is said to have had great sums of money out on loan in Britain. Nearer home, in Rome and Italy, you must not be a professional money-lender; he was the man whose occupation was not *honestum*, respectable, in the eyes of the elder Cato.[35] On the other hand, short-term lending and borrowing among friends was perfectly in order; it was the kind of thing that Atticus was arranging every day for his respectable acquaintances. If it was not for the existence of banks, people would be doing the same thing today – as, indeed, they did between a hundred and two hundred years ago.

Cicero made an exception for the professions of architects, doctors and teachers. These were suitable occupations for 'men of that class', 'iis quorum ordini conveniunt', for freedmen, in fact.

Men 'not of that class', the gentry, if their wealth vanished, had no option but to try to bamboozle a money-lender, to sponge on relatives or friends (even on the Emperor, if they were lucky), to become gladiators, if they were young enough, or, if all else failed, to commit suicide. At a distance from Rome, however, they might be driven to earn money, if the alternative was starvation. After he had left Domitian's Rome in a huff, Florus set up as a schoolmaster at Tarraco in Spain. 'What a terrible shame,' his friends from Baetica said; 'how

---

* In the *De finibus* (5,52) he refers to artisans as the lowest of the low (*infimâ fortunâ*): how remarkable that even people of that sort should be interested in history. (One is reminded of Polly in the *Beggar's Opera*: 'Even butchers weep'.)

do you put up with sitting in school and teaching boys?' Florus answered that it had been hard at first, but that he had become a dedicated teacher.[36] And there were men in exile who had no option but to earn a living (see p.112).

It is a striking fact that there was so little change in outlook through the centuries. One might have expected that with the expansion of the senatorial class to include, eventually to consist predominantly of, Italians and then provincials, depreciation of Italians and of provincials would cease. But that was not the case, for the City of Rome never ceased to be the social centre of the Roman universe, and those who came from outside caught its infection. Snobbery always began at Rome. Horace was a freedman's son; Juvenal was an Italian; Martial and Tacitus were provincials of no particularly eminent extraction. Yet all of them express contemporary upper-class Roman senatorial snobbery. Listen to Tacitus on the debate after the fall of Sejanus. Stern proposals were made by men with great names, a Scipio, a Silanus, a Cassius. Then Togonius Gallus spoke to the same effect, 'pushfully associating his own undistinguished name with the names of the great', 'dum ignobilitatem suam magnis nominibus inserit'.[37]

We have Ammianus Marcellinus' description of the top Roman senatorial society which he found in the fourth century AD. Rich, narrow-minded, uncultured and conceited, its members looked down their noses at an outsider, even a respectable outsider like Ammianus himself. 'Inanes flatus quorundam vile esse quicquid extra urbis pomerium nascitur aestimant', 'There are people who, with empty bombast, treat anything born outside the city as simple dirt'.[38]

In the modern world occupations once discreditable have come with time to acquire high social respectability – doctors, for instance, and solicitors. ('Dr Johnson did not care to speak ill of a man behind his back, but he believed the gentleman was an attorney.')[39] In Rome, on the other hand, there was perhaps only one significant occupational social change, when at the end of the first century AD and the beginning of the second Equites decided that it was compatible with their dignity to hold posts previously monopolised by freedmen and to be chief-secretaries, heads of departments in the imperial civil service.

CHAPTER THREE

The Roman Outlook,
1: Greeks[1]

With the Greeks the Romans had a love-hate relationship. For the broad mass of contemporary Greeks, the majority of Romans at all times in their history felt unbridled contempt. Yet at the same time, confronted by the spectre of Greek genius, the Romans had a profound inferiority complex; if they despised the Greeks, the Greeks – they knew – despised them as much, thinking them earthy, not 'spiritual' at all. They had not to wait for the witty writing of Lucian in the second century AD to discover this.

The Greeks had always divided and, Roman empire or no Roman empire, were always to divide humanity into two sections, Greeks and barbarians, and the Romans were on the wrong side of that divide. Translation from Greek into Latin was 'vertere barbare'.

The Greek division of mankind into Greeks and barbarians might be explicable as simply a division into those who were and those who were not Greek. But in Greek the word 'barbaros' had overtones, and its Latin equivalent 'barbarus' meant 'barbarous'.[2]

As the best Roman families had decided already in Republican days, and as Augustan propaganda (with Virgil as its euphonious mouthpiece) trumpeted, the Romans were not in origin Greek; they were Trojan. And Trojans had this great advantage that they belonged to the remote heroic past; they had not littered the eastern Mediterranean world with decadent and dissolute descendants who in one way or another got into the Romans' hair.

But still there was the Greek-barbarian smudge – and this friendly Greeks did their best to remove. Dionysius of Halicarnassus asserted, and tried to prove, that in their origins the Romans themselves were Greeks.[3] Aelius Aristides declared that the Greek/barbarian dichotomy was outmoded, that it had been revised and modernised into a Roman/non-Roman dichotomy.[4] Or perhaps the division should be a division into three: Romans, Greeks, barbarians.[5] Or go back to Eratosthenes and divide humanity into 'goodies' and 'baddies', with the Romans on the right side of the divide and some bad Greeks on the wrong side.[6]

Yet, for all this, the old division of humanity into Greeks and barbarians was instinctive. It was still made by Greek writers friendly to Rome – by Strabo, Josephus, Dio Chrysostom (even in his speeches on kingship addressed to Trajan), Pausanias and Galen.[7] Even Arrian made it when in the introduction of his *Anabasis of Alexander* he wrote that Alexander was a *nonpareil*, that no Greek or barbarian had ever matched his achievements. There is no need to see this as a dirty stab in the back at the Romans, at the dead Trajan perhaps, on the part of one of their Greek friends (see p.208), a man who was himself a distinguished Roman citizen.[8]

If you forgot about administration and law (a thing which literary men and scholars have always found easy), there was no doubt at all, as Cicero admitted at the start of his *Tusculan Disputations*, that Rome lacked an indigenous cultural heritage comparable with that of the Greeks. However much it absorbed from the Greeks (and, Cicero averred bombastically, improved in the process), Greece was where *doctrina*, where literature, started.

In the fourth century AD came the *trahison des clercs*. Alexander at an orgy had once said to a Greek that he must be disgusted by Macedonian ill-manners; now a Roman emperor, Julian, mocked things Roman in his admiration for everything that was Greek, to the delight of the talented Greek rhetorician Libanius of Antioch, who never thought of Romans as anything but barbarians, and was even shocked when in Syria prominent Greeks allowed their daughters to marry Roman soldiers.[9]

(ii)

Romans admired success and, while their own history was a continuous success-story, the history of every Greek state was, at the best, one of ephemeral glory and, after that, long obscurity. Rightly had Philopoemen been called 'the last of the Greeks'.[10] The Roman looked at the contemporary Greek world and despised it, with all the silliness, vanity, bickering and self-importance of its city-politics.[11]

In particular, Greeks were no good as fighters, being, as Tacitus thought, both idle and undisciplined.[12] On one of the first occasions when Greeks and Romans fought side by side in battle, the second Macedonian war, Flamininus held no high opinion of his Aetolian allies. Later at Alexandria in Caesar's civil war the Rhodian admiral was an exception: 'You could not find a Greek to match his spirit and courage; your standard of comparison had to be Roman.'[13]

Greeks were light-weights, unreliable, irresponsible, flighty people – *leves* (playboys), *molles* (sloppy); their national character was in sharp contrast to Roman sturdiness, *gravitas*. *Gravitas*, Cicero declared, was a quality born in Rome.[14]

Greeks were crooks – 'You scratch my back and I will scratch yours' was a saying of theirs – and they were sycophants who could never be trusted on oath to tell the truth, for they regarded the giving of evidence on oath as 'a great game'. They were light-fingered in money matters and, as Polybius himself admitted, they lacked the scrupulous honesty, particularly in the handling of public funds, which had distinguished Romans in their better days. With them, Cicero wrote, 'deceptiveness was second nature': *ingenia ad fallendum parata.* 'Loose and unscrupulous,' Lucian was to write later; 'that is the picture that the Romans have of us.'[15]

Indeed there is plenty of evidence of peculation and dishonesty on the part of magistrates in the public life of Greek cities and also in native Greek courts. This was a problem which confronted Cicero when he governed Cilicia under the Republic and the younger Pliny when he governed Bithynia under the Empire – and it has been suggested, not implausibly, that a clause in Verres' edict as governor of Sicily (which Cicero, of course, pilloried) was prompted by this very problem.[16]

There was too much talk, *loquacitas*, and too little common sense in Greeks. Verbosity – words, words, words.[17] On their public monuments the most trifling achievements were the subject of interminable panegyric.

Not only did Greeks talk too much – the world's greatest chatterboxes, Strabo called them[18] – but they talked at the wrong time. The learned Greek did not wear his learning lightly but was often gauche, *ineptus*, a bore. Greeks had a great intellectual conceit, *inanis adrogantia.* They talked shop, their own shop, in a manner offensive to polite conversation. 'Wherever they are and whatever the company, they launch into abstruse argument about the most difficult and inapposite topics.'[19]

A prize case of ineptitude was that of the Peripatetic Phormio who at Ephesus gave a lecture on generalship, with Hannibal present among his audience. Hannibal said that he had met many old fools in his life, but never such an old fool as this. The hysterical thanksgiving for Pompey's recovery from illness in 50 BC at Naples and Pompeii, predominantly Greek cities, was 'ineptum sane negotium et Graeculum'.[20]

Greek literature included works of sheer fantasy: 'Democritus'' book on the chameleon,* stories in conflict with ascertainable fact on the origin of amber, all shamelessly presented as factual truth. 'Graeculi quidem multa fingunt'; unlike the Romans, in fact, they had a genius for fiction.[21]

There was a pettiness about some of their customs, for instance that the equivalent of a Roman triumph should be accorded in his home town to an athlete who had won an event at one of the major panhellenic contests; that on his return home he should be allowed to drive a chariot through a breach in the walls and receive a public

---

* Really by Bolos, an Egyptian Greek of the third century BC, who thought to give prestige to his writing by publishing under the name of the great fifth-century scientist Democritus (*RE* III, 676f.)

pension for the rest of his life. But then the Greeks attached importance to a number of things (works of art, for instance) which in his heart of hearts the normal Roman regarded as being of trifling importance (see p.177).[22]

The dreadful thing about the Greeks was that they were so clever, thinking and talking twice as fast as any Roman who confronted them.[23] Brainy Greeks, delighting in the exercise of proving a thesis and then, by clever argument, destroying it, were capable of proving that black was white, like the philosopher-diplomats from Athens in 155 BC (see p.5), or they would go off at a tangent and raise irrelevant questions of principle. When the Aetolians surrendered 'to the Roman faith' – surrendered unconditionally – in 191 BC, the Roman commander demanded the handing over of their politicians. To which the Aetolian envoy answered, 'But this demand is in keeping neither with Justice nor with Greek Tradition.' 'There you go,' the exasperated M. Acilius answered, 'playing the Greek, talking about Honour and Duty.'[24] (On this incident, see also p.124.)

There was also Greek cultural conceit, *insolens Graecia*. Greeks were aware that the achievement of no other people could match theirs, whether in literature or in art; and culturally the Romans gave them plenty to laugh or to sneer at (see p.176). They were just a little too much interested in themselves, in the view of many Romans. Not enough was made of the German Arminius in their history books, Tacitus felt, 'because Greeks admire nothing that is not Greek'. Josephus makes the same criticism: rather than interest themselves in a startlingly important contemporary event, the war of Vespasian and Titus against the Jews, Greek historians preferred to write accounts of ancient history, on which books – and far better books – had already been published.[25]

(iii)

To Rome they exported both their practices and themselves.

One of the earliest impressions created by the Greeks on the Italian mainland and in Sicily, which had long been notorious in Greece itself for such a style of living, was of base self-indulgence in private life – feasting, drinking, whoring; and the Romans had a word for this kind of living, *pergraecari*, 'to play the Greek', a word understood by Plautus' audiences but which soon went out of use (because, the moralists would have said, the infection spread quickly to Italy and decadent youth could be said to be 'playing the Roman' as much as 'playing the Greek'). And in these early (second century BC) days, repeating Greek verses was for a Roman something like telling dirty stories.[26]

Greek influence was corrupting and, at the worst, the Romans returned the corruption to the Greeks – with interest. It was from the Greeks that male Roman youth learnt to strip naked at the baths and at exercise. Romans then went further and, in mixed baths presumably, nudism was practised by men and women in company, a debased habit which, in its turn, spread from Rome to Greece; so Plutarch states.[27]

In the view of the elder Cato, who was censor in that year, the corruption which was to undermine and destroy conventional Roman morality had arrived already in 184 BC:* homosexuality (which Cicero also believed to be a by-product of nudism and of Greek origin, in spite of the fact that the practice was recorded in Rome from a time earlier than Rome's entry into the Greek world) and other sexual profligacy. Fantastic sums were paid for an attractive girl, ten thousand sesterces and more for a slave-boy under twenty. So Cato imposed a thumpingly heavy tax on such purchases. This was not, in the event, a particularly effective deterrent.[28]

A generation after his censorship Cato was still on the warpath, and his fear of Greek infection was shared by another conservative statesman, Scipio Nasica Corculum. Dangerous encouragement was given to free thinking by the presence in Rome in 155 BC of the philosopher-diplomats from Athens; so Cato ensured their quick departure. Then the censors of 154 let out a contract for the building of a permanent stone theatre in Rome. Every Greek city had a permanent stone theatre, and what use did its citizens make of it? To sit down day after day for their footling, ineffective public debates. Public business should, on the contrary, be dispatched with responsible expedition by men standing on their feet. So Nasica declared war on the project, and with success. The building, which had already started, was dismantled; its material was sold by auction, and the Senate resolved that no such building should ever be erected within a mile of Rome – 'one of the most splendid illustrations of public feeling in history', Velleius Paterculus thought. The resolution was effective for nearly a century, until Pompey.[29]

First among Greek demoralising exports were the baths and the palaestra, Greek exercises and public games.

Greek exercises and physical training – wrestling, discus-throwing, hoop-trundling (to say nothing of 'foreign exercises like rolling in the mud in order to stimulate thirst')[30] – were contrasted unfavourably with traditional upper-class Roman exercises like riding and hunting and, generation after generation, they were sneeringly abused by old-fashioned Romans on the ridiculous ground that they made men soft. 'Gymnasiis indulgent Graeculi,' Trajan wrote to the younger Pliny.[31] There was greater truth in the claim that they did not fit men for 'the long slog' and so were not the best of training for an infantry soldier.[32] This abuse of Greek athletics is monotonously repeated by a whole succession of Roman writers: Horace, Seneca, Lucan (in a highly

---

* See p 5 for differing views of when the rot set in.

rhetorical speech put into Caesar's mouth on the eve of Pharsalus) and the elder Pliny. 'The Greeks, from whom every degenerate practice originates, turn the use of oil to luxury by spreading the habit of using it in the gymnasia.' 'Young Romans now increase their bodily strength at the expense of character.' The younger Pliny joined the chorus: 'In these days when physical training instructors are no longer old soldiers with military decorations, but Greeklings, *Graeculi magistri.*'[33]

Public games in the Greek fashion met similar criticism; 'accita lascivia.' So far from consisting of the ennobling spectacle of men killing one another or slaughtering wild beasts, they involved sloppy events like oratory, poetry-reading and music, together with athletic events in which men ran completely naked, while in Roman games, as Dionysius of Halicarnassus records approvingly, men wore loin-cloths. Augustus had introduced such games to Rome; so did Nero and, after him, Domitian – in both cases as 'quinquennial' events – and Gordian III. The younger Pliny was delighted when Trajan's Privy Council invalidated a legacy at Vienna in Gaul and put an end to the holding of such games there. 'Would that they could be abolished at Rome too.' Tacitus dilated on the subject in connexion with Nero's new games, giving the arguments advanced in favour and, by a minority, against. The arguments of the critics are a near-approach to imbecility. They deplored the fact that theatrical performances had ever been introduced to Rome and, because Nero's games continued into the night, conceived of their degeneration into a debased sexual orgy. 'What, in all that glare of artificial light?' the advocates of the games retorted. In fact, as Tacitus admitted, the new games took place with very little fuss and excitement. There was no pantomime-dancing, the only thing the public cared about; so there were no scenes of disorder.[34]

Everything in its proper place. Where the traditional games held in Greece were concerned, the Romans were delighted and flattered in the early days when they were first accepted as competitors – at the Isthmian Games in 228 BC. An Italian was victor at Lebadea in 220 BC.

But soon the great Greek festivals (the Olympic, Pythian, Isthmian and Nemean) lapsed and lost a great deal of their international flavour until revived under imperial encouragement, first by Augustus, later – with typical idiosyncrasy – by Nero and finally, with genuine enthusiasm, by Hadrian and Antoninus Pius. New games (some ephemeral) had sprung up in some three hundred different places in mainland Greece and Asia Minor, offering prizes more substantial than the bare crown of leaves offered at the Big Four. Professional athletes travelled from one engagement to another and if particular games, like the Big Four, were declared 'eiselastic', the victor returned home to drive a chariot through a breach in the walls, in the anticipation of receiving a pension for life from the community.

Training had become a science and, according to Galen, a very bad science. Philostratus went further, attributing some of the responsibility to the medical profession which had introduced a four-day training system which, whatever its theoretical merits, led athletes to eat far too much food at the wrong times. Seneca had written about athletic training in the same disparaging terms.[35]

As for the baths, the one advance in civilisation whose benefits were enjoyed by men and women of all classes, Seneca drives himself to such a pitch of absurdity that he can accord nostalgic praise to Scipio's bath house, still after two and a half centuries on exhibition to tourists, because it was so dark and squalid.[36]

Juvenal deplored the fact that certain Roman women thought it smart to look Greek and to talk Greek rather than Latin. Some of the language which he deplored was no doubt the language of Greek prostitutes; in other cases, too, this adoption of foreign speech and manner was thought by Roman women, however mistakenly, to make them appear younger than their true age.[37]

The Greeks exported professional expertise – *doctrina*. By the end of the Republic practically the whole of Roman education was in their hands – grammar, rhetoric and philosophy. At first there was opposition. Two Epicurean philosophers were expelled in 173 BC; in 161 there was an expulsion of philosophers and rhetoricians. But Carneades and the other two Athenian philosophers made an abiding mark when they visited Rome between 160 and 150. And when censorial disapproval was expressed in 92 BC, it was of Latin rhetoricians who, it was claimed, lacked the broad cultural basis of their Greek counterparts and were simply tricksters, encouraging their pupils to be impudent idlers. It was, anyhow, a political as much as a cultural issue, a side-blow at Marius who knew no Greek and was not particularly embarrassed by the fact. Latin teachers were not put out of business; one of them was the 'Auctor ad Herennium'.[38]

The profession which above all others has always been vulnerable to ignorant criticism, medicine, was almost exclusively a Greek preserve, and was thought to be incompatible with Roman *gravitas*. The first Greek doctor arrived in Rome in 219 BC; he came from the Peloponnese and was called Agatharchos. He started well, being given Roman citizenship and a surgery at public expense, but, so brutal was his use of the knife and the hot iron that he was given the name Butcher (Carnifex).[39]

Some Greek doctors had a further taint in that they had been educated in Egypt, in the excellent medical school of Alexandria. Doctors were Greek, and the use of the Greek language in medicine was an offensive status-symbol. Cato in one generation* and the elder

---

* Cato had the half-baked idea that the Hippocratic oath prevented Greek doctors from treating 'barbarians' (which the Romans, of course, were).

Pliny several generations later launched out at Greek doctors, 'the only people in the world who can do murder and get away with it'. Others too. Why did the Emperor Tiberius live so long? Because he kept out of the doctors' clutches.[40]

Cato and Pliny looked at the medical world with a layman's eyes and were shocked. They would have been more deeply shocked still if they had known the secrets of the profession, the intrigue, caballing and in-fighting which is revealed to us by rich, skilful and cantankerous doctor Galen, particularly in his book on Prognosis.[41] Success had its risks as well as failure. A clever young doctor, making his reputation, was found poisoned. Antonius Musa, Augustus' successful doctor, failed to save the life of Marcellus and was never heard of again. And there was Martial's doctor who, with no significant change, abandoned medicine and turned undertaker.[42]

Whose skilled hand – according to rumour – finished off the poisoning of the emperor Claudius, when the poisoned mushrooms proved anything but fatal? His doctor, of course, C. Stertinius Xenophon, *so it was said*. He came from the best medical background, the island of Cos and, after distinguished military service in the invasion of Britain and other employment at Court, he joined his brother Q. Stertinius, who was already established as Court doctor. Though his brother complained of his salary (half a million sesterces a year), they built up considerable private fortunes and, unaffected by malicious rumour about the circumstances of Claudius' death, Xenophon lived in prosperous retirement in Cos, incumbent of a priesthood, greatly respected by his fellow-citizens, and rightly; for, thanks to his influence with Claudius, the island paid no taxes.[43]

In the Roman imperial civil service Greeks quickly made their mark, meddling in, even controlling, politics and administration, making fortunes for themselves (Narcissus was worth four hundred million sesterces, Pallas three hundred million),[44] achieving prominence in the best Roman society, honoured even with magisterial decorations.[45] Efficient they might be; but they were also, of course, corrupt. Who could doubt it?

They were freedmen, these civil servants, and in the common disparagement of freedmen the Greek origin of the most prominent of them aggravated their offensiveness. Pallas boasted royal blood, for kings of Arcadia were, supposedly, among his forebears (the three successive wives of his brother Felix were all princesses). In private households, too, the Greek freedman easily gave offence, like Milichus, who betrayed his master Scaevinus and the whole Pisonian conspiracy to Nero; he assumed the *cognomen* Saviour (Sôter), a title of Hellenistic kings.[46]

In the social rat-race of imperial Rome Greeks edged deserving Romans out of position. That was why, victim of an almost universal xenophobia, Juvenal* so much disliked the Greeks. They were sharp-

---

* Juvenal was, it appears, an 'authoritarian personality', such a personality being

witted, quick to come up with an apt remark (*ingenium velox, sermo promptus*); they were Jacks of All Trades (*omnia novit Graeculus esuriens*); they were sycophants and clever sycophants at that; they were actors (*natio comoeda est*), the playboys of the ancient world.[47]

Greeks were spoken of disparagingly, not as Hellenes or Greeks (*Graeci*), but as 'Graeculi'. This word the most cultured of Romans like Cicero used naturally with little thought, it seems, for the offence which it could cause.* Petronius even devised 'Graeculio'. The phrenetic Cato might have said that they only received their deserts, since in early days Greeks referred to Romans not as Oscans but as 'Opici', clowns.[48]

But when, after the defeat of the Achaean League in 146 BC, Greece was made a province, it was called Achaea by the Romans, not Hellas or Graecia.

(iv)

Still, if you thought or spoke seriously of Greeks, all this was obviously less than half the story.

Apart from the treasure-house of classical Greek literature, Roman literature and education themselves were based on Greek, and no educated Roman could deny the fact; Greece was the home of *humanitas*; and even in the contemporary world the *humanitas* of the Greek set him apart from the *barbarae nationes*.[49]

There were three ways out of the dilemma.

It could be claimed that Greeks were part-good and part-bad, an amalgam of contrasting qualities. On the good side were their literature and aesthetic culture, their attractive conversational qualities, the sharpness of their minds, their oratorical gifts; on the other, their innate dishonesty, the fact that they had no respect for truth or for the sanctity of oaths.[50]

The second way out of the dilemma was to draw a sharp contrast between ancient Greece – 'Graecia vetus', the home of *humanitas* – and modern Greece, 'iam languens Graecia'.[51] Contempt for contemporary Greeks should not blind a man to the magnificence of the Greek past. This, according to report, was expressed crudely by Sulla and by Caesar when, in showing leniency to Athens, a city which had fought against them, they said, 'You have your fathers to thank for this, not yourselves.' Cicero revered the past of the Greeks and the younger Pliny thought it entitled contemporary Greeks to

characterised by general ethnocentrism, also by excessive conformity, rigidity, concern with status, a tendency to see the world as harsh and unfriendly and an inclination to favour strong punishment of deviants and offenders. See 'International Relations', *Encycl. Brit.*, ed. 1964, quoted by T. Reekmans, 'Juvenal's views on social change', *Anc. Soc.* 2, 1971, 161, n.153.

* 'Poenulus', for a Carthaginian, was similarly disparaging, Cic., *Defin.* 4, 56.

particularly considerate treatment. When Maximus was commissioned by Trajan to order the affairs of Greece, Pliny begged him to respect the gods of the Greeks, their ancient glory, their old age. Germanicus, attended by only one lictor when in Athens in AD 18 showed his respect for the ancient history of this allied city, and few Romans would have had the mannerless effrontery to abuse Athenians for their past and present alike as Cn. Piso did when he arrived hot on the heels of Germanicus and called the Athenians to their faces, 'the dregs of the earth'.[52]

Philosophy itself reflected the decline. Epicureanism, the doctrine that pleasure was the highest good, was in Cicero's view a marked deterioration from the teaching of the great Greek philosophers, Plato and Aristotle.[53]

At the same time, certain of the weaknesses of the Greeks were congenital and could be traced back even to the Greece of its great days; in ancient Athens 'absolute power was in the hands of the ignorant, inexperienced mob'.[54] Greek democratic government was at fault. So far from being controlled by the system of checks and balances which Polybius admired in Rome, policy emerged from the impetuosity of unprepared and ignorant assemblies. Such assemblies were responsible not only for the chaotic policies which had caused such a series of headaches to Rome in the first half of the second century BC, but, far earlier, had destroyed the glory of Greece in its golden age, promoting idiotic projects like the Sicilian Expedition which had brought Athens to her knees, exiling good politicians and replacing them by bad.

In the eyes of the upper-class Roman, Greek politics exemplified democracy gone mad.[55] Decisions were taken by the *faex*, while the better men, the men of property, *inter suos nobiles*, men whose conservative instincts resembled those of Roman capitalists themselves, did not, or could not, make their influence felt.

Under Roman control the effective power of the Greek assemblies ended; in some cities they still formally elected magistrates and ratified legislation, but only to the degree of approving the list of candidates and such other business as was put before them.[56]

Thirdly it was possible to draw a distinction between contemporary Greeks themselves, between 'good Greeks' and 'bad Greeks'.

Greeks themselves, of course, in their compartmentalised city-state existence, had never been uncritical of other Greeks. A Rhodian, representative of a state which in less troubled times was the object of widespread admiration, had said in the Senate in 167 BC, 'Some people are irascible, some headstrong, others pusillanimous. Some drink too much and some are over-sexed. The Athenians are traditionally impetuous and indulge in bold enterprises which are beyond their power; Spartans procrastinate. Nor can I deny that, as a whole, Greeks living in western Asia Minor are empty-headed and that we open our mouths far too wide.'

Even between neighbouring cities there were wide diversities. 'The Boeotians say that greed lies in Oropus, envy in Tanagra, quarrelsomeness in Thespiae, insolence in Thebes, covetousness in Anthedon, curiosity in Coronea, braggadocio in Plataea, fever in Onchestus, stupidity in Haliartus.' This was perhaps written in the second half of the third century BC or in the second.[57]

For the Romans the distinction between good Greeks and bad Greeks was generally economic and social. The good Greeks, generally, were the leading citizens of states enjoying responsible conservative as against intemperate democratic government. There were but few who could be compared with the Greeks of antiquity: the Massiliots in Gaul, Spartans and Athenians in Greece itself and, of course, when Cicero was prosecuting Verres, his vital Sicilian witnesses who, so far from being idle and extravagant like most Greeks, were paragons of virtue, 'just like the Romans in the good old days'.[58]

The 'bad Greeks' were to be found chiefly in Asia Minor – including Carians, Mysians, Phrygians, Lydians, many of whom were not Greeks at all. This was the line taken by Cicero in his defence of Flaccus, attacking those who gave evidence for the prosecution. Their history was against them for, unlike the Greeks on the mainland, they had been subject through the centuries to one alien power after another. Long subjection had taught them to be deceitful, sycophantic, fickle – to run with the hare and hunt with the hounds. It was the Greeks of Asia who, cooperating with Mithridates, had slaughtered Romans by the thousand. Yet, Pausanias asked, a Greek himself, were the Ionians in this respect so different from the rest of mankind?[59]

(v)

From the early second century BC there was Ennius; and there were the second-century Roman dramatists; but, in general, it was not until the late Republic and the age of Augustus that Roman literature offered anything to match the masterpieces of the Greeks. Greek literature, Greek mythology and Greek history, therefore, were the basic part of Roman education. Greek writers set the standard in style, Greek philosophers in abstract thought, Greek heroes in action. The younger Scipio was not the only Roman who read and re-read Xenophon's *Cyropaideia*;[60] Harmodius and Aristogeiton, Leonidas, Epaminondas were the Roman schoolboy's heroes.

Good enough; but had Rome not its own heroes? Why, Cicero asked, instead of reading the *Cyropaideia*, were young Romans not rather poring over the Memoirs of Aemilius Scaurus?[61]

In fact there was very soon to be a series of books which closely linked the two cultures, Greek and Roman, comparisons of the great men – generals in particular, and statesmen – in Greek, Hellenistic and Roman history, starting with Varro's illustrated *Hebdomads*, joint *Who was Who?* books about Romans, Greeks (and even other foreigners), the partly surviving *De viris illustribus* of Cornelius Nepos, the *De vita rebusque illustrium virorum* of Julius Hyginus and later the surviving compendium of *exempla*, Valerius Maximus' nine books of *Memorable Deeds and Sayings*, Roman and non-Roman.[62]

If such books were successful, they not only educated Romans, particularly pupils in the rhetorical schools, in the facts of world-history but broadened their outlook, encouraging cosmopolitanism. For there is always a temptation to criticise the foreigner on the ground that his habits are not the same as your own, and this was the basis of much Roman criticism of Greeks. This attitude was attacked by Cornelius Nepos in the introduction to his book on outstanding foreign generals. If Romans criticised Greeks because Greeks thought dancing respectable, it was just as reasonable, he claimed, for Greeks to criticise Romans because of the freedom which Romans (unlike Greeks) accorded to women in social life.[63]

From as early as the third century BC promising literary men of Greek extraction were brought as part of the spoil of war to Rome and there, under the patronage of an enlightened patron, encouraged to give a Latin twist to their talents. First of all soon after the mid-third century BC there was Livius Andronicus from Tarentum who set up as a schoolmaster and, needing a classical text in Latin for the benefit of his pupils, translated the Odyssey into Latin. At the end of the century Cato brought Ennius back from Sardinia; he was a native of Messapian Rudiae with three languages at his command (Greek, Oscan and Latin), and he was to write, in verse, the first history of Rome in Latin and to accompany Fulvius Nobilior on his campaign in Greece in 189 BC. (Terence, a north African, not a Greek, arrived – we do not know how – as a slave in Rome and was encouraged by his master, a senator Terentius Lucanus, who gave him his freedom.)[64]

From the second century it became customary for distinguished Romans to take into their households as personal friends Greek men of culture, writers, masters of public speaking, philosophers.* The writers could be expected to employ their talents in publicising in readable form the exploits of their patrons, as Archias from Antioch wrote of Lucullus' campaigns and those of Marius, and Theophanes of Mytilene wrote of Pompey's.[65] Orators and philosophers were tutors to the younger members of their patron's family. After his victory over Macedon Aemilius Paullus applied to the Athenians for a painter to supply the illustrations for display at his triumph and for a tutor for his younger sons, and the Athenians were able to kill two birds with one stone when they supplied him with the artist-philosopher Metrodorus.[66] At the same time Polybius was brought

* See Appendix at end of Chapter.

into service as a companion-tutor for his elder sons, Scipio and Fabius
Maximus. Tiberius Gracchus was believed by his enemies to have
been strongly influenced – and for the bad – by the tuition of the Stoic
philosopher Blossius of Cumae and by the orator Diophanes of
Mytilene.[67]

In particular, philosophers. A healthy young man, in the
Hellenistic tradition, had three commendable interests: horses, dogs
and philosophy; and though philosophers were scorned by the crude
soldiery and the common man in Lucilius might declare that a horse
and a good warm cloak were better value as possessions than a
philosopher, cultured Romans in general were not so basely
materialistic.[68] The younger Scipio was a close associate of the
distinguished Stoic philosopher Panaetius; M. Pupius Piso (consul in
61 BC) as a young man had Staseas of Naples in his household, the
first Peripatetic – as far as we know – to settle in Rome; Piso, consul in
58 BC, had the very distinguished Epicurean philosopher Philodemus
of Gadara in his house in Campania. The younger Cato, when on
service in Macedonia, collected Athenodorus of Tarsus, by this time a
very old man, from Asia Minor, and brought him back to live with
him in Rome. Diodotus, a Stoic, was a member of Cicero's household.

Patronage of such men was evidently something of a status-symbol
and, more important, the function of the philosopher in the household
was comparable with that in Europe later of a private chaplain to a
great family. With his insistence on high moral standards, his
preaching against such failings as superstition, avarice and anger, he
encouraged – or should have encouraged – high moral standards in
the family.

Later on, in the Empire, in wealthy Roman households the resident
Greek tutor in philosophy, literature or rhetoric no longer enjoyed the
privileged status which he had held in distinguished aristocratic
families under the Republic, and he was often no better treated than a
poor client. After the first insincere welcome, he enjoyed the contempt
of master, guests and servants alike, overworked on a miserable
pittance which itself, on one excuse or another, was paid irregularly or
not at all. He lost his health, he lost his self-esteem. With strong
overtones of Juvenal, Lucian described the poor man's miseries in his
The Dependent Scholar (see p.186).

In public life Rome's debt to Greek technical skill, from Julius
Caesar's use of the calculations of the Greek scholar Sosigenes in his
revision of the calendar to Trajan's employment of the engineer-
architect Apollodorus of Damascus in bridge-building on the Danube
and for his great building programme in Rome, was immense. Indeed,
as Trajan stressed more than once in his correspondence with Pliny in
Bithynia, architects and surveyors were for the most part Greeks.[69]

How great was the influence of the first tide of Greek culture on

Roman policy and Roman public behaviour? Was Roman policy in any sense humanised?

Cicero was influenced to a degree by all that he had read. Yet, though in Cilicia he succeeded for the most part in administering with fairness and justice, he shows little interest in the large problem of imperialism, the responsibility of an imperial power to its provincial subjects. Scipio Aemilianus, extolled by Cicero in fiction and by Velleius Paterculus as the Roman patron of Panaetius and a man happy to soak himself in Greek culture, showed both at Carthage and at Numantia the same ruthless cruelty that had marked the character of his father Aemilius Paullus.[70] That Pompey's generosity in resettling the captured pirates on the land (instead of killing or enslaving them) owed anything to the influence of the Stoic Posidonius is no more than a guess (see p.196). And, as his behaviour in Athens showed, Memmius' Epicureanism was scarcely even skin-deep (see p.51).

(vi)

By the end of the second century BC Greek was a first language in Roman education – schooling began with Homer – and it was in Greek, not Latin, that the young pupil started his declamation. Greek teachers were utterly self-confident, as little impressed by Roman attainment in fields like rhetoric, in which they were confident of their own mastery, as by the powerful majesty of the leading figures of the new imperial Roman world.[71]

The conqueror had to learn the language of the conquered, a language whose use was far more widespread than his own, and he learnt it very quickly and very well. Soon Greek was 'the other language', and the educated Roman was bilingual, at home 'utrâque linguâ'.*

In the cultured Roman household the two languages will have been spoken above and below stairs, for most of the slaves spoke Greek as a first language and had had to learn Latin as slaves.

Greek was admitted to be a prettier language than Latin and, once it had been made the basis of Roman education, there was a danger, Quintilian thought (and he advised teachers to be on the look-out for this), that Roman pupils might speak Latin with a slight foreign accent.[72]

From quite early in the second century BC most prominent Roman men of affairs spoke Greek fluently: Flamininus; the elder Tiberius Gracchus (who in Rhodes made a public speech in Greek); both the great Scipios; Aemilius Paullus; P. Licinius Crassus Mucianus, consul of 131, who in Asia conducted cases in court in five different

---

* Compare the eighteenth-century remark, whether of an Englishman or an American, 'Every civilised being has two languages, his own and French'.

Greek dialects. At the end of the century L. Crassus spoke Greek as if
it was his native language, and the Greek accent and idiom of the
elder Catulus, consul in 102 BC, was admired by Greeks themselves.[73]

There was at first a certain ambivalence in the life of cultured
Romans. Among themselves they cultivated a Greek background,
with statues of Plato and other Greek notables in their grounds –
whether or not, as Cicero once suggests, they felt twinges of
conscience about their possession[74] – and the major Greek classics in
their libraries. They might chaff one another for this, as in Cicero's *De
oratore*, and amuse themselves by mocking apologies for their tastes,
but in fact it was a very strong bond that they had in common, the
feeling of belonging to an educated class.

By the end of the Republic and the start of the Empire the chaffing
will have stopped. All educated men had Greek as well as Latin books
in their libraries and, for those who were not particularly well
educated, the possession of Greek books was something of a status-
symbol. So in Petronius' *Satyricon* Trimalchio boasted of his two
libraries, one Latin and one Greek.[75]

In public life, however, Greek scholarship, fluency in the Greek
tongue and appreciation of Greek culture were never things to boast
about. Though both L. Crassus and M. Antonius, the two great
orators at the turn of the second century BC, were widely read in
Greek literature, in public Crassus professed a scorn for Greek and
Antonius pretended not to know it. When Cicero, the Hellenist *par
excellence*, spoke in court of Verres' thefts of works of art, he was
appropriately coy: 'Canephorae they were called, and said to be the
work of the sculptor – the sculptor – what's his name? – oh, thank you,
sir, for reminding me – of Polyclitus.'[76]

Roman administrators like L. Crassus in 110, M. Antonius in 102 and
later General Cicero – 'Athenis imperator' – stopped in Athens on
their way to and from the East and sat in on seminars of leading
scholars, drinking in the words of the master or, if they were brave,
arguing against him. L. Crassus, who in Asia had received instruction
from the distinguished Metrodorus of Scepsis, even read Plato's
Gorgias with Charmadas, leading figure in the Academy in Athens.[77]
And at about this time it became the regular practice of clever young
Romans of means who were bent on a public career to finish off their
education in Athens and in Rhodes, attending the lectures of
distinguished philosophers and teachers of rhetoric. Cicero did this;
so did Pupius Piso, Quintus Cicero, Atticus and Julius Caesar. They
were all, like Sulla and Lucullus, accomplished Greek scholars and
fluent Greek speakers[78] – as, in the tradition, was nearly every Roman
emperor. Though, despite his distinguished Greek tutors, Augustus is
reported to have spoken Greek falteringly and, in writing, to have
made a Latin draft which he handed over to an expert for translation,
his surviving letters are as thickly bespattered with Greek words and

phrases as is any letter from Cicero to Atticus.[79]

After his long stay in Rhodes, Tiberius must have spoken Greek perfectly, but as an old-fashioned Roman and linguistic purist, he disapproved of Greek being spoken or of Greek words being used at all in the Senate; in this he differed from his nephew Claudius, a talented Greek scholar who enjoyed the opportunity of making a set speech in Greek when Greek envoys appeared before the Senate.[80]

Trajan may not have understood Greek well; Hadrian and Marcus Aurelius were completely bilingual. Of later emperors, Constantine could speak Greek, but preferred to make his speech at the Council of Nicaea in Latin and have it translated. Valens did not know Greek well. Julian, on the other hand, a polished Greek scholar, hardly understood Latin.[81]

Tiberius Gracchus the elder was not the only Roman who was qualified to make public speeches in Greek; Cicero did this before the Senate at Syracuse, and in AD 69 Vespasian won high praise for his speech in Greek in the theatre of Antioch in Syria. But on momentous occasions, anyhow in early days, it was thought that, if Roman *dignitas* was to be upheld, the public speech of a Roman of rank should be in Latin. So Aemilius Paullus announced the peace settlement of 167 BC at the end of the third Macedonian war in Latin; one of his officers then read a Greek translation.* [82]

Educated Romans wrote Greek as well as speaking it, even if they did not always write it perfectly. In a painstaking examination of a number of public letters written in Greek by high-ranking Romans as if they were compositions of his own pupils, a late nineteenth-century scholar faulted Titus Flamininus' letter to Cyretiae in 196/4 as lacking both elegance and clarity, approved the letter of M. Valerius to Teos in 193 BC and of the Scipios to Heraclea ad Latmum (189 BC), and awarded very high marks indeed to the letter of Q. Fabius to Dyme (? 115 BC) and to those of the emperor Augustus to Mylasa (when he was Octavian) in 31 BC and to Chios in 6 BC. But, of course, these letters may well have been drafted or at least polished up by these great men's Greek secretaries, as is commonly assumed to be the case with the elegant Greek letter of Paullus Fabius Maximus, proconsul of Asia, in 9 BC, about the introduction of a new calendar to Asia; it looks like an excellent free composition based on the proconsul's short Latin draft. How, otherwise, if Augustus' Greek was imperfect, should he have written such faultless letters?[83]

The first Romans to write and publish Roman history in prose in the late third and early second centuries BC, Fabius Pictor and his

---

* On the other hand the momentous announcement of the freedom of the Greek states made by the herald at the Isthmian Games of 196 BC must have been in Greek, for it was immediately understood by the vast audience (p.18, 46).

successors, wrote in Greek. This they may have done without great conscious deliberation since the tradition of historical writing into which they were stepping was a Greek tradition. In any case there was a large reading public for books in Greek (the language in which histories of the Punic wars seen from the Carthaginian point of view had been written, in particular by Philenus and Silenus) and writers could hope to put across their own – the Roman – view of Rome's institutions and Rome's past to foreigners, in particular to Greeks, if they wrote in Greek, a thing which they did not find difficult. The last of this first school of Roman historians was A. Postumius Albinus, who prefaced his book with a polite apology in case his readers found anything in his Greek idiom to criticise.

There was not necessarily much wrong with the Greek which he wrote; but Cato pounced. Cato's own *History* was written as, to his mind, any patriotic Roman's history should be written, in his native language. Albinus, he scoffed, was like a boxer at a championship bout who apologised to the spectators for not being up to championship standard. Polybius, who had his own private reasons for hating Albinus, was delighted to repeat Cato's remark.[84]

Albinus, anyhow, was not the last Roman to write history in Greek. It was in Greek that the blind Cn. Aufidius, probably at the start of the first century, wrote some historical work or other. Rutilius Rufus published a Greek version of his *History* and Lucullus did a history of the Marsic war in Greek. Cicero also produced an account in Greek prose of his consulship.[85] It is an interesting fact that King Juba II of Mauretania, who from the age of about six had received the whole of his education in Rome and must have spoken and written Latin perfectly, wrote his many books on geography and anthropology in Greek; and that was the language in which the emperor Claudius wrote his Etruscan and Carthaginian histories. Suetonius published two works in Greek, one on Greek games, the other on terms of abuse.[86] And Marcus Aurelius wrote his *Meditations* in Greek.

Roman poets, self-conscious heirs of a Greek literary tradition, whether of early lyric or of Hellenistic poetry, were, of course, translating, adapting and imitating Greek masterpieces all the time. But there were a variety of other Greek books which were being turned into Latin by one man of culture or another. Cicero translated Aratus (as did Germanicus later), some dialogues of Plato and the *Oeconomicus* of Xenophon, the latter earning at one point a criticism from the elder Pliny. Sisenna had done Aristides' bawdy *Milesian Tales* into Latin. Pompey commissioned the translation of Mithridates' note-books on herbs, an encyclopedia of antidotes to poison, and this was done into Latin by his freedman Laenas.[87] Lucretius worked on a Greek original.

We are in the fortunate position of being able to watch a Roman translator at work, Livy. For the history of Roman expansion into the East in the first half of the second century BC, Livy wisely accepted the published account of Polybius which, with occasional omissions and adaptations (on account of the fact that he was writing for a Roman and not, like Polybius, for a Greek public) he translated literally. Where Polybius' text survives, we can compare the translation with the original. There are occasional mistakes – one, and only one, a first-class howler – but the comparison shows beyond question that Livy knew Greek very well indeed.[88]

Yet the only really famous translation had been done in the third century BC, Livius Andronicus' Latin version of the *Odyssey*, and it is evident that from the time when Greek became a fundamental part of Roman education and the cultured Roman was bilingual, there was no large reading public for Latin translations of the great Greek classics. Borrowing and recasting – as Plautus did for the stage and Cicero in his own philosophical dialogues – was a different matter. So translations were done as a pleasing and testing relaxation – testing because, particularly in philosophy, Greek had so much richer a vocabulary than Latin. Lucretius stressed this difficulty and so did Cicero.[89]

Cultured men, good Greek scholars themselves, had no use for published translations; they preferred to read the Greek classics in the original.[90]

In the early Empire writing Greek as well as Latin verse was a polite social accomplishment. Ovid's friend, the senator Tuticanus Gallus, wrote erotic verses in Greek. The emperor Tiberius had a particular liking for certain Alexandrian poets and made them his models in the Greek verse which he composed. The younger Pliny completed a Greek tragedy at the age of fourteen and a friend of his aspired to compose a Greek epic on Trajan's Dacian wars. Among the younger Pliny's acquaintances, Vestricius Spurinna at seventy-seven was writing Greek lyrics and so, in old age and retirement, was another consular, Arrius Antoninus.[91]

If we believe Suetonius, officers and troops of the Praetorian Guard had, anyhow, a smattering of Greek; for Claudius is said on occasions to have issued a password to the Guard in Greek – a line of Homer.[92]

Foreign languages always have expressions which are not easily translated, and so they are borrowed. French and Italians speak of 'un week-end'; English may speak of 'le mot juste'.* Indeed among cultured people there is a great temptation to introduce an occasional foreign word into speech or writing not simply for ostentation but

* Mrs Thrale (*Thraliana*, Oxford 1942, 982): 'The modern French Method of introducing Anglicanisms spoyls their language ... The Gallicisms used by our own Puppies are frequent and intolerable' (6 Oct. 1797).

because it is more apt than anything in their native tongue. So the cultured Roman often used a Greek expression. Cicero's correspondence with Atticus and with his brother Quintus is bespattered with Greek words and expressions. Indeed, referring to the speech by which he reconciled the tyrannicides and the Caesarians in the Senate two days after Caesar's murder, 'I used,' he said, 'a Greek word.'[93]

When the emperor Tiberius reproved his daughter-in-law Agrippina on one occasion, he did it by means of a Greek quotation; he used another when he darkly forecast the future which was in store for Galba; and when he disparaged the servility of the Senate, he used a Greek, not a Latin, expression. When Augustus made his smart remark about Herod, 'Better be Herod's kine than Herod's kin', the words he used were obviously Greek, for this play on words was not possible in Latin. Apt use of Greek quotations was a mark of Vespasian's witty conversation.[94]

Marcus Aurelius had frequent recourse to Greek words and expressions in his correspondence with Fronto, and Fronto, who did the same, took great pride in the two letters in Greek, a display of tedious exhibitionism, which he wrote to Marcus Aurelius' mother, Domitia Lucilla. He also wrote in Greek to other people, including Herodes Atticus and Appian.[95]

All the time Greek words were creeping into the Latin language and Latin words into Greek. From the early Empire onwards, for 'Bravo' after a recital, people in Rome no longer shouted 'Bene' in Latin, but 'Sophôs' in Greek (just as we shout 'Encore' in French and the French shout 'Bis' in Latin). To use a Greek word or phrase in Latin was sometimes a convenience, sometimes – like 'acoenonêtos', which Juvenal mocks – an affectation, a determination to be smart. Horace condemned the tendency; in poetry it might be pardoned (as treading in the footsteps of Lucilius), but could anybody be fool enough to think that Greek words and expressions were appropriate to the course of public pleadings in court? And, as has been seen, Juvenal was to protest against the way in which Roman women not only wore Greek clothes but used Greek the whole time in their conversation; Martial too.[96]

In the Republic there were naturally die-hards like the elder Cato and Cicero's grandfather, men capable of saying that, as with Syrian slaves, the better a man spoke Greek, the greater rascal he was likely to be. And there were philistines – the occasional senator who, once Greek envoys were allowed to address the Senate in their native language (after 87 BC), muttered and growled and called for an interpreter. Though the elder Cato learnt Greek, he mistrusted Greek philosophers just as he mistrusted Greek doctors.[97]

Marius had only the most elementary knowledge of Greek, a fact which was rightly thought significant; he was 'durior ad haec studia'.[98] Indeed it was Marius, no doubt, who was behind the attempt to arrest the Greek influence in education by the setting up of rhetorical schools in which Latin and no Greek was taught, the most famous of them under L. Plotius Gallus, who was his close friend — those schools of which the censors disapproved.* As we know from Cicero, a boy at the time, they had a great appeal to his contemporaries (no doubt because they seemed to make rhetoric easier).

In the course of the Empire a change took place in the western world. For one thing, the 'classics' were no longer exclusively the old Greek masterpieces; there were Latin masterpieces too, the poems of Virgil and all the writings of Cicero; philosophy and rhetoric could now be studied in Latin. Greek instructors in rhetoric sometimes taught in Latin, sometimes in both languages.[99] So, though Greek continued to be taught as before and there were Romans, especially in the aristocracy, for whom Greek had as great an appeal as ever and who mastered Greek and were thoroughly versed in Greek literature, there was an increasing superficiality about the study of Greek and many grown men in Rome and the West remembered little of the Greek that they had learnt at school. By the fourth century, apart from occasional self-conscious stars like Ausonius in Gaul, the familiarity with Greek which had marked the educated Roman at the end of the Republic and start of the Empire had disappeared, and this is evidenced by the growing difficulty which the prelates of the western and eastern Christian church found in understanding each other.[100]

Learned Greeks made fit companions, but to surround yourself with young Greeks, as Cicero's *bête noire* P. Clodius did, was to invite criticism.[101] And absorption in Greek culture must not be overdone; Roman considerations of *dignitas* intervened.

Philosophy was a Greek import to Rome, and once culture became a respectable attribute of the Roman gentleman, it was as proper for him to have a philosophy as, in civilised periods of European history, it was necessary for an educated man to have a religion, even to the degree of being a confirmed atheist or agnostic. The various philosophies explored, and gave widely differing answers to, the fundamental problems of human existence: the nature of the Universe, its creation and the question of human survival after death; the principles of ethical conduct, and the validity of the thought-process. These were respectively the fields of natural philosophy, moral philosophy and logic.

Intellectuals like Cicero might follow in the tradition of Plato and/or Aristotle and be Academics or Peripatetics, advocating a certain scepticism because knowledge was based in the first instance

---

* See p. 36 above.

on sense-data which belonged to the world of appearance, not to reality itself. But for most Romans the alternatives were Stoicism or Epicureanism. The fact that the prose writings of both schools lacked elegance and clarity and were of little educational value for the embryo orator is not likely to have worried many people as much as it offended Cicero.* [102]

Whatever was thought of Stoic physics (the periodical dissolution of the Universe in a fiery cataclysm, followed by its recreation; temporary survival of the human soul after death until its extinction at the next conflagration), Stoic morals, with virtue and vice the only realities (virtue being a matter of 'living according to nature' and doing your duty) and all else (pain, for instance, and fear of death) being 'indifferent', matters to be treated 'with calm indifference and philosophic contempt', despite a lack of compassion which was often inhumane, accorded with the best of traditional Roman *mores*. [103] Whatever fun might be poked at Stoic logic (the paradoxes), Stoicism won constant respect among Romans.

But not Epicureanism, whose sheer materialism (belief that the Universe was created by accident, 'the atomic swerve', and that the human soul was extinguished at death)† was widely disparaged, whose creed that pleasure was the highest good it was all too easy to travesty as the creed of the voluptuary, and whose teaching that the wise men sought to avoid embroilment in public life was unacceptable to most educated Romans who if, like Cassius, Brutus' associate in Caesar's murder, they accepted Epicureanism, simply disregarded it. In that one respect they were better Romans than Epicureans. [104]

And if Stoicism turned good Romans into better Romans still, Epicureanism tended somehow to unromanise its devotees, to turn them into Greeklings, only in a few cases pardonably – in the case of Cicero's friend T. Pomponius, for instance. He went to Greece to escape the unsettled conditions of the mid-eighties BC and, once there, made profitable investments and acquired a perfect Greek accent; it was twenty years before he returned to Rome, with his new third name 'Atticus'. Greece remained his second home – 'Athenae tuae' – and he never disguised his affection for it or for Greek manners and culture. Nor did he pretend to be anything but an Epicurean. [105]

But there were other Roman Epicureans who were notorious as degenerates: Clodius' associate Gellius who squandered a fortune and then sought the reputation of a Greek of leisure, 'Graeculum se atque otiosum putari voluit'; [106] and at the end of the second century BC, T. Albucius, who is reminiscent of a type of young American to be found today in Paris or in Rome. Living for a long time as a young man in Athens, he disparaged his Sabine origins and became more

---

* Cicero read, and was impressed by, Lucretius' great poem, the *De rerum natura*, when it came out in 54 BC (*Ad Q.f* 2, 10(9),3), but never referred to it when writing about Epicureanism later, for instance in the *De finibus* or *Tusculan Disputations*.

† Cicero mocked Epicureans for their adoption of the atomic theory (e.g. *TD* 1, 22; 2, 45).

Greek than the Greeks; and so in 120 BC, he was mocked by Q. Scaevola, a keen Stoic on his way out to govern Asia, greeted publicly by Scaevola and his staff in Greek – *Chaíré* – and not in Latin. After a public career at Rome which ended with condemnation for extortion as a provincial governor, he retired to spend the rest of his life in the tranquillity of his beloved Athens, even writing a poem on the Epicurean faith.[107]

And there was C. Memmius, praetor in 58 BC, who, as governor of Bithynia in 57, incurred the hatred of at least one member of his staff, Catullus (see p.75). A *littérateur*, he was in the tradition of esteeming Greek literature more highly than Latin – 'perfectus litteris, sed Graecis, fastidiosus sane Latinarum'. An Epicurean of Epicureans, it might seem from the fact that Lucretius honoured him with the dedication of his *De rerum natura*. The dedication, however, is belied by the facts of his career: corruption, intrigue, exile in 52 BC to Athens where, to the horror of Atticus and all good Epicureans, he acquired the house of Epicurus for demolition, in order to build a modern residence for himself on the spot. Like Albucius, an unbalanced man.[108]

Certain Romans, however, developed profound Greek sympathies without at the same time losing their respectability. P. Rutilius Rufus, consul of 105 BC, was the first; after his scandalous condemnation in the courts in 92 BC, he spent the rest of his life in Greek Asia Minor, a popular figure in the province which he was so shamefully condemned for plundering. It took a venomous pen, that of Pompey's protégé and historian Theophanes, to suggest that Rutilius abetted Mithridates in his massacre of Roman citizens in Asia in 88 BC, and no credence was given to the libel.[109] Nor was it held against Rutilius that he saved his life at the time of the massacre by passing himself off as a Greek or that later he refused Sulla's offer of a safe return to Rome. This was understandable; the man had his pride. If in the Greek world Rutilius had 'gone native', that was the consequence of Roman injustice; martyrs must be allowed to obey their own rules. There was even a paradoxical satisfaction in the fact that he played his new part so well, perhaps renewing the acquaintance of his earlier fellow-student Posidonius.[110]

Roman 'Graeculi' – before Nero – were never on the grand scale. So Antony was not really a 'Graeculus', in spite of the fact that in Athens and in Alexandria he frequented the palaistra, wore Greek dress and attended philosophical lectures which, given his far from academic equipment, he must have found difficulty in understanding.[111] He was something far more menacing, a distinguished Roman general who cracked his skull against the sky, posing as the 'new Dionysus', a man who publicly travestied the most sacred of Roman ritual when he held a Roman-style triumph in Alexandria, a man who gave part of the empire away to foreigners as if it was his to give, a man who behaved as the caricature of a generous, well-meaning Hellenistic potentate while being, all the time, the Queen of Egypt's lapdog.

In the Empire things changed and, despite the vigorous broadsides of Juvenal and Tacitus against Greeks in general and Martial's abuse of a Roman girl whose mannerisms reduced her to the level of a second-rate Greek prostitute, there was little criticism of those westerners, in particular professional sophists and philosophers, who adopted Greek ways and, indeed, found themselves more at home in Greece than in Italy: Musonius, that much-banished man, in the first century and, in the second, Favorinus of Arles, to whom Athens and Corinth erected portrait statues (which they subsequently demolished). This man, whom Hadrian knew and banished and whom Antoninus Pius pardoned, the tutor of Herodes Atticus and acquaintance of most distinguished contemporaries both in Rome and in Greece, 'affected', in his own words, 'not only the thought, manner and dress of the Greeks ... with mastery and manifold success' but 'aimed not only to seem Greek but to be Greek too'.[112]

An emperor's first devotion, on the other hand, must be to his own native Roman culture. There was no sympathy in the West with Nero's Greek proclivities and Hadrian, warmly praised by Pausanias and greatly revered in the East for his benefactions to Greece, was criticised in Rome for his devotion to Greek culture; he was a Graeculus'.[113]

(vii)

Roman prejudice against the admission of Greeks to the Senate and to the opportunity of careers in the top flight of Roman administration was slow to die, and there was little to show that at first Greeks themselves aspired to such careers. The foundations, however, were being laid. From the time of the late Republic and the Civil Wars citizenship was granted to envoys from Greek cities, usually men of literary or academic distinction, who often secured privileges for their home towns and were there honoured as Benefactors (*Euergetai*) in consequence.[114] Citizenship, often of equestrian status (with procuratorial posts and the opportunity of minor commissions in the army) was conferred on talented Greeks closely associated with the Court and on members of prominent Greek and oriental families by Augustus, Tiberius and Claudius (or Nero), as is evident from their names: C. Julius Eurycles and Ti. Claudius Brasidas in Sparta,[115] Ti. Julius Alexander in Egypt, Ti. Julius Celsus of Ephesus (father of Polemaeanus, consul in AD 92) and Ti. Claudius Herodes, great-grandfather of Herodes Atticus.[116]

The son of Pompey's Greek associate Theophanes, M. Pompeius Macer, was a Roman knight, procurator of Asia and a talented literary figure, on very good terms with Tiberius, and his great-grandson Pompeius Macer held the praetorship in AD 15, but he, together with his father, also a Roman knight, was driven to suicide in AD 33.[117] Ti. Julius Alexander, son of an alabarch of Alexandria, a renegade Jew, was Prefect of Egypt under Nero;[118] but Nero's affection for things Greek had little to do with administration, and it was Vespasian on his accession in Alexandria in AD 69/70 who brought Ti. Julius Celsus Polemaeanus of Ephesus, already an equestrian legionary tribune, and C. Antius Aulus Julius Quadratus of Pergamon – he was to be consul twice, once under Domitian, once under Trajan – into the Senate, presumably because of the good reports which he received about both men.[119] There were further admissions into the Senate by Trajan and Hadrian, though there is little evidence in Plutarch of widespread enthusiasm among Greeks for a Roman public career,[120] but it was under Antoninus Pius and Marcus Aurelius that the flood started. The men to emerge and give the empire distinguished service, particularly in the administration of eastern provinces,* were members of families which had held the citizenship for more than a generation; they were generally of distinguished, often of royal,† families which had intermarried with members of prosperous families of Roman settlers,[121] and they were extremely rich, for Claudius was not the only Roman who believed that a 'good man' was also a 'rich man', *bonus vir et locuples*.[122] Of them all, the one whom we know best, perhaps, is the Bithynian Cassius Dio, a senator from the time of Commodus, twice consul, proconsul of Asia and a rigorous governor of Upper Pannonia and the author of the very long and good Roman history which, happily, in large part survives (see p.211).

These were men chiefly from Asia Minor, not from the impoverished mainland of Greece itself. Their public success did nothing to weaken their pride in their origins, and it is largely from inscriptions recording the gratitude of their native eastern cities for their extensive benefactions that we know as much about their careers as we do.

The end of the first century AD, in fact, opened up a new chapter in Greco-Roman relationship. In Greek literature there was what has been called a Renaissance, the Second Sophistic, a period which has bequeathed writings as fascinating and brilliant as Lucian's, as interesting and important as Plutarch's, Arrian's and Cassius Dio's and as tedious to modern taste as most of those of Dio of Prusa and of Aristides. While the rich aristocrats of the eastern Greek world who entered the Roman Senate and took an increasing part in Roman

---

* 'The chief reason why eastern senators were usually used in the eastern provinces was not so much that they were resented in the West, as that they were irreplaceable in the East', S. Mitchell, *JRS* 64, 1974, 38.

† The Julii Severi and L. Servenius Cornutus had the blood of the Attalids and also of Deiotarus in their veins.

administration necessarily spent considerable periods of time in Italy, the literary men and the orators, the sophists, visited the West for longer or shorter periods, the latter often, in the established Greek traditions, as ambassadors to Rome from their cities. They themselves were generally rich men. From Syria there was Euphrates, *bête noire* of Apollonius of Tyana, a man for whom the younger Pliny had warm admiration, a man who feathered his nest well. The wealthy Dio of Prusa moved in Court circles at Rome, was exiled by Domitian and recalled and encouraged by Trajan; eighty specimens of his verbosity survive. And there was the ostentatiously wealthy Polemo (see p.27).

Whoever they were, leading Greeks of the new world consorted as equals with Romans at high levels of society (one has only to consider the number of Plutarch's attested Roman friends, and Lucian's) and they and their Roman friends shared common tastes and common prejudices. If in their writings Greeks condemn features of Roman life which sensitive Romans themselves condemned, that is no evidence of hostility to Rome or to the Empire; it is simply evidence of a cultural fusion between educated Greeks and educated Romans, whose roots went very deep.

In the late first and the second century AD a quiet revolution was taking place; and this, if you please, was the period of Juvenal's and Tacitus' splenetic writings.

Appendix
Late Republic: Greek and Greek-speaking scholars etc. attached to prominent Romans *

M. Livius Salinator, father of consul of 219, 207 BC
> L. LIVIUS ANDRONICUS, playwright, from Tarentum, employed as tutor to his sons (see *RE* XIII, 891, no.32).

M. Porcius Cato, cos. 195 BC
> ENNIUS, Calabrian, brought to Rome from Sardinia in 198 (CN, *Cato* 1, 4); friend of elder Scipio Africanus (Cic., *Pro Arch.* 22), M. Acilius Glabrio, cos.191, (Cic., *De orat.* 2, 276) and Ser. Sulpicius Galba, pr. 187 (Cic., *Lucull.* 51).
>
> CHILON, *grammaticus*, one of his Greek slaves (Plut., *Cato mai.* 20, 5).

Q. Fulvius Nobilior, cos.189 BC
> ENNIUS, taken in his suite on his campaign in Greece (Cic., *TD* 1, 3), which he wrote up (*Ambracia*).

---

* See A.H. Hillscher, 'Hominum litteratorum Graecorum ante Tiberi mortem in urbe Roma commoratorum historia critica', *Jahrb.f.kl.Philol.*, Suppl. 18, 1892, 335-440.

L. Aemilius Paullus, cos.168 BC
> METRODORUS, painter and philosopher, brought from Athens to tutor his boys (Plin., *NH* 35, 135); cf. Plut., *Aem.* 6, 8-10 on their Greek education.

P. Scipio Africanus, cos.147, 134 BC
> PANAETIUS (*RE* XVIII, 422-4), house-guest of Scipio (Cic., *Pro Mur.* 66; VP 1, 13, 3 etc.) and accompanied him on his eastern embassy, 140/39 (Plut., *Mor.* 777A).
>
> POLYBIUS, house-guest and tutor (cf. P. 31, 23-25, 1).

Tiberius Gracchus, tr.pl. 133 BC
> DIOPHANES of Mytilene, orator, and BLOSSIUS of Cumae, philosopher, his tutors, (Cic., *Brut.* 104; Plut., *Ti.Gr.* 8, 6).

C. Gracchus, tr.pl. 123, 122 BC
> MENELAUS of Marathos, orator of the Asian school, his tutor (Cic., *Brut.* 100).

Q. Lutatius Catulus, cos. 102 BC
> ARCHIAS his friend; LUTATIUS DAPHNIS, *grammaticus*, bought for high price and freed (Cic., *Pro Arch.* 6; Suet., *Gramm.* 3).
>
> ANTIPATER of Sidon, poet, possibly a friend (Cic., *De orat.* 3, 194).

M. Antonius, cos.99 BC
> MENEDEMUS, rhetorician, his guest in Rome (Cic., *De orat.* 1, 85).

L. Crassus, cos.95 BC
> ASCLEPIADES of Bithynia, his friend and doctor (Cic., *De orat.* 1, 62).

L. Cornelius Sulla, cos.88 BC etc.
> ALEXANDER POLYHISTOR of Miletus, wide-ranging, unoriginal historian brought to Rome as slave by a Lentulus, given citizenship by Sulla (Serv. Dan. on Virg., *Aen.* 10, 388; *RE* I, 1449-52, no.88; *FGH* 273); taught Julius Hyginus.
>
> CORNELIUS EPICADUS, librarian to Sulla, author, completed Sulla's autobiography (Suet., *Gramm.* 12).

L. Lucullus, cos. 74 BC
> ANTIOCHUS of Ascalon, philosopher, founder of 5th Academy, with him at Alexandria in 87/6 (Cic., *Lucull.* 11) and later in Mithridatic war (Plut., *Lucull.* 28, 8). (Elder) TYRANNION of Amisus, Aristotelian scholar, grammarian, geographer and librarian, captured in Amisus in 71, brought to Rome by Murena

and Lucullus; taught Strabo (12, 548); friend of Atticus (Cic., *Ad Att.* 12, 6, 2); used as librarian by Cicero (*Ad Att.* 4, 4A); tutor to Cicero's son and nephew (*Ad Q.f*, 2, 4, 2). First to work on books of Aristotle and Theophrastus brought to Rome by Sulla (Plut., *Sull.* 26, 2; Strabo 13, 609).

Patron of A. LICINIUS ARCHIAS of Antiocheia, who wrote epic on his conquests (Cic., *Pro Arch.* 21), also on Cimbric war of Marius; friend of Q. Metellus Pius (Cic., *Pro Arch.* 7).

ARCESILAUS, sculptor whose maquettes fetched high prices, sculptor of statue of Venus Genetrix in Julius Caesar's temple, a friend of his (Plin., *NH* 35, 155).

Cn. Pompeius Magnus, cos. 70, 55, 52 BC

CN. POMPEIUS THEOPHANES of Mytilene, close personal friend, adviser on eastern affairs, historian of Pompey's eastern campaigns (Strabo 13, 617; *FGH* 188).

POSIDONIUS, on close terms of friendship since 67 and wrote monograph on Pompey's achievements (Strabo 11, 1, 6, 419f.; *RE* XXII, 638-41).

LENAEUS, *grammaticus*, devoted freedman, accompanied him on nearly all his campaigns (Suet., *Gramm.* 15).

DEMETRIUS of Gadara, immensely rich freedman, who accompanied him in the East (*RE* IV, 2802f., no.50).

CURTIUS NICIAS, *grammaticus* and writer (Suet., *Gramm.* 14), associate also of C. Memmius and of Cicero (*RE* XV, 1868f., no.22).

M. Crassus, cos. 70, 55 BC

ALEXANDER, austere Peripatetic philosopher, his teacher and friend (Plut., *Crass.* 3, 6-8), accompanying him abroad.

M. Tullius Cicero, cos.63 BC

Elder TYRANNION (v.s., under 'Lucullus')

PHILON of Larissa, head of Academy fled to Rome from Athens, 87/6. Cicero studied under him, as did many prominent Romans (*Brut.* 306; *TD* 2, 9); P. died *c*.86/5.

DIODOTUS, blind Stoic philosopher and mathematician, lived in Cicero's house, died *c.* 60 (*Brut.* 309; *Lucull.* 115); left Cicero a legacy (*Ad Att.* 2, 20, 6).

POSIDONIUS (v.s., under 'Cn. Pompeius').

M. POMPONIUS DIONYSIUS, freedman of Atticus, tutor to Cicero's son and nephew (as were slaves CHRYSIPPUS and PAIONIUS, *Ad Att.* 7, 2, 8; *Ad Q.f.* 3, 3, 4) and close associate in Cicero's studies and writing (*RE* XXI, 2328-40, no.14a).

M. Pupius Piso, cos. 61 BC

STASEAS of Naples, his house-guest; first Peripatetic philosopher to settle in Rome (Cic., *De fin.* 5, 8).

C. Iulius Caesar, cos. 59 BC etc.

THEOPOMPUS of Cnidus, father of Apollodorus, a close and influential personal friend (Strabo 14, 2, 15, 656).

SOSIGENES (*RE* IIIA, 1153-7, no.6), Caesar's adviser on reform of calendar (Plin., *NH* 18, 211f.).

JULIUS HYGINUS, librarian, scholar, writer, may have been brought as a boy to Rome by Caesar from Alexandria (Suet., *Gramm.* 20); freedman of Augustus, close friend of Clodius Licinus, cos. AD 4, historian.

L. Piso, cos. 58 BC

PHILODEMUS of Gadara, Epicurean philosopher, had Piso for his patron (Cic., *In Pis.* 68-72; ed. R.G.M. Nisbet (Oxford, 1961), 183-8).

Ap. Claudius Pulcher, cos. 54 BC

L. ATEIUS PHILOLOGUS of Athens, grammarian, rhetorician, writer, probably brought to Rome by M. Ateius, officer of Sulla; accompanied Ap. Claudius when he governed Cilicia and C. Claudius Pulcher, pr. 56 BC when he governed Asia, associate of Sallust and Asinius Pollio (Suet., *Gramm.* 10).

Younger P. Crassus (on Caesar's staff in Gaul)

APOLLONIUS, writer, his freedman, recommended by Cicero to Caesar (Cic., *Ad fam.* 13, 16).

M. Porcius Cato, pr. 54 BC

SARPEDON, his tutor when a boy (Plut., *Cato mi.* 1, 10).

ATHENODORUS CORDYLION, Stoic philosopher and librarian, brought to Rome by Cato from Pergamum and died in Cato's house (Strabo 14, 5, 14, 674; Plut., *Cato mi.* 10; 16; P. Grimal, *REA* 47, 1945, 264-6).

M. Junius Brutus, pr. 44 BC

ARISTUS, philosopher, and EMPYLUS, *rhetor*, lived in his house (Plut., *M. Brut.* 2, 1-4).

STABERIUS EROS, tutored him and also C. Cassius (Suet., *Gramm.* 13).

APOLLODORUS, son of Theopompus, who warned Caesar on the Ides of March, an associate of Brutus (Plut., *Brut.* 65, 1).

STRATON of Aigae (Edessa), a trusted companion of Brutus (as he was later of Octavian; Plut., *Brut.*, 52, 6-53, 2).

M. Antonius, cos. 44 BC etc.

 SEX. CLODIUS from Sicily, his tutor, a *rhetor* (Suet., *Rhet.* 5).

Cn. and Sext. Pompeius (sons of Pompey)

 ARISTODEMUS of Nysa, *grammaticus*, grandson of Posidonius, brought to Rome by their father, taught them and also taught Strabo later at Nysa (Strabo 14, 1, 48, 650).

C. Octavius (later the emperor Augustus)

 APOLLODORUS of Pergamum, founder of a rhetorical school, Atticist, his tutor (who stayed in Rome and had many pupils, Suet., *DA* 89, 1; Strabo 13, 4, 3, 625; *RE* I 2886-94, no.64).

 ATHENODORUS, son of Sandon, Stoic philosopher from near Tarsus, Pupil of Posidonius, his tutor (Strabo 14, 5, 14, 674; *RE* II, 2045, no.19; P. Grimal 'Auguste et Athénodore', *REA* 47, 1945, 261-73; 48, 1946, 62-77).

 AREIUS DIDYMUS of Alexandria, Stoic philosopher, and his two sons his associates (Suet., *DA* 89, 1; *RE* II, 626, no.12).

 Later XENARCHUS from Cilicia, philosopher and scientist was a close friend of Augustus when emperor (Strabo 14, 5, 4, 670, who was his pupil).

CHAPTER FOUR

The Roman Outlook,
2: Other Peoples[1]

(i) North and South

If you were decently educated, you knew that the inhabited world was only in a sense 'flat', being part of a rounded, though not completely spherical, earth: it was an island, as it were, but not quite circular, measuring just under 9,000 miles from East to West and under 4000 miles from South to North, and surrounded by Ocean, as peripheral voyages of discovery had in large part proved. Were it not for the isthmus connecting Egypt with Arabia, it would consist of two islands. There were various inland seas opening out into Ocean: the Persian Gulf, the Arabian Gulf, the great *mare internum* – the Mediterranean, Adriatic, Aegean and Euxine – and also, opening into the northern Ocean, the Caspian or Hyrcanian Sea.[2]

At one extreme was the frozen North, home of the Hyperboreans; Ireland, whose inhabitants were completely savage and led a miserable life because of the cold, being a fringe-country, due north of Britain. There was the Danube, in summer a river, in winter a frozen highway. There were the long summer days and short nights of the far North, Britons 'content with minimal darkness'. About the North you could believe what you liked; Cassius Dio thought there were people in Scotland, the unclad Caledonii and Maeatae, who, in flight from their enemies, lived for days on end in marshy bogs, only their heads protruding above the surface, kept alive by a diet of marsh weeds.[3] At the other extreme was the torrid South, the country of the Ethiopians, the 'cinnamon country'.[4]

The physique and character of the inhabitants of the southern and northern extremities of the world were profoundly different, the difference deriving from proximity to the sun or remoteness from it.[5]

The southern people – the Ethiopians, the Numidians, the Mauretanians, whose name was thought by a false derivation to derive from the Greek word *mauros*,[6] 'black' – were small (though Pliny oddly describes them as tall) and burnt black by the sun; they were shrill-voiced, strong-legged. The sun drew the blood to their heads; so they were quick-witted. On the other hand they suffered from blood-deficiency and were therefore afraid of losing the small amount of blood that they possessed. In consequence they were like haemophilics, terrified of being wounded; so they made bad fighters in hand-to-hand battle.[7]

The South was the snake country, its menace graphically described by Lucan.[8] It was where the spotted cats and so many of the wild beasts (and hunters) for the Games came from, their transport vividly illustrated in the mosaics at Piazza Armerina in Sicily.

Northerners, on the other hand, were deep-voiced palefaces, full-blooded and as fighters courageous to the point of foolhardiness, warlike but undisciplined. Their humours sank into their legs (so they were tall) and, in the absence of sun, not drawn up into their heads.[9]

Romans were superior to northerners in intelligence, to southerners in physical strength.

(ii) East and West

There was a great rift between East and West, partially bridged by the Greeks who, though regarded by unsympathetic Romans as easterners, shared – indeed were themselves the origin of – many Roman prejudices.

Together with the prejudices of one half of the world against the other there went a very considerable ignorance. When told of Nero's Olympic victories, the simple Spaniards thought that he had fought and defeated people called Olympians.[10] Greeks in general were as ignorant of the West as they were unanxious to visit it. Germans, of course, and for many the British, were beyond the pale. Galen stated, 'I am no more writing for Germans than for wolves and bears.' And there was disparagement even of a highly cultured city like Lugdunum in Gaul. The younger Pliny was surprised that there were bookshops in the town and Cassius Dio considered its citizens crude and unsophisticated even by Roman standards. Aulus Gellius describes the mocking of a Spanish-born Latin *rhetor* by a number of Greek smarties from Asia Minor, men who were the embodiment of Greek cultural conceit.[11]

East and West had their marvels, often exaggerated in the telling.

In the far East India was a kind of never-never land which you could read about in books as fantastic as *Gulliver's Travels*, in particular in the work of the over-credulous Megasthenes who had actually travelled to Bengal at the time of Seleucus I and had spent a period at the Court of king Candragupta. No story about India was too fantastic to be true – there were people who slept in their ears, for instance – and the country literally flowed with milk and honey. It was the country of the great rivers, the Indus in particular and the Ganges, and of the great animals, elephants and tigers. It had its caste system, the most interesting being the wondermen, the Brahmans, vegetarians, wearing no wool or leather, indeed often no clothes at all, men of immense physical self-control, completely celibate for thirty-seven years (after which they married as many wives as they could, careful not to impart the secrets of their philosophy to them, and bred earnestly) and the Garmanes, medicine men who could determine the sex of unborn children. And there were the naked sophists who made prophecies until they had been proved wrong three times, after which they had to be quiet.[12]

Nearer home was Egypt, whose history extended further into the remote past than that of any other country. Peculiar to Egypt were the pyramids and, greatest wonder perhaps of the whole world, partly because its origin was so uncertain, the Nile flood.[13]

Chief wonder of the West (and North) were the great Atlantic tides; it has even been suggested that Posidonius' prime purpose in going to Cadiz was in order to study them. Many people believed that the migration of the Cimbri from the sea coast in the late second century BC had been caused by a specially large high tide from which they fled.[14]

If westerners were crude and uncultured, they were tough and warlike; softness, effeminacy, lack of enterprise and courage marked the unwarlike oriental. If Roman soldiers on the western frontier of the Empire were tougher than those in the East, that was because the enemy whom they might at any time be called on to confront was so much more formidable. This was something that Tacitus stressed. For roughly 210 years, he wrote in AD 98, Rome had been in conflict with the Germans, and the history was one of recurrent Roman disasters. What comparable threat was offered by the Parthians?[15]

Valerius Maximus, describing the decadent conduct of Metellus Pius and his suite in Spain in the seventies BC, wrote, 'And this not in Greece or Asia, by whose luxury severity itself might be corrupted, but in rough (*horrida*), warlike (*bellicosa*) Spain.'[16]

Martial contrasted the tough Spaniard (himself) with the cissy Greek. Troops recruited in the East were shocked in AD 69 by the rough appearance and crude speech of delegates from the western legions. For themselves, conscious of the good things of life which they enjoyed, the eastern legions greeted with horror the thought of transfer to the West; they had only to think of the weather for a start.[17]

The oriental's dress was unmanly, the burnouse, and so was his way of fighting with bow and arrow, a matter of tip and run, in contrast to cold steel, which was the essence of fighting in the West and the North, 'where men were men'.

The softness of the oriental was partly a matter of heredity, the result of subservience through long generations to the rule of kings – 'Let Syria be slave, and Asia and the East, which is accustomed to kings'* – and it was partly environmental, induced by the soft climate and by the luxury products of the East, the rich and extravagant things in life,† the scents, the preservatives, exotic tastes, exotic

---

* Never having enjoyed 'liberty', orientals did not, like the Romans, know the bitterness of losing it, Lucan observed, *Phars.* 7, 442f.

† Appropriately enough, the word *gaza* (treasure) came to Latin from Persia.

smells, rich jewels. Silk came from the East, and fine linen, by contrast with the coarse but serviceable woollen garments, smelly cloaks in particular, which came from Spain and Gaul, greasy and so waterproof. Amber was unusual, an elegant extravagance which came from the North, not from the East.[18]

Easterners displayed all the decadence of over-civilisation, as Tacitus might have written when he belittled the 'eastern peril' by contrast with the menace which was constituted by the free Germans.

Of that 'decadence', a stern Roman might have said, there were two outward and visible signs.

The first was the ecstatic character of all the eastern mystery religions, so different from the man-to-man relationship of a Roman with his traditional gods.

The second – not that a Roman would so have described it – was a surfeit of good manners, a tendency to agree, however insincerely, with what was said rather than commit the rudeness of disagreement, a readiness to give presents and to give them so charmingly that, if a Roman was half-asleep, he failed to recognise that what he was receiving was, by Roman standards, nothing less than a bribe. Sometimes, of course, the presents were in fact gross bribes and recognised as such by both parties to the transaction; but sometimes the Roman law against receiving bribes was almost unduly strained – in the case of Julius Bassus, for instance, 'that simple and incautious man', who as governor of Bithynia technically broke the law, but whose action had plenty of precedents. People in Bithynia sent him presents on his birthday and at the Saturnalia and he in return sent presents to them. What he called presents the prosecution in Rome described as 'theft and extortion'.[19]

Flattery may be an exaggeration, it may be a corruption, of good manners, and flattery which had come easily to suggest to the Hellenistic monarchs that they were more than human and in fact divine, which had created the institution of ruler-cult, could not easily adopt a different attitude to Roman administrators, once Rome annexed the Hellenistic kingdoms into her empire. Good men, Flamininus in Greece, the admirable Mucius Scaevola in Asia, were so treated, Flamininus being made the object of religious cult, Scaevola giving his name to newly established games, the 'Mucia' in Asia. Even better men (perhaps) remembered that they were Romans and refused the proferred honours – Cicero, for instance, who in Cilicia refused to accept the dedication of statues and four-horse chariots in his honour. Bad men were just as likely to be honoured, in the hope that such flattery might effect an improvement in them. 'Verria' were established by the Greeks in Sicily.[20]

The embarrassment which attended such honours in the Republic ended with the institution of the principate, after which there was at Rome, to eastern eyes, one super-Hellenistic king, the Emperor. His name was associated in cult with Rome (itself already a somewhat nebulous object of worship) and all was well. The new imperial cult was an acceptable form of loyalty, an effective bond of unity, which was allowed, with government encouragement, to spread even into Italy, and the western provinces.

Not, of course, that the emperor was a god in his lifetime; official policy was absolutely clear on that point. But in the East the exuberance of good manners (or flattery) could not so easily be checked. We possess the edict in which on his accession the emperor Claudius explained, in accepting certain honours and refusing others, from the city of Alexandria, that he was not a god or anything like it. The edict was published, introduced with a short preamble, by the Prefect of Egypt, 'that everybody might have the chance of reading the words of the god Caesar'. The governor obviously chose to forget for a moment that he was a Roman and instead to address the Alexandrians in their own language.[21]

There were, of course, ways of honouring people short of cult. In the second century AD we know that the Rhodians greatly enjoyed erecting statues in honour of individuals from whom they had received benefits. As a result the island was littered with such statues, three thousand of them, and as new statues cost money, what could be better (or cheaper) than to take an old statue, the statue of some forgotten worthy of the past, erase the dedication and give it a new name and inscription?[22]

No manners are so good as to be able to resist evil communications; and so, to western thinking, the influence of the East on the West was always a corrupting influence. This was shown by the degeneration of Macedonians in the Hellenistic world and by the disintegration of the migrant Gauls after they settled down in Asia Minor. And in the eyes of the Roman moralist this was the source of the degeneration of Roman morals from the time when Roman troops penetrated the Greek East in the early second century BC (see p.5).

The intellectual and cultural tide flowed all the time from East to West. Astronomy and arithmetic were discoveries of the Phoenicians, geometry of the Egyptians; humane culture was derived by Rome from Greece. Then from the East came oriental religions, astrology and the false trickery of magic (*magicae vanitates*).[23] All that the West exported to the East, the Roman legal system apart, was a taste for gladiators, a taste which, for all its cultural heritage, the East was anything but reluctant to acquire.

If a Roman looked round the world, he saw *humanitas* in Greece and – not every Greek would have agreed with him – in Rome (perhaps, also, in a vague way in distant India), and he found it elsewhere in those who had been properly romanised (in some cases, Tacitus would have said, over-romanised). These were the children of light;

everywhere else was shrouded in the darkness of barbarism. Inside the Empire Cicero contrasted the barbarous Africans, Spaniards and Gauls on the one hand with the Greeks of Asia Minor on the other; the Sardinians, too, were *homines barbari*.[24] Northern peoples were particularly barbaric in Strabo's opinion, having no civilised traditions, though in religion at least the Romans had eliminated some barbarisms from Gaul.[25] Once you crossed the Rhine, there was no civilisation whatever: *immanitas barbariae*. Germans, by Velleius Paterculus' account – and he had fought against them – were able to talk (they were born liars) and were physically recognisable as human beings,[26] but that was all. Thracians were particularly uncivilised, a people without comprehension of freedom in the view of Apollonius of Tyana, best left to tyrants,[27] the only form of government they were fit for. In the East, Armenians were *barbari*, and so were Parthians.[28]

(iii) *Other peoples in particular*

The nearest non-Romans were the inhabitants of Sicily, Sardinia and Corsica. Sicilians, who were largely Greek, were famed for their sharp intelligence and clever wit.[29] At the other extreme, Sardinians, ferocious, unattractive brigands and congenital liars, this being a part of their Punic legacy, had no better name than had the climate of their island.[30] There was an old saying in Rome, 'Sardinians for sale; if one is bad, the others are worse.' Yet, as inscriptions show, they were recruited in large numbers for the Roman navy; they evidently made good sailors.[31]

Corsicans were less notorious, as their island was less productive and more thinly populated. They spoke a barbarous language. Diodorus said that they made good slaves, Strabo that they made very bad slaves indeed, since it was impossible to train them satisfactorily; you might buy one for a trifling sum, but you would always regret your purchase.[32]

Spain and Gaul alike were divided into an early civilised and romanised South (Baetica, the earliest district outside Italy to receive Roman settlers, and Gallia Narbonensis which was 'more like Italy than a province') and a tougher North and West, the effort of whose conquest was not forgotten – Caesar's campaigns in Gaul and, in Spain, two centuries of horrible warfare before Augustus beat the Spaniards to their knees in 25 BC (and Agrippa had to beat them to their knees again six years after that). The fine military qualities of Spaniards were never depreciated by Roman writers.[33] However, they settled down quickly, adopted the Latin language, provided Rome with soldiers, literary men* and administrators and were, in general, the

---

* In the first century of the Empire, Julius Hyginus, who taught Ovid (Suet., *Gramm.* 20) may have been Spanish. Tarraconensis produced Quintilian (from Calagurris on the Ebro) and Martial from Bilbilis on the Salo; in the South, Baetica produced Porcius Latro, whose rhetorical exercises in Rome Augustus at least once attended, the Senecas and Lucan from Corduba, Columella from Gades and Pomponius Mela from Tingentera (?Algeciras).

best possible advertisement for romanisation. They had only one colourful peculiarity, apart from the golden wool of their sheep and the infestation of their country by rabbits, *cuniculosa Celtiberia*:[34] they cleaned their teeth in urine, and even bathed in it.[35]

Gauls were the better – the more civilised, that is to say – the nearer they were to Rome. Nearest of all were the Gauls of the Po valley who after 90 BC were not Gauls any longer, but Latins and, after Julius Caesar, Romans. These were the Gauls whose highest ambition it was, according to the elder Cato, to be good soldiers and good talkers – Carcopino's Frenchmen who, under Julius Caesar, conquered France and did so much to build the Roman empire.[36] They did indeed form the bulk of Caesar's legionaries, and they provided the first Gallic senators whose elevation so deeply shocked the fastidious, Cicero chief among them. And it was Cisalpine Gaul which supplied late Republican and early imperial Rome with the outstanding literary talent of a Catullus, a Virgil and a Livy.

Over the Alps, Narbonese Gaul, unique already in being a western outpost of Greek civilisation, soon caught the Roman infection. Massilia (Marseilles) had been Rome's oldest ally in the days of the city's freedom[37] and, after Claudius, the province's Roman senators, like those from Sicily and, to the end of the second century, those of no other province, were allowed to return home on visits to their property without having to seek the emperor's permission.[38] The reputation of Marseilles' highly respected university was established early, with prominent Romans among its students[39] and from here culture was to spread northwards into the backwoods, where one day there would be important universities at Bordeaux and at Trier.

To the north of Narbonensis, the huge, long-haired, pale, often blue-eyed and trousered Gauls (see p.221f), addicted – unlike the Romans – to the wearing of gold and silver ornaments, necklaces and bracelets,[40] had two weaknesses: they were impetuous and improvident and, therefore, terrifying as they might be, men and women alike,* at first confrontation, they collapsed quickly if faced by resolute opposition; they lacked staying power.[41] Moreover, they were not adaptable to climates and conditions apart from those in which they were nurtured (see p.214) and in particular were unable to support heat or thirst or to exercise moderation in the enjoyment of – for them, exotic – luxuries like hot baths, cooked food and wine.[42]

Northern Gauls were not clever; they were highly credulous and they were braggarts (and yet, with all this, Diodorus thought them intelligent).[43] They had their bards and their Druids whom, as the focus of Gallic nationalism and as perpetrators of human sacrifice, the Romans made it their policy to eliminate.[44] Their young men, willing participants in homosexual practices, were liberal with their favours (see p.225).

---

* The fighting woman was a feature of northern peoples, Plut., *Mar.* 19, 9; Florus 4, 12, 5.

A sportsman would urge you not to forget that Gaul produced the finest breed of sporting dog in the world, appropriately enough since every kind of hunting flourished in Gaul, beagling, fox-hunting and stag-hunting. Fine hounds, and fine horses.[45]

The British were hardly civilised and were inhospitable, only better than the Irish, who were without any redeeming virtues whatever. The one fact generally known about the British was that they painted their bodies with woad. A girl of British extraction who could pass at Rome as city-born – and there was one in Martial's time – was a prodigy. Still, Agricola saw virtue in some of the better-class young men in Britain who accepted the new educational opportunities which he offered; they might not acquire the same depth of culture as their counterparts in Gaul, but they were more quick-witted. We have an instance of the quick wit of one prominent Scotch woman, who in repartee was more than a match for the empress Julia Domna.[46]

Thought of Britain provoked the question: had the place really been worth conquering at all? Would the empire not in fact have been the better without it? There was kudos in the fact that, by including it, the Roman empire extended beyond Ocean; but economically it brought no gain and was, in fact, a dead loss.*[47]

The Roman view of Greeks has already been examined (chap. 3).

The inhabitants of the Balkan countries up to the Danube were generally considered to be rough, tough and uncouth. It was unusual, Polybius wrote, to find a Thracian who was sober or gentle. Velleius Paterculus, who served under Tiberius in the suppression of the Pannonian revolt of AD 6, had the poorest opinion of Pannonians, as indeed of other northern peoples; the Pannonians were not to be trusted; they had adopted Roman ways too quickly and, as a result, their culture was only skin-deep.[48] We have Ovid's unflattering account of the people who lived on the western shores of the Black Sea.

Once you moved into the hinterland of Asia Minor, you were in the country that the slaves came from, the people so roundly abused by Cicero in his defence of Flaccus. What were the common sayings? 'A Phrygian is the better for a beating'; 'Try the poison on a Carian.' But Cappadocians were the commonest target of abuse. They spoke vile Greek, if they spoke Greek at all, and though they were often tall and made good litter-bearers (as did Bithynians and Syrians), they were as a general rule both stupid and dumb. Abusing Piso, in whose consulship he had been exiled, Cicero said, 'Insensitive, tasteless,

---

* It is a sad thought for a Briton that on the first of the only two occasions in history in which Britain has been part of the extensive European community, this should have been an European view of its economy.

tongue-tied, a dawdling apology for a man, a Cappadocian, you might think, who had just been picked out of a crowd of slaves under the auctioneer's hammer.'[49] Paphlagonians, according to Lucian (who, as a Syrian, should have known what he was talking about) were 'rich and uneducated'.[50]

The Syrian was the slave *par excellence*. 'Like Jews,' Cicero said, 'Syrians were born slaves'; some had been sold into slavery by their families. Indeed Syria and Asia Minor supplied the largest number of slaves whose country of origin can be identified.[51]

Syria provided Rome with tall litter-bearers[52] – also with bakers, cooks, hairdressers, singers and dancers.[53] Syrians were sharp, quick to learn but not always impressively honest. Artful Dodgers, in fact.[54]

But there was a very positive side to Syrian enterprise. The Phoenicians, after all, had been the greatest sailors in Mediterranean history, and in the early Empire Syrians (like Arabs in the East) were great traders. 'The Syrian slave came early to the West; the Syrian trader followed.'[55]

From being provincial subjects, some acquired the Roman citizenship, the gallant ship-captain Seleucus of Rhosos from Octavian as triumvir.[56] Finally, by the end of the second and start of the third centuries AD there was Syrian blood in the imperial family itself.

An origin by which a man might feel embarrassed? So Severus Alexander is said to have felt. Lucian, on the other hand, made no bones about it.[57]

With the Syrians as natural slaves Cicero coupled the Jews. Jews were 'superstitiosi' and their 'superstition' involved a great number of distasteful peculiarities – the recurrent Sabbath, an excuse for idleness, circumcision, dietary tabus (see p.223f) and there was Jewish proselytising activity,[58] for the exposition of their scriptures in the synagogue had the attraction of a philosophy lecture and was something unparalleled in other cults. But what was worse was Jewish exclusiveness, their division of humanity into Jews and Gentiles, just as the Greeks divided humanity into Greeks and Barbarians. This exclusiveness, easily construed as misanthropy, was nowhere more evident than in their refusal to participate in the gaiety and rejoicing of imperial festival-days.[59] Greeks had never liked Jews and, where there were large Jewish communities in a single city, Alexandria for instance or Antioch in Syria, they were like oil and water; there was no mixture. Nor was any love lost between Jews and their Arab neighbours. No pagan writer, Greek or Roman, had any great sympathy with the Jews.

Concerning the Arabs there was a nice fable that once upon a time the god Hermes' cart, loaded with mischief of all sorts, broke down in their country and was plundered by the natives. This explained why

Arabs were 'liars and impostors, who did not know the meaning of truth'.* [60]

Egyptians generally were regarded by the Romans with hatred and contempt, and sometimes little distinction was made between Egyptians proper and Egyptian Greeks. 'An unwarlike and treacherous people', according to Florus; basely abject at one extreme, rashly foolhardy at the other, according to Achilles Tatius. [61]

Romans of the senatorial class can have known little of Egypt itself except at second hand. In the Republic it was a foreign country and in the Empire senators were not allowed to visit the province without the express permission of the Emperor. It is significant that the younger Pliny, a prominent figure at the Roman Bar, did not know that Roman citizenship could not be given to an Egyptian unless he first possessed the citizenship of Alexandria. Augustus had barred the Roman Senate to Egyptians and it was not until the time of Caracalla that the rule was broken. [62]

Yet clever Egyptians – 'eruditi' is Apuleius' epithet for Egyptians (*Flor.* 6), and nobody doubted the existence of such men – climbed to positions of importance in Rome, favourites of the emperor to whom they owed their position, but of few others. There was the teacher Apion under Gaius, an Egyptian who had acquired Alexandrian citizenship, and, more important, Crispinus, a native of Memphis, who was perhaps Prefect of the Praetorian Guard under Domitian, a man to whom Martial toadied and whose memory Juvenal flogged, and there was the renegade Alexandrian Jew, Tiberius Alexander, also perhaps Prefect of the Guard at the end of his very distinguished carrer, a man whose statue, Juvenal suggested, was best used as a public lavatory. [63]

Roman writers who visited Egypt, not being senators, were Seneca as a young man (his uncle was Roman governor) and Juvenal, who was exiled by Domitian, perhaps to Syene; his unqualified hatred for Egypt and Egyptians is expressed in his fifteenth satire. [64]

In the eyes of most Romans Egypt consisted of Alexandria and a vast hinterland, the country inhabited by native Egyptians, [65] while the population of Alexandria consisted predominantly of Greeks and Jews who were always at one another's throats. The Jews had the bad qualities of Jews everywhere; the Alexandrians, whether slave-children from the gutter or garrulous public representatives, were smart-alecs, boastful, ineffective, cheekily impertinent, particularly to those in authority whether in Egypt or in Rome, [66] where their puerile abuse of Roman emperors who sat in judgment on them is recorded in the surviving *Acts of the Pagan Martyrs* (see p.188). Particularly in the fact that until Septimius Severus they had no senate, they thought

---

* Gibbon, *Decline & Fall*, ch. 7, on the emperor Philip: 'He was an Arab by birth and, consequently, in the earlier part of his life, a robber.'

that they were discriminated against by Rome.[67]

Concerts and horse-racing roused them to a pitch of frenzy.[68]

A Roman who was in Egypt at the time of Julius Caesar was the author of the *Bellum Alexandrinum*. He wrote, 'If I was briefed to defend Alexandrians and to establish that they were neither treacherous nor irresponsible, I could make a long speech, but it would be a wasted effort.'[69]

Yet the Alexandrians' very beautiful city was the largest in the empire after Rome, and the most cosmopolitan, a gateway to the deep South and to the far East.[70]

Egypt was the home of the cult of Isis and of Serapis, which attracted converts in all parts of the Mediterranean. It was the home also, and the fact was notorious, of fantastic animal-worship of a widespread parochial kind; here one animal or bird was worshipped, there another: the cat, the ichneumon (which ate crocodile eggs), the dog, the hawk, the ibis, the wolf, the crocodile, the eagle and the goat. Besides which there were the great cults of the bull Apis at Memphis and, second in importance, of the bull Mneuis at Heliopolis.

'Who knows not what monsters demented Egypt worships?'[71]

The devotion of Egyptians to animals was such as to inspire the admiration of the most sentimental of English spinsters. They denied themselves food for the animals' sake.

They did not display such considerate affection towards their fellow-men but instead behaved frequently as bloodthirsty fanatics. A Roman soldier was lynched in the late Republic because he accidentally killed a cat.[72] The frenzied conflict of two villages described by Juvenal in his fifteenth satire ended in a cannibalistic orgy and blood was often shed as a result of religious animosity. When the Kynopolites (inhabitants of Dogstown and dog-worshippers) ate a snouted fish (*oxyrhynchus*), the Oxyrhynchites had their revenge by sacrificing and eating a dog. This in Plutarch's time, who records that peace was only restored after intervention by the Roman authorities.[73] In the days of Egyptian independence the bestial savagery of civil conflict in Alexandria – where many of the offenders must have been Greeks – was recorded with horror by Polybius.[74]

Africa, though it was in due course to produce lawyers, administrators, even emperors, and writers of genius[75] and to possess in architecture the finest of Roman monuments, was a province whose inhabitants did not enjoy the highest cultural esteem. There were Numidians, Berbers and descendants of the Carthaginians, whose language was still widely spoken (see p.117), fickle and untrustworthy, surviving examples of *Punica fides*.[76] Africans, too, were thought of as over-sexed,[77] like some of their wild animals whose mongrel offspring from male animals of other species produced the famous Greek observation which in Latin has become proverbial, 'Ex Africa semper aliquid novi'. Africa was the country of two women of fatal charm,

Dido in legend* and Sophonisba in romantic history, to whom the
young Massinissa so badly lost his heart that Scipio had to lecture
him on the virtue of self-control – Massinissa who survived a broken
heart when young and was still fathering children in his late eighties.[78]
Such was Hannibal's self-control in refusing the enjoyment of captive
women as bedfellows that, Justin states, nobody would believe that he
had been born in Africa.[79]

African women were very fertile, commonly producing twins, just
as Egyptian women, thanks to the water of the Nile, produced
triplets.[80]

(iv) Patrons and clients

Popular generalisations apart, anthropological curiosity about
different peoples on the part of educated Romans was satisfied by
books like Strabo's or Pomponius Mela's on Geography, by wide-
ranging histories like that of Posidonius or by encyclopedias like the
Natural Histories of the elder Pliny. Much of the information available
to such writers came from the first-hand records of Roman
administrators; we have seen what Velleius Paterculus thought of the
Germans and Pannonians and what the author of the *Bellum
Alexandrinum* thought about the character of the Alexandrians. More
importantly, there were the memoirs of important generals like
Suetonius Paulinus and Domitius Corbulo in the Empire, who
naturally took a vivid interest in the character of the peoples against
whom they campaigned, just as Caesar, whether or not all that
appears in the *Bellum Gallicum* was written by him, showed an
anthropological interest in the Gauls, the Germans and the British.[81]
There were Romans, obviously, who had a great gift for
understanding and getting on well with particular native peoples, the
elder Africanus and Sertorius in Spain, Rutilius Rufus in Greek Asia
Minor and Agricola in Britain.

Among the aristocracy in Rome there were individuals and families
who enjoyed a particular relationship with particular provinces, a
relationship derived from personal administration in a province
(Cicero's close relationship with Sicily dated from the year when he
was one of the two quaestors in the island) or inherited,[82] perhaps as a
consequence of the achievement of an ancestor in the province's
conquest; in this way the Fabii and Domitii Ahenobarbi had a
particular interest in southern Gaul and the Claudii Marcelli in Sicily.
Or it might derive from a leading Roman's appearance on behalf of
the provincials in the Roman law courts. In such cases the
relationship was, in Roman language, the relationship of patron and

---

* And, according to legend, there was Callirhoe, daughter of king Lycos of Libya who, in her
infatuation, did not hesitate to murder her father to save the life of Diomede, who had fled to
Libya after the Trojan war; she was then deserted by him, as Dido was deserted by Aeneas, and
hanged herself (*FGH* 275, F.5).

clients. And though this relationship lost much of its reality in the Empire, when the Emperor emerged as a universal father-figure, leading advocates in the courts might still establish a close connexion with a particular province as a result of their advocacy of that province's interests, as was the case – *patrocinii foedus* – of the younger Pliny and Spanish Baetica.[83]

Through administration in a province a Roman might have a bond of hospitality (*hospitium*) with particular provincial families,[84] and provincial cities and even provinces themselves sometimes adopted a senator or Eques as 'patron', a relationship for which there is much inscriptional evidence, which descended from generation to generation in the patron's family.[85]

Such relationship might give a boost to *dignitas* and be something to boast about in the courts, but there is no evidence that it resulted in any particularly close knowledge of the provincials themselves.

CHAPTER FIVE
Romans Abroad[1]

There were many categories of Romans in any province. Exiles apart (on whom, see p.102), there were men in private life, traders, business-men, farmers, money-lenders, bankers. There were Romans present in a semi-official capacity, concerned in particular (more under the Republic then under the Empire) with the supervision of tax-collection.[2] There might be military units, temporarily or permanently stationed in the province. There were sometimes delegates on official commissions from the central Roman government, sticking their noses into one thing or another, senatorial big-wigs normally under the Republic but, under the Empire, sometimes men of startlingly different stamp, freedmen even,[3] and there might be important Romans travelling on private or semi-private business with special privileges (*libera legatio*).[4] There were Roman officials of all ranks from lictors to adjutants (*legati*) in the entourage of the governor. And, at the top, there was the governor himself, exposed to criticism from every quarter.[5]

Romans (or men of Roman extraction) were sometimes birds of passage: members of the administration on a temporarily limited tour of duty, Roman employees of the tax-collecting syndicates and, of course, a large number of business men. On the other hand there were the settlers, *provinciales*, Roman residents in the provinces as opposed to the 'natives', who were *socii*.

There were soldiers who on discharge settled down in the province where they had served, often, no doubt, because they had taken up with some native woman (though, unless the man had received *conubium* (see p.91), their association could not constitute a legal marriage). Our best evidence is early, from Spain in the second Punic war, where Scipio Africanus left a number of his wounded and disabled soldiers at Italica and where in 171 BC the first Latin colony outside Italy was founded for over four thousand sons of Roman soldiers who had remained in Spain and married Spanish women.[6] In the course of his eastern campaign in 66 BC Pompey settled wounded and over-age soldiers of his army at Nicopolis in Armenia Minor and this was a flourishing city in Strabo's time.[7] Indeed a reason why we hear so little of Pompey's veterans after his eastern campaign may well be that many of them had remained in the East and had not returned to Rome. We even know that, when Parthia set about identifying and returning Roman prisoners in accordance with its agreement with Rome in 20 BC, some of them went to ground because they preferred to remain where they were.[8]

There were the foundation-members of Roman and Latin colonies in the provinces sent out by the government in Rome, themselves very largely ex-servicemen, and their descendants, who embraced as wide a variety of occupations as did the inhabitants of any Italian town. Often a number of natives were incorporated in the new settlement if it was on an already occupied site, these natives sometimes being given Roman citizenship and sometimes not (see p.84).

There were individual Roman businessmen and traders who settled down and made a new home for themselves in the provinces and, indeed, sometimes outside the imperial frontier. 'If it is a wretched thing to be away from your country,' Cicero wrote, 'the provinces are full of unhappy wretches, only a few of whom ever return to Rome', and Tacitus, writing in the convention, described such people (in Bohemia) as first involved in business dealings, then obsessed by avarice, and finally no longer conscious of being Romans – going native, in fact.[9]

There were Romans who acquired land and settled down to farm in the provinces, many in Sicily (these are the 'aratores', innocent victims, according to Cicero, of Verres' rapacity) and many in southern Gaul, one of them the brother of the P. Quinctius whom Cicero defended in the courts; he 'went in for cattle on a considerable scale and was also a successful arable farmer'.[10]

Roman businessmen took their lives in their hands when they crossed the frontiers into foreign territory or moved into land which had been freshly conquered and was not yet fully pacified. Or when there was rebellion in a province and Roman military protection was not immediately available. So we know of massacres of Roman traders in Jugurtha's Numidia, in the big Gallic revolt of 52 BC, in Pannonia in AD 6, in the Gallic rising of AD 21[11] as well as at numerous cities in the East;[12] and the greatest holocaust of all was the massacre of – Memnon says 80,000 – Romans which Mithridates ordered in 88 BC in Asia, a province which had been under Roman administration for nearly half a century.[13] After that, the most terrifying massacre must have been that of Romans and Greeks alike in Cyrene, Egypt, Cyprus and Mesopotamia in the great Jewish revolt of AD 115-17, when captives suffered unspeakable bestialities; and Romans were among the victims of the Jewish rebellion in Palestine in AD 132-35.[14] In 133-131 BC in Sicily (as in south Italy between 73 and 71 BC) the brutalities which Romans suffered were fruit of the pent-up vengeance of slaves who had been grossly maltreated.

The victims of Boudicca's revolt in AD 60 in Britain – 70,000 Romans and British collaborators – paid the penalty for Roman maladministration and corruption at all levels, in the disregard of king

Prasutagus' will, the treatment of his widow and daughters, in the bestialities practised by the Roman veteran-colonists at Colchester and the corrupt behaviour of the procurator who, when the revolt broke out, advisedly fled the province.[15]

The murder of Roman ambassadors to foreign countries, where recorded, was the result of their own arrogance or of the offensive nature of their commission. The young Coruncanius, whose murder in 230 BC was followed by the first Illyrian war, had spoken to queen Teuta as if she was a slave-girl rather than a queen. And Cn. Octavius, murdered in the gymnasium at Laodicea in Syria in 162 BC by a certain Leptines, was commissioned to burn Syrian ships and hamstring Syrian elephants, a condition of the Peace of Apamea a quarter of a century earlier which the Romans had not tried to enforce until there was a young boy on the Syrian throne. Leptines was a fanatic, convinced that he acted under divine guidance; his associate Isocrates, a demented academic, declared that all Roman envoys should be murdered on principle, so that an end might be brought to arrogant Roman demands and to Rome's unbridled power.[16]

There was a limit to what provincial subjects could tolerate in the abuse of power by Roman officials. When Verres, enjoying the diplomatic privilege of an official member of the staff of the governor of Cilicia, instigated one of his creatures to abuse the hospitality of a Greek citizen of Lampsacus in the province of Asia, popular feeling was roused, the house was attacked and a lictor was killed. Later, when governor of Sicily, Verres came near to being burnt alive.[17] This, indeed, had been the fate in 82 BC of C. Fabius Hadrianus, governor of Africa, when his official residence at Utica was set alight, not indeed by native Africans but by resident Romans. The man was a Marian, but the act was condoned by the Sullan government in Rome not for that reason so much as because it had been patently provoked by his cruelty and avarice.[18]

Though wounded both times, Q. Cassius Longinus, a monumentally extortionate Roman official, survived two attempts to murder him in Further Spain as quaestor in 54 BC and later, when Julius Caesar foolishly appointed him governor of the province; he was drowned in escaping from it with his loot. In AD 26 the governor of Hispania Tarraconensis was murdered by a native Spaniard; 'his greed was greater than even barbarians could stomach.'[19]

Not all Roman administrators were cruel, lustful and avaricious. Many, like Cicero, did their best to act justly. But, particularly in the Republic, the best of governors was pulled in two opposite directions, by the duty of which he was conscious to natives and provincials and by pressure from Rome which was shameless (Cicero asking Vatinius in Illyricum to befriend a man who was a notorious criminal), time-wasting (Caelius importuning Cicero for panthers for his Games in Rome) or unprincipled (Brutus' agent pressing Cicero to ensure fulfilment of a contract which was quite illegal). Justice or no justice, there were powerful influences in Rome which must not be antagonised, as Cicero reminded his brother when he was governor of Asia.[20] In the Republic in particular there was the difficulty of holding the balance between the tax-collectors (the antennae of politically powerful agencies in Rome) and the provincials and natives who paid the taxes.

The governor had not only to watch himself, he had to watch his staff, for they expected to line their pockets, as Cicero discovered sorrowfully; 'how hard it is to be good'. Catullus, on the staff of Memmius in Bithynia, was furious at being denied the opportunity.[21]

Evidence of a real liking by Roman administrators for the peoples for whose welfare they were responsible is rare. Sertorius evidently liked Spaniards (and they liked him) and Agricola liked and understood the British, in whose island he completed three separate tours of duty. Julius Caesar liked his soldiers, but there is little evidence that he liked anybody else; indeed one may suspect that the only Gaul whom he really admired was Dumnorix, whom he hunted to death, the man who died with the cry, 'I am a free man, member of a free country'; he had something of Caesar's own spirit.[22] Quinctilius Varus was a Roman who believed too easily in the goodness of other people (the Germans) and three Roman legions were destroyed in AD 9 because he disregarded warnings that the Germans to whom he was communicating the civilised blessings of Roman law, so far from happily submitting to the process, were in fact exploiting his simple folly, sharpening their swords and waiting for the moment to pounce.[23]

Roman civilians no doubt differed in their attitude to natives of a province. Those who lived or spent long periods abroad, particularly in the Greek East (Cicero's friend Atticus was one of many)[24] must have found people as well as places to their taste. On the other hand there are likely to have been many who, with Roman conceit, used the harsh language about provincial natives that Velleius Paterculus (see above, p.66) used in writing of the Pannonians and Germans, even the intemperate abuse which in the courts in Rome Cicero showered on Gauls in his defence of Fonteius and, in defending Flaccus, on the Greek natives of Asia Minor.

Resident Romans in civilian life were registered by assize districts (*conventus.*) and were fetched in to sit on the Bench with the Governor when he came round on assizes to their neighbourhood. So that the natives might well see the world as divided into 'Them' and 'Us'; in an emergency the Romans would all stick together, even gang up on the rest. This was shockingly revealed when Augustus discovered that in Cyrene Roman jurors and Roman prosecutors and witnesses had worked together to secure the condemnation of innocent Greeks to death.[25]

In the Empire there was an increasing assimilation of Romans and others in the provinces through a steady increase in the number of those who received Roman citizenship and through mixed marriages, especially on the frontiers and in new colonial settlements. We are fortunate in having the splendid evidence of the case of Cologne (Colonia Agrippinensis) in AD 70. When it joined the rebels, the Tencteri suggested that for a start its Gallic (once German) inhabitants should cut the throats of any Romans they could lay hands on. 'What?' they retorted in horror, 'cut the throats of our relatives?'[26]

CHAPTER SIX

Enslavement and the Purchase of Slaves[1]

Aristotle had said that slavery was a fundamental feature of civilised life and it occurred to few people apart from the Essenes in Judaea,[2] not even to the Christians, to doubt the fact.

The pipe-dream of a world without slaves may have occurred often to slaves themselves, but it makes little showing in literature. Only, it seems, in the idealisation of life in India by Alexander's journalists and their successors and, in another idealisation, in Ceylon. Megasthenes declared that slavery was unknown in India, Onesicritus that this was the case only in the kingdom of Musicanus, which got on very well without them.[3] There were few slaves in Arabia Nabataea, a country so democratic that the king waited on his guests; nor, because native labour was so cheap, were there large numbers of slaves in Egypt – only concubines and male house-slaves.[4]

If Stoics felt momentary qualms about the existence of slavery,* they had only to think for a moment and they were reassured. A slave lacked freedom, as being the possession of his master; but, in one way or another, people who were not slaves lacked freedom too. A passenger on board ship was subject to the captain's orders.[5] A high administrator born of free parents was, in a sense, a slave; he had to obey the emperor's orders. And everybody was the slave of Fortune which he feared because at any moment Fortune might strike and a man might lose his wealth and be pauperised, lose his health or his wife or his children – indeed lose his own 'freedom', be kidnapped and himself sold as a slave.[6] Kings and queens had become slaves in the course of history and even Romans, prisoners of war, of Hannibal; after Carrhae, of the Parthians; and, after AD 9, of the Germans.[7] Anyhow, it would be a rash man who asserted that there was no slave-blood in his veins; how far back could anybody trace his own genealogy?[8] And were there not people who opted for what was virtual slavery, the ignominious position of a private tutor in a rich vulgarian's household?[9] Seneca knew all the arguments, and so did Epictetus and Aelius Aristides. There was really nothing to worry about.

---

* Posidonius suggested (*FGH* 87, F.38) that in being enslaved by Mithridates the inhabitants of the island of Chios suffered their just deserts, for they had been the first people to introduce slavery to Greece.

There was more than one door to slavery.[10] There were prisoners of war and victims of pirates and kidnappers, free one moment and slaves the next, up for purchase in the open market.[11] Once a slave, you might change masters, being put up for sale again or being given away as a present;* or you might be bequeathed, like any other object, by will. You might be the child of slave parents, born in your master's household, a *verna*, brought up from infancy as a slave. You might have been an exposed child of freeborn parents, picked up off a dunghill by someone who then brought you up as an investment and sold you; in which case you might wonder about your origins, but never have the chance of finding out.[12] You might have been sold into slavery by your parents when you were an infant; you might even when adult, and with your eyes wide open, have sold yourself into slavery.[13]

First, capture: the lot often of women and children, their menfolk having been killed fighting or executed after being made prisoners. But sometimes the men were made slaves too.

At first, as with wealthy folk captured by pirates or kidnappers, there were hopes of ransom, particularly in the early days, in the third and second centuries BC. One of the most notable cases was the ransoming by the Greeks themselves of the 1,200 Roman slaves (prisoners of war) whom they had bought from the Carthaginians in the second Punic war and the handing over of them in a wonderful gesture of appreciation to the Roman general Flamininus.[14] And in Sicily in 104 BC, there were Bithynians (free men seized and enslaved for debt by Roman tax-collectors, whose sins had subsequently found them out), summoned before the governor of Sicily and told that they were free to go home; and eight hundred of them actually went before the rich landlords of the island paid the governor to suspend his enquiry.[15] Yet hope often turned into disappointment. In fiction, a *declamatio* of pseudo-Quintilian, we have the story of a rich man's son who was kidnapped by pirates and, when his father refused to meet the demand for a ransom, he was sold to be a gladiator.[16]

After the great military *coups*, victories in battle or the capture of cities, there were slave-sales *sub corona* (so called, perhaps, because the slaves' heads were garlanded)[17] and human beings were bought up by the wholesalers (*mangones*) and often transported great distances to be put on the market as *novicii*, first-timers, at one or other of the big slave emporia,[18] where they were sold to the retailers.

Finally, put up for sale for the third time, they were offered to purchasers by the retailers, either as individuals or in lots, and the law insisted that they should be tabbed, so as to reveal their nationalities, because certain people were known to make good slaves and certain people to make bad ones.[19] To say that 'Syrians and Jews were peoples born for slavery' did not mean that in all cases they made

---

* It was an unwise man who looked a gift slave in the mouth, Claudian, *In Eutrop.* 1, 29-41.

good slaves.[20] Syrians, however, were naturally submissive and deferential, and from extensive surviving evidence of Syrian slaves – 'Syrus' was a common slave-name – Syria has been described as being at all times in antiquity *par excellence* the homeland of slaves.[21] For the rest, three-fifths of all slaves whose nationality is known came from Asia Minor. These, then, with the advantage that in many cases they spoke Greek, must have been in large demand.[22]

Sometimes a purchaser was in search of a particular skill which was more likely to be found in natives of one part of the world than in those of another. Litter-bearers, for instance, needed to be tall and strong, and such people, it seems, came chiefly from the eastern Mediterranean, largely from Syria or, more particularly, from Bithynia, where the litter was supposed to have originated.[23]

According to Varro, masters in search of herdsmen for their cattle were wise to avoid Spaniards and to buy Gauls, who were particularly good with draught cattle.[24]

From the moment of enslavement to this last stage, assignment to an owner, men, women and children must have suffered a hideously traumatic experience, but nobody was interested in describing the psychological sufferings of the victims; one did not, after all, have animal-psychologists.

The sale itself must have been to most victims a thing of horror: the bawling voice of the auctioneer (in a language which most of them could not understand), the indignity of standing on a platform (*catasta* or *lapis*) with bare white-chalked feet,[25] of being slapped, punched, pinched, even made to jump by a potential purchaser who wanted to make sure of the quality of the human flesh that he was buying. Burnt jet might be thrust under their noses to find if they were epileptic. They might be made to strip for a medical inspection.[26]

These slave-auctions were all humiliation for the vendibles, and all noise.

The *novicii*, of course, were not the only slaves who were put up for sale, and a slave might find himself up for sale by public auction more than once in his life because, for any one of a variety of reasons, his master might want to dispose of him (or her); he might be overstaffed; he might need to raise money, or he might want to rid himself of a particular slave because of his inefficiency, his dishonesty or his tendency to abscond, if he was a *fugitivus*. Indeed, the more often a slave had appeared in the sale room, the more suspect he was. These slaves were much more informatively tabbed than the *novicii* (of whom little can have been known in most cases but their nationality), for the law dealt severely with any vendor who misrepresented the skill or withheld vital information about the proved shortcomings of a slave whom he sold.[27]

Or a slave might be sold privately; here is Horace's account of such a transaction:

Imagine someone wanting to sell you a slave born at Tibur or at Gabii and saying to you, 'He is fair and handsome from tip to toe, and you can have him for eight thousand sesterces. He is house-born (a *verna*), good at doing whatever his master wants, with a smattering of Greek, qualified for any use, soft clay out of which you can mould whatever shape you want. He hasn't a trained voice, but his singing will sound sweet enough when you have a drink in front of you. Recommendations often raise doubts, when a vendor praises in exaggerated terms whatever he is selling, because he wants to get rid of it, but I am under no such constraint. No professional slave-dealer would make you such an offer, and there are few people to whom I would make it. He did clear off once and hid from terror of the whip that hangs on the stairs. Do pay up – unless you are worried by this fact of his absconding.'

Well, he would get his price without fear of punishment. You have bought a faulty object with your eyes wide open. The legal position is clear. And are you still going to launch a prosecution?[28]

The slave-auctions in Rome were held in the Forum near the Temple of Castor,[29] but for an exotic pricey slave you went to a dealer in the Saepta (see p.16). And all over the Empire there were local slave sales. At Tithorea in Phocis in Greece on the third day of the Festival of·Isis there was a fair at which slaves were on sale as well as animals, clothing, silver and gold.[30]

Slaves were wanted for a number of purposes: for sex (pretty boys for homosexuals, prostitutes for the brothels), for public entertainment (gladiatorial trainees), for administration (imperial and municipal slaves), for the internal and external needs of.the city-dwelling family (household servants and employees in family business and trading interests), for work on the farms and for hard labour (the mines and quarries). Different purchasers were in search of different qualities: good looks, intelligence, physical strength, previous experience of one sort or another.

If a slave boy had a smattering of letters, he was advertised as 'litteratus'. Slave boys seeking household employment as jesters or wits recited set pieces and showed off their tricks.[31]

The slave in Horace's *Epistle* cost eight thousand sesterces, which Columella gives as the price of a skilled vine-dresser. (Cato had been prepared to pay up to six thousand for a good labourer.) Davus in Horace's *Satire* cost two thousand. Martial writes of a man selling a slave for twelve hundred, so as to raise the price of a good dinner, and of a coachman with the great asset of deafness* fetching twenty thousand. Twelve hundred was what Habinnas in Petronius' *Satyricon* paid for the squint-eyed Jew-boy who snored by night and played the fool by day. Highly literate slaves are mentioned by Seneca as costing a hundred thousand and the same figure (or even two hundred thousand) is given by Martial as an extravagant outlay on a singularly pretty boy, particularly Greek.[32] At Rome prices were obviously

---

* Herod Agrippa would not have suffered the ignominy of imprisonment in the last days of Tiberius' rule if the coachman driving him and the prince Gaius had not listened to (and reported) their conversation, Jos., *AJ* 18, 168-91.

considerably higher than on the periphery of the empire.[33]

Once bought, the slave usually required training; he also had to be taught Latin. So that it is easy to understand why most masters preferred slaves born in the household (*vernae*). Atticus, who employed a highly skilled household both in his business dealings and in his book-publishing, employed none but house-born slaves.[34]

CHAPTER SEVEN

Admission: Becoming a Roman[1]

Thanks to the survival of an inscription, we have an early tribute paid to Rome by a foreigner – King Philip V of Macedon, no less – on account of the liberality with which Roman citizenship was extended; and Roman history is in fact a story of continuous extension of the citizen body until under Caracalla in AD 212 the climax was reached and all the free inhabitants of the Empire were made Romans. Against conservative opposition, this policy was pursued by a series of enlightened liberal statesmen, Gaius Gracchus and Livius Drusus under the Republic, Julius Caesar and, later, the emperors Claudius ('who had resolved to see the whole population of the world in togas – Greeks, Gauls, Spaniards, Britons, the lot')[2], Vespasian and Hadrian in particular.

(i) Enemy deserters, allied fighters

Under the Republic, the Romans frequently rewarded foreigners who made a substantial contribution to their own success in war, whether as traitors in the enemy camp, as deserters from the enemy to Rome or as allies fighting on the Roman side.

The reward to a high-ranking deserter might consist of land or of money, enrolment as 'a friend of the Roman people', with the erection of an inscription on the Capitol in Rome recording the grant and, within the Empire, exemption from taxation.[3] Or it might consist of the grant of Roman citizenship, the earliest cases dating from the second Punic war. In 211 such a grant was made to a Syracusan and a Spaniard whose treachery had enabled Marcellus to capture Syracuse and in the following year to Myttones, a man half-Phoenician and half-Libyan, who betrayed Acragas in Sicily to M. Valerius Laevinus and, with his Numidian cavalry, went over to the Roman side. He became M. Valerius Mottones and he and his Numidians fought for the Romans against Antiochus in 190 BC.[4] In the civil war Pompey gave citizenship to a Gaul who deserted to him from Caesar's army.[5] Octavian gave full Roman citizenship (and indeed knighthood) to that professional deserter, the freedman admiral Menodorus, when he came over to him from Sextus Pompeius for the first time.[6]

These were rewards to useful deserters from the enemy.* Of more general significance were the grants of citizenship to Roman allies and supporters, originally by popular decree or plebiscite at Rome, later by the award of a Roman general with the approval of his staff under the terms of a special enabling bill of the people in Rome (by Pompey, for instance, in Spain in 72 BC under the terms of a law passed at Rome in that year in the names of the two consuls, the *lex Gellia Cornelia*). In the period of the civil wars such awards were made by the dynasts (Caesar, Pompey, Antony and Octavian) on their own authority;[7] after the establishment of the Empire, by the emperor alone.

In this Marius was something of a law to himself, enfranchising on his own authority two cohorts of the Camertes (Umbrians; this before the enfranchisement of Italy after the Social war) on the battlefield for their courage in fighting the Cimbri in 101 BC. Later he dismissed the illegality of the act by an epigram: 'in the din of battle he could not hear the voice of the law'†[8]

Our best information on such grants concerns Cn. Pompeius in Spain in 72 BC and his father Pompeius Strabo seventeen years earlier than that. A surviving inscription records the grant of Roman citizenship by Pompeius Strabo, with the agreement of his officers, fifty-nine of them, in council, to thirty Spanish cavalrymen in 89 BC,[9] on the authority of the *lex Iulia* of 90 BC. His son, authorised by the consular bill of 72 BC, made similar grants after his successful conflict with Sertorius in Spain.

Remarkable honorands of the last days of the Republic were the two Spaniards, uncle and nephew, each taking the name L. Cornelius Balbus (see p.90), from Gades; together with their fathers they received Roman citizenship from Pompey in Spain in 72 BC. They were to be staunch supporters of Caesar, the elder acting as his agent in Rome from the time of the Gallic wars onwards** (he was suffect consul in 40 BC), the younger ultimately receiving consular status from Octavian. No less remarkable, from the Greek world, was Theophanes of Mytilene who, from being Pompey's expert adviser on eastern affairs in his campaign in the eastern Mediterranean, became Pompey's closest and most intimate adjutant in Rome. Pompey

---

* Valuable, however, as were the services of Pullus Numitorius who betrayed Fregellae to the Romans in 125 BC, his name was universally execrated, according to Cicero (*De fin.* 5, 62; *Phil.* 3, 17) and we hear nothing of his being rewarded; but Cicero's own abuse of him may not have been unconnected with the fact that his daughter was the first wife of Antonius Creticus, the father of Antony.

† Marius showed similar impetuosity in Rome itself in 100 BC. Authorised by a bill of the tribune Saturninus to name three Roman citizens for each of the Latin colonies established by the bill, he named his men – and they assumed Roman citizenship – although the bill itself was repealed or shelved. His act was subsequently challenged unsuccessfully in the courts.[10]

** In a forlorn move to discredit Caesar and Pompey, his citizenship was challenged unsuccessfully in the courts in 56 BC on the ground that by the terms of Rome's treaty with Gades the agreement of the government of Gades was essential, and the formality of consulting Gades on the grant had been disregarded.[13]

conferred citizenship on him at a full military parade in Mytilene.[11]

Ornospades, a Parthian in exile, fought under Tiberius in his Pannonian campaign in AD 6 and was given Roman citizenship; later, probably with Roman consent, he returned to Parthia and became a satrap of king Artabanus III.[12]

(ii) *Automatic grants of citizenship*

Latins, of course, always ranked second after Romans and until late in the second century BC they could acquire Roman citizenship by change of domicile, by leaving their home town and making a new home in Rome (see p.99). Gaius Gracchus had proposed without success that all Latins should receive Roman citizenship and that all other Italians should move up to receive Latin citizenship. In the event the issue was decided by the Social war which broke out in 90 BC and all free inhabitants of the Italian peninsula south of the Po were given Roman citizenship, those north of the Po Latin citizenship; these last had to wait for Julius Caesar to be made full Romans like the rest.

In the provinces citizenship (Roman and Latin) was acquired through the change in status of old towns or the status of newly founded communities in which people lived. When in the first case an existing town was given municipal status, constituted a 'municipium', its inhabitants became Romans overnight, as happened to Volubilis in Mauretania in AD 44, a reward for its loyalty to Rome during the rising of Aedemon at the moment of the establishment of Mauretania as a province.[14] In the second category were 'Roman colonies', the earliest to be proposed (by C. Gracchus) being the restored Carthage (Iunonia) and the earliest to be realised being Narbo in Gaul in 118 BC. Such colonies were established in considerable numbers, particularly in the western Empire, by Caesar and Augustus, largely in order to settle military veterans, who were chiefly Roman citizens already, but those who were not Romans, accepted as settlers in a Roman colony, became Roman citizens as soon as they registered at a census in that colony. Sometimes colonies were sent to enlarge existing communities, whose native citizens sometimes were made Roman citizens and sometimes not. In Latin colonies the settlers acquired Latin citizenship (discarding their Roman citizenship, if they happened to be Romans), but in them there was a regular creaming off of members of the upper class to be full Roman citizens, for from the late second century BC Roman citizenship was acquired automatically on retirement from office by the annual magistrates, of whom more often than not there were six, and their families.

Apart from new colonies, existing cities might be given Latin status. This happened to Italy north of the Po after the Social war,* to the

---

* The grant of Latin rights to Sicily was proposed by Julius Caesar and, after his death, Antony claimed that Caesar intended full Roman citizenship for the island (Cic., *Ad Att.* 14, 12, 1). But Augustus quashed the proposal; see Brunt, *o.c.* (n.1), 239-41.

Maritime Alps under Nero and to Spain under Vespasian.*[15] In that case service as annual magistrates in the cities, as in Latin colonies, was rewarded with the grant of full Roman citizenship, a privilege which in the course of time came to be known as *Latium minus* for, perhaps during the principate of Hadrian, a greater privilege might be conferred on Latin cities and colonies: not only their magistrates but all their city councillors (*decuriones*) received Roman citizenship.[16]

C. Gracchus devised a new qualification for the acquisition of Roman citizenship by a provincial subject. If, after trial at Rome, a Roman senatorial administrator was found guilty of extortion (*repetundae*), the provincial who was judged to have played the most active part in his prosecution received Roman citizenship for himself and his descendants, together with exemption from military service, and this concession was presumably repeated in later laws on the subject. The number of men acquiring citizenship in this way, however, cannot have been large.[17]

Together with the enfranchisement of slaves (see p.86), the greatest increase in the Roman citizen body from the time of the civil wars which ended the Republic to AD 212 was a consequence of service in the armed forces, the army and navy. Indeed the fighting services were a great factory for the production of Roman citizens both from inside the Empire and, surprisingly enough (if one does not start from a knowledge of the late Empire when Roman military service was to all intents and purposes handed over to the barbarians) from outside it.

First the legions, in which long tradition, and indeed religion, decreed that Roman soldiers alone should serve. So in times of crisis, when Julius Caesar raised his famous legion of Gauls, with a lark for their crest (the legion V Alaudae), when Nero in AD 68 and Vitellius in AD 69 raised new legions from the marines, I Adiutrix and II Adiutrix respectively, the new legionaries were necessarily given Roman citizenship.† [18]

These were extraordinary events in time of crisis. In addition it often happened in normal times that when legions fell below full strength and, particularly in the East, satisfactory recruits, Roman citizens already, were not forthcoming, whether from volunteers or from levies, attractive recruits presented themselves, good material in every way but one – they were not Roman citizens. There was a simple solution, to give them citizenship and to enlist them. We have evidence from as early as the time of Augustus, a list of men seconded

---

* This grant of Vespasian, it is calculated, necessitated the drafting of some three hundred and fifty city charters for Spain. Portions of two of them, for Salpensa and Malaca, survive (*FIRA*³ 1, 23f.).

† This is attested for V Alaudae (Suet., *DJ* 24, 2). In the case of I and II Adiutrix we have evidence of citizenship granted to men signed on from the navies and soon after discharged because they had done full service already as marines (*ILS* 1988f.); their younger fellow-servicemen will have received citizenship and continued to serve as legionaries.

from their legion in Egypt, every one of them having the same first name (*praenomen*) as his father, which suggests that the father's name was fictitious and he was not a Roman. While on the official military records a soldier's home town was normally given as his place of origin, some of these newly created Romans, illegitimate sons of Roman legionaries, were recorded as hailing 'from the camp'.[19]

A far bigger part in the creation of new Roman citizens was played by the auxiliary forces, infantry and cavalry, whose total strength equalled that of the legions, and by the navy, which together constituted one of the greatest mercenary armies of the ancient world. Their recruits were in the main *socii, peregrini*, non-Romans, mostly from inside the Empire but some from outside its boundaries. If they did twenty-five years good service,* [20] whether they then took their discharge or continued to soldier on, they automatically received Roman citizenship, and it has been calculated that the Roman citizen body was increased by over ten thousand a year in this way,[21] new Romans who for the most part settled down in civilian life on the frontiers where they had served, some even returning (as Roman citizens) to their native environment outside the Empire.

(iii) Freedmen

The very remarkable feature of Roman civilisation which, when he was at war with Rome in 214 BC, king Philip of Macedon (see p.82) commended as something that Greeks would do well to imitate[22] was the automatic grant of citizenship to slaves who were freed with the proper formalities; touched by the lictor's rod (*vindicta*) in the presence of a magistrate with *imperium*; enrolled on the census list of citizens with the master's approval (*censu*), or granted freedom by a clause in their master's will after his death (*testamento*). Other slaves in the Republic were freed without full formality and presumably did not acquire full citizenship.

In certain circumstances the emancipation of slaves in the late Republic was universally deplored – when, for instance, young male slaves were freed and then enlisted as soldiers to fight on one side or other in the civil wars; and the emancipation of slaves was regarded as a deplorable feature of Sulla's proscriptions. He selected over ten thousand young and strong slaves of prominent Romans whom he had proscribed and turned them into citizens, calling them by his own name, *Cornelii*; they were a protective Nazi-type guard of thugs for himself in his lifetime and a general menace to society after he was dead.[23]

---

* Some received citizenship far earlier than this, for instance the German Arminius, for he had done his service and received Roman citizenship before he was 25 (his age in AD 9, when he led the attack on Varus' camp, *TA* 2, 88, 4). The Numidian Tacfarinas, another one-time auxiliary, who led an insurrection against Rome in AD 17, will not have achieved Roman citizenship since he was a deserter from the Roman army (*TA* 2, 52, 2).

Still after the civil wars a number of slaves of bad character were being emancipated, as Dionysius of Halicarnassus made clear when writing his history (see p.199). Augustus confronted the problem; Suetonius states that 'he was chary of granting Roman citizenship and set a limit on manumission'.[24]

It was clear, first of all, that with a view to increasing the number of ostentatiously and enthusiastically heart-broken mourners at their funerals, some Romans were inclined (with little consideration for their heirs) to free far too many slaves by their wills. So by a law of 2 BC, the *lex Fufia Caninia*, a man was forbidden to emancipate more than half his slaves by will if he possessed between two and ten, more than a third if he had between ten and thirty, more than a quarter if he had between thirty and a hundred, a fifth if between a hundred and five hundred, and in no circumstances whatever more than a hundred (a limitation which could only affect the very rich).[25]

A law of AD 4, the *lex Aelia Sentia*, dealt with some of the cases by which no doubt Dionysius of Halicarnassus was chiefly shocked: slaves with a criminal record, runaways, men who had been imprisoned or consigned to the arena. These, known as *dediticii*, were in no circumstances to acquire full Roman citizenship if they were freed. They might not inherit under a will or make a will or live within a hundred miles of Rome. There was to be no chance for such men to turn over a new leaf.[26]

Between the *dediticii* on the one hand and the regularly emancipated slaves on the other were those whose emancipation was informal (*minus iusta*); their master had indicated a change in their status by the simple act of allowing them to sit down in his presence, or he had declared them free in the presence of friends (*inter amicos*).[27] The position of these half-and-halfers was regularised, presumably by legislation of the consul of 17 BC, C. Junius Silanus, for they were known as *Latini Iuniani*. They died as slaves, their master inheriting the whole of their estate. In AD 4 by the *lex Aelia Sentia* the class of *Latini Iuniani* was enlarged to include slaves under the age of thirty at the time of emancipation and slaves emancipated by a master under twenty.[28]

In cases other than those resulting from the specified age limit, whether of slave or master, this type of informal emancipation might proceed from the selfishness or indecision of a master, but in many cases it simply reflected the fact that, except in Rome 'where you might catch him on his way to the baths or to the theatre',[29] a magistrate with *imperium* was not on the doorstep whenever a master wished to emancipate a slave. So in a great many cases the master doubtless promised full emancipation – and complete Roman citizenship – as soon as a Roman magistrate was available (in rural Italy, the next time an outgoing or returning provincial governor passed that way,[30] in the provinces as soon as a provincial governor was in the neighbourhood, perhaps for the conduct of assizes).

In the case of the slave under thirty or the master under twenty, a claim for full emancipation could be submitted to a Panel of responsible Roman citizens (ten, half senators half Equites, in Rome; twenty regardless of status in the provinces).* If the Panel approved the case, all was well.[31]

Or the *Latinus Junianus* might achieve full emancipation (and Roman citizenship) by his own effort. First of all, by marriage and fatherhood. The freedman under thirty (or with a master under twenty) and, after Vespasian, the man freed 'among friends' acquired full freedom and citizenship if he could demonstrate to a magistrate that he had married a Roman or Latin wife and fathered a child, son or daughter, who had lived for a full year (which, given the incidence of infant mortality, was by no means the same thing as fathering a child); so, if the wife was Latin, did she and the child.†[32]

Other avenues to full emancipation for the *Latinus Junianus* opened up with time. After AD 24 he could acquire it through national service, six (later three) years service in the Roman fire brigade (the Vigiles); after Claudius, through investment in ship-building for the corn-supply (once his ship had been in service for six years); after Nero, through building operations in Rome; after Trajan, through running a bakery of a certain size in Rome for three years.[33] In all these cases there was an exclusive concentration of interest on the *Latinus Junianus* in Rome itself.

More generally, it was always open to the *Latinus Junianus*, on condition that his master agreed, to petition the Emperor for full citizenship. Or the petition could be made by the master, as the younger Pliny petitioned Trajan in the case of some *Latini Juniani* whom he had acquired as a legacy; and, if Trajan's answer is anything to judge by, the emperor was extremely accommodating in granting such requests.[34]

We have no means of knowing the average annual increase in the Roman citizen body on account of the freeing of slaves,[35] for we do not know what proportion of slaves was emancipated – the proportion of household slaves to be freed was presumably far higher than the proportion of slaves employed on the land – or, on an average, at what age.**

* By the charter of Salpensa, following Vespasian's grant of Latin rights to Spain, a slave enfranchised by a master under the age of twenty received full Latin citizenship if the grant was approved by a quorum of members of the city council (*FIRA*[2] 1, 23, 28).

† After Hadrian the child acquired Roman citizenship at birth if the mother was Roman.[36]

** It is not safe, on the strength of a remark of Cicero about the emancipation of enslaved prisoners of war (*Philippics* 8, 32), to think that emancipation came normally after only six years of slavery. Emancipation of the under-thirties was evidently frowned on, and numbers of slaves who were eventually emancipated had been members of the slave-household from birth (*vernae*). Augustus laid down that certain prisoners sold into slavery were not to be emancipated for twenty (CD 53, 25, 4) or thirty (Suet., *DA* 21, 2) years. Petronius, *Sat.* 57, 9, mentions a slave freed after forty years. Lucian, *De merced. conduct.* 24, suggests emancipation when slaves were quite old.

(iv) Some general reasons for granting Roman citizenship

The grant of Roman citizenship, whether or not by the emancipation of slaves, was not always a disinterested act.* On the lowest material plane an enfranchised slave in the city of Rome, still closely bound (see p.92) to his former master, and after that to his master's descendants,[37] became a literal bread-winner for his master's household since, now registered as an independent Roman citizen domiciled in Rome, he qualified to be put on the list of those entitled to receive the monthly grain allowance which from 58 BC onwards was given free.[38] In the Republic, when voting assemblies in Rome were sovereign, he was expected to vote as his master, now his 'patron', told him to vote, and a patron who was involved in politics and had a large number of clients wished to gain a maximum advantage from their votes. That was why interested attempts were made from time to time, though with little success, to alter the rule by which freedmen were automatically allocated to one of the four city tribes. The thirty-one country tribes were naturally less well represented in the voting assemblies and in any of them a single vote counted for more than in one of the over-represented city tribes.[39]

In the case of aliens there was a trafficking in citizenship-grants. This was one of the charges which Cicero brought against Antony. And the practice continued under the Empire. Claudius Lysias, the captain who arrested St Paul at Jerusalem, made no bones of the fact that he had bought his citizenship and had had to pay a considerable sum of money for it. His name suggests that he acquired his citizenship under Claudius, during whose rule, according to Cassius Dio, there was widespread trafficking in Roman citizenship on the part of the imperial freedmen; the sum had been expended in bribes to get his name on to a list submitted by those freedmen to the Emperor for his approval.[40]

For in the Empire, except when slaves were emancipated or citizenship was acquired legally under some law or other, all grants required the formal approval of the Emperor, and the correspondence of the younger Pliny gives us a typical specimen of the sort of applications which the emperor received: in one case on behalf of an Egyptian Greek doctor by whom Pliny had been treated, in another for a centurion in the auxiliary army who wanted citizenship for his daughter.

Roman citizenship was granted to direct petitioners, men who submitted *libelli*, by the Emperor in consultation with his Privy Council (*Consilium*), just as in 89 BC Pompeius Strabo had acted in consultation with his staff, and inscriptional evidence has recently come to light of such grants to two Mauretanian chieftains, father and

---

* In many cases, no doubt, a *dediticius* was given his – qualified – freedom by his master in Rome because he was a troublesome character and a bad influence in the slave-household. Anything to place the distance of a hundred miles between him and the city.

son, to the father by M. Aurelius and Lucius Verus and to the son by
M. Aurelius and Commodus, citizenship going also in both cases to
the men's wives and children, all of whose names were recorded.[41]

The grant of citizenship by the Roman state was clearly of benefit
to both parties to the transaction. For the slave and the auxiliary
soldier its achievement had for many years been an incentive and a
goal, bringing freedom in the first case and, in both cases,
opportunities for sons and daughters to better themselves in the
world. At the same time the State benefited. Bad freedmen apart
(and, as has been seen, Augustus legislated to meet this problem), the
new members of the Roman body politic were generally of 'good
type': in particular, men responsible for local government, ex-
servicemen (who had learnt discipline and acquired a measure of
education, particularly in becoming Latin-speaking, during their
military service) and individuals whose cases the emperor had
personally examined and approved. On the highest plane the grant of
citizenship was an instrument of imperial policy; hence its conferment
on client princes, particularly in the East, by Augustus* and the early
emperors; though they could not foresee the ultimate consequence of
their act, the incorporation of the descendants of these princes a
century or so later into the senatorial aristocracy and governing class
of Rome.

Acts like Nero's grant of citizenship to Greek dancers were
exceptional and generally criticised.[42]

(v) Becoming a Roman

For the freedman in particular the first moment was perhaps the best:
parties, letters of congratulation. We possess the letter in which
Quintus Cicero expressed his delight at the news that his brother had
emancipated Tiro;[43] presumably he also wrote a letter to Tiro himself.

The new citizen had to buy a toga and learn how to wear it, though
he might perhaps reckon (like a newly fledged M.A. at the University
today) that he could get away with it by borrowing on the rare
occasions when he would have to wear it.

He had to accustom himself to the strange possession of three
names, two of them certainly, perhaps all three of them, new. For a
man emerging from slavery the first two names were normally those of
his old master (see p.154). An allied soldier given citizenship in the
Republic (see p.83) might take the first names of the Roman
commander-in-chief under whom he had fought; so numbers of Iulii
in Gaul were descended from Gauls enfranchised by Julius Caesar.[44]
Or they might take the names of a subordinate Roman officer. The
Cornelii Balbi, enfranchised by Pompey in 72 BC, evidently took the

---

*Augustus gave citizenship to, among others, Eurycles of Sparta, Ariobarzanes of Media,
Mithridates of Commagene (almost certainly, see Goodfellow, *o.c.* (n.1), 104), Samsigeramus of
Emesa, Juba of Mauretania and Cottius of the Alps.

name of one of Pompey's officers, Cornelius Lentulus Crus (the future consul of 49 BC). And the list of Spaniards enfranchised by Pompey's father in 89 BC tells an interesting story. Most of the men are listed by their native Spanish names, names like Umarillun, Atullo, Balciadin. But three have new Roman names: Otacilius, Cn. Cornelius, P. Fabius. Now on the officers' council which approved Pompey's grant were two Otacilii, a Cn. Cornelius and a M. Fabius. Here, then, are three men who beat the gun by losing no time in applying to particular officers who had commanded them for permission to adopt their names.[45]

In the Empire the first names taken by auxiliary soldiers who had completed their military service were more often than not those of the ruling emperor who authorised their citizenship-grant. The name given on their citizenship certificates (*diplomata*) was their old, not their new, name.

The new citizen must often have felt very lonely, a stranger in a new world. He was formally estranged from his parents and, unless they had been included in this grant, from his wife and children. The men who acquired citizenship through the tenure of magistracies in Latin towns or colonies came off best, for their parents, children and sons' children shared in the grant.[46] The wife of a *Latinus Junianus*, if she was Latin herself, shared in her husband's present and future status.

Strictly speaking, at the expiry of their military service soldiers and sailors (*classiarii*) did not possess wives because in every branch of the Service (legions, Praetorian and Urban Guard, auxiliary units and fleet) they were not, until Septimius Severus, allowed to contract a legitimate marriage, *matrimonium iustum*, during service (and even after Septimius Severus Guardsmen might not marry).[47] In fact, however, large numbers of them kept women in the civilian quarters adjacent to their barracks and had children by them. In the case of auxiliaries and sailors, such children were given citizenship at the end of their fathers' military service, as we know from the explicit language of the surviving certificates of citizenship (*diplomata*) issued to auxiliaries and sailors at the completion of their service. In exceptional circumstances the same concession might be made in the case of the children of legionaries born during their fathers' service; it seems not to have been made ever in the case of regular legionaries or members of the Praetorian Guard.[48]

The ex-serviceman might wish to give respectability to the woman with whom he had been living (who in the diplomata is flattered with the title of 'wife') and, though she did not share in his new citizenship, he was granted *conubium*, which meant that, if he continued to live with her, any children subsequently born to them would be Roman. This is explicitly stated in the *diplomata* for auxiliaries, sailors and Guardsmen[49] and was the case also with ex-service legionaries (who themselves, of course, like the Guardsmen, were Roman citizens

already), though in their case *diplomata* seem not to have been issued.[50]
The *conubium* (with legitimisation of subsequent offspring) was
granted also to any serviceman who, on discharge, was a bachelor and
who married subsequently.

From the time of Antoninus Pius a change was made – for whatever
reason – and children of auxiliaries born during their fathers' service
no longer received citizenship on their fathers' discharge. This
privilege was retained henceforth only in the case of sailors.[51]

As for the emancipated slave, all turned on the amount remaining in
his purse (*peculium*), particularly if he had had to pay for his own
emancipation. Could he afford now to free the woman (the
contubernalis) with whom he had been living, and his children –
assuming, of course, that their master was cooperative?

In every respect the emancipated slave came off worse, for though his
sons and grandsons would fare better, he would never be more than a
second-class citizen. Various careers open to the freeborn Roman
were closed to him; he could not, though he was of the right age,
volunteer for service in the legions or in the Praetorian Guard; except
in Julius Caesar's colonies, he could not be a town-councillor (*decurio*)
or a magistrate. Down to the third generation members of his family
were barred, after Augustus, from marriage into a senatorial family.
And in the bond which had attached him to his former master and his
master's family, not every strand was cut. His old master retained a
certain interest in his estate, to the extent of inheriting one half if the
freedman left no direct descendants. His old master, now his patron,
demanded dutiful obedience (*obsequium*),* he also required specific
services (*officia*) which had been made a condition of his
emancipation.†

The freedman who displayed gross lack of deference, who was
ingratus, might discover that he had not escaped from his old master's
clutches. There were cases in which Claudius ordered the re-
enslavement of such men, and the general question of 'ingratitude' on
the part of freedmen was debated in the Senate under Nero. In the
second century the government took over the investigation of such
charges and offending freedmen might be exiled or, in particularly
grave cases, condemned to hard labour in the mines. And the
freedman was always in danger of severe punishment, however great
his innocence, if he remained a member of his former master's

---

* An indication of such deference was the fact that by Augustus' legislation a freedwoman
who was married to her patron, and then left him, was not allowed to marry again without his
permission (*Dig.* 38, 11, 1, 1).

† For instance a freedman who was a qualified doctor might be bound, as a condition of his
manumission, to continue to give medical attention to his patron and his patron's family. At the
same time he might owe his start in independent practice to the master who had freed him, just
as very many freedman-artisans and shopkeepers set up in business with the help, perhaps on
some sort of profit-sharing basis, of their former master.

household and that master was murdered.[52]

Yet the further estranged he was from his old habitat and from direct association with his old master, the greater might be his immediate problems. As a slave, he had been kept, fed and clothed; he had had little cause to worry about the economics of existence. Now, as Epictetus pointed out, he had to find work and earn an income in order to survive.[53]

When his name was written or inscribed officially, the second-class nature of his citizenship was evident. Normally his tribe was not mentioned, as it was mentioned in the case of other citizens, nor was the name of his father. He was not 'the son of X', but 'the freedman of Y'. Yet, despite all these handicaps, pride in achievement prevailed; this is evident from the great number of surviving freedmen's epitaphs.

The enfranchised foreigner (*peregrinus*) on the other hand, mentioned his tribe and also his father's name – a nice Roman name if his father was a fiction, as in the case of certain legionary recruits (see p.86), an outlandish name often, if it was his father's real name, as is the case more often than not in the military *diplomata*.

On paper the most valuable element in the new citizen-package was, perhaps, the right of appeal (*provocatio*) which in Italy, at the end of the second century BC,[54] had been held by some to be a preferable alternative to Roman citizenship (even without its attendant disadvantage, after Augustus, of liability to certain taxation and to death duties).

In the provinces this gave the Roman citizen real advantage. His statement, 'I am a Roman citizen' or later, 'I appeal to Caesar', should always have been enough to prevent him from being summarily imprisoned, tortured for the extraction of evidence or from being tried on a criminal charge – or, perhaps, suffering capital punishment after condemnation – by the governor (or his deputy) in a province (instead of having his case referred to Rome), and his rights in this respect were stated in the (probably Augustan) *lex Iulia de vi publica*.[55] How often recourse was had to such an appeal we do not know. It might offer temptation to any blithe spirit anxious to see Rome and something of the world at the government's expense, and it was a wise precaution where there was local prejudice or a notoriously dishonest governor (though governors of the type of Verres ran a very small risk generally if they overrode or disregarded such an appeal);* but in the case of a good governor there might be little reason to expect a fairer trial in Rome. If every Roman citizen on a capital charge had appealed to Rome and his transport to Rome had involved

* And there were doubtless underlings of the Verres type. Or did St Paul submit to scourging and imprisonment at Philippi and only reveal his Roman citizenship when the authorities subsequently ordered his release (Acts 16, 37)? In Jerusalem he revealed his citizenship to the Roman officer as soon as he was threatened with scourging, and the officer took immediate notice of his statement (Acts 22, 25-9).

all the trouble and vicissitudes of St Paul's journey, the business of transferring all cases of appeal to Rome would have been a fantastic exercise.[56]

So, not unnaturally, with the number of Roman citizens in the provinces perpetually on the increase, the number of cases transferred to Rome decreased. From the end of the first century AD it has been claimed that where a man's alleged crime was one fully defined in the statute-book at Rome, the subject in Rome of a special criminal court, the governor himself tried the case and sent a report to Rome, deferring the execution of sentence until he received the emperor's agreement. The cases involving Roman citizens which he transferred for trial to Rome were of those accused of a somewhat indeterminate crime. Whether they had appealed or not, we know that the younger Pliny quite automatically sent the Roman citizens among those arrested for Christianity in Bithynia for trial in Rome.[57]

With the wholesale grant of Roman citizenship by Caracalla in AD 212, this particular privilege of Roman citizens inevitably came to an end; for criminal purposes there remained the horizontal stratification of imperial subjects, not into Roman citizens and others (*peregrini*) but into the upper and lower class of Roman citizens themselves, *honestiores* (in the provinces, chiefly decurions) and *humiliores*, condemned members of the upper class receiving upper-class punishments (like deportation), those of the lower class lower-class punishments, consignment to the mines or exposure to wild beasts in the arena.[58]

There were certain disadvantages about becoming a Roman citizen and we know that by the terms of C. Gracchus' extortion law (the *lex Acilia*) a successful plaintiff might opt to receive the right of appeal (*provocatio*) instead of full Roman citizenship, if he so preferred.[59] And there is the engaging story of a Cretan involved somehow or other on the enemy side in the Social war of 90 BC who, offered Roman citizenship by the consul in exchange for his volunteering to play the traitor, answered, 'Citizenship is so much clap-trap; I want money.'[60]

The five per cent death duty (*vicesima hereditatis*), instituted by Augustus, was particularly resented. In established Roman families this was not levied in the case of legacies to near relatives, but in cases when an individual received Roman citizenship for himself but not for his parents or children, it was levied on inheritances which they received from him or he received from them. Protests were sometimes made successfully in individual cases to the emperor; but Trajan did well, completing a reform begun by Nerva, when he put an end to the exaction of death duty in all cases between near relatives.[61]

In highly favoured cases – Octavian's honouring of Seleucus of Rhosos, for instance – Roman citizenship was granted with *immunitas*, exemption from all the obligations to which a Roman citizen was normally liable.[62]

In AD 212 Caracalla granted citizenship to all free men living within the borders of the Roman empire. The·starry-eyed accounts of this liberal measure which brighten the pages of so many modern history books find no reflection in the *History* of Cassius Dio. It was simply a means of increasing the State's income from taxation, which in the case of death duties, he raised sharply; so Dio wrote.* [63]

What of a man's position in his home town or his native community within the Empire if he became a Roman citizen? Could he retain his civic honours? Was he liable still to local obligations of service and taxation? In the late Republic Cicero claimed that Roman citizenship was incompatible with any other form of citizenship, honours and duties alike. But clearly, if widespread local resentment was to be avoided, that position could not be held. In the triumviral period the freshly made Roman citizen was allowed to retain local honours, but exempted from local chores. Very soon, however, this exemption was abolished, as seems evident from the third Cyrene edict of Augustus. Later emperors were at pains to emphasise that in no case were a man's local obligations changed by his new status.[62] Julius Caesar, it seems, had earlier played with the idea of making established Roman citizens who resided in cities of the Empire contribute to local taxation – which from· time to time and place to place a number of Romans perhaps did as a good-will gesture calculated to win local popularity.[65]

All the time, until the climax was reached with Caracalla's grant, the number of Romans in the provinces, especially the western provinces, was increasing regularly. There are a few pointers to the process of change.

There is a certain significance, for instance, in the evidence for recruits to the auxiliary service from Trajan's time onwards. Formerly the great majority of such recruits had been non-Roman. Now men who were already Roman citizens joined up. Six recruits for the third cohort of Itumaei in Egypt under Trajan are shown by their possession of three names to have been Roman,[66] and a change in the official language of *diplomata* from Antoninus Pius onwards is significant. Instead of the grant of citizenship being made on each occasion to all men who had completed their service in certain named units, citizenship was now granted 'to such men as did not possess it already'.[67]

And why do no certain *diplomata* for auxiliaries survive from later than AD 178? Because by now recruits to the auxiliary forces were largely Roman citizens already and, perhaps, those who were not, on

---

* Yet could this object not have been achieved more simply within the existing tax structure? Caracalla was certainly not well cast for the part of enlightened imperial benefactor. Was vanity a motive? Did he want to go down to history as an unrivalled benefactor, an emperor in a class of his own, an outstanding *exemplum*? (see J.H. Oliver, *AJP* 76, 1955, 293).

the example of the legions, were made Roman citizens at the moment of enlistment?

Somewhere or other, the grant of Roman citizenship was officially registered – on the Capitol in Rome in the case of all enfranchised auxiliary ex-servicemen, at provincial headquarters in the case of any provincial civilian, as we know from Trajan's instruction to Pliny to send him the relevant information about the Egyptian doctor freshly enfranchised at Pliny's request, for transmission to the central government offices in Egypt. And from the start of the Empire, the imperial archives in Rome held a complete list of individual civilians who had received Roman citizenship with the emperor's personal sanction.[68]

The ex-service auxiliary was supplied with a copy of the relevant part of the public inscription at Rome as concerned himself and this, in the convenient form of a small diptych (*diploma*), he could carry about with him. Indeed he was the only Roman to possess irrefutable evidence of his citizenship – except for men who had received Roman citizenship in an imperial rescript to a personal petition.

A legitimate child of Roman citizens whose birth had been registered as, after Augustus, the law required,[69] could have carried a diptych certifying the registration of his birth (and probably did), but its evidence was not irrefutable any more than the appearance of a man's name on the census lists (he having registered as a Roman at the census), for in neither of the two cases was there any official check on the *bona fides* of the registration. A child was registered within thirty days of birth, normally by one or other of the parents, but their statement was not checked officially, and in the case of the census, as Cicero pointed out, impostors could well have registered as Roman citizens.[70]

A considerable amount of enquiry must have been necessary, therefore, to verify many statements by men that they were Roman, and it is surprising at first sight that St Paul's statement that he was a Roman was seemingly not challenged by the officer to whom he made it. It is possible, of course, that it was and that reasonable evidence, perhaps a birth certificate, was readily available.[71]

CHAPTER EIGHT

Expulsion from Rome, Italy or your Homeland[1]

(i) Deprivation of citizenship

Citizenship was lost automatically by Romans who were made prisoners of war but, if they were freed and returned to Rome, by what was called *postliminium* they automatically recovered it. Until the late Republic (see p.110) they surrendered it of their own free will if they became citizens of another state, and that was why Atticus was said to have declined the offer of Athenian citizenship.[2] Also if he joined a Latin colony, a Roman ceased to be a Roman and became a Latin.

A Roman once lost his citizenship if the people (i.e. the popular assembly at Rome) decided to sell him into slavery – which, in theory at least, might happen if without good reason he failed to appear at the census or if he shirked military service. Cassius Dio, indeed, states that when, after the Varian disaster in Germany in AD 9, men of military age in Rome refused to volunteer for military service in the emergency, Augustus picked by lot one out of every five men under thirty-five and one in ten of those between thirty-five and forty-six, and that the unfortunates were stripped of their property and disfranchised.[3]

Automatic, too, was the loss of citizenship by any Roman who, as a punishment and an example, was handed over to the enemy as a kind of scapegoat, so absolving the Roman state of any public guilt which might be thought to have been incurred through his transaction.

The Roman history books recorded how in 321 BC, trapped in the Caudine Forks, the two consuls T. Veturius and Sp. Postumius surrendered and made peace with the Samnites, in consequence of which the entire Roman army escaped with their lives. This desirable result achieved, Postumius in the following year pointed out to the Senate that the Roman people alone was entitled to make a valid peace treaty, and so the war could be resumed at a moment's notice; all that had been made was a *sponsio*, the sole responsibility of the two consuls, Veturius and himself. So let them both be handed over to the Samnites naked and in bonds with all the refinement of august priestly ceremony and Rome could wash its hands of them (for they would automatically become Samnites) and, with an easy conscience, it could resume the war. Similar action was taken in the case of the consul of 137 BC, C. Hostilius Mancinus who in Spain surrendered his army and signed a peace with the Numantines. To succeed, of course, this extraordinary game required cooperation from the enemy. The Samnites received the Romans and even heard Postumius declare that he was himself now a Samnite and saw him behave in what he thought was a suitable Samnite manner (see p.4); they then told them to get out. The surrender of Mancinus, naked and bound, was more ineffective still. The Numantines did not even open their gates to receive him. What were the Romans to do in face of such non-cooperation? They could not leave him to die; after all, he was still a fellow-citizen, a Roman. So they picked him up and brought him home. A dilemma immediately arose. *Was* he still a Roman? The lawyers scratched their heads and in the end it required a law of the people to assert that, by a kind of *postliminium*, he was.[4]

Could a Roman act in other ways so as to deprive himself of his Roman citizenship? Obviously, if he deserted and, joining Rome's enemies, he fought against his country, as Coriolanus had done in legend and as Labienus, the son of Caesar's adjutant in Gaul, did in fact when, at the time of the civil wars, he joined the Parthians. Cicero even claimed that this could happen nearer home. By his summary execution of the Catilinarian prisoners in December 63 BC he denied them the citizen's fundamental right of appeal and trial. But no, Cicero argued; they had no such right because they were no longer citizens; they had behaved in such a way as to change themselves from citizens to enemies (*hostes*) of Rome.[5]

In the Empire a man could be stripped of his citizenship by the Emperor, as Claudius disfranchised a Lycian because he could not speak Latin;[6] the Emperor gave, the Emperor could take away. Also, as will be seen, loss of Roman citizenship in the Empire was an automatic consequence of deportation.

(ii) Expulsion of aliens from Rome

The expulsion of aliens (*peregrini*) – and sometimes of Roman citizens – from the city of Rome in the Republic could be ordered by law, by decree of the Senate, by the edict of a consul or by a decision of the censors. The censors had no effective means of enforcing their decision, and it is difficult to see how in other cases the expulsion order can have been carried out effectively. Foreigners had no passports and Romans no identity cards; there was no police force of any effectiveness, no C.I.D. The state must have depended on the common informer, the keen young prosecutor.

There were two occasions when, to our knowledge, foreigners were expelled at the outbreak of war. In 171 BC war had not in fact been declared against Macedon, and Macedonian envoys were in Rome trying to dispel the Senate's suspicion of king Perseus of Macedon, particularly its suspicion that Perseus had engineered the recent unsuccessful attempt on the Pergamene king Eumenes' life at Delphi. They had no success. They were ordered to leave Rome before night and to be out of Italy within thirty days; and the order was extended to cover all Macedonian residents in Rome, of whom, surprisingly, there seems to have been a number. Appian gives a graphic account of their dilemma. How were they to collect their possessions in the time? How were they to find transport? 'Some threw themselves on the ground at the city gates with their wives and children.'[7]

In AD 9 there was hysteria in Rome on the news of the annihilation of three Roman legions under Varus in the Teutoberg forest in Germany. The emperor's German bodyguard was disbanded and its members removed to the islands (from which they were recalled before very long to resume their duties); 'Gauls and Celts' living or staying in Rome were ordered out of the city.[8]

If we disregard a fanciful suggestion of Dionysius of Halicarnassus that Latins and Hernici not domiciled in Rome were ordered out of the city in 486 BC,[9] the first of the many 'expulsions' of Latins and Italian allies from Rome occurred in the period 187 to 172 BC and was a step taken by the Roman government in response to a request from the authorities of the Latin cities themselves, a request which it would have been difficult to refuse.

By the constitution of the Latin League it was open to the citizen of any Latin town (Rome included) to migrate to any other city within the League; in which case he relinquished his former citizenship and without any difficulty acquired the citizenship of the city to which he migrated, technically *per migrationem et censum*. Now by the beginning of the second century BC with the growth and increasing attraction of Rome, this was in danger of becoming a one-way traffic. Latin cities were alarmed by the reduction in their own population, particularly in the number of young men of military age, for they were under obligation to supply a fixed number of soldiers every year to the Roman army; and it was on the prompting of the Latin cities themselves that the Romans acted.

The first request was made in 187 BC, and the Senate gave orders for the return to their own cities of all Latins who (or whose fathers) had registered at home and not in Rome in the census of 204 BC or in any subsequent census. The praetor peregrinus was made responsible for the carrying out of the decree. Twelve thousand Latins were identified (from lists which can only have been supplied by the Latin cities, who must have kept tabs on the men) and sent home.[10] This was a very considerable operation, and we are at a loss to know what staff the praetor employed for the purpose.

However, those who are determined to beat the law can usually beat it. There was an old agreement, probably in the constitution of the Latin League, that a man could change cities (and citizenship) within the League if he left a son behind in his home town. The letter of the law was observed and its spirit broken if the migrant adopted some one for the purpose and left him behind or if he left a son but before migration sold him into slavery to a Roman on the understanding that the Roman would proceed to enfranchise him; the son would then be a freedman, but beyond question a Roman.

So after only ten years, in 177, delegates from Latin cities were knocking again on the doors of the Senate. Again the Senate did everything possible to stop up the holes, and a law was passed ordering the return to their homes of all who registered, or whose parents registered, in a Latin city at the census of 189, 184 or 179, and a senatorial decree forbad the device of selling a son in order to secure his enfranchisement. The praetor L. Mummius was given the task of bringing to trial any one who was suspected of evading the new law.[11]

But there were still determined law-breakers, Latins who, while they waited for fresh opportunity, would claim, presumably, if challenged, that Rome was simply their business address. So in 172 there was a consular edict forbidding such men to register at the census in Rome; they had to return for the purpose to their home towns.[12]

That is the last that we hear of the matter.

Towards the end of the Republic, always when proposals were in the air to extend the franchise – Roman citizenship, that is to say – there were, it appears at first sight, a whole series of expulsions of aliens from Rome;* in 126 BC (a bill of the tribune Junius Pennus); in 122 BC (a bill of the consul C. Fannius); in 95 (a law of the two consuls L. Licinius Crassus and Q. Mucius Scaevola which caused intense resentment) and in 65 BC (a *lex Papia*, which we know to have been operative for at least eleven years).[13] Yet, as far as expulsions were concerned, the bills were, it seems, as effective as the Red Queen's monotonous, 'Off with their heads'; there is no evidence that they resulted in any expulsion at all of aliens from the city of Rome.

In a famous passage Cicero stated that the expulsion of aliens from Rome was all wrong; on the other hand, to take measures against aliens masquerading as Roman citizens, people who tried to vote in the elections when they were not entitled to vote at all, was all right.[14] And this, it seems, is what the 'alien acts' were about. They were a deterrent before 90 BC to Latins and Italians attempting to vote in Rome (otherwise than, as Latins were entitled to vote, in one only of the thirty-five tribes, chosen by lot), in 65 BC to non-Roman residents domiciled north of the Po, when the extension of Roman citizenship to that part of Italy was under consideration. The bills may, indeed, have gone as far as to instruct unenfranchised aliens to keep out of Rome to a distance of five miles on the polling days when the enfranchising bills were being voted on.[15] This was not unreasonable,

---

* None of them, curiously, thought worth a mention by the author of the *Perioche* of Livy.

a precaution against rioting and interference by aliens who themselves had no voting rights.

These 'alien acts' were strong irritants not only to those against whom they were aimed, because they provoked malevolent informants and were manipulated for political purposes. The *lex Licinia Mucia* of 95 BC, for instance, evidently gave the opportunity of challenging the citizenship of certain people who had been registered as *bona fide* citizens by the censors two years earlier. One (T. Matrinius) was a protégé of Marius and, if the case against him had been established, proceedings would no doubt have been taken against a number of Marius' other clients.[16] Prosecutions under the *lex Papia* in 62 BC against Archias and in 56 against Cornelius Balbus were moves against Lucullus, Pompey and Caesar respectively.

What, then, happened to the culprit, the man who under one or other of these bills was prosecuted in a criminal court and found to have been passing himself off falsely as a Roman citizen? His punishment, it seems, was very mild indeed; he was merely forbidden to continue to live in the city of Rome.*

Republican history, therefore, shows no evidence of hostility to foreigners as such or any wish to prevent them from living in Rome. Nothing could be more untrue or nonsensical than what Cassius Dio wrote of the bill of Papius in 65 BC: 'All those residing in Rome, unless they had homes in Italy south of the Alps, were expelled from the city on Papius' motion because there were too many of them and they did not seem to be suitable people for Roman citizens to consort with.'[18]

To masquerade as a Roman citizen under the Empire was a grave criminal offence. A number of such men were detected and executed under Claudius and later. Such was Claudius' distorted sense of humour – or propriety – that in one case he insisted on the defendant wearing Greek (foreign) dress when the prosecutor spoke and changing it for a Roman toga when his own advocate argued in his defence.†

Yet when it came to light in the early Empire that certain people on the southern foothills of the Alps had in all innocence acted on the mistaken assumption that they were full Roman citizens (some even serving – and at non-commissioned rank – in the Praetorian Guard**

---

* An inference from the extraordinary story of the Etruscan Perperna family. After M. Perperna, consul of 130 BC, campaigned in Asia and was lined up for a triumph (but he died before he could celebrate it), the citizenship of his father, who himself had won distinction as an officer in the Illyrian war of 168, was successfully challenged; so he left Rome to live in the country. Yet this did not prevent his grandson, consul in 92, from enjoying an eminent public career.[17]

† Other forms of masquerading were punishable: a slave masquerading as a free man (if such an impostor was accepted as a volunteer for military service and subsequently detected, he merited execution by Trajan's ruling); a freedman passing himself off as a knight, even sitting in the 'fourteen rows'.[20]

** What had the recruiting officers been doing, to accept such men as recruits?

and sitting on juries), Claudius decided very sensibly to confirm their citizen status, and to confirm it with retrospective effect.[19]

(iii) Exiles

It is a long-established Russian tradition to use Siberia as a dumping-ground for Russians whom, on one ground or another, the Russian government has found unacceptable. Britain once sent Britons condemned of criminal offences to Australia. Mussolini dispatched the enemies of fascism to the islands, and recent authoritarian Greek governments have treated critics of their regime in a similar way.

As a result of the instability of political life in ancient Greece, considerable numbers of men were driven into exile from time to time – aristocrats or oligarchs at the establishment of a tyranny or radical democracy, radical democrats under an oligarchy. In Athenian history Themistocles and Alcibiades are the most famous names. In 404 BC there were the moderates who rallied outside the country and fought their way back to overthrow the Thirty at Athens. One of Alexander's greatest anxieties was to secure the return of exiles to all Greek cities, and in the confusion of Spartan-Achaean relations in the early days of Roman involvement in Greece, there were always exiles struggling to get back to Sparta and to overthrow the government.

Because of the smooth course of Roman constitutional development, wholesale exile was not a feature of Republican life at all. When revolution came, in the eighties BC and after Caesar's death, the victor killed his opponents and seized their property; there were the proscriptions of the eighties, first of Marius then of Sulla, and with the formation of the Triumvirate in 43 BC there was a greedy massacre both of the innocents and of the not-so-innocent. In the interval there had been the prodigious victory of Julius Caesar, who preferred to spare his enemies and who initiated no proscription at all.

In a variety of ways individuals could be forced to leave their homes and to live elsewhere. From the earliest times the head of a Roman family was evidently entitled to treat his son in this way;* and he could compel any of his freedmen who offended him to put the distance of a hundred miles between himself and Rome.[21]

From the remote past of the fifth and fourth centuries BC there were the legends of Coriolanus and of Cincinnatus, both banished (or choosing to retire) from Rome when charged with partiality in the distribution of booty. And then, in real history, there was the record of the sad end of the great Africanus, hounded out of Rome to live in retirement at Liternum.

---

* For attempted parricide, for instance. When the son of L. Tarius Rufus, a man who rose from humble origins to be consul in 16 BC, was detected in a scheme to murder him, he held a private Council (with Augustus present) and the son was exiled to Massilia. But, kind-hearted and forgiving, Rufus made a regular allowance to his son, so that his exile was attended by little material discomfort, Sen., *De clem.* 1, 15; Plin., *NH* 18, 37.

At one extreme a Roman lived out of Rome of his own free will; at the other he was stripped of his belongings and transported to live the rest of his life outside Rome and Italy often on some devil's island which was not his choice, indeed was not likely sometimes to have been anybody's choice, for a home.

In the first case a Roman remained a full Roman citizen, whether he lived in a community of Roman citizens (a Roman colony or a *municipium*) or lived in some other sort of community, whose citizenship he did not adopt; he might or might not intend at some time or other to return and live in Rome. If he joined a Latin colony, he surrendered his Roman and acquired Latin citizenship.

Apart from the Latin cities down to the Social war, there were others, bound to Rome by treaty (*civitates foederatae*), and therefore independent of Roman jurisdiction – cities in Italy itself down to the Social war (for instance Praeneste and Tibur at the very gates of Rome, Tarquinii, Nuceria and Naples) and, in the provinces, Massilia in Gaul, Gades and Tarraco in Spain, Athens and Patrae in Greece. If a Roman migrated to one 'of these and acquired its citizenship, he ceased to be a Roman and was outside the reach of Roman law; from the Roman point of view, he was *exul*, an exile.

Here were very convenient bolt-holes for Romans who, on capital charges before the people in Rome, knew from the way the voting was going that condemnation was inevitable and, after Sulla, for those who anticipated condemnation on capital charges in any of the new permanent criminal courts; they escaped in time and saved their skins. Others, whose lives were not in danger, saved their fortunes. These were senators who, after the establishment in 149 BC of a permanent court for the trial of men of senatorial rank, chiefly those who had been provincial governors, were accused of exacting money illegally from the people in whose interest it was their duty to administer and now anticipated condemnation and the sentence to repay the whole sum – after 123 BC twice the sum – which they were proved to have stolen. Of such criminals Verres was the tarnished exemplar. If prosecution threatened or a trial started and condemnation seemed inevitable, with the quick and efficient co-operation of those bankers and businessmen of whom in public in his happier days he had spoken so contemptuously, an accused man could salt away his illegal takings and escape to enjoy them; saying good-bye to any thought of a further career in Rome, he could live in his new home without anxiety in comfort and safety. Had he stayed in Rome and paid the penalty, he might well have had to face life in poverty and, even in Rome, as a disgraced man, branded with *infamia*, he could not have looked forward to a further public career.

After Sulla, such a man had greater cause still to put a distance between himself and Rome, for condemnation for extortion did not close the book on a senatorial administrator's wrong-doing; it could lead to other more serious – capital – charges (treason, for instance).

And after Julius Caesar extortion itself, if accompanied by violence (*saevitia*) became a capital crime.[22]

So far, exile was voluntary. Cicero said in 69 BC: 'Exile is not a punishment. Men who seek to avoid some penalty or disaster change their residence. So in Roman law, unlike the laws of other states, you will not find that any crime has ever been punished by exile. To avoid imprisonment, execution or degradation – all legal penalties – men escape into exile as if taking sanctuary at an altar.'[23]

The voluntary exile therefore evaded Roman justice, but Roman justice then caught up with him by making it impossible for him to return to Rome if he had departed already when the court pronounced sentence or, if he was still in Rome, by condemning him to leave Rome (and normally Italy) without the possibility of returning. This, from the late Republic, was done by passing the 'interdict', forbidding him fire or water on Roman (and Italian) soil. After which, still in Cicero's life time, the interdict was passed as a sentence in capital trials (for instance, arson, murder, forgery, violence and treason); so that in 46 BC Cicero could write, 'Do you not know that exile is a penalty for crime?' More than this, by Caesar's regulation half the condemned man's property was annexed to the State.[24]

Under the Republic a man could be banished from Rome without trial by a popular bill or by the administrative act of a magistrate. Cicero in 58 BC abandoned Rome of his own free will before the storm burst, but then Clodius secured the passing of a bill forbidding him fire and water within the distance of 600 miles of Rome. Later in the same year when Aelius Lamia took up the cudgels on Cicero's behalf, he was banished by the consul Gabinius. Such happenings were rare because the terrorist regime of 58 was rare; normally a man threatened in this way would have secured the veto of a friendly tribune on his behalf and, at the worst, would have been called on to face proper legal proceedings.

In the Empire such administrative action to banish a man – to forbid him to live in certain territory or to command him to live in a particular place, was taken from the start by the Emperor (by Augustus, for instance, against Ovid) and could be taken later by the Prefect of the Praetorian Guard and by the Prefect of the City or, in the provinces, by a provincial governor. Such men and women and those sentenced by the courts at Rome for an offence which did not carry a capital penalty, were technically 'relegati', enforced émigrés, and not, as Ovid protested in his own case, exiles (*exules*), though the word was commonly used then, as for convenience, it is used of them by the historian today.

Such relegation could be without a time limit or it could be temporary as, under Cicero's bribery law, a man was, as it seems, banished for ten years from Rome, after which he could return with no reflection on his character, no *infamia*, and resume a public career. Under the Empire temporary relegation was for ten years or for a shorter period and, in its milder form, when imposed at Rome, it was merely negative and precluded residence in Rome and, generally, Italy and, later, in any province in which the Emperor might be present; sometimes other parts of the empire were also barred, often, in the case of a man of provincial origin, the province in which he was born. After Claudius, a man banished from his province by a provincial governor might not enter Italy.[27] Outside the forbidden territory a man or woman could live where he or she chose.

As for the time limit, under Tiberius a society woman of bad character was banished from Rome for ten years as a precautionary measure; she had gravely corrupted her elder son, who had killed himself, and it was assumed that at the end of ten years her younger son would be mature enough to resist his mother's seduction.[28] An instance of a man banished from his native province as well as from Rome and Italy was Dio Chrysostom, forbidden by Domitian to live in Italy or in Bithynia.[29]

The penalty was more severe when the place of banishment was fixed. When Augustus discussed the matter, he named as suitable in general, places where living conditions were anything but disagreeable: Cos, Rhodes, Lesbos and Samos.[30] But, when incensed, he showed no such generosity. His daughter Julia was banished to the diminutive wind-swept island of Pandateria (Ventotene) off the Campanian coast,* and Ovid was sent to pursue love in a very cold climate indeed, at Tomis on the Black Sea. And little consideration was shown for Seneca's comfort when the emperor Claudius banished him to Corsica. (Sardinia was chosen under Nero for the monstrous Anicetus, Agrippina's murderer, and he evidently accommodated himself to its conditions.)[31]

Such men and women did not lose their Roman citizenship; nor, in general, did they suffer any confiscation of property. If found guilty, however, on certain criminal charges (adultery, for instance, or violent conduct, *vis privata*), they had to surrender a certain portion of their wealth and in other cases they were evidently mulcted of sums on one excuse or another until Trajan firmly prohibited any such stoppage.[32]

Far more serious under the Empire was the condition of the exile proper, the *deportatus*, the man or woman who was 'deported' or, as the English said, when imposing a similar punishment, 'transported'. These deportees were men or women who had been pronounced guilty of an offence which carried the death penalty; and under the Empire the number of such offences rose sharply as in the cut-throat senatorial atmosphere the sinister allegation of treason (*maiestas*) was attached to nearly every criminal charge. Deportation, which gave a

---

* It had a sizeable imperial villa and was therefore, throughout the early Empire, considered an appropriate place of exile for members of the imperial family.

sinister twist to the 'interdict', was normally to a particular place, in particular to an island, and it involved the accompaniments of a capital execution, loss of Roman citizenship and confiscation of property to the exchequer, usually to the imperial *fiscus*, though *ex gratia*, normally through the emperor's intervention, a certain sum (*viaticum*) was sometimes retained.

It was better to rid Rome of the physical presence of such convicted men or women than to take their life by execution. For, though there was nothing to offend anybody in the sight of slaves or members of the lower class dying in the torment of crucifixion or being thrown to make a meal for wild animals in the arena, the notion of execution of members of the upper class, however criminal, was offensive to the members of that class, who constituted the government. Executions took place, of course, under military discipline in the army and once upon a time a man prosecuted for treason (*perduellio*), if he failed in his defence before the people, was strung up and hanged on the spot. Religious anxiety might sanction the public flogging to death of the detected paramour of a Vestal Virgin, and on the sensational exposure of conspiracies to overthrow the republican government (by Catiline in 63 BC) or later to assassinate the emperor (by Sejanus, it was alleged, in AD 31, by Piso and his associates in AD 65) current hysteria was satisfied by nothing less than execution. But one has only to consider the public horror after the event in 63 BC; better by far to give the convicted criminal the opportunity of taking his own life or to deport him right out of sight to some devil's island where he could live on, tortured by the agony of remorse.[34]

The exiles so far considered suffered or were punished as individuals, men or women who were criminals or at least believed to be criminals.

There were also banishments (relegations) *en masse* from Italy of persons whose religious or philosophical beliefs were considered to threaten the structure of established society (as if in western Europe today a country should expel all anarchists or communists). In every case it was the well-being of Rome and Italy that was the main consideration; the expelled persons were free to preach their pernicious doctrines or to pursue their objectionable practices elsewhere, except in cases where the attempt was made to exterminate a religious cult entirely – Christianity, for instance, during the Persecutions before Constantine.

On more than one occasion in the early Empire Jews were forbidden to live in Rome.[35] They were expelled from Italy (unless they forswore Judaism) in AD 19 after a public scandal (a spurious Rabbi and his friends lining their pockets with money extorted from a rich Roman woman-convert, supposedly for transmission to Jerusalem) and again by Claudius in AD 48 because of disorders which may have had to do with the arrival of the first Christians in Rome; earlier he had forbidden them to meet in their synagogues. In

AD 19 Isis-worshippers were expelled too, also because of a public scandal (a respectable Roman woman debauched in the temple of Isis by a Roman knight whom, believing what the well-bribed priests told her, she thought to be the god Anubis). In this year AD 19 four thousand Jews and Isis-worshippers of military age and freedman status were conscripted for military service, to put down brigandage in Sardinia. The climate might kill them, but that would be no great loss, Tacitus wrote.[36]

At the time of the jurists relegation, even deportation, was standard punishment in the case of socially respectable people (the *honestiores*) for anyone introducing 'new sects or religions unknown to reason'.[37]

Astrology (see p.242) was a treasonable practice when a private citizen asked the experts for the horoscope of the reigning emperor, for if this suggested that the emperor had not long to live, a conspiracy against his life might appear timely. Death was the penalty for any such detected enquirer (as for a slave who showed a similar interest in the death of his master) and for the astrologer who responded to the enquiry; the astrologer who answered the slave's enquiry was deported or sent to the mines.[38]

When astrologers were expelled, they were expelled not only from Rome but also from Italy – first, it was thought, in 139 BC, then by Agrippa as aedile in 33 BC and, under the Empire, after evidence of their involvement in treasonable conspiracies, real or alleged (of Libo Drusus in AD 16, of Furius Scribonianus in AD 52) and finally, perhaps, under Vitellius* and Vespasian.[39] Astrologers were a worthless lot, but people could not dispense with them; how, without them, was anybody to know what was the right moment for embarking on any kind of important enterprise? So, like the Jews between AD 19 and 41, they crept back, turning up again and again like bad pennies. The more often they had been expelled, the higher their reputation – and, no doubt, their fees. So after Vespasian – or, perhaps, Domitian – there were no more wholesale expulsions. It was up to the individual; the law was the law, and he practised at his own risk.

Actors, the lowest dregs of society, were not as dangerous as astrologers, but their indiscretions on the stage could cause disrespect for authority and be the cause of popular disorder in Rome; so from time to time – by Tiberius in AD 23 and by Nero in AD 56 – they were expelled from Italy.[40] They returned more quickly even than the astrologers.

Philosophers were more important people than astrologers or actors, and they were the more dangerous because they made their appeal to the educated classes. They might threaten Roman *mores*, traditional practices and beliefs. There were expulsions in 173 BC (of Epicureans) and in 161.[41] In the powerful influence exerted on the

---

* He fixed a day before which they must clear out; they are said to have retorted with a poster announcing (accurately, as it transpired) the day on which Vitellius would die.

young by Càrneades with his challenge to the high-minded ethic of
Roman imperialism in 155 BC, Cato will have seen the wisdom of
both moves. But then with Panaetius and later Posidonius Stoicism
established itself in Rome as a creditable philosophy for a Roman and
a gentleman, and other philosophies established themselves too.

There was an outbreak of trouble under Nero and the Flavians both
for professional philosophers and for philosophical devotees: Seneca
and Thrasea Paetus forced to death and Musonius Rufus banished
together with Helvidius Priscus and the Cynic Demetrius under Nero;
under Vespasian, Musonius Rufus banished again and Helvidius
Priscus banished for the second time and then executed in exile;
Epictetus, Apollodorus (Musonius Rufus' son-in-law) and the
mother-in-law and widow of Helvidius Priscus banished at the end of
Domitian's rule. If they were top members of the senatorial class like
Helvidius Priscus, they addressed the emperor in public with studied
offensiveness; lesser men, like Diogenes the Cynic, shrieked abuse of
Titus and Berenice in the theatre in AD 75.[42]

Then, after Domitian's death, the storm blew over and the
philosopher-exiles were recalled; Helvidius Priscus' womenfolk came
home and Epictetus could have returned from Nicopolis, had he
wished. And before long Dio Chrysostom, given access once more to
Italy and to his native Bithynia, was addressing the emperor Trajan
as a well-meaning friend and admirer in his orations on Kingship (see
p.206).

The trouble, it seems, had been over the principle of hereditary
succession, which could not be said to have produced 'the best man'
for emperor in Nero, a principle which, with his two sons, Vespasian
was determined to uphold. With Nerva a senatorial choice and Trajan
adopted and, with no son of his own, likely to choose his successor by
adoption, Cynics and Stoics could claim to have established their
point.[43]

(No political significance attached to the temporary expulsion from
Rome of slaves and foreigners, doctors and teachers excepted, in the
great famine of AD 6 or, in another famine in AD 353, of those who
had not a Roman domicile, dancing-girls and dancing-masters
excepted.)[44]

What of the lives of these Roman exiles?

Wherever they were, they were still under observation by the
Roman provincial administration and, apart from the lesser fry, Jews,
actors and the like, if they entered forbidden territory or moved from
their appointed place of detention, they were likely to be detected.
Punishment followed: temporary relegation was made permanent;
men already sentenced to permanent relegation were sent to an
island; if sent to an island already, they were deported; if already
deported, they were put to death.[45] The provincial governor had also

to be on the look-out for men banished (*relegati*) from his province, whether by himself or by one of his predecessors, who returned before the proper time, if their banishment was temporary, or, if sentenced to perpetual banishment, slipped back and hoped to evade detection. Such behaviour was *contumacia* and merited the severest punishment.[46]

If a man broke the terms of his exile in this way, his further punishment was not undeserved; nor was that of Cassius Severus who in banishment (*relegatio*) in Crete continued to publish the kind of offensive lampoons against public figures in Rome for which he had been banished under Augustus. So in AD 24 he was stripped of his property and deported to Seriphos.[47]

Grim as the exile's fate might be, there could always be worse in store. Deported to Amorgos for vicious conduct, Vibius Serenus was brought back in chains to Rome to face a further charge of having, when proconsul of the Spanish province of Baetica, sympathised with, even supported, the rising of Florus and Sacrovir in Gaul in AD 21. His son brought the prosecution and popular disgust at the son's behaviour saved him; he was allowed to return to Amorgos; but there had been a proposal to transfer him to the devil's island of Gyaros.[48]

Worse still, with no warning a party of troops might land, ready to execute a death warrant. This was the fate of members of the imperial family whose survival was an embarrassment to the ruler, of Agrippa Postumus on Planasia when Augustus died – did Augustus give the order, or Tiberius, or neither? – and in AD 62 of Rubellius Plautus, who was not technically an exile, but he had been advised by Nero to leave Rome and live in Asia. His only crime was that he was a great-grandson of the emperor Tiberius. It was the fate in AD 14 of Sempronius Gracchus on the island of Cercina, a man who, as Julia's paramour, was believed to have done his best to sour the relationship of her father Augustus and her husband Tiberius. It was the fate of the man who governed Egypt at the time of the great pogrom in Alexandria in AD 38 and who was subsequently banished by the emperor Gaius – Avillius Flaccus, who is so colourfully reviled in the writings of the Jewish scholar Philo. And it was the fate, under Vespasian, of Helvidius Priscus.[49]

Many exiles, obviously, suffered such nightmares as Philo described with picturesque imagination in the case of Flaccus. On the other hand there were others, particularly the philosophers, who were without apprehension, unless they were marked men like Helvidius Priscus; they looked forward to a turn in fortune's wheel.

A large part of the pathos of Ovid in exile lies in the fact that he never gave up hoping for return. Would the empress Livia not use her influence on his behalf? When Augustus died, would Tiberius not recall him? Would Germanicus not use his influence? Vain hopes, all of them. Particularly for those exiled by a 'bad emperor', there was hope, because for bad emperors assassination was an occupational hazard. After the deaths of Gaius Caligula, Nero and Domitian numerous exiles were recalled; but the 'bad emperor' had to die first. There is a story, not true perhaps but *ben trovato*, that a sycophant of a man banished by Tiberius was asked by Gaius, who recalled him, how he had spent his time in exile. 'Praying for Tiberius' death and your accession', was the man's misguided answer. So Gaius, imagining his own exiles to be engaged in similar prayer, sent round and had the whole lot executed.[50]

The *relegatus* might be accompanied into exile by his wife, but more often than not she remained in Italy, partly no doubt to look after his financial interests. His sons, whose political advancement was normally not prejudiced by their father's misfortune,* and his daughters, who were either married or needed to find husbands, generally remained in Rome. The example of Gracchus, exiled (*relegatus*) to the island of Cercina in 1 BC, was a warning to any exile against taking a young son with him. When Tiberius sent and had the father executed, the son, brought up without any proper education, eked out a living as a small trader and it was only through the influence of powerful friends of his father that he was not run in for supplying provisions to the rebel Tacfarinas in Africa in AD 23.[51] Sometimes the exile was accompanied by a loyal friend. Musonius Rufus, later to suffer exile himself, was in Asia with Rubellius Plautus and, thanks to Martial, we know that Caesennius Maximus went to Corsica to share his friend Seneca's exile and that, when he himself was banished by Nero and went to live in Sicily, he too was accompanied by a friend, Q. Ovidius.[52]

We do not know of many cases in which an exile, free to choose his new habitat, selected a city whose citizenship he could acquire and cease to be a Roman (see p.97), as in the Republic Rutilius Rufus became a citizen of Smyrna. In the early Empire Volcatius Moschus, settling in exile in Massilia, adopted Massiliot citizenship and, when he died, bequeathed his property to that city.[53]

Massilia was not the only place to benefit from giving a new home to a Roman exile. P. Glitius Gallus, exiled to Andros for his supposed involvement in the Pisonian conspiracy of AD 65, was accompanied by his rich wife Egnatia Maximilla and they evidently contributed generously to local charities, for the island honoured him as its patron and both as its benefactors. And the few poor fishermen who inhabited the bare waterless rock of Gyaros had lasting cause for

---

* This was generally true even if the father had been deported. In AD 397 (Arcadius and Honorius), a son shared his father's disgrace, if his father was condemned for treason (*Cod. Theod.* 9, 14, 3; *Cod. Instin.* 9, 8, 5).

gratitude to Musonius Rufus, who discovered a spring of water on the island. Also he brought them a small tourist industry, first young people who came to Gyaros to enjoy Musonius' tuition, later people who came to see the now famous spring. How the inhabitants of Cephallenia viewed the residence in exile among them of C. Antonius, Cicero's colleague in the consulship, we can only guess; he is said to have treated the island as if it belonged to him.[54]

Philo in his imaginative way pictures the ship which carried Avillius Flaccus into exile landing at successive ports in the Peloponnese and people, attracted to the harbours by curiosity, some abusing Flaccus, others sympathising. But curiosity was probably the dominant motive. Vienne in Gaul and Lugdunum Convenarum in the Pyrenees must have been surprised to find Jewish princelings wished on them by Augustus and by Gaius. In Asia in the late Republic Rutilius Rufus received in exile the warm welcome that he deserved; the province had known him as an honest and sympathetic administrator. At Tomis, after hearing Ovid recite his poem in Getic in honour of the imperial family, people no doubt felt the surprise which Ovid himself described; what was the Roman government doing, punishing such a fervent patriot with exile?[55]

If the exile had plenty of money, he could resign himself to the enjoyment of whatever advantages his new home offered. P. Suillius, retiring in exile to the Balearic Isles at the age of nearly eighty in AD 58, is said to have led a comfortable relaxed life, as did Anicetus in Sardinia. Milo at the end of the Republic found that Massilia offered at least one advantage as against Rome, its delicious red mullets. Sometimes for a serious man there was the opportunity of self-improvement: philosophy lectures on Rhodes, which Metellus Numidicus frequented in exile, as later, in his semi-exile under Augustus, did Tiberius.[56] Ovid in Tomis learnt a new foreign language and wrote a book on Pontic fish (p.141).

But, whether for the politician or the man of culture, there was no place like Rome. Lucian's Nigrinus (see p.186) was exceptional in wanting to get away from it all. Even as he strolled about Cilicia with all the importance of a provincial governor, Cicero was continuously homesick for Rome; he missed it more bitterly still in exile, uncertain whether he would ever be able to return. He found it surprising that there were Romans, 'good men', who lived in the provinces from choice, just as Seneca found it remarkable that there were people who actually chose to live in Corsica. For Ovid civilised life was to be led in Rome and nowhere else. It was not easy for Statius to persuade his wife to leave Rome and retire to Naples.[57]

Hardest was the lot of the deported who, apart from any small sum which they had been allowed to keep, had been stripped of their possessions. Unless they could sponge on rich friends (under Nero, for instance, the astrologer Pammenes continued to be professionally employed and received an annual stipend from the consular P. Anteius Rufus in Rome), they had – usually for the first time in their lives – to earn a living. Flaccus acquired a small plot of land on Andros and was learning to be a farmer in the short time before he was executed. In a civilised community an educated man might lecture and give lessons in rhetoric. This was done in Massilia by Volcatius Moschus, condemned as a poisoner and banished perhaps in 20 BC, and done successfully to judge by the legacy which Massilia received from him years later (see p.110), also by the ex-praetor Valerius Licinianus in Sicily, wearing a Greek *pallium* and not a Roman toga (for he had been deported), a man implicated in the scandal of the Vestal Virgins under Domitian; it was Nerva who allowed him to live in Sicily.[58] And a notable philosopher continued to attract pupils, Musonius Rufus on Gyaros, Epictetus at Nicopolis. (Annaeus Florus, who found great satisfaction in the life of a schoolmaster at Tarraco in Spain, was not an exile; he had retired of his own free will in chagrin from Rome.)[59]

For members of the 'working class', who in any case were unlikely to suffer expulsion except en masse from Rome, the problem was no problem at all. They settled down in a suitable place and worked as they had worked in Rome, the Jews Aquila and Priscilla in Corinth, making tents.[60]

Dio Chrysostom, was not deported; he was 'relegatus'. But, whether of necessity (because he could not draw funds from Bithynia) or from simple philosophic ostentation, he worked, to keep himself, as an unskilled labourer (when he was not reading the works of Plato and Demosthenes which he carried round with him).[61]

In the case of exile as of other human misfortunes, philosophers, Stoics in particular, produced dissertations in which, if they persuaded nobody else, they presumably persuaded themselves that exile was no worse a condition of life than any other; it did not hinder the practice of virtue. Exile involved a change of habitat, but if moving house within your own city was no disaster, why was it worse to leave one city or country in order to live in another? Secondly the exile, having to work for his living as he had never done before, had the chance of greatly improving his own health. Thirdly the 'disgrace' of banishment was unsubstantial for, if a man was justly exiled, how could he rail against the justice of his sentence? If he was sentenced unjustly, then the shame and disgrace rested with those responsible for his exile, not with himself. Comfort, however cold.[62]

Unpleasant as was the penalty of being forced to leave your home and live elsewhere, it was in the later Empire to become the even more unpleasant experience of masses of people of all ranks, from the labourers on imperial estates at one extreme to city-councillors at the other, not to be allowed to move away at all. Earlier we know of one occasion, the German invasions of the late second century BC, when, reasonably enough, the emigration of Romans of military age (under 35) from Italy was stopped – insofar as the instruction to all ship-captains not to take such men aboard could prove effective.[63]

As a class, senators alone were always subject to certain restrictions. Except on official state duties, they could not leave Italy under the Republic unless they had been given an exeat (a *libera legatio*) by the Senate. In the Empire, anyhow from the time of Claudius, such a permit had to be obtained from the Emperor except, as has been seen, in the case of Sicily (for those who owned property there) and, after AD 49, Narbonese Gaul (again for those who had property to visit). Both provinces were counted for this purpose as part of Italy. Senators too (as well as high-ranking Equites) were forbidden to enter Egypt (see p.68) except with an imperial permit.[64]

Individuals, too, could be forcibly confined to certain residences in Italy, as Octavian kept Lepidus cooling his heels in ignominy at Cerceii and Claudius 'banished' a man (as diplomats in the modern world are sometimes 'banished' by the governments of the authoritarian societies to which they are accredited) to within the third milestone from Rome, beyond which he was forbidden to travel.[65]

Appendix
Known places of exile

Spain

Tarraco. C. Cato, cos. 114 BC, moved here to forestall prosecution 109 BC Cic., *Pro Balbo* 28.

Balearic Isles
P. Suillius, consul under Claudius in AD 58, aged about eighty, *TA*, 13, 43, 6.

Gaul
Lugdunum Convenarum. Herod Antipas, AD 39, Jos., *AJ* 18, 252; *BJ* 2, 183; Hirschfeld, *Kl. Schr.* 174n.
Vienna. Archelaus of Judaea, AD 6, Jos., *AJ* 17, 344.
Massilia. L. Cornelius Scipio, cos. 83 BC, Cic., *Pro Sest.* 7; Schol. Bob. 126St.
   T. Annius Milo, tr. pl. 57 BC, on condemnation in 52 BC, CD 40, 54, 3.
   Volcatius Moschus,? 20 BC, *TA* 4, 43, 8; *PIR*, 'v' 621.
   Faustus Cornelius Sulla, cos. AD 52, in AD 58, *TA* 13, 47, 4; 14, 57, 6; PIR,[2] 'c' 1464 (explicitly confined to the city; murdered AD 62).

Southern Mediterranean
Island of Cercina. Sempronius Gracchus, for adultery with Julia, 1 BC; executed AD 14, *TA* 1, 53, 6.
Italy
Rhegium. Julia moved here by Augustus from Pandateria, *TA* 1, 53, 1.

Islands off Italy

Corsica. L. Annaeus Seneca, AD 41, CD 60, 8, 5; Schol. Juv. 5, 109. Recalled, AD 49, *TA* 12, 8, 3.

L. Pompusius Mettius by Domitian; subsequently executed, CD 67, 12, 3.

Lipara. Plautus and Plautilla (wife of Caracalla), children of Plautianus, AD 205; executed on accession of Caracalla, CD 76, 6, 3.

Pandateria. Julia, daughter of Augustus in 2 BC, CD 55, 10, 14; after five years moved to Rhegium, CD 55, 13, 1; *TA* 1, 53, 1.

Agrippina, widow of Germanicus, AD 29; died (? hunger strike), AD 33; *TA* 5, 3, 5; 6, 25.

Julia Livilla, daughter of Germanicus, AD 41, *TA* 14, 63, 2 (her second exile); she was soon executed, *PIR*,[2] 'I' 674.

Octavia, wife of Nero, AD 62, TA 14, 63, 1; execution followed quickly.

Flavia Domitilla, wife of Flevius Clemens, AD 95, CD 67, 14, 3.

Planasia. Agrippa Postumus (Agrippa Julius Caesar), AD 6; executed AD 14, PIR,[2] 'I' 214.

Nero, son of Germanicus, AD 29, Suet., *Tib.* 54, 2.

Pontiae Insulae. Julia Livilla (her first exile) and Agrippina, sisters of the emperor Gaius, AD 39, CD 59, 22, 8; recalled in AD 41.

Sardinia. Freedman Anicetus, prefect of the Fleet at Misenum, murderer of Agrippina, false witness against Octavia, *TA* 14, 62, 6.

Rufrius Crispinus, Prefect of the Praetorian Guard 47-51, first husband of Poppaea, AD 65, *TA* 15, 71, 8; 16, 17, 2; forced to suicide, AD 66.

C. Cassius Longinus (descendant of the tyrannicide), cos. AD 30, banished AD 65, recalled by Vespasian, *TA* 16, 9, 2; *PIR*,[2] 'C' 501.

Brother of Aratulla, Mart. 8, 32.

Sicily. Valerius Licinianus, ex-praetor, exiled by Domitian, allowed by Nerva to reside in Sicily, Plin., *Ep.* 4, 11.

Trimerus (north of Monte Gargano). Julia, granddaughter of Augustus, AD 8; she died there in AD 28, *TA* 4, 71, 6.

Eastern Adriatic

Cephallenia. C. Antonius, cos. 63 BC, in 59; recalled by Julius Caesar as dictator, Strabo 10, 2, 13, 455.

Dyrrhachium. L. Opimius, cos. 121 BC, exiled in 109 BC, Cic., *Pro Sest.* 140.

Nicopolis. Epictetus, AD 89; remained there till his death, AG 15, 11, 5.

Mainland Greece

Athens. T. Albucius, ex-praetor, 103 BC; Cic., *TD* 5, 108.

C. Memmius, ex-praetor, 52 BC.

Aegean Islands, 'rocks crowded with our noble exiles',* Juv. 13, 246f.

Cluvidienus Quietus, Julius Agrippa, Blitius Catulinus, Petronius Priscus, Julius Altinus, AD 65, *TA* 15, 71, 10 (? allowed to make their own selection). .

Amorgos. C. Vibius Serenus, ex-praetor, AD 23, 24, *TA* 4, 13, 2; 4, 30, 2.

Andros. A. Avillius Flaccus, Prefect of Egypt 32-8, AD 38; executed a year later, Philo, *C. Flac.* 151-91.

P. Glitius Gallus, AD 65, *TA* 15, 71, 6; *SIG*,[3] 811f. Probably recalled by Galba.

---

* Aut maris Aegaei rupem scopulosque frequentes/exulibus magnis.

Cos considered by Augustus a suitable place of exile, CD 56, 27, 2.

Crete. Cassius Severus, orator (for his lampoons), AD 12; deported to Seriphos in AD 24; *TA* 1, 72, 4; 4, 21, 5.

Cythnos. C. Junius Silanus, cos. AD 10, procos. Asiae AD 20, 22, *TA* 3, 69, 8.

Delos. Mummius Achaicus under *lex Varia* in 90 BC, App., *BC* 1, 37, 168.

Donusa proposed at first for C. Vibius Serenus in AD 24, *TA* 4, 30, 1.

Gyaros ('Narrow Gyara', 'brevia Gyara', Juv. 1, 73)

    C. Musonius Rufus, equestrian philosopher, AD 65, *TA* 15, 71, 9; Philostr., *VAT* 7, 16; recalled by Galba; banished again by Vespasian and recalled by Titus.

    proposed (but rejected) for C. Iunius Silanus, AD 22, *TA* 3, 68, 2; for Vibius Serenus, AD 24, *TA* 4, 30, 1; for Avillius Flaccus, Philo, *C. Flac.* 151.

Lesbos. 'A famous and charming island', 'nobilis et amoena', too good a place for a criminal, *TA* 6, 3, 3; but Augustus had considered it suitable, CD 56, 27, 2.

Naxos. L. Junius Silanus, AD 65, *TA* 16, 9, 2 (but he was executed before he set sail).

Rhodes considered suitable by Augustus, CD 56, 27, 2.

Samos recognised as suitable by Augustus, CD 56, 27, 2.

Seriphos. Vistilia, high-born woman punished for prostitution, AD 19, *TA* 2, 85, 4.

    Cassius Severus, moved from Crete, AD 24, *TA* 4, 21, 5.

Asia. Rubellius Plautus retired to Asia in AD 60 at Nero's prompting, and was subsequently executed, *TA* 14, 22, 5; 14, 58f.

Smyrna selected for residence after banishment by Q. Servilius Caepio in 103 BC and Rutilius Rufus after 92 BC, Cic., *Pro Balb.* 27.

Euxine

Tomis. Ovid banished (*relegatus*) for life, AD 8, *Trist.* 1, 5, 83; *Ex Pont.* 4, 13, 39f. etc.

Egypt

Syene. Juvenal (under Domitian); see G. Highet, *Juvenal the Satirist*, Oxford 1962, 27-31.

CHAPTER NINE

Communication,

1 : Mainly Latin and Greek[1]

(i) Survival of a variety of spoken languages

Latin arrived as a new language in southern Italy where Oscan was spoken inland and Greek on the coast; in Bruttium, indeed, both languages were in use. So Latin became a second language and in the early second century BC Lucilius referred to Tarentum, Consentia and Sicily as places where there were people speaking a mixture of Greek and bad Latin. Before this Q. Ennius of Rudiae in Calabria knew three languages, Greek, Oscan and Latin. Over the Alps, too, in Massilia, an old Greek colony which never lost its nationality, people were trilingual, speaking Greek, Latin and Celtic.[2] In Italy Cumae changed its official language from Oscan to Latin in 180 BC, having received Rome's official sanction for the change;[3] evidently the non-Latin allies of Rome (cities with *civitas sine suffragio*) required Rome's permission in such a matter.

It was by a gradual process that through the third and second centuries BC Italy, previously multilingual, became predominantly Latin-speaking and, though we cannot trace the stages, it is clear that by the start of the first century BC Latin was the dominant language in the peninsula. Legends on the coins of the Italian insurgents in the Social war were in Latin and, once that war was over and Italy south of the Po was unified, municipal inscriptions all over Italy were in Latin.[4] Greek, of course, survived in Naples and some other cities in the South and so did Oscan and other Italic languages locally, but by the end of the Republic there can have been few people of any education at all anywhere in Italy who could not speak Latin.

In Sicily Greek remained a first language under the Republic and there are no inscriptions in Latin apart from those set up by Romans. Of Caecilius' many disqualifications for acting as the prosecutor of Verres, according to Cicero, one was the fact that he had learnt his Latin in Sicily, not in Rome, and therefore he had an imperfect knowledge of the language. With the Empire things changed. Latin was naturally a first language in the six new colonies and it was spoken, though not enforced, in other cities of the island.[5]

Apart from the indirect result of the settlement of colonies, which would be Roman speech-centres, the Roman government had no deliberate policy of eliminating other languages in Italy; nor had it any policy later of enforcing the everyday use of Latin on the whole empire.

From the Roman point of view there were two civilised languages, Latin and Greek and, beyond these, a variety of *barbarae linguae* which inspired little interest or investigation on the part of Roman scholars except in the case of words which were borrowed and became a part of Latin.

So native languages survived, particularly among country people, in all parts of the Empire, and indeed from the third century onwards many of them were to enjoy a wide renaissance, particularly as Christianity spread from the towns, where Latin or Greek was spoken, to the countryside.[6] In the West there was Iberian (recorded as spoken by a country-dweller of Nearer Spain under torture in AD 25),[7] Germanic, Celtic (which in the third and fourth centuries AD almost had the status of an official language in northern Gaul),[8] Illyrian and Thracian in the Balkans, Coptic in Egypt, Aramaic (including Syriac) and Armenian in the East.*

In Africa there was Berber, but the common spoken language of the province was Punic. When the process of his corruption started, Apuleius' stepson spoke nothing but Punic and Punic later was Septimius Severus' first language and St Augustine's.[9]

But though it survived as a spoken language, particularly in country districts, Punic disappeared from public use. In the early first century AD there were great public monuments like the four-horse chariot at Lepcis carrying Germanicus and Drusus with an inscription in Punic, but no Punic inscription has been found which dates from later than the end of the first century AD.[10]

Strabo records that at Cibyra in Lycia you could hear four different languages spoken: Pisidian, the language of the Solymi, Greek and Lydian (which was already a dead language in Lydia itself). At Derbe St Paul heard people speaking Lycaonian, and this with Phrygian, Mysian and Isaurian is known to have survived as a spoken language (mainly outside the towns) until the sixth century AD. Apollonius of Tyana wrote a book in Cappadocian. And the Galatians were speaking the same kind of Gallic as the Treveri in Gaul.[11]

Towards the end of the second century AD Irenaeus spoke of Christianity being expounded in a variety of different languages in Germany, Spain, Gaul, Egypt and the East and, as for himself, at Lyons he apologised for imperfections in his Greek on the ground that he was surrounded by Celts and was generally expressing himself in their barbarous tongue. From Ulpian we learn that in the early third century AD a *fideicommissum* (a charge on the trustees of a will) could be executed not only in Latin or Greek but in Punic, Gallic or, indeed, any other language.[12] In this one respect, that is to say, the law recognised the existence of people who were familiar with neither of

* Illyrian was a 'semi-barbarous language' for Jerome, and so was Syriac (*CCSL* 73, 292; *EP.* 7, 2).

the main imperial languages.

In America, Britain and France many immigrants continued, within their own families, to talk their own native languages, and the same thing must have happened within the Roman empire. The Cheruscan Flavus, who settled down in Roman territory, spoke fluent Latin (see p.165); his son Italicus, sent to be king of the Cherusci in AD 47, had been born in the Empire and obviously spoke Latin. Yet it is unthinkable that the Cherusci would have accepted him at all if he had not spoken perfect German too. The same is true of Vonones, the Parthian prince, sent with his brothers to Rome between 11 and 7 BC, who returned to be an unsuccessful king of Parthia in AD 16. Every kind of charge was levelled against him by the Parthians, but there was no suggestion that there was anything the matter with his native speech.[13]

(ii) The spread of Latin in the West

While doing nothing to stamp out native languages, it was Roman policy to encourage their replacement, wherever possible, by Latin in the West and by Greek in the East. Latin established itself in the West as a common language and educated men from all parts of the West could 'communicate' with one another for the first time. This was no small achievement on Rome's part, as St Augustine acknowledged; he only questioned the price in human blood which had been paid in the course of the Roman conquest to make this achievement possible.[14]

In the East Greek had begun to perform a similar function from the time of Alexander the Great and under the Romans this was a continuing process. Libanius reflected sadly on what was lost by Julian's failure to conquer the Persians; as well as being made to cut their hair, they would have had to learn to speak Greek.[15]

Acquiring Latin as a first language – and, for those who enjoyed the new higher education, Greek too – was more than a linguistic readjustment; it was a matter of entering fully into the Graeco-Roman cultural tradition and acquiring a new personal background. So that when in the second century AD an African like Apuleius appealed in court to the example of Manius Curius and the Grand Old Men in early Roman history, he felt that he was appealing to his own ancestors, his own historical tradition.[16]

Military service was a powerful agent in the spread of Latin in the West. Numbers of auxiliaries knew little Latin or no Latin at all when they joined up; at the time of their discharge they must all have spoken and understood the language reasonably well. There is plenty of evidence of the spread of Latin through military service in the West. Tacitus gives a vivid picture of the German Arminius engaged in AD 16 in a slanging-match with his brother Flavus, who was serving in the

Roman auxiliary army. From opposite banks of the Weser they addressed each other in Latin, not in their native language. Arminius, like Flavus, had learnt Latin while serving as a Roman auxiliary.*[17]

Earlier when Tiberius reached Germany in AD 5 and advanced as far as the river Elbe, Velleius Paterculus was serving under him and, giving one of those vivid personal reminiscences with which he embellished his history, he tells us how an elderly German of distinguished appearance sculled himself across the river and asked if he might land and set eyes on Tiberius. The request was granted and, deeply impressed, the German made a little speech, declaring that the Germans were mad not to submit to the Roman might. He was allowed to shake Tiberius' hand and he rowed back, eyes fixed on the representative of Roman majesty. Was it in Latin that he spoke? Or was there an interpreter? Velleius does not tell us.

It is not impossible that the man could speak Latin; for in AD 16, when Germanicus' army had crossed the Weser, a German soldier approached the Roman lines and, in Latin, offered fantastic bribes to Roman soldiers who deserted to Arminius.[18]

In the West troops, particularly in auxiliary units, no doubt often conversed among themselves in their native languages, but they must all have possessed a reasonable fluency in Latin. In this respect, however, they have come under frequent fire. Tacitus found it difficult to believe that an effective alliance to stop the civil war in AD 69 should have been made between Otho's and Vitellius' armies, 'so different in language and habits', and he states that the German army soldiers sent by Vitellius after his victory to other units provoked revulsion both by their rough appearance and by their coarse speech; they were 'horridi sermone'. And, though Tacitus makes no such disparaging remarks about the men drafted into the Praetorian Guard from the Rhine armies in AD 69, Cassius Dio said that it was terrifying to listen to the voices of the new type of guardsman brought into Rome from the legions by Septimius Severus at the end of the second century AD. In no case can the historians' statements be taken to imply that the men could not speak Latin; they evidently spoke it with a strong northern accent.[20]

Army Latin is a fascinating subject in itself.[21] Its vocabulary included numbers of colourful technical words, *verba castrensia*, often animal names: ram (*aries*), scorpion (*scorpio*, a siege-engine), tortoise (*testudo*, a shield-covering to soldiers advancing under an enemy wall). A body

---

* It is always a sad thing when a good joke is spoilt by being taken seriously. Some joker mocked the humble origin and early lack of education of M. Bassaeus Rufus, whose spectacular military career culminated in the prefecture of Egypt and the command of the Praetorian Guard under M. Aurelius. He declared that on an occasion when a soldier failed to understand some instruction of the emperor given in Latin, Rufus said, 'Naturally he does not understand; he does not know Greek'. The story has come down in a small fragment of Cassius Dio who cannot himself have believed, as some modern scholars have done, that the Praetorian Guard was in fact commanded in the second century AD by a man who did not understand Latin.[19]

of men advancing in wedge-formation was a 'pig's head', *caput porci.* Other army words had social connotations; 'muger' was a bad knuckle-bone player, 'focaria' a soldier's kept woman.[22] There was also a camp-word for somebody from your own part of the world – probably corrupt in its received form – which the elder Pliny playfully made use of as one soldier to another ('agnoscis et hoc campestre verbum') at the start of the dedication of his *Natural Histories* to Titus.

Roman soldiers, like most other soldiers in history,* had a keen wit. At Caesar's siege of Alesia in 52 BC they had their own names, 'lilies' for one, for the lethal traps which were buried under the surface of the ground. Later when soldiers in Gaul had noticed that the young prince Tiberius (Tiberius Claudius Nero) drank more than was good for him, they called him 'Biberius Caldius Mero'. And when the disciplinarian Galba took over on the Rhine from the lax Gaetulicus, soldiers summed up the new situation, 'Disce, miles, militare; Galba est, non Gaetulicus.' 'High time you fighters learnt to fight.'[23]

Further, soldiers, whose life was spent on the frontiers and in fighting foreign people, brought foreign words into the Latin language – the Carthaginian *mapalia* (huts) and *mappa* (a napkin), a number of Celtic words for vehicles (*essedum*, a chariot; *raeda* and *petorritum*, brands of four-wheeled carriages), while from Spain came the word *gurdus*, a fool. Arrian, who greatly admired Roman readiness to take lessons from its enemies, pointed out, in his description of Roman cavalry fighting, that many of the technical words in cavalry manoeuvre and the names of many weapons were not Latin at all, but the foreign words of the peoples from whom the Romans had done their borrowing, chiefly Spanish and Celtic.[24] And many of the Greek words bandied about in Plautus' plays had no doubt been brought into the Latin language by troops serving in south Italy, Sicily and the Greek mainland.

In Africa at the time of the Roman conquest Greek came second to Punic, for the Carthaginian government's decision in the early fourth century BC to ban the learning of Greek was evidently not long effective. The pro-Carthaginian histories of the first and second Punic wars were written in Greek, a language which Hannibal understood, just as out of necessity he came to understand Latin.[25] Cleitomachus (Hasdrubal), who studied under Carneades at Athens in the second century BC, had probably started his philosophy in Greek in Carthage;[26] and in the second century AD Pudentilla, whom Apuleius married, wrote to her son in Greek. But in general Latin replaced Greek and from the early days of Roman administration it was no doubt picked up in childhood, as St Augustine picked it up easily; Greek, taught when children went to school, was learnt with greater difficulty.[27] In the big

---

* When a terrorist is blown up by his own bomb, British soldiers call the mishap 'own goal'.

towns well-educated people evidently spoke both languages, with Latin enjoying primacy. Apuleius, for instance, was mocked for his knowledge of Greek by his prosecutor, a man who evidently knew no Greek himself. Apuleius had perfected his Greek in Athens and his Latin (without a tutor) in Rome.[28]

In Narbonese Gaul, which was already flooded with Roman citizens both in and outside Narbo (a Roman colony), it is evident that Latin was commonly spoken by the end of the Republic. 'The country was more like Italy than a province', as the elder Pliny was to write later, a statement which the great number of surviving Latin inscriptions confirms.[29]

In Spain and southern Gaul there were numbers of Roman and Italian residents, the citizens of the colonies which Julius Caesar and Augustus established,* the families of Roman settlers who had left Italy to seek a future in the new world (Diodorus says that large numbers were attracted to the mines in Spain) and in Spain there were, from the time of the second Punic war, soldiers who had remained there instead of returning to Italy for discharge. There were the war-wounded left by Scipio in 206 BC at Italica, the home later of Trajan and of Hadrian, and at Carteia, the first Latin colony overseas, there were the descendants of the Roman soldiers who had stayed behind in Spain and married Spanish wives. Already in 122 BC three thousand Roman citizens from Spain – some, perhaps, but by no means all, men discharged from his own army – were settled by Q. Metellus Balearicus in the Balearic islands.[30]

On the evidence of inscriptions, Noricum became far more romanised than Raetia. In Pannonia Latin was evidently picked up very quickly. Velleius, who fought against the Pannonians in their revolt in AD 6 says that, though less than twenty years had elapsed since the Roman conquest, they not only spoke and read Latin but they had absorbed the fundamentals of Roman discipline.[31]

Further East in the province of Upper Moesia Latin made no such extensive conquest. It was the language of the administration and the courts, and in colonies which had a mixture of peoples – and languages – at their foundation, it became a first language and in due course Latin was spoken by the upper municipal class. But it does not seem to have spread widely into the countryside, where native Thracian, *lingua Bessica*, survived.[32]

Yet what could be more remarkable than the case of Dacia, a province of the Roman empire for no more than a century and a half, from the conquest by Trajan to the withdrawal of Roman forces by Aurelian? Latin established itself so firmly in that short time that Romanian is a Romance language.[33]

---

* Up in the North, Emporiae (Ampurias) was half-Spanish, half-Greek. Julius Caesar dispatched Roman colonists. First the Spanish, then the Greeks (why in that order?) received Roman citizenship. So it became a Latin-speaking town (Livy 34, 9).

The British, on the other hand, were stubborn and before the governorship of Agricola, if Tacitus is to be believed, their young men jibbed at learning Latin at all. The effect of Agricola's new schools, however, was revolutionary; the young men were on fire not only to speak Latin, but to speak it well. 'Eloquent Gaul has taught British lawyers and Ultima Thule talks of having a rhetorican.' Greek, even, may have been taught at York in Britain at the time of Domitian.[34]

In encouraging education and, in particular, the spread of Latin, official Roman interest was directed in the first place to potential officers and administrators from the social and propertied class which in every province of the empire the government chiefly supported – the sons of chieftains, where there were chieftains, and of other prominent families.* Our earliest information is of Sertorius in the seventies BC:

Nothing appealed to the Spaniards more strongly than Sertorius' provision for their sons. He brought the noblest of them from the tribes to the large town of Osca. They may have been hostages in fact but, for all to see, they were given a schooling by the teachers of Latin and Greek whom he had appointed, on the clear understanding that, when they reached manhood, they would receive Roman citizenship and enter the Roman administration. The fathers were delighted by the sight of their sons dressed like Roman boys and going to school in an orderly way, all at Sertorius' expense, with frequent examinations and prizes for the successful, the gold lockets which Romans call *bullae*.

We hear of a similar school at Augustodunum (Autun) in Gallia Lugdunensis in AD 21; the boys were of the same social status, 'nobilissima Galliarum suboles', and they were receiving similar education in the *liberalia studia*. A little later there is mention of a school, a *litterarius ludus*, near the Rhine. And we have evidence of schools at Emona in the Julian Alps and at Savaria in Pannonia.[35]

The only education which the Romans practised, the *liberalia studia*, was education both in Greek and Latin, and in Gaul this will have spread up from the South, from Massilia, largely a Greek-speaking city, with an established University of great repute, to which Augustus sent his great-nephew L. Antonius, to get him out of the way, and which Agricola attended. The Greek alphabet spread even further than the Greek language, since Druids used it for their most secret documents. In the second century AD when Lucian was in Gaul – he does not say where – and was mystified by the Gallic representation of Hercules˙ in art, he asked a Gaul, who was able to give him the explanation in Greek.[36]

Already in the early Empire Latin was spoken on the Rhone by

---

* The Latin words which were absorbed into the Brittanic languages (Welsh, Cornish, Breton) have in many cases an upper-class pedantic respectability, from which it is inferred that they passed from the conversation of the upper class (the people whose education Tacitus describes) down through the servants' hall into the native vernacular; see K.H. Jackson, *Language and History in early Britain*, Edinburgh 1953, 108f.

Gallic tribesmen and in Spain Latin had replaced Spanish as a first language among the Turditani on the Baetis and even among the Celtiberians, 'once the wildest folk in Spain'.[37]

Spain, which had already exported a consul in Cornelius Balbus (a true Spaniard, not of Roman descent),[38] exported distinguished teachers and men of letters: Porcius Latro, the elder and the younger Seneca, Lucan, Mela, Columella, Quintilian and Martial (see p.64, n.). Southern Gaul was exporting speakers, Domitius Afer, 'the best orator of the day' and Julius Africanus.[39] Already in the time of Augustus, Pompeius Trogus, a Roman of the third generation, whose father had been Julius Caesar's secretary, published the first history in Latin of the Hellenistic period (see p.183), for which he must have had to read a great many books in Greek. Martial's books were on sale in Vienne and those of the younger Pliny at Lugdunum, and Martial claimed a reading public in the far North, even in Britain. The process of romanisation continued until in the fourth century Gaul was the home of a vigorous culture in both languages at Bordeaux and other academic centres, as we appreciate from the poems of Ausonius. While Ausonius himself wrote in Latin, his doctor-father had evidently found Greek a more sympathetic language than Latin, just as two centuries earlier in the second century the sophist Favorinus of Arles, a Roman knight, though clearly at home in Latin, left nobody in any doubt about his preference for Greek, the language of his public speeches and writings.[40]

(iii) Greeks and Latin

We have seen how words from the native languages of the West passed into the Latin vocabulary. To an even greater degree the Romans adopted Greek words when they adopted novel Greek practices, physical exercise, for instance, of the kind for which there was no Roman precedent – *cerôma*, the soft floor of a wrestling ring, is an example – and when they penetrated new and utterly unroman territory, seafaring for instance in early days* and philosophy later. There were purists like the emperor Tiberius, who viewed Greek loan-words like *monopolium* with suspicion.[41]

'Just as,' Quintilian wrote, 'the Greeks borrow from us.' Greek borrowing was, naturally, on a far more extensive scale. There were the Latin words for coins, weights and measures which became standard through the Empire. And there were all the names of the different elements of the Roman constitution, military organisation and imperial administration. Sometimes the Greeks simply transliterated: *augour* (augur), *kentorion* (centurion), *saiklareis* (ludi saeculares). When Cassius Dio wanted to explain the highly technical

---

* The Latin words for 'seasickness' (*nausea*) and 'a helmsman' (*gubernator*) are Greek in derivation.

connotation of 'senatus auctoritas', he pointed out that the expression could not possibly be translated into Greek.[42]

Sometimes Greeks gave their own version of a Roman name or expression, for instance *dêmarchos* for *tribunus plebis* (*plêtharchos* would have been better). *Strategos* at first seemed an admirable Greek name for the commander-in-chief of a Roman army, but then it was realised that there were two sorts of commander, a praetor (a six-lictor man, *hexapelekus*, each lictor carrying rods and axe) or a twelve-lictor man, a consul. So they called the first a *strategos* and the second a 'top *strategos*', *strategos hypatos*, and he in the end became '*hypatos*' *tout court*.[43]

And there were distinctive Roman social practices. What was a Greek to make of the great Roman patron's matutinal reception of his clients in the hall of his house, the *salutatio* in the *atrium?* *Atrium* was transliterated into Greek and so was patron (*patronês*), and for *salutatio* the Greek word *proskynesis* (grovelling obeisance) seemed adequate.[44]

Sometimes when direct translation seemed easy, Roman *fides* into Greek *pistis*, the danger was greatest, as the Aetolians discovered in 191 BC. Surrender to the *fides* of the Romans was, the Aetolians thought, a basis for gentlemanly negotiation; but in Latin the expression signified unconditional surrender.[45]

All these difficulties in hellenising Roman concepts had been real difficulties since the fourth century for the Greek inhabitants of south Italy into whose territory the Romans encroached. This explains why certain Greek words – *thriambos* for a triumph and *tebenna* for a toga – are almost certainly of Etruscan origin. The later corruption of the Greek language started in the West and spread East. In the first century BC the Alexandrian scholar Tryphon noted Italicisms in the Greek speech of the inhabitants of Rhegium and Syracuse.[46]

There were continuing pockets of Greek speech in the West. In Marseilles and in Naples you were more likely to hear Greek spoken in the streets than Latin. And immigrants from the East among themselves clung to their own native language. In Rome, for instance, the language of the Christian Church, the majority of whose converts were cosmopolitan – compare the list of names in St Paul's Epistle to the Romans 16, 3-15 – and did not rank high in the social scale, was Greek in the first two centuries as, in the main, was the language of the synagogues in Rome (some three-quarters of the surviving Jewish inscriptions in Rome are in Greek). The same was true of the Church in Gaul until in the middle of the third century Latin replaced Greek, though well-educated members of the clergy were still able to read Greek and in most cases to write it.[47]

Many people whose first language was Greek learnt Latin as a matter of necessity. Greek-speaking household slaves in Roman families, even in families whose masters cultivated the affectation of speaking to their slaves in Greek, had to learn Latin, (a reason, as has been seen, for preferring home-bred slaves, for whom Latin was a native language);[48] so had Greek-speaking recruits to the Roman army. Among slaves and freedmen were some who evidently became very good Latinists. Sulla's freedman Cornelius Epicadus completed Sulla's autobiography, left unfinished when Sulla died, and Pompilius Andronicus from Syria wrote a book on Ennius. Pompeius Lenaeus, a freedman of Pompey, translated Greek medical writings into Latin and the younger Tyrannio wrote on the origin of the Latin language which, like Dionysius of Halicarnassus, he took to be Greek.[49]

Others learnt Latin by their own choice and went to Rome in search of employment as educationists (*grammatici*, rhetoricians and philosophers) and doctors, and in the former category there were teachers of rhetoric who had achieved sufficient mastery of Latin to give instruction in Latin rhetoric. Sextus Clodius from Sicily practised as a rhetorician in Latin as well as in Greek and at the time of Augustus there were teachers of Larin rhetoric who came from the East, like Cestius Pius who, despite an inadequate Latin vocabulary, made a great reputation as a critic of Cicero's speeches, and Arellius Fuscus, who taught Ovid, both from Asia. At the end of the first century AD the scholarly Latinist Valerius Probus, a Roman citizen, indeed an equestrian, came from Berytus in Syria.[50]

And there were the literary men who wanted not only to find out about Rome and the Romans but to write books about them, conspicuously Dionysius of Halicarnassus and Diodorus during the principate of Augustus and, at the end of the first century, Plutarch.

At a lower social level there were Greeks in the eastern provinces who learnt Latin by their own choice because they sought employment in government offices, where there must always have been a considerable staff of men employed in the translation from Latin of official documents whether they emanated from Rome or from the provincial administrative headquarters. And there was always a demand for interpreters (see p.139).

For a long time well-educated Greeks of good social position were constrained by no necessity, and in the late Republic and early Empire felt no desire, to learn Latin. There was little reason for wishing to visit Rome or Latin-speaking Italy as a tourist, for there was no architecture, or, save where it had been filched from the Greek East, any art of consequence. Nor was there any temptation to learn the Romans' barbarous language in order to read the masterpieces of Latin literature in the original. Until the late Republic there were no such masterpieces; and even after that what had Cicero to offer that was not to be found far better in Demosthenes and Plato, what was there in Virgil which could face comparison with Homer? For the educated Greek, as for the modern Frenchman, there was no language, no literature, comparable with his own.

The world, of course, had not stopped dead with Alexander, and an educated Greek could hardly close his eyes to the history of Rome's growth to empire, however distasteful a subject this might be, or to the facts of Roman civilisation, character and institutions, but anybody

interested in history, sociology and politics could find what he wanted
in books written for him in his native tongue – in Polybius,
Posidonius, Dionysius of Halicarnassus (Plutarch's source for his Life
of Coriolanus), Timagenes, Diodorus and others. In the second
century AD Sallust's *Histories* were translated into Greek.[51]

How much of what was written about Rome in Greek and primarily
for Greek readers by such authors was absorbed by educated Greeks,
and how widely? How many Greeks had the knowledge which the
educated Roman possessed (see p.43) of the two cultures? Plutarch
evidently took such knowledge for granted in his readers, for the
Praecepta reipublicae gerendae, for instance, is littered indiscriminately
with references to Greek and to Roman history; the reader was
expected to know quite a lot about the elder and the younger
Africanus, about Marius, Sulla, Pompey and the younger Cato.

Yet the frequency with which Greeks who wrote about Rome –
Dionysius of Halicarnassus, for instance, and Plutarch – thought it
necessary to give the Greek translation of not particularly uncommon
Latin terms suggests that there was, among Greeks, a considerable
reading public which knew little Latin. Though it is hard to think of
any Greek city which did not have public inscriptions in which the
Greek word *Sebastos* occurred, Pausanias considered it necessary to tell
his readers that the founder of the Roman Empire was called
Augustus and that 'Augustus' was what the Greek word *Sebastos*
signified.[52]

Few Greeks were called upon to speak Latin in public life. Roman
governors and high-ranking members of their staffs spoke fluent Greek
and even if diplomatic business took a Greek to Rome, he could get by
without being able to speak Latin. Until the eighties BC, it is true, he
was not allowed to address the Senate in his own language, but there
were plenty of Roman senators who were happy to act on his behalf,
as C. Acilius acted for the three distinguished Greek philosophers in
155 BC, and after the eighties, however offensive this might be to a few
diehard Romans, Greeks were allowed to address the Senate in their
native language. Agrippa I and his brother Herod spoke to the Senate
in Greek in AD 41, and Claudius often replied in the Senate in a set
speech in Greek when a delegation of Greeks was being received.[53]

Dio of Prusa is significant. Though he appreciated the *pax Romana*,
spoke with admiration of the Roman character and of Trajan as
emperor, and indeed boasted – perhaps a little too loudly – of his
powerful Roman friends, he shows no knowledge of or interest in
Roman history or culture; all his *exempla* are Greek. Numa, indeed, a
philosopher-king of Greek copy-book type, is the only character in
Roman history whom he mentioned by name.[54]

Particularly in Asia Minor in the families of distinguished Greeks and
the descendants of families which had once ruled client kingdoms, the
second century AD witnessed very great change. It was now that men

with such backgrounds turned their eyes to the West and to a career in Roman government (see p.53). They held magistracies in Rome and belonged to the Senate; they must have had houses in Rome (just as, since Trajan, they were required to invest a portion of their capital in real estate in Italy). So the historic process was reversed. With the conquest of the East the Latin-speaking Roman administrator was of necessity bilingual; now his counterpart, the Greek-speaking Roman administrator was of necessity bilingual too.[55]

Though we hear much of the success of numerous Romans in mastering the everyday use of the Greek language (see p.43), we have no more concrete evidence of this than the splattering of Greek terms in Cicero's Letters to his brother and to Atticus until we come to Fronto's prize compositions in Greek and the *Meditations* of Marcus Aurelius. From the late fourth century we have specimens of the Latin writings of two remarkable men whose first language was Greek. Ammianus Marcellinus, a Greek from Antioch, after an effective military career settled down in Rome in AD 378 to undertake the most ambitious of enterprises, a Roman History in Latin, starting where Tacitus left off, at the death of Domitian, and coming down to his own times. His Latin is turgid and often obscure, but the book is galvanic. Ammianus was a born historian, diligent in research, acute in historical judgment; he was, in fact, Rome's last great historian.

Claudian, a Greek born probably in Alexandria, author in Latin of panegyrics, epics and epigrams and a master of invective in the best Roman traditions started publishing in Rome in AD 395, but must have been writing in Latin some time before this. He was 'inter ceteras artes praegloriosissimus poeta', and the emperors Arcadius and Honorius ordered his statue to be erected in Trajan's Forum.[56]

It is difficult in general to know how hard a language Latin was for a Greek to master. Lucian's 'Dependent Scholar', tutor in a rich and boorish Roman family, 'murdered the Latin tongue with his dreadful foreign accent'. Plutarch certainly found Latin difficult. He admitted that he was not a good enough Latinist to comment on the finesse of Cicero's oratory and he criticised the 'youthful effort' of the great scholar Caecilius of Caleacte in Sicily who had published a comparison of the oratory of Demosthenes and Cicero. Caecilius evidently, like his friend Dionysius of Halicarnassus, knew Latin well. Plutarch, on the other hand, knew no Latin when he first came to Italy. 'I proceeded,' he wrote, 'from things to words, not from words to things.' It is unlikely that even for his Roman *Lives* he read Roman historians who wrote in Latin, and it is plausibly conjectured that he was heavily dependent on assistants whose knowledge of Latin was greater than his own (see p.206).[57]

Itinerant Greek orators who visited Rome like Dio Chrysostom and

Aelius Aristides may have known no Latin at all. In the case of other distinguished Greek writers, it is difficult to know how much Latin they knew. Nicolaus of Damascus is likely to have known it well. Strabo, who spent considerable time in Rome and in Campania and who travelled with Aelius Gallus in Egypt in 24 BC must have had reasonable knowledge of the language; whether or not he read Asinius Pollio and Q. Dellius in the original, he twice quoted passages from Cicero. Lucian records questioning boatmen on the Po, was familiar with Juvenal and his *Pro Lapsu inter Salutandum* implies a knowledge of Latin; anyhow he is unlikely to have been appointed to a respectable post in the civil service in Egypt if he knew no Latin. Josephus, we know, had trouble with his Greek; whether he achieved any proficiency in Latin we do not know at all.[58]

(iv) Spoken Latin

Inspired by Agricola, the young Britons aimed, as we have seen, not only at speaking correct Latin but at speaking good Latin; *eloquentia* was what they sought to achieve. How far, one wonders, was this within their powers?

Nowhere in the Empire, of course, was Latin ever a static language; like all other living languages, it was changing all the time.

The most perfect French is – or was – spoken on the Loire, the best Italian in Tuscany. In ancient Rome perfect Latin, *sermo dulcis*, Latin with a top-class accent, as the two Catuli spoke it, was Roman Latin, *certa vox Romani generis urbisque propria*. You should speak 'ut oratio Romana plane videatur, non civitate data', not something thrown in with your citizenship in a package-deal. But, of course, it was Latin, not Roman, that you talked; your aim should be 'perbene Latine loqui'.*[59]

There was the question of your accent in speaking,† and there was the question of the Latin that you spoke.

There were, in Italy itself, broadly two different kinds of Latin. There was the Latin of polished refinement (*eruditus, perpolitus, urbanus*), like the French sanctioned by the Academy. This was the Latin of public speeches and of the bulk of Latin literature which has survived, and certain educated conversational speech might avoid neologisms and current slang, 'incorrupta antiquitas', which was a particularly attractive trait in a woman.[61] On the other hand there was the wide spectrum of spoken everyday Latin (*cotidianus, plebeius, vulgaris*, even *inconditus* and *rusticus*). Cicero, the most polished of

---

* Greeks, however, spoke of 'talking Roman' (*rhômaïzein*) and referred to written Latin as *rhômaïka grammata*, though they too referred to 'the Latin language' (*phônê, dialektos, glôssê*), not 'the Roman language'.[60]

† When Mestrius Florus criticised Vespasian for mispronunciation (saying 'plostra' instead of 'plaustra'), Vespasian retorted by addressing him as 'Flaurus', Suet., *D. Vesp.* 22.

Latinists, might sometimes employ this in writing letters to his friends, though he would not use it in a public speech. It included a wide variety of vocabulary (including foreign words and words with unusual suffixes like *gaudimonium, cruciabiliter*) and of syntax, ranging from the talk of the educated at one extreme to that of the uneducated at the other,[62] and within it there were great differences of dialect. Our inadequate knowledge of such spoken Latin comes from a limited number of literary sources (Plautus, the authors of the *Bellum Africum* and the *Bellum Hispaniense*, Vitruvius and Petronius) and from inscriptions;* it includes words and expressions which, though never found in correct written Latin, have passed into one or other of the Romance languages; *multum* as an adverb, for instance; 'multum loquaces' (in Plautus' *Aul.* 124) is at the background of an Italian's 'molto poco'.[63]

And there was considerable uncertainty and, indeed, change of 'correct' practice in the use of aspirates, both before vowels at the start of words and in juxtaposition with consonants (*triumpus, triumphus*).† As in English, faulty aspirates often revealed lack of education in a speaker and still in St Augustine's time a faulty aspirate was enough to condemn a man socially; on the other hand, the emphasis on or omission of an aspirate in educated speech might simply be old-fashioned or new-fangled, as the case might be (as it was once the smart thing in England to slur the 'h' in 'Your humble servant'). Practice was evidently changing fast in the Ciceronian age and Cicero himself at first followed tradition in saying 'pulcer' and 'triumpus' when 'pulcher' and 'triumphus' had become a part of general correct speech; and Catullus mocked Arrius who, at this time of changing pronunciation, overdid things with his 'chommoda' as well as with his idiosyncratic initial aspirates.[64]

Then there was the Latin which, while not ungrammatical, was what we should call 'dialect', *peregrina insolentia*. Local words of Gallic, Etruscan or, in Campania, Greek derivation were used; for the last, witness Petronius' *Satyricon*. The dour Pliny apologised to Titus for the crude vocabulary of much of the technical language of the *Natural Histories*. In particular, technical terms in agriculture will have differed in different districts, as they do in any modern country. Sometimes perfectly good archaic Latin words survived which had gone out of general use, like 'mane' for 'good' at Lanuvium. Praenestines used abbreviated words, according to Plautus. And there was Livy's *Patavinitas*; he wrote 'sibe' and 'quase', according to Quintilian.[65]

All this in Italy; outside Italy there were greater differences still. In

---

* E.g. *CIL* IV, 1895, a graffito from Pompeii has turned Ovid's 'quid magis est saxo durum, quid mollius unda' (*AA* 1, 475) into 'quid pote tam durum saxso aut quid mollius unda?'

† As in Co. Durham in England the 'h' in 'which' is emphasised, while elsewhere in England it is not pronounced.

the *Brutus*, whose fictional date was 46 BC, when Brutus was about to leave Rome for Gaul, Cicero told him that, when he got there, he would not only find a different vocabulary in spoken Latin but a marked difference in people's speech from that to which he was accustomed in Rome.[66]

Even among the educated, there must have been great differences both in accent and vocabulary from one part of the empire to another; and in view of the snobbishness of the genuine Roman which is reflected in our sources in references to *municipales* as such,* it is surprising that there are not more disparaging references, particularly in Martial, to the Latin spoken by those who hailed from the provinces.

When a stranger who met Tacitus at the Games asked him whether he came from Italy or from the provinces[67] (and what a lot of modern speculation would have been saved if Tacitus had given him a straight answer), it was evidently from hearing Tacitus speak that the man realised that he had not been born in Rome.

Spaniards were evidently recognisable; and Africans.

Poets from Corduba in Spain, according to Cicero, had a heavy foreign accent, 'pingue quiddam sonantes et peregrinum' – a remark which, among Spaniards, was not forgotten – and when Hadrian, who had been brought up in Spain, became quaestor to Trajan in Trajan's fourth consulship, and read a speech of the emperor in the Senate, there were titters of laughter; he spoke at that stage with a *rustica vox et agrestis*, a defect which he was soon to correct. And there is a good story in Aulus Gellius of the rhetorican who spoke Latin with a Spanish accent (*Hispano ore*) and, when he was offensively criticised by some young Greeks at a dinner party, he turned the tables on them showing that, whatever might be the nature of his accent, he was, in wit and culture, the master of his critics.[68]

To the end of his life Septimius Severus spoke with an African accent – 'Afrum quiddam usque ad senectutem sonans' – and his sister spoke such terrible Latin that she had to be sent home from Rome.[69] African Latin was marked not only in accent and vocabulary but perhaps also in style, that style for which Apuleius himself apologised. 'Rude and rustic', he called himself, 'exotici ac forensis sermonis rudis locutor'. Macrobius, too, who may have been African in origin, apologised if he lacked 'the native elegance of Roman speech'.[70]

Seneca who, during his exile, had plenty of time to interest himself in the Latin spoken in Corsica, noted the prevalence of Spanish, Ligurian and Greek words; it was anything but pure Latin (*patrius sermo*).[71]

There was not in fact one vulgar Latin, but there were numerous

* See p. 24 above.

vulgar Latins, with the general standard much lower in some provinces (Moesia for instance) than in others, and with great variations everywhere between the educated and the half-educated. Jerome admitted that Illyrian Latin was contaminated by native idiom: 'externis vitiis sermo patrius sordidatur.'[72] Inscriptions supply us with most of the information that we possess, and in the crudest cases it is impossible to know how the responsibility for abnormalities is to be apportioned as between the stone-cutter and the patron by whom he was commissioned.[73]

(v) Latin in the eastern Empire

In Roman colonies in Greece, Asia Minor and Syria (few, except in Syria and Palestine, founded later than the time of Augustus and none later than Hadrian) Latin was preserved until the third century AD as the proper language for official, particularly complimentary, inscriptions. How long after the foundation it remained a first language depended chiefly, no doubt, on whether the colonists or their descendants were married to Roman or to native women,[74] in which latter case the Roman families caught the infection of their environment and Latin ceased to be their first spoken language.[75]

Outside the colonies, there were Roman families which had settled all over the East (and, as in the West, soldiers at the end of their military service, quite a lot probably from Pompey's armies for a start), and in many cases their descendants remained sufficiently Roman to be given military and administrative appointments in the western empire if they entered on a public career. It is an interesting fact that out of 69 identifiable senators from Asia Minor down to the time of Commodus, 55 came from Roman colonies or from places where there were settlements of Italians.[76]

As has been noted, the increasing number of rich Greeks, particularly from Asia Minor, who entered the Senate in the second century AD must have been competent Latin speakers. Yet in the fourth century, in recording the appointment of Libanius' friend Flavius Strategius Musonianus to be Praetorian Prefect in the East in AD 354, Ammianus Marcellinus stated that the distinction, greater than he had expected to receive, was due to the fact that he spoke Latin fluently, just as he spoke Greek.[77]

In the East as in the West Latin was the language of the army,* and in the early Empire must have been learnt and understood up to a point by all serving soldiers,[78] not all of whom will have known much Latin before joining up. All official military documents were in Latin, as we know from inscriptions and papyri which survive in Egypt: imperial edicts addressed to the army (other imperial edicts to Egypt

---

* In his account of the circumnavigation of the Euxine dedicated to Hadrian and written in Greek, Arrian referred (6, 2; 10, 1) to official military reports which he had sent in, written in Latin.

were published in Greek translation), rosters of troops, duty rosters and military accounts.[79] All commands were given in Latin, a practice which survived even at the end of the sixth century, when Latin otherwise can hardly have been understood at all. As we know from the *Strategicon* of Mauritius (about AD 600), the command 'Quick march' was still 'Movê', not 'Kineson', and 'Sta' was the order to halt.

How well, except in military officialese, soldiers in the East understood Latin and to what degree they spoke it among themselves, rather than speaking Greek (or, indeed, spoke either of those languages) is impossible to know. On one occasion a soldier was called on in Greek, to give evidence, and was ordered by Tiberius to give his evidence in Latin, not Greek. In second-century fiction there was the legionary soldier in Apuleius' *Metamorphoses* (and Lucian's *Ass*) who in Greece, though able to speak Greek, addressed a peasant in Latin and beat him for not understanding what he said.[80]

Of the graffiti on the statue of Memnon at Thebes composed by soldiers on leave from regiments in Egypt, thirteen are in Latin and only two in Greek. On the other hand, letters from serving soldiers to their parents in Egypt were naturally written in Greek, for this was the language which their parents knew, though until their sons became soldiers they may not have understood such words as *principalis, librarius, cornicularius*, written in Greek letters.[81]

How many Roman citizens were there, particularly in the eastern half of the empire, who could not speak Latin, including descendants from Roman colonists or men enfranchised through military service, who had themselves in a Greek-speaking environment lost familiarity with Latin? Under Claudius we hear of the Lycian who had himself received Roman citizenship but who could not understand Latin, or at least could not understand the emperor's Latin when cross-examined by him in the Senate in AD 43; he was one of a Lycian delegation. 'Nobody has a right to Roman citizenship who can not speak Latin', Claudius pronounced, and cancelled the man's citizenship forthwith.[82] It is to be suspected, however, that, as there was a great trafficking in Roman citizenship, there were in fact a great many Roman citizens in the East who could not speak Latin.[83] Could St Paul, before he went to Rome?

Outstandingly versatile linguists like Mithridates and Cleopatra, will have had no difficulty in picking up Latin; Cleopatra, unlike earlier Ptolemies, had even mastered Egyptian. In the third century Zenobia is reported (by a not very good source) as being only a moderate Latin speaker though her sons, instructed in Latin at her insistence, spoke Latin better than they spoke Greek.[84]

In public life in the East Latin was employed in a variety of different fields. All imperial constitutions and edicts and public letters of provincial governors down to the early sixth century were issued in

Latin and, in the East, they had to be translated or adapted for publication either in Greek alone or in both languages. Down to the third century in Egypt (except for soldiers or ex-soldiers who from the middle of the second century could use Greek if they preferred)* and elsewhere in the East before AD 439 (Theodosius II) wills had to be executed in Latin, save where special exception was made by the emperor; however, when a will, instead of making legacies, established a deed of trust (*fideicommissum*), Latin, Greek or any other language might be employed.[85]

The administration of law in the East was a curiously mongrel affair. The law itself was Roman law, in Latin – witness the *Codex Theodosianus* and the Corpus of Civil Law of Justinian – and after Caracalla's gift of universal citizenship was binding on all free members of the Empire. Before AD 397 judgments in court were published in Latin, as was the reported preamble of a case; as a general rule, however, proceedings were conducted and reported in Greek. This is clear from the recorded adjudication of imperial procurators in Phrygia in the first half of the third century AD and from the surviving record of a case which was tried on appeal by Caracalla in Antioch in AD 216.[86] Barristers were engaged for their oratorical gifts and often had a poor knowledge of law (just as at Rome in the Republic many barristers had little or no knowledge of Roman civil law). So that often both they and the judge were dependent on the trained lawyers, men, according to Libanius, of inferior social standing, 'the sons of labourers'.[87]

In the middle of the fourth century there was a profound change, though we cannot tell for how long it lasted. Our evidence comes in the main from Libanius' jeremiads. Oratorical study (the *logoi*) was losing ground; students were undisciplined and inattentive. Worse still, good well-born young men, instead of devoting themselves to the kind of education which Libanius gave, were studying Latin and law – obviously it was impossible to study law without a knowledge of Latin – either at the famous law school at Berytus or, worse still, at Rome, to which they were going in the further hope of making good social contacts, even at Court.†[88] This was because of a new – and belated – ruling that advocates had to be registered and to know Latin; and since registration as an advocate was a way of escape from curial duties, the hook was well baited. Already towards the middle of the fourth century Jerome and his rich friends had been sent from northern Dalmatia to receive the whole of their education in Rome.

Egyptian papyri teach us something which we could not learn from

---

* Which clearly indicates that not every soldier became fluent in Latin.

† To what extent had boys been sent to Rome earlier than this to study law (and learn Latin in the process)? Philostratus, *VAT* 7, 42, describes a boy sent to Rome for this purpose by his father from Messene in Achaea at the time of Domitian.

any other source, how Latin was actually taught to those who already knew Greek. The number of such papyri is not large – if papyri survived from Alexandria, the centre of the Roman administration, where Latin was much used, it would obviously be considerably larger – and only a few date from the first two centuries AD, most belonging to the fourth century or later.[89] There was Latin writing practice (lines of Virgil, second/third century and – fourth/fifth century – Virgil, *Aeneid* 2, 601, written out a number of times); there were texts of literary, philosophical and historical works (e.g. Livy, late third century). There were glossaries of Latin words, sometimes written in Greek letters, with their Greek equivalents; Latin classics with scholia and vocabulary, the earliest of them Sallust on a fourth-century papyrus. From the fourth century or later there is a not very accurate translation into Greek of the first book of Virgil's *Aeneid*; a model Latin alphabet, the letters named in Greek; a list of Latin numbers written out in full with their Greek equivalents and repeated several times, evidently as a writing exercise.[90]

Of Latin authors, passages of Virgil appear on nineteen papyri, passages of Cicero on eight and passages of Sallust on five.[91]

Most of this after Diocletian and Constantine had given a fillip to the use of Latin in the East, illustrated in Egypt by the fact that the journals of high government officials, previously written in Greek, were now written in Latin.[92]

The most fascinating evidence of instruction in Latin in Egypt comes from a sixth-century papyrus giving two exercises, each in three languages (Latin, Greek and Coptic, the Latin and Coptic words being written in Greek letters.[93] The exercises themselves are admirable and closely comparable with the kind of fiction used today by the British Broadcasting Corporation in its highly entertaining instruction in foreign languages.

Here, in English, is the first:

A. If everybody has finished his drink, wipe the table, bring the candles and light the lamps. Let us have the sweets and the scent.
B. Now, everybody, say, 'Bless you; you have entertained us well and royally, as befits you'.
A. It is getting late. Would you like to spend the night here?
B. That is a kind offer, and we are grateful. But no, thank you very much.
A. As you will. I have done what was up to me. Now light the lamps, and let me see you out.

And the second:

A. Somebody is knocking at the door. Go out and find who it is.
B. It is someone from Aurelius with a message.
A. Ask him in. What is it, boy, what is your message?
Slave. All is well. Maximus sends you his greeting.
A. Where is he?
Slave. He is outside.

A.	Let him come in ... I am delighted to see you.
Maximus.	Greetings from the children and their parents. They have sent this letter by a slave.
Letter.	I am extremely worried, brother, at having had no letter from you for so long. Send me a letter, to put my mind at ease. Greeting to all your family.

(vi) Spoken Greek

There were all sorts of Greek too. There was the commonly spoken and written Greek, the *koinê*. There was Attic Greek (which Arrian himself wrote, though in playing Boswell to Epictetus' Johnson he reported the Master's utterances as they were spoken, in the *koinê*).[94] There was Doric which, according to Pausanias, survived at its purest in Messenia. And there were the survivals of other traditional dialects, the five dialects of Asia, for instance, all of which the consul of 131 BC, Licinius Crassus, could speak (see p.43) – one of them Aeolic, in which the formidable poetess Balbilla, who travelled in Hadrian's company in Egypt, wrote epigrams which survive on the statue of Memnon. During the first century Eirenaeus, the Alexandrian scholar (Minucius Pacatus), wrote a book on Attic Greek and another on the dialect of Alexandria, both, no doubt, in relation to the *koinê*.[95]

And all the time Greek was loading itself up with a wide variety of loan-words, in particular from Latin.[96]

Cappadocian Greek was notoriously bad and at Tyana, a Greek city amid a population of Cappadocians, it was remarkable that the cultivated Attic accent of that young paragon Apollonius was not corrupted by his surroundings. (His esoteric book on divination was written in Cappadocian, not in Greek.)[97] At Tomis on the Black Sea, according to Ovid, nobody understood Latin and the few people who spoke Greek spoke it with a strong Getic accent; and we are told by Dio Chrysostom that, though the natives of Olbia knew Homer's epics by heart, their own spoken Greek suffered greatly from their barbarian surroundings.[98]

There were still Greek-speaking cities, Hellenistic foundations, in Parthia (Seleuceia on the Tigris, for instance, and Susa), and the Parthian Chancellery corresponded with the authorities of those cities in Greek. Greek (unlike Latin) was evidently well understood in the Persian Court, by Orodes in 53 BC (as by the Armenian king Artabazus, who even wrote tragedies and histories in Greek) – there was the famous performance of the Bacchae after Carrhae, in which Crassus' head served as a prop – and by king Vardanes, with whom Apollonius of Tyana conversed. Plutarch observed, indeed, that many of the Arsacids had Greek mothers, Ionian courtesans.

Apollonius' Indian king conversed freely in Greek (and even exercised himself in the Greek manner), as did the Indian Sages. Indeed the letter brought by the Indian envoys from king Porus to Augustus was in Greek.[99]

Of the Greek of a third-century inscription from Phrygia it is observed that 'the language is beginning to resemble Modern Greek'.[100]

A fourth-century Latin-Greek word-list on papyrus from Egypt shows how in Latin by that time 'o' and 'u' were interchanged and 'b' had replaced 'v' (*binu* for *vinum*, *bile* for *vile*), while classical Greek words had been replaced by others, *neron*, for instance, meaning 'water', as it does in Greek today. 'Wash your hands' – 'Labamanos', 'Nipson'.[101]

The ancient world not having discovered the fascination of bedevilling itself with statistics, we have no conception at all of the proportion of people who could read and write in any part of the Roman empire in any language at all;* or, indeed, in any province of what proportion of people habitually spoke, or were able to speak, what languages. Nor in the case of the unrecorded, but certain, survival of native languages do we know how far this was the consequence of conservatism or laziness and how far it indicated (as in some parts of Russia's modern empire it is said to indicate) a hostility to the imperial power.

---

* We might have some bad shocks. In Egypt, where from Ptolemaic days Greek was the language of local administration, papyri have revealed the surprising fact that at the end of the second century AD (AD 184-7) at least two important local officials in the Fayum, *kōmogrammateis*, men whose days must have been spent in handling and issuing documents in Greek, could neither read nor write the language; they were *agrammatoi* (though able, both, presumably to write and speak Coptic). In one case the patient efforts of the man to write his name in Greek characters, so as to sign official documents, have been preserved. He must have placed great trust in his clerks, *scribae*, of whom he had at least nine, and in his other subordinates to tell him the truth about what he was signing.[102]

CHAPTER TEN

Communication,
2: 'Barbarous Languages' and Interpreters

Mr Wharton Senior: I remember a waiter at an hotel in Holborn who could speak seven languages. It is an accomplishment very necessary for a Courier or a King's Messenger.
Mr Wharton Junior: You don't mean to say, Sir, that you disregard foreign languages?

Trollope, *The Prime Minister*, chap. 4.

We hear surprisingly little of language difficulties in antiquity; only in the Bible does the story of the Tower of Babel point to the segregation of humanity through differences in language; while the story of Pentecost describes the miracle of unity when language barriers are broken down. In Persian dualism the world of peace to be established after the ultimate triumph of Ahuramasda would be a world which spoke a single language.[1]

In his pastiche, *The Council of the Gods*, Lucian might have made more of the idea that proceedings could not be conducted without the presence of a celestial interpreter. He merely observes that it was a polyglot assembly and that Mithras could not speak Greek and converse with those who did. When the late emperor Claudius arrived in Heaven in Seneca's skit, the *Apokolokyntosis*, nobody could understand his speech; it did not sound like Latin and it did not sound like Greek. So Hercules, as a much-travelled god, was sent to see if he could identify his nationality.[2]

In Herodian's highly coloured story of Caracalla's suit to the Parthian king for the hand of his daughter, Artabanus at first ridiculed the proposal on the ground that neither Caracalla nor his bride would understand a word that the other said.* [3]

In Paphlagonia anyone speaking what we should call Double Dutch 'was making unintelligible noises, as if speaking Hebrew or Phoenician'. When Alexander set up his bogus oracle at Abonuteichos in Paphlagonia in the second century AD and enquiries were made in writing in Syriac or Celtic (this last, presumably, by Galatians), there was, according to Lucian, an uncomfortably long interval before the oracle supplied an answer, because Alexander had difficulty in finding a translator.[4]

In Heliodorus' *Aethiopica* (third century AD), when the Egyptian

* Would the Parthian princess not speak Greek (cf. p.35)?

bandit Thyamis, whose Greek was not particularly good, addressed his trusty comrades in Egyptian and was anxious that his paean of self-praise should be appreciated by his Greek prisoners, he employed a young Greek who had learnt Egyptian to translate his speech, as he delivered it, into Greek.[5]

Skilled interpreters have always had their vital importance, but they never occupy the limelight. When the Heads of the American and Soviet states are shown in animated conversation, the camera is careful not to include the two skilled interpreters without whom there could be no conversation at all. In the same way in antiquity historians rarely concerned themselves with language problems.

What languages did Jesus speak? Was Aramaic or Mishna Hebrew his first language? Was Greek generally understood in Galilee? In which case Jesus and Pilate will have conversed directly in Greek. If not, their conversation at the trial must have been conducted – though this is nowhere stated – though an interpreter skilled both in Aramaic and in Greek or Latin. In Acts we are told that at Jerusalem Paul spoke to the Captain of the Guard in Greek and then proceeded to address the crowd in Aramaic (Hebrew).[6]

In an aristocratic society certain foreign languages are sometimes spoken well by members of the upper crust, as in the nineteenth century French was spoken fluently in Czarist Russia and in the eastern Mediterranean, and Greek was spoken by the upper classes of ancient Rome. But, in general, proficiency in foreign languages has all too easily been considered an achievement of the second order. This, Josephus tells us, was the Jewish assessment in Palestine. Ability to speak a foreign language idiomatically was often possessed by slaves, so why should a gentleman compete? *His* education should be in subjects which no slave could aspire to master, Jewish scriptures and Jewish law.

Josephus should not be taken to imply that knowledge of Greek was unusual in Palestine, for the very opposite appears to have been the case. The Cave of Letters in the Wadi Habra, for instance, has produced a letter almost certainly from Bar Cochba written in Greek, 'because he felt no impulse to write in Aramaic (*hebristi*)'. Josephus must mean that little effort was made to achieve a high idiomatic standard in Greek; so Josephus himself, who spoke Greek better than most of his compatriots, spoke it with a bad accent and with no great refinement.[7]

Fluency in two languages was, in the Italian peninsula, at first the mark of the southerner, able to speak Oscan and Greek. Further North the first Romans to be bilingual will have spoken Etruscan as well as Latin, but our earliest reference to such proficiency does not suggest that it was a common achievement. Livy writes of the year 310 BC:

When, with the memory of the Caudine Forks fresh in their minds, no Roman dared penetrate the Ciminian Forest, the consul's brother – or perhaps half-brother – volunteered to scout out the position and return soon with a reliable report. He had been educated at Caere among friends and was an Etruscan scholar who spoke the language fluently. I have read in books that in those days Roman boys were educated in Etruscan literature, as today they are educated in Greek, but it is more probable that this was an individual achievement on his part, considering the audacious disguise in which he entered enemy territory accompanied, it is said, by a single slave who had been brought up with him as a boy and knew Etruscan. They went disguised as farm-labourers with a countryman's tools, hooks and a couple of spears. What saved them was not so much their linguistic performance, their clothing and weapons as the fact that it was beyond belief that any outsider should set foot in the Ciminian Forest.[8]

For how long the Etruscan language was spoken, written or understood even in Roman families as proud of their Etruscan origins as some Scotch families are aggressively proud of their Caledonian origins today is something that we do not know. It is thought that, despite his researches into Etruscan history, the emperor Claudius did not understand the language. In the case of Latin words of Etruscan (as of Oscan) derivation, Roman etymologists showed a certain interest and knowledge which only communicated itself to a wider public when something sensational happened – when, for instance, shortly before Augustus' death lightning struck off the letter C in CAISAR on a statue of Augustus, leaving AISAR, the Etruscan word for God.[9]

Greek did not count as a 'foreign' language; it was 'the other language', and from the second century BC onwards, as has been seen, an educated Roman was fluent 'in both languages', *utraque lingua*. When as early as 282 BC a Roman envoy, the distinguished ex-consul L. Postumius, made bold to speak publicly in Greek in a Greek city, Tarentum, there were flaws in his idiom and his mannerless Greek audience mocked the slips that he made;[10] a hundred and fifty years later his Greek would have been as good as theirs; for it is one of the least loudly trumpeted virtues of the educated Roman from the second century BC onwards that he spoke Greek extremely well (see p.43).

On official occasions, however, Roman magistrates, ambassadors and generals in the Greek-speaking world were accompanied by interpreters, at first Greeks who had acquired Roman citizenship.

There was a legend – not recorded by the Roman annalists – that the Roman embassy sent in 454 BC before the Decemvirate to study the laws of Athens and other Greek states was accompanied by an interpreter, the distinguished Hermodorus who lived in exile in Italy after banishment by the egalitarian democracy of his native Ephesus; but this was a fiction built round the statue of a certain Hermodorus in the Comitium at Rome.

At the end of the third century, however, Cn. Publilius Menander is a historical figure. He was a Greek slave who had acquired Roman citizenship, and special provisions were made to ensure that he should not lose his Roman citizenship through returning to his Greek city of origin on an official mission in which he served as a Roman interpreter.[11]

Such professional bilingual Greek and Latin speakers were used on occasion when it was thought more becoming to Roman dignity that a Roman commander or official should not demean himself by speaking publicly any language other than Latin; or, indeed, the interpreting might be done by a junior officer. Valerius Maximus gives his own pompous explanation:

It was a regularly observed Roman custom never to reply officially to Greeks except in Latin. In Greece and Asia as well as in Rome they compelled Greeks to dispense with that volubility in which they are so practised and to speak through an interpreter, so that greater respect should be accorded everywhere to Latin. Not that the Romans themselves were not good Greek scholars; but they considered that there was no field in which the Greek cloak should not take second place to the Roman toga. It was improper, they thought, that the weighty authority of Roman imperialism should be surrendered to the claims of Greek literature with all its deceitful charm.

So, after the third Macedonian war, Aemilius Paullus, who spoke Greek fluently (and spoke privately in Greek to Perseus), announced the peace settlement of 167 BC publicly in Latin; it was then translated into Greek by Cn. Octavius, a propraetor on his staff. Earlier, in 191, Cato's public speech at Athens had been followed by a Greek translation and it was acutely observed by the Greeks that Greek was a more verbose language than Latin, though this did not necessarily imply, as Cato thought, that Greeks spoke from the lips and Romans from the heart.[12]

Considerations of Roman dignity, no doubt, induced Scipio to conduct his conversation with Hannibal before Zama through interpreters, for they could perfectly well have spoken in Greek, which Hannibal knew well. In the story, probably fictional, of their meeting at Ephesus in 193 BC Scipio was out of uniform; so their conversation could have been in Greek.[13]

In the Republic there must have been 'Treasury draughtsmen' at Rome, capable of translating Roman official enactments from Latin for publication in eastern provinces in Greek, and there was increasing need of such translators in the imperial household from Augustus' time onwards even before, probably under Marcus Aurelius, a separate bureau for Greek correspondence under the *ab epistulis Graecis* was set up.[14] The men employed were presumably for the most part Greeks who had learnt Latin, slaves, freedmen or free Greeks who had received Roman citizenship. As has been seen, there was similar employment for a similar type of man at the provincial headquarters of the eastern Greek-speaking provinces.

Sometimes, even in the Republic, it was in Rome that the Greek translation of an official document, normally a decree of the Senate, was made and from Rome it was circulated in full to the governors of interested provinces in the East who then published the whole' or extracts. On other occasions the Greek translation was made (as the translation of governors' edicts and letters was made) at the provincial headquarters. There were standard Greek versions of technical Latin constitutional and administrative terms, and these were no doubt available for consultation in all offices, not merely in Rome, where translations were made. Sometimes the Greek of the translator was good, sometimes it was not of a very high standard and sometimes the translator was not perfectly at home in the Latin language, especially in Latin technical abbreviations.[15]

Making an exception, of course, of their own language, the Romans followed the Greeks in dismissing any language at all but Greek as barbarian. In a rhetorical declamation, one of the major horrors to be apprehended if the Cimbri had defeated Marius was that the Romans would have had to learn to speak their conqueror's language: 'an Cimbrice loquendum sit.'[16]

It is hard to know to what extent Romans interested themselves in learning barbarian languages.* The fact that Q. Terentius Culleo, the senator who was a Carthaginian prisoner in the second Punic war, was subsequently used frequently in diplomatic negotiations with Carthage may suggest that he had learnt Punic as a prisoner.[17]

In the mid-second century BC the Roman D. Junius·Silanus (about whom we know only this single fact) headed a team of experts in Punic who translated Mago's treatise on agriculture into Latin and in 88 BC a certain Cassius Dionysius of Utica made a fresh abbreviated translation, which Varro used later, this time into Greek.[18]

Decimus Brutus learnt to speak Celtic, presumably when serving under Caesar in the conquest of Gaul, and he must have spoken it reasonably well since he hoped, when things grew too hot for him in north Italy in 43 BC, to make his way over the Alps to join Brutus and Cassius, disguised as a Gaul.[19]

At Tomis, where, as has been seen, nobody spoke Latin and only a few people (very bad) Greek, Ovid had to learn Getic,† and he learnt it with the utmost reluctance (while talking to himself in Latin for fear that his Latin might grow rusty). Had he been a Varro, he might have written usefully about the Getic language; but all that he recorded was the rapturous applause of his fully-armed native audience listening, the arrows rattling in their quivers, to his recitation of a poem in Getic extolling the virtues of the imperial family.[20]

---

* In his section on 'Application and Hard Work' (*De Studio et Industria*, 8, 7) Valerius Maximus listed two non-Roman linguistic feats (Themistocles learning Persian and Mithridates' 22 languages), but no comparable Roman achievement.

† At the end of the first century AD the Greek Dio Chrysostom spent part of his exile on the Danube and subsequently published a *Getika* (*FGH* 707; *RE* V, 873f.). Did he learn anything of the language?

Whether Ovid was ever used by visiting Romans or Greeks as an interpreter, we do not know.

Two qualities were called for in an interpreter; he must be a good linguist, and he must be absolutely trustworthy and discreet. Sometimes linguistic skill was enough, as in the case of the interpreter who questioned the Gallic deserter (or prisoner) who was to be executed at L. Quinctius Flamininus' infamous dinner-party in north Italy in 192 BC, or the man who conducted that masterpiece of tragic irony, Marius' discussion with the Cimbri before Vercellae in 102 BC about the Teutones whose arrival as reinforcements the Cimbri expected from minute to minute, not knowing, as Marius knew, that they were all dead or captive.[21]

But very often there was need of more than linguistic skill, discretion. There were, for instance, the interpreters who made possible the intrigue of Sulla with king Bocchus for the trapping of Jugurtha. There is, indeed, the story that the interpreters whom Caracalla employed in his conversations with the delegates of northern peoples were subsequently eliminated by him, so that there should be no record of the indiscretions which he had committed in the course of the talks.[22]

In the West most interpreters were no doubt men of native origin who – or whose fathers or grandfathers – had received Roman citizenship. Such were the interpreters on Caesar's staff in Gaul, chief among them C. Valerius Troucillus, son of a former chief of the Helvii who was given Roman citizenship by C. Valerius Flaccus in 83 BC, after which his name was C. Valerius Caburrus. Troucillus was probably killed during Caesar's conquest of Gaul, as was his brother C. Valerius Donnotaurus; but not before, in the first year's campaign, he had been used by Caesar as the most .trustworthy of his evidently numerous staff of interpreters (*cotidiani interpretes*), first in dealings with the Aedui; later he was sent to Ariovistus with M. Mattius, a guest-friend of Ariovistus, as a confidential envoy chosen for his reliability and his knowledge of Celtic which by this time Ariovistus spoke fluently. They were arrested on arrival as spies, and were lucky to escape execution. Both men were recovered after Ariovistus' defeat, and the recovery of Valerius, 'as honest a man as was to be found in Gaul', gave Caesar, by his own account, as great delight as the victory itself.[23] Other interpreters, doubtless of Gallic origin, were Cn. Pompeius and C. Arpineius, used – with Q. Junius, whose origin was Spanish – in the forlorn negotiations between Titurius Sabinus and Ambiorix in Gaul in 54 BC.[24]

Before attacking the Alemanni in AD 369, Julian used as a spy the military tribune Hariobaudes who spoke German and was, no doubt, in origin a German himself.[25]

In Greek-speaking provinces like Sicily interpreters were a convenience. On the frontiers, for negotiations with Gallic, German and trans-Danubian peoples, in north Africa, Spain and in the East they were vitally necessary. So the headquarters of provincial administration had their official interpreters, more often than not Roman citizens of local provincial origin, and from the establishment of the Empire military units on the frontiers had their own professional interpreters, enlisted soldiers. Two men are specified as interpreters on a list of discharges from legion VII Claudia (stationed on the Danube) in AD 195, and there are epitaphs of other soldiers who in their military service had been so employed.[26] It was, perhaps, such uniformed interpreters who were employed when Trajan commanded on the Rhine in his second consulship in AD 98, for Pliny records that on most of the occasions when Trajan made a public speech, it had to be translated.[27] When at a late stage in the siege of Jerusalem Titus spoke to Simon and John and rejected their proposals, he had an interpreter to turn his own Latin into Aramaic, whether a soldier or a civilian we are not told.[28]

The presence of foreign auxiliary troops in the Roman army, the most intelligent of whom will have learnt a reasonable amount of Latin (and might be used as spies) meant that even without professional interpreters on the spot, it was possible for the Romans campaigning on or outside the frontiers to understand something of local speech. The Romans under Antony were forewarned of an impending Parthian attack by a Roman in Parthian hands, a prisoner after Carrhae, who rode into the Roman lines dressed in Parthian clothing and conveyed the message to them in Latin; but there are numerous anecdotes in the Roman history books which are evidence of the translation of foreign speech by somebody or other into Latin. When in this very Parthian attack Roman soldiers lay on the ground under cover of their shields like some vast dead tortoise and so were unharmed by the volley of Parthian arrows and then, when the enemy ran out of arrows, rose as if from the dead and made off, a Parthian shouted, 'Be gone and good riddance, Romans. Well do you deserve your reputation as victors when you have managed to escape from the Parthian volley.' There is another story of Antony's flight from the Parthians, that a Parthian rode up and asked to speak to someone who could talk Parthian or Syrian, and a Greek from Antioch, a companion of Antony, was produced. When Crassus fought the Moesians in 29/8 BC, an enemy commander shouted, 'Who are you?' 'Romans, masters of the world', was the answer! 'That may well be,' the man replied, 'but you have to beat us first.'[29]

At the prestigious ceremony in the Forum in AD 66 when Tiridates made formal submission to Nero and received back the diadem which he had previously deposited before the Roman standards at the time of his compact with Corbulo in the East, a Latin version of his speech was read to the crowd by a man of praetorian rank.[30]

Apart from officials in full-time employment, there were also free-lance interpreters to whom ordinary people came in the provinces when they had to use Latin (which they did not understand) in order to approach the Roman administration with a claim or to fill in official papers.

In the eastern Christian Church, particularly from the fourth century onwards, there was plenty of work for interpreters of all kinds. Though from ignorance – and deep-seated Greek disparagement – of Latin, the language of the government and administration, even the important writings of the luminaries of the western Church were little known in the East,* there were communications in Latin from the West to be translated. At the Council of Nicaea Constantine courteously opened his address in Greek but after that spoke Latin, which was at once translated by an interpreter into Greek. And there was the two-way exchange between Greek and the native languages of the East, translating and interpreting. When St John Chrysostom preached in Antioch, there were Syriac-speaking members of his congregation who could not understand him. When he preached as bishop in Constantinople, his sermon was at once translated into Gothic for the benefit of Gothic-speaking members of the congregation.[31]

How about Roman staffs at custom-houses on the borders of the Empire? How about traders, those for instance who attended the great trade fair at Batnai near Edessa or those who sailed to India?[32] In Asia Minor and the country east of the Black Sea it is evident that a great number of different languages were spoken; Mithridates spoke twenty-two, some no doubt dialects of the same language.[33] In the district round Dioscurias in northern Colchis there were, according to the account which the elder Pliny swallowed (from Timosthenes), three hundred tribes, each with its own language; Strabo says there were seventy. Pliny speaks of 130 interpreters used by Roman merchants in the district.[34] Further south there were said by Strabo to have been twenty-six different languages in Albania.[35]

We hear of sensational episodes – of the freedman employed in collecting dues in the Red Sea early in the first century AD who was caught by the monsoon and found himself in Ceylon, where in six months he learnt to speak fluent Sinhalese,[36] and of an Indian stranded in Egypt in the second century AD who succeeded in learning Greek.[37] There must have been countless others. The agents of the Macedonian businessman Maës Titianus, who traded with the Chinese well east on the silk route at the Stone Tower in the country of Kômedon, returned with an authentic account of the habits of the

* St John Chrysostom knew no Latin.

Chinese people, and Bardesanes round AD 200, who spoke fluent Greek and Aramaic, knew about Chinese customs.[38] Quite a lot of translating must have been going on somewhere, particularly into and from Aramaic, 'the commercial language of the East from Egypt and northern Arabia to north-west India'.[39]

And there were the diplomatic contacts with the far East, the reception of embassies from India under Augustus and Trajan and one from Ceylon under Claudius; and, as is known from a Chinese source, an embassy was dispatched to China by Marcus Aurelius in AD 166.[40]

The fictional Damis, allegedly author of the notes on which Philostratus' *Life of Apollonius of Tyana* was based, had to be a considerable linguist. He was given a working knowledge of Greek – not a perfect knowledge for, born at Nineveh, 'he had been raised among Barbarians'. He also spoke Armenian and Persian.[41]

CHAPTER ELEVEN

A Problem of Names;
The Polyonymous Romans[1]

(i) Romans, the people with three names

The Romans came to be known as 'the people with three names' –
they could well have been known as the people with three names or
more – and their brand of nomenclature, rooted as it was in Etruscan
and other Italian usages, distinguished them from all other peoples in
the world who, as a general rule, had only one name with, perhaps, a
patronymic. The founder of the Ptolemaic dynasty in Egypt was
Ptolemy Lagu, Ptolemy son of Lagos. The Macedonian monarchs
whom we know as Philip II and Philip V were distinguished as Philip
son of Amyntas and Philip son of Demetrius.

As written with full formality, a Roman's name gave you his
patronymic too (with, if he was of good birth, the names sometimes of
his grandfather and great-grandfather as well) and also the name of
whichever of the thirty-five tribes it was to which he belonged – all this
in a series of conventional abbreviations, which made things still more
difficult. L. Funisulanus L.f. Ani. Vettonianus, for instance, was
Lucius Funisulanus Vettonianus, son of Lucius Funisulanus and a
member of the tribe Aniensis.[2]

Varro was probably right in stating that at the start the Romans
themselves had only one name apiece[3] as, however fictional their
characters, Ascanius, Romulus and Remus had single names. Very
soon, however, a Roman had two names, a *praenomen* (Gaius, Lucius
or whatever might be) and a gentile (clan) name, *nomen*, Cornelius,
Fabius etc. The first name marked the individual and was given to a
boy by his father nine days after birth. In late Republican times,
Varro reckoned, the number of traditional *praenomina* was thirty,[4] but
only about half that number were in general use, with Gaius (C.),
Gnaeus (Cn.), Lucius (L.), Marcus (M.) and Publius (P.) the most
common.

The *praenomen* Spurius had a fascinating history. Though it had
been the first name of two stock villains of early Roman history,
Spurius Cassius and Spurius Maelius, it was employed in aristocratic
families in the Republic; one Spurius Postumius Albinus was consul
in 174 BC, another in 148, another in 110. It was still a perfectly
respectable name in the middle of the first century AD; we have an

inscriptional record of a certain Spurius Turranius, grandson of another Spurius. Then it went out of use – because 'spurius' acquired the meaning of 'born out of wedlock', which it certainly possessed by the time of Trajan. For, it seems, just as 'the son of Marcus' was 'Marci filius', 'M.f.', children born out of proper wedlock (*matrimonium justum*), who took their civil status from their mother, were recorded as fatherless, 'sine patre filii', abbreviated to 's.p.f.' which, with the stops not plainly marked, became 'Sp.f.', 'Spurii filius'. And so, by a further twist, 'spurius' meant 'a bastard'.[5]

Families tended to be conservative in their use of *praenomina*, and it was a general rule that the first son had the same *praenomen* as his father.* On rare occasions a traditional *praenomen* was ostentatiously abandoned by an aristocratic family because one of its members to whom the name belonged had incurred disgrace. So, since the early fourth century, no patrician Manlius was called Marcus. Later such prohibitions were made by public resolution; after Mark Antony's death the Senate ruled that no Antonius should have the first name of Marcus, and after the disgrace of Cn. Piso in AD 20 his elder son's *praenomen* was changed by senatorial resolution from Cnaeus to Lucius.†[6]

After Sulla the *praenomen* ceased to be the distinguishing part of a man's name and at the same time new *praenomina* came into use. Sulla's son had Faustus (Fortunate) for his first name, and in the imperial family later third names like Nero became first names.

Antiquarian scholars at the end of the Republic and start of the Empire speculated on the origin of family names (*nomina*). Were they occupational in the main, reflecting the primitive agricultural life, like Farmer in English, Bauer in German? The Fabii, for instance; were they originally Diggers (*Fodii*)? Or had they something to do with beans (*fabae*)? Or did their name commemorate their descent from Hercules? Had the ancestral goddess or girl, whichever it was, enjoyed the embraces of Hercules in a pit (*fovea*)? Or was it a wolf-pit that the name commemorated, since the Fabii constituted one of the panels of the Luperci, the wolf-priests?

Had the Suillii and the Porcii, in their origin, anything to do with pigs?[7]

A peculiarity – and to other peoples a very puzzling peculiarity – of Roman nomenclature was 'the third name', the *cognomen*; indeed not only the third name because, given this start, names snowballed until the consul of AD 169 established a record with thirty-eight of them.

---

* It seems likely that, if the first son died, his next eldest brother then assumed his (and the father's) *praenomen*.

† Similar public resolutions were made about *cognomina* in the early Empire: by the Senate after the Libo Drusus affair in AD 16, that no Scribonius should be called Drusus (*TA* 2, 32, 2); by the emperor Gaius to force Cn. Pompeius Magnus to abandon his pretentious *cognomen* (*CD* 60, 5, 8).

The third name was in origin more often than not a descriptive nickname (*agnomen*) such as had parallels of a sort both in Greece and in the Hellenistic monarchies (see p.158). In Rome such names were evidently used first for identification ('Maximus', Lofty; 'Glabrio', Bald). Sometimes they were inherited, like double-barrel family names among the British, to distinguish one family within a *gens* from another. This was markedly the case in the extensive clan of the Cornelii, of which there were at least nine different branches. The Cornelii Scipiones were one of them; then they themselves subdivided into the Cornelii Scipiones and the Cornelii Scipiones Nasicae. But there were other families too where, without performing any function of marking a particular subdivision within a *gens*, a *cognomen* descended from generation to generation, as with the Tullii Cicerones.

Even to these established third – and sometimes fourth – names others, personally descriptive, could be added. The great Q. Fabius Maximus in the second Punic war, the hero who 'by doing nothing restored Rome's fortunes', had a surprising fourth name, 'Verrucosus', Warty, a name which, naturally enough, was not inherited by his son any more than his later fifth name, recording his performance as a general, 'Cunctator', Slowcoach. P. Cornelius Scipio Nasica, who achieved historical fame through his opposition to the destruction of Carthage, was given a flattering fifth name, 'Corculum', Wise-Guy, which was not passed on; yet the unflattering name of 'Serapio', the name of a pork-butcher, given to his son, was inherited in the next generation.* [8]

Indeed the majority of *cognomina*, if not simply descriptive ('Sabinus', for instance, denoting origin), were anything but flattering, and efforts were sometimes made to explain them away; in the case of 'Gurges', 'Glutton', for instance, the story was spread that in its origin it was given to a man who, having once been a glutton, had seen the light and had reformed. [9]

Yet with the precedent of the Hellenistic kings ('Soter', Saviour, 'Philadelphos', Loving Brother), flattering third names appeared in due course. Sulla became L. Cornelius Sulla Felix, 'Sulla the Fortunate'; Pompey became Pompeius Magnus, 'Pompey the Great' and, most splendid of all, Julius Caesar's adopted son became C. Caesar Augustus, and the name Augustus was inherited by his son Tiberius and his grandson Gaius and, after that, was assumed by successive emperors. Trajan became 'Optimus', the Nonpareil.

By a practice which was perhaps central Italian, even Etruscan, in origin, a son might be given a *cognomen* based on his mother's family

---

* Soldiers, of course (cf. p.120), were always inventing nicknames, which were bandied about in speech, but went no further than that. A sadistic centurion who broke cane after cane in beating soldiers was called 'Hand me Another' (*Cedo Alterum*), *TA* 1, 23, 4; the young son of Germanicus, later the emperor Gaius, was called 'Bootie' (*Caligula*), Suet., *C.Cal.* 9, 1; and the smart young tribune, later to be emperor, Aurelian was 'Hand on Sword' (*Manu ad Ferrum*) because he was so quick on the draw, SHA, *Aurel.* 6, 2. Schoolchildren too, e.g. *CIL* VI, 16932, '*Benedictus*'.

name. So in the second century BC the two sons of Cato by different mothers, (Licinia and Salonia respectively,) were Licinianus and Salonianus. While the emperor Vespasian's elder brother was, like his father, Flavius Sabinus, Vespasian's third name was taken from his mother Vespasia Polla. Domitian's name, too, came from his mother's family.[10]

A very honourable *cognomen* (or *agnomen*) was that given to a military conqueror by the Senate, the name of the people whom he had defeated in war: Africanus and Asiagenes to the brothers Publius and Lucius Scipio respectively, Creticus to Caecilius Metellus the consul of 69 BC.* Such a name, almost a title, was normally hereditable only by a man's first son.[11] The last commoner to achieve eminence of this kind was Cossus Cornelius Lentulus, consul in 1 BC, who took the title 'Gaetulicus' later for his successes against the Gaetuli in Africa, yet did not use it himself but passed it on to the younger, not the elder, of his two sons, from whom it descended to his three grandsons. After this, such honourable titles were reserved for the imperial family. 'Germanicus', which had been given to Augustus' stepson Drusus, was inherited by Drusus' elder son (Germanicus) and by his grandson, the emperor Gaius, and, after his elder son's death, it was assumed by his younger son, who was to be the emperor Claudius. After the conquest of Britain Claudius did not assume the name Britannicus for himself – why? – but, though it was voted to him and to his son by the Senate, he reserved it for his son.[12] Domitian was Germanicus for his supposed successes in the North; Trajan at the end of his life was Germanicus, Dacicus, Parthicus, and M. Aurelius was Armenicus, Medicus, Parthicus, Germanicus, Sarmaticus.

Great generals who never received such honorific titles – again, why? – were C. Marius, Julius Caesar and the emperor Tiberius.

Marius, of course, not only failed to acquire an honorific title; he had no *cognomen* at all. This was a mark of certain plebeian families, and very distinguished families at that, the Antonii, for instance, and the Etruscan Perpernae (see p.101 n.). And, in the Empire, of the Vitellii; the emperor Vitellius had no third name.

The *cognomen* had long been in use before it was officially recorded. Our first inscriptional record of a personal *cognomen* is of the consul of 298 BC, L. Cornelius Scipio Barbatus, but it is not until 123 BC that we have evidence of its official adoption as a constituent of a man's name in the higher ranks of society.† On the official list of equestrians qualified for jury service at Rome required by the *lex Acilia* of that

---

* The father of Mark Antony, M. Antonius, praetor in 74 BC, whose campaigns against the pirates were a series of disasters, was called 'Creticus' not officially but as a joke.

† Earlier appearances of *cognomina* in the official lists (*fasti*) of consuls are not historical; they reflect the belief (how well justified, we cannot tell) of those who drafted the *fasti* for cutting on stone late in the first century BC.

year, the style of a juror was to be given in full, *praenomen, nomen,* father's name, tribe and *cognomen*.[13] The general official use of the *cognomen* in the upper classes dates from the time of Sulla. Among ordinary people, the *plebs ingenua*, its use had started by the time of Augustus (for it is assumed, for census purposes, in Julius Caesar's draft municipal law) and in the army it was adopted later still. An army list from Egypt in the time of Augustus gives in each case only the man's first and second (gentile) names, his filiation and tribe and his home town.[14] Though there are occasional earlier instances of a soldier's inscribed name including his *cognomen*, its regular use in the army is thought to date from the principate of Claudius.

Roman women[15] – like Etruscan women, it seems – had once had two names, the first a personal name (*praenomen*) like Gaia, the second the family (gentile) name, and this made sense of a girl's being named on the eighth day after birth, just as a boy was named on the ninth day; but by the late Republic a woman generally had only one name, the feminine of the gentile name (Claudia, for instance, or Tullia), though within the family, especially if there were a number of daughters, she had a second name for identification (Prima, for instance, or Secunda). Then at the end of the Republic, as an indication perhaps of growing emancipation, a woman commonly had two names again, the first her gentile name, the second a form of *cognomen*, being the feminine form of the family *cognomen* – Caecilia Metella, for instance – or else one which recalled some family ancestry. Often in the early Empire the second name was a diminutive of her father's (or perhaps grandfather's) *cognomen*; so the first daughter of M. (Vipsanius) Agrippa, who married Tiberius (who was later to be emperor) was called Vipsania Agrippina and his daughter who married, and achieved notoriety as the wife of, Germanicus was called Agrippina, whether or not she was also called Vipsania.

Or the second name might derive from her mother's family. Claudius' earlier wife Plautia Urgulanilla was, on her mother's side, a grand-daughter of Urgulania. Poppaea Sabina, whom Nero married, had taken both her mother's names, recalling her maternal grandfather, the distinguished Poppaeus Sabinus and also her Etruscan ancestry, rather than label herself with the cacophonous name of Ollia, her father having been T. Ollius.

While women did not change their names on marriage as they do in most countries of the modern world, numerous women are known to us from inscriptions, particularly from the city of Rome, whose name was the same as that of their husband: Aurelia Messia, wife of T. Aurelius Aris, Terentia wife of T. Terentius Lapidarius.[16] In most cases a common slave background supplies the explanation; both parties had been, or were descended from, slaves in the same household, and so both had the same gentile name, the name of the enfranchising master or mistress; or a free man may have emancipated a slave woman, giving her his name, and then have married her. In the provinces the explanation may sometimes lie in the commonness of certain gentile names – the Julii in Gaul, for instance – on account of the large number of men enfranchised by a particular Republican general or, later, by a particular emperor.

In the case of families which emerged from the provinces to take a prominent position in Roman life, families whose members assumed historical importance, the modern historian turns detective, anxious to discover whether they are foreign stock which has acquired Roman citizenship or, on the contrary, families whose ancestors had emigrated long ago from Italy. Here proper names may provide valuable clues. The gentile name of an eminent Roman family (Valerius, Fabius) suggests the enfranchisement of foreigners; so do imperial names.* Roman-type gentile names which occur very rarely, if at all, in Italy suggest emigrants – in Spain, for instance, Annaeus (the name of the Senecas) and Ulpius, the gentile name of Trajan.

In particular provinces Roman families often had distinctive names which were not found, or were rarely found, elsewhere. In the western provinces, for instance, there were a number of gentile names (*nomina*) formed from recognised *cognomina* and given the termination '–inius', for instance Faustinius, Frontinius. Spaniards fancied animal names like Lupus and Taurus as *cognomina*. African names, too, were distinctive, adjectival third names like Datus, also Saturninus, Martialis, some based on Punic equivalents, Venerius from Astarte. An inscription records two African brothers, Valerius Donatus and Valerius Muthunus, one with a Punic *cognomen*, the other with its Latin equivalent.[17]

(ii) Changing names

On adoption into a different family – by *adoptio*, if his father was still alive, by *adrogatio* if he was grown up and *sui iuris*, (i.e. legally independent – which adopters anxious to secure the continuance of their families usually preferred) – a Roman naturally altered his name. The manner of alteration changed with time. Before Sulla, he assumed the first and second names of the man by whom he was adopted, and he added a new *cognomen* ending in '—anus', denoting the family of his birth.† The sons of Aemilius Paullus, adopted respectively into the families of the Fabii Maximi and the Cornelii Scipiones, became Q. Fabius Maximus Aemilianus and P. Cornelius Scipio Aemilianus.

* Which indicate either that the family was enfranchised by a particular emperor or that it was enfranchised through someone whose family had received citizenship from that emperor.

† This same termination could have different explanations. In families of central Italian extraction it could (see p.148 above) indicate the family name of a man's mother; in the case of a freedman (see p.154 below) it could indicate the name of a former master.

After Sulla, the adopted man might turn his adoptive *cognomen* into a *nomen* and add his original *cognomen*, as M. Junius Brutus, Caesar's murderer, adopted by Q. Servilius Caepio, became formally Q. Caepio Brutus (though generally referred to still, and addressed, by his old name); or he might add one or more of his original names to the new names which he assumed on adoption, as at the end of the Republic that aristocrat of aristocrats Scipio Nasica, whose daughter Pompey was to marry, became, after his adoption by Metellus Pius, Q. Caecilius Metellus Pius Scipio Nasica. This practice continued into the Empire and among the aristocracy, men and women* alike, even without adoption, names might accumulate in this way, the name of one ancestor (or benefactor) being pinned on to that of another from both sides of the family, to create that monstrosity, the consul of AD 169, 'the polyonymus of Tibur' who, like a snail with its house on its back, carried his extensive family tree about with him, a man with thirty-eight names.[20] His grandfather, consul in AD.108, had thirteen; his father contented himself with four, his son with three.

In the case of adoption there was never absolute rigidity,† and an individual had room for manoeuvre. The aristocrat Servius Sulpicius Galba, adopted by his stepmother Livia Ocellina, changed his name to Lucius Livius Ocella Servius Sulpicius Galba and this, substituting 'Augustus' for 'Ocella' and dropping the 'Servius, was the name which the Prefect of Egypt gave him in issuing an edict immediately after the news of his proclamation as emperor. But in fact Galba reverted at that moment to calling himself Servius Sulpicius Galba.[21]

With his new uniform a recruit to the Roman armed forces frequently acquired a new name. Though a foreigner joining the fleet or an auxiliary unit did not acquire Roman citizenship until after a long period of service, normally twenty-five years, he was occasionally given a Roman name at the moment of joining up. Thanks to papyri, we know of an Egyptian Greek Apion who, when he joined the Roman navy at Misenum and received the Roman equivalent of 'the king's shilling' some time in the first half of the second century AD, wrote to his parents in Egypt to give them all his news, including the fact that he had acquired a new name, Antonius Maximus (which as yet he could not spell). He signed his letter with his old name, but before long he was writing to his sister under his new Roman name. Sailors were recorded sometimes on their epitaphs under both their names: *C. Ravonius Celer qui et Bato natione Del [mata]*.[22]

As has been seen (p.86), the man who received Roman citizenship

---

* The wife of the wealthy sophist Herodes Atticus, consul in AD 143, had six names; one of his daughters had seven. And an inscription records, from the time of Trajan, a lady called Servenia Cornuta Calpurnia Valeria Secunda Cotia Procilla Porcia Luculla Domna.[19]

† Indeed when Julius Caesar's close associate L. Cornelius Balbus was adopted by Pompey's opposite number, the Greek Cn. Pompeius Theophanes in or round 59 BC, Balbus did not change his name at all. 'Balbus Cornelius Theofanes' is an aberration of SHA XXI, 7, 3.

when he signed on for service in a legion in the early Empire was given two Roman names, as well as a patronymic and a tribe, for instance 'C. Iulius C.f. Pol.', Gaius Iulius, son of Gaius, of the tribe Pollia.[23] This up to the time of Claudius. After Claudius, when legionary soldiers first adopted the regular use of a third name, there was still the *cognomen* and, while the first two names were assigned to him, the third name was largely his own choice.[24] Many recruits, too, who were bona fide Roman citizens now acquired a *cognomen* for the first time or changed their old *cognomen* for a new one. The *cognomen* might indicate a soldier's place of origin; one soldier born at Lugdunum, for instance, had the Celtic *cognomen* Salica.[25] Some legionaries in north Africa had Punic *cognomina*, names such as Hiddibal and Motthunus, and the centurion M. Porcius Eacustan's third name was Berber.[26] There was a great variety of favourite names, particularly popular being those indicative of sterling moral quality or of remarkable physique.

The auxiliary who received citizenship after completing his statutory military service normally took the first two names of the ruling emperor and added his own barbaric name as a *cognomen*: Tiberius Iulius Sedebdas, for instance, or Tiberius Claudius Congonetiacus.[27]

The foreign civilian admitted to Roman citizenship might take the first two names of the Roman to whom he owed his enfranchisement; so Pompey's protégé was Cn. Pompeius Theophanes and Plutarch was L. Mestrius Plutarchus.[28] Increasingly, however, they took the first two names of the ruling emperor. This Cassius Dio declares to have been an insistence of the emperor Claudius,[29] but he may be mistaken, for the general rule seems to date from the end of the first and start of the second century AD; after Caracalla's extension of the citizenship in AD 212 – his official name was M. Aurelius Antoninus – the name M. Aurelius broke out like a rash all over the Roman world.

As *cognomen*, the new citizen normally (like the auxiliary soldier) retained his original (non-Roman) name. In Greece it was by this third name that he continued to be known; he often added to it, in the genitive, the Greek name of his father. His son would have a different Greek third name which, from the Greek habit of treating a Roman *praenomen* as hereditable, like the *nomen*, identified the individual.[30]

A slave, not being a Roman, had only one name. In the earliest days he was known as the slave (*puer*) of his master, Lucipor, Publipor;[31] but it was not long before he was known by his individual name. Of slave names there was a rich variety exceeding the customary range of Roman names. A slave might retain the name which he possessed before enslavement or he might, on enslavement, have been given a new one, a name indicating his national origin (Syrus, Thraex) or his appearance ('Rufus', Redhead; 'Flavus', Blondie).

There was a variety of participial slave-names (Crescens, Amatus etc). His name might reflect the caprice of his master; Varro pictured three slaves purchased at Ephesus, one given the name Artemas (from Artemidorus the auctioneer who sold him), the second Ion (Ephesus being in Ionia), the third Ephesius. Herodes Atticus, in the hope of educating his wayward son, called twenty-four of his slaves by the names of the letters of the alphabet. Or, very commonly, the slave might receive an euphoric name like Eutychus, Felix, Hermes, Onesimus or Phoebus.[32] With his master's agreement, presumably, a slave could give whatever name he liked to his child, and some slave children's names are a *jeu d'esprit*. A slave called Lykos ('wolf' in Greek) called his son Lupus ('wolf' in Latin); the son of a Lucifer was given the Greek version of his father's name, Phosphoros; and a Phoebus called his son Mercurius.[33]

Artemidorus' Manual of Dreams drew to an end on a suitably fantastic note:[34] a slave who dreamt that he had three genitals. This signified that he would be emancipated and would have three names.

On emancipation his new second name was the gentile name of the master (or mistress) who freed him and so, normally, was his new *praenomen*, though there were occasional exceptions. When T. Pomponius Atticus, for instance, enfranchised his slave Dionysius, Dionysius' new first name was not the first name of his master, Titus, but, in flattery to Cicero, with whom he had the closest of links, it was Marcus. The possession of a *praenomen* was a constituent of his new status of which the freedman was particularly proud.[35]

The freedman never took the *cognomen* of his master, so that there was never any possibility of his being thought – or his descendants being thought – to be blood-members of the *gens* whose name they bore. More often than not his new third name was the name which he had had as a slave.

His old name, of course, whether Greek or that kind of Latin name that a free-born Roman would disparage, like Fortunatus or Amatus, revealed to the world that he had been a slave.* Some freedmen tried to efface this blot. The distinguished *littérateur* L. Crassicius Pasicles at the time of Augustus changed his third name to Pansa; and Martial writes of a freedman who changed his give-away name Cinnamus to the respectable Roman name of Cinna. Greek doctors in particular seem to have adopted Roman names; P. Decimius Eros took a fourth name and a very good Roman name at that, calling himself P. Decimius Eros Merula. Octavian's doctor Asclepiades may, after emancipation, have gone by the name of M. Artorius.[36] The freedman always could, and often did, give his son a *cognomen* different from his own, a respectable Roman sort of name like Proculus or Maximus.[37] Or the son could drop his father's name completely, like Claudius

---

* The fact was more apparent still if, on emancipation, he acquired a fourth name like Othonianus, Poppaeanus, for this revealed the fact that he had had two masters, the second the man whose gentile name was now his own, the first the man whom this fourth name recorded; Trimalchio in Petronius *Satyricon* was C. Pompeius Trimalchio Maecenatius. There were plenty of other indications that he was a freedman: no mention of his tribe in his official nomenclature and no mention of a father, but instead the first name of the man who freed him, Gai.l (ibertus).

Etruscus, to whom Statius wrote a poem of condolence on the death of his father; he adopted the name of his mother's evidently highly respectable family (as a result of which, we have no idea what his enormously important freedman father was called).[38]

In very many cases, therefore, to a man of intelligence, the name, including filiation and tribe, like the speaking voice, of a Roman, whatever his rank in society, revealed a great deal about him and about his provenance and background.[39]

There were people in the Empire who, without being Roman citizens, adopted Roman names. Greeks sometimes took single Roman gentile names, sometimes with a Roman, sometimes with a Greek, patronymic – 'Antonius, son of Antonius' or 'Antonius son of Menander'. Apollonius of Tyana spoke of their assuming names like Fabricius or Lucullus. About this there was considerable pretentiousness, but as they did not give themselves a Roman tribe, they were not actually masquerading as Roman citizens. The practice was regarded with strong disapproval by Apollonius of Tyana. More important, it had been condemned by the emperor Claudius, who forbad non-Romans to call themselves by Roman gentile names.[40]

On the other hand, there were very good Greek families from the first century AD onwards, families possessing Roman citizenship, whose utterly Roman names revealed nothing of their Greek origin, the Cornelii Pulchri, for instance, who came from Epidaurus.

(iii) How Romans referred to other Romans

It is clear from Cicero that by the time of the late Republic it was normal Roman practice for grown men to address one another by their third names: 'mi Caesar', 'mi Rufe' (his friend Caelius Rufus), 'mi Attice', 'Brute', 'mi Dolabella'. As soon as the validity of Julius Caesar's adoption of Octavius by his will was recognised, Octavius became C. Julius Caesar and would normally be addressed as 'Caesar'. Hence Cicero's dilemma when he first encountered him after Caesar's death. Should he call him 'Caesar', thereby recognising the validity of the adoption? In Cicero's dialogues the speakers regularly address one another by their *cognomina*; in the Dream of Scipio in the *De republica* the elder Scipio is made to address his adoptive grandson as 'Scipio'.[41]

He might, however, have addressed him by his first name, for this, it seems, was used between close relatives, particularly when a younger man was being addressed. Cicero addressed his brother, 'mi Quinte', and his son (at the start of the *De officiis*) as 'Marce fili' (though at the start of the *De partitione oratoria* he calls him 'mi Cicero'). In all three dialogues of the *De finibus* the speakers regularly addressed one another by their *cognomina* except that in the third

Cicero's young cousin, who is treated as the baby of the party, is addressed by his first name, 'Luci noster', 'Luci'.[42]

It was only on formal occasions, in the Senate for instance, that a man was addressed by his first two names, 'Dic, Marce Tulli'.

This habit of addressing people by their third names greatly eased the social life of new citizens because, as has been seen, their third name was more often than not the single name which they had possessed before they acquired Roman citizenship. The acquisition of Roman citizenship, therefore, will not have made any change in the manner by which they were addressed by their relations and friends.

When writing of others in the third person also it was only on the rarest of occasions that Romans used the *praenomen* alone. Occasionally Cicero referred to Pompey as 'Gnaeus noster', hardly ever as 'Gnaeus'. He once referred to Publius Clodius as 'Publius', but only when there could be no doubt to whom he was referring. His son was 'Cicero meus' and his nephew, when he wrote to the boy's father, was 'Cicero tuus'.[43] Friends and acquaintances were referred to generally by *praenomen* and *nomen* or by *praenomen* and *cognomen*; Cicero referred normally to 'Quintus Mucius' or to 'Quintus Scaevola', or even to 'Mucius' or 'Scaevola' simply.

In the *Bellum Gallicum* Julius Caesar usually gave a man's name in full (all three names, if he had three) at the first mention; after that he used whatever means of identification was clearest, *praenomen* and *nomen* or *nomen* or *cognomen* alone.

In official nomenclature the Republican practice survived; in naming the consuls of any year Tacitus used *praenomen* and *nomen* generally, or *nomen* and *cognomen*.[44]

In general speech, however, something of a change evidently took place in the early Empire and there was an increasing tendency to refer to men by *nomen* and *cognomen*: Virginius Rufus, Herennius Senecio. Indeed a patient count has shown that of seven hundred Romans with two names in Tacitus, more than two-thirds are referred to in this way.[45] The younger Pliny likewise. For Greeks he gives their single name unless they were Roman citizens, in which case he uses the Roman gentile name with the Greek *cognomen*, 'Claudius Ariston', for instance.[46] Epictetus always refers to Musonius Rufus simply as 'Rufus'.

In the Empire the order of the first two names might be reversed, if those were being used. One of the consuls of AD 25 was Cossus Cornelius Lentulus, father of Cossus Cornelius Lentulus, consul in AD 60. In both cases Tacitus gave the name as 'Cornelius Cossus'. *Nomen* and *Cognomen* might change places too, and the order of *cognomina*, where there were more than one, could be varied. (P. Clodius) Thrasea Paetus was sometimes Paetus Thrasea in Tacitus; (Junius) Arulenus Rusticus was 'Arulenus Rusticus' and 'Rusticus Arulenus' only a few lines apart in a letter of the younger Pliny.[47]

The absence of any rigid convention in the use of names for the purpose of reference is well illustrated in the case of the early emperors. Tiberius, Gaius, Nero and Titus were known, as they are known today, by their first names; Claudius and Vitellius by their second; and Augustus, Galba, Otho, Vespasian, Domitian, Nerva, Trajan and Hadrian by their third.

(iv) Foreigners and Roman names

From this (the capture of Corioli) he acquired the third name of Coriolanus. So it is clear that the first name 'Gaius' was the personal name, the second, 'Marcius', the family or gentile name, while the third name which the Romans came to use later was an epithet from a man's achievement or fortune or appearance or character. In exactly the same way the Greeks added a name which indicated a man's achievement (*Sôter*, 'Saviour'; *Kallinikos*, 'Fine Victor'), his general appearance (*Physkon*, 'Pot-Belly'; *Grypos*, 'Hook-Nose'), his good character (*Euergetes*, 'Do-Gooder', *Philadelphos*, 'Fond Brother') or his good fortune (*Eudaimon*, 'Prosperous'). Some kings received their second names jokingly (Antigonos Dôsôn, 'Generous Tomorrow', Ptolemy Lathyros, 'Peasecod'). The Romans employ this kind of name extensively. They called one of the Metelli 'Diadumenos', since for a long time he went about with a bandage on his forehead because of a wound. Another Metellus got the name 'Celer' (Nippy) for admiration of the speed with which he gave funeral gladiatorial games after the death of his father. Some they still name after circumstances attending their birth: Proculus (born in the absence of his father), Postumus (born after his father's death), Vopiscus (the sole survivor of twins). Names derived from physical features like Sulla,* Niger (Black), Rufus (Red-Head) include also Caecus (Blind) and Clodius,† from the praiseworthy habit of not regarding blindness or other physical defects as grounds for reproach or censure, but of answering to such names as their own.

Plutarch, Coriolanus 11.

We cannot give a third name for Gaius Marius any more than we can for Quintus Sertorius, who held out in Spain, or for Lucius Mummius, who captured Corinth (for the name Achaicus was given to him specifically for this achievement; compare 'Africanus' in the case of Scipio and 'Macedonicus' in the case of Metellus).

On this ground Posidonius thought to refute people who held that a Roman's third name (like Camillus, Marcellus, Cato) is his vital name; for on that theory people with only two names would have no name at all. But he did not see that on his theory Roman women would have no names, for no woman has a *praenomen*, that being, in Posidonius' view, a Roman's real name. Of the other two, one (the *nomen*) is a family name (Pompeius, Manlius, Cornelius, like the Herakleidai and the Pelopidai in Greek); the other is an epithet descriptive of character, achievement or physical or psychological peculiarity (Macrinus,** Torquatus,† Sulla, like the Greek Mnemon, Grypos or Kallinikos).

Plutarch, Marius 1, 1-5.

To the foreigner their complicated naming system was one of the most incomprehensible peculiarities of the Romans. There were nicknames, of course, in Greece: Aristeides had been called 'the Just',

---

* Pale and blushing.

† From *claudus* (*clodus*), 'lame'.

** Derived from 'macer', 'thin', presumably. But there is no evidence at all of this.

† Inherited by the Manlii from T. Manlius who, after killing a Gaul, stripped him of his necklace (*torques*).

Diagoras 'the Atheist' and Metrodorus, the historian of Mithridates, was called *Misorhômaios*, 'Rome-Hater';*[48] but these never became part of a man's official nomenclature as 'Gurges' or 'Serapio' did at Rome.

As for the names of the great, it was only among the Hellenistic dynasts that something of a parallel was to be found. Some of these were given slighting nicknames very like many Roman *cognomina* in their origin, 'Ptolemy Physcon' (Pot-Belly), or 'Ptolemy Auletes', 'Ptolemy the Piper', which might be used in common speech but were never written officially. There were, however, the official and honorific titles of Hellenistic kings, 'Sôter' (Saviour), 'Euergetes' (Benefactor), names which, as has been seen, probably influenced the introduction to Rome of names like Felix (for Sulla), Magnus (for Pompey) and Augustus.

When the Greeks first encountered the Romans in south Italy in the fourth century BC and in Sicily and mainland Greece in the third and second centuries, Romans who possessed *cognomina* made as yet no official use of them; so the problem was to know which of a Roman's two names to select – the Greeks being accustomed to the idea of one man, one name – whether in addressing him, speaking of him or mentioning his name in a dispatch or an honorary decree. Fatally the Greeks seized on the first name which came to hand, the *praenomen*. The first important Roman arbiter of Greek affairs, Titus Quinctius Flamininus, was 'Titus' in his lifetime to the Greeks and it was as Titus that he was subsequently remembered. Three centuries after his death you could see dedications in Chalcis in Euboea to 'Titus and Heracles', 'Titus and Apollo'; there was a priest of Titus and, at the annual ceremony of his cult, people sang of 'Great Zeus, Titus and the Roman Faith', 'Hail Paean, Titus our Savour'.[49]

As has been seen, the number of Roman *praenomina* was not very large; so the ancients must have encountered the same difficulty which we often encounter today in trying to identify a Roman named in an inscription by *praenomen* alone.[50] It was not until the end of the second century BC – and not always even then – that Greeks in general learnt sense and used a Roman's *nomen*.

Polybius shared the contemporary Greek affection for Roman *praenomina*. At the first mention he gave a Roman his full name, but after that he used the *praenomen* alone. Scipio was 'Publius'; an embassy consisted of 'Lucius and his colleagues'. As the last thirty-four of Polybius' forty books survive in fragments alone and the first mention of a Roman is often missing, there would be constant difficulty in identifying Polybius' references if we had not the good

---

* The Cyrenaic philosopher Hegesias in Egypt was nicknamed 'Death-inducer' (*Peisithanatos*) because – until the government (Ptolemy II) reasonably put an end to his lecturing – he gave so vivid an account of the horrors of life as to induce many of his listeners to commit suicide (Cic., *TD* 1, 83).

fortune to possess, anyhow for the period 200 to 167 BC, Livy's translation of a great deal of Polybius' full text; Livy, of course, named Romans in the Roman manner of his own time.

Living for so long in a distinguished Roman household, Polybius might have been expected to conform with Roman practice. Was it the case that in the second century BC the *praenomen* was, even in Rome, used far more commonly than was later the case? Did people at large speak of the younger Scipio Africanus and his brother as 'Publius' and 'Quintus'? Was Cicero wrong in a second-century fictional context, in his *De republica*, in making the spirit of the elder Africanus address the younger, as he would have done in Cicero's own time, as 'Scipio'?

Yet this kind of uncertainty persisted, and not only among Greeks. Who was 'the proconsul Tiberius' whom, writing in AD 197, Tertullian named as the man who stopped the ritual murder of children in Africa (see p.246)? The emperor Tiberius? A proconsul of of about 97 BC? Or a proconsul in Tertullian's own time?

Roman nomenclature, which seems to have caused Polybius little concern, was, because of its peculiarities, a matter of interest to later Greeks who wrote of Rome and Romans. Cicero's contemporary Posidonius evidently went into the subject in considerable detail in the Introduction to his *History*. Being a philosopher, he asked himself what any Roman clot could have told him was a silly question: which of a Roman's three names was the fundamentally important one? He evidently decided on the *praenomen*. In which case, as Plutarch pointed out, Roman women had no *real* name at all.

Plutarch, who had occasion to interest himself in inherited and acquired names in many of his Roman *Lives*, dipped extensively into what Posidonius had written on the subject,[51] and he also discovered what had been written by Roman antiquarians and etymologists of the late Republic and early Empire in their speculations about the origin of Roman names.* [52]

Appian, too, refers to Roman nomenclature in the Introduction to his *History*. The Romans, he stated, had originally had one name, then two and finally three, 'the third derived from some personal incident or else a distinction for bravery'. His own sensible practice was sometimes to give all three names, in other cases the name which was commonly used and made identification easy. Pausanias normally did the same.[53]

Other peoples, to whom in the matter of nomenclature the Romans presented such great problems, themselves presented the Romans

---

* The first chapters (on *praenomina*) of a Roman monograph on *Names* has survived by a curious chance, appended to an epitome of Valerius Maximus, the work of the 'Auctor de Praenominibus' quoted in the first notes on this chapter.

with no problems at all. They had single names like Orgetorix or Dumnorix or Cassivellaunus or Apollodoros. Cacophonous names they might be sometimes, grotesque in shape, tongue-twisters when it came to pronunciation (Sdapezematygus, for instance), but single names with, at the most, a patronymic, Bato Scenobarbi.

CHAPTER TWELVE
A Bad Press for Rome[1]

(i) Greeks (in particular) and Romans

There were features of life under the Roman Empire, in particular the relegation of war to the distant frontiers and the improvement in communications (which, among other things, reduced the incidence of starvation) of which no sane man, wherever in the Empire he lived, could disapprove. But approving of the Roman Empire did not mean that you had to like Romans.

There might be a good deal to say for the much-advertised Roman Justice, if it was ever properly administered; and for the vaunted Roman Integrity, if it was ever practised. All that you could say, without fear of contradiction, of the Romans was that they were powerful and that they were rich and indeed that some of them, never the most popular men in their own country, appreciated the Greek point of view.

From Philopoemen in the second century BC to Libanius six hundred years later there were always Greeks who for differing reasons despised or actively disliked qualities in the Roman character. To educated Greeks Romans never appeared anything but a race of upstarts. In architecture and the fine arts they had no native possessions which were ancient at all. In literature they had nothing comparable with the Homeric bible; and if, as Dionysius of Halicarnassus stressed,[2] Rome was better than Greece for not boasting a religion and mythology of its own which commemorated divine exploits of extravagant crime and lust, its literature, a reflection of the Roman character, lacked that richness of imaginative fancy whose brightness, in Greek writing, was never completely extinguished. Moreover, compared with Greek, Latin was a crude, shallow and inflexible language.

There was a startling vulgarity, self-indulgence and immorality in the social life of the rich at Rome as was evident from Roman books (those of Martial, for instance and, heavily underlined, in Tacitus' book on the Germans) which were on sale on the provincial bookstalls, and even the wife of the Caledonian Argentocoxus knew (and showed the empress Julia Domna that she knew) of the degrading sexual practices of smart society women in Rome.[3] Rome was Babylon, the Great Whore, in the language of excitable Christians.[4]

The impact of Greek on Roman culture made itself felt once and for all in the last centuries BC. The romanisation of the East, as far as it occurred at all, came later, though as early as 175 BC Antiochus Epiphanes introduced gladiatorial fighting to Syria, and this was to prove the one highly successful Roman 'cultural' export to the East.[5]

There were fundamental differences in social conventions, as Cornelius Nepos indicated: Roman contempt for, Greek approval of, dancing; the free movement of women in Roman society and mixed Roman dinner parties, which offended established Greek prejudice.[6] But as more and more Greeks entered the Roman senate in the late first and second centuries AD, the social life of their families presumably took on a Roman colouring and their womenfolk emerged from purdah.

(ii) Liberty, servitude: words, words, words

'Man is born free and is everywhere in chains': the antithesis of 'freedom' and 'servitude' was inescapable. 'Other peoples can bear servitude', Cicero said; 'liberty is a Roman perquisite'. For the clever cynic like Tacitus, life at Rome under the Republic was 'freedom', life under the Empire 'servitude';* sycophancy, *obsequium* in its bad sense, had replaced freedom of speech. When Nero mounted the Capitol to give thanks for the successful murder of his mother, 'he was celebrating a triumph over the servility of Rome', *publici servitii victor*. To get rid of a tyrant like Nero (without any regard to the political consequences of his death) was to strike a blow for 'liberty'.[7]

In the language of hyperbole, servitude within the empire affected even those whose social position might have seemed most enviable. Senatorial 'freedom' was virtually extingushed when the Republic ended; it was revived only in an occasional and ineffective flicker by men like Paetus Thrasea and Helvidius Priscus.[8] Senators tumbled over themselves to be slaves, as Tiberius said in a moment of disgust: 'O homines ad servitutem paratos.'[9] The younger Pliny confirmed the judgment when he said to Trajan, 'You bid us be free, and so we will be.'[10]

Hypocrisy, hypocrisy, all was hypocrisy, to Tacitus' thinking. An apparently liberal concession made to the Senate by the Emperor had the appearance of liberty, but its consequence was greater servitude than ever.[11] Except, of course, for the occasional moment of felicity, 'rara temporum felicitas', when on the accession of Nerva there was 'a reconciliatiorr of previously irreconcilables', the principate and liberty, or when his successor Trajan 'recalled liberty and restored it'.[12]

The antithesis of slavery under the Roman empire and freedom

---

* For 'liberty' had fled to the far banks of the Rhine and (oddly enough) the Euphrates; so Lucan, *Phars.* 7, 433f.

outside it is stated by Caesar himself: 'It is human nature to strive after independence (*libertas*) and to hate subjection (*servitus*)'. This antithesis pervades Tacitus' writing and was no doubt expressed frequently both inside the empire and outside its boundaries.[13] For if, universally, imperialism confers benefits and provokes discontents, it also produces, or at least produced in antiquity, the same emotive language.[14] The Persian empire, the Athenian and the Roman were described by their critics in similar terms. The subjects of these empires lived in servitude; freedom was the rich possession of those who lived outside their boundaries or who escaped from inside them. When Augustus demoted Cyzicus from the status of a free city, Dio says, 'he enslaved it'.[15]

The poor Armenians, strangers to 'liberty', were confronted by the grim alternative of slavery to Parthia or slavery to Rome. When his pregnant wife was stolen from him by her father and given a home in Roman Gaul, Arminius was driven mad by the thought of 'his wife's womb subjected to servitude'. The symbols of servitude were the rods and axe, tribute and the licentious Roman soldiery. What the critic called imperial servitude, the Roman called dutiful obedience, '*obsequium*', and with it went security and 'such liberty as rulers allowed to their subjects'.[16]

The days of Greek independence were gone for ever, and there was no greater scope for the political leaders in Greek cities than to achieve concord (*homonoia*), to ensure that their (subject) communities lived in peace, without strife (*stasis*).[17] For in Greek cities *stasis* was endemic. Thucydides wrote of it as a contemporary political evil and so, five centuries later, did Plutarch. If the issue was between the rich and the poor, the rich had the backing of the Roman administration; if the ruling class was itself divided and one side had Roman backing, its opponents were inevitably Rome's enemies. In the second century BC and at the time of the Mithridatic wars in the first, an anti-Roman party might not unreasonably bank on success; the Romans might be driven back to where they came from. Then there was the forced involvement of the East in three civil wars, always on the losing side. The significance of Augustus' final victory may have taken a little time to seep through, but by the end of Augustus' principate it was clear enough that the Roman empire was firmly established and in no danger from any local – inevitably small-scale – opposition. But Roman rule was not the more acceptable on that account to many people – to the poor and dispossessed in Greek cities, whose hardships Rome did little to alleviate except on the occasion of sensational disasters like earthquakes, or to parties with particular grievances like the Alexandrians, who chafed at the insult of being denied (until Septimius Severus) what every other Greek city possessed, their own senate.

Those outside the Empire boasted of their freedom. The Caledonians, according to Calgacus, were the last survivors of a free world, 'nos libertatis extremos'. The Germans boasted of their freedom, and Roman writers like Tacitus took them at their word. In the revolt of AD 69 the Gauls were invited to secede from Rome and recover their old freedom; beating up support for revolt in Africa against Tiberius, Tacfarinas had used the same catchwords, and so did Caratacus to the Ordovices in Britain in AD 50, and Boudicca eleven years later. In Critognatus' speech in beleaguered Alesia in 52 BC (the only direct speech in Caesar's *Gallic War*) when he urged cannibalism for the sake of preserving independence, 'servitus' occurs four times and 'libertas' twice.[18]

Psychologically the transition from 'liberty' to 'servitude' did not take place overnight; so the Trinovantes in AD 60 joined Boudicca's revolt for freedom; 'they had not yet been broken by slavery'.[19]

Most of the fine speeches, of course, about liberty outside the empire and servitude inside it were given to princelings and chiefs; and as far as they themselves were concerned, there was a large measure of truth in what they said. At the best, the once independent king became a client-king when he entered the sphere of Roman influence; it was by the grace of Rome that he continued to rule. Let Rome be dissatisfied and he would quickly be dispossessed. In the early days of Rome's imperial conquests it was believed that monarchy was something to which Romans objected in principle because of their own unhappy experience when they were subject to kings.[20] So kings like Antiochus the Great and Mithridates urged other kings to join them in common self-defence against Roman aggression. They were right, for all the effort that the elder Africanus and his brother put into their propaganda that, so far from disliking kings on principle, Romans in fact supported them and even increased their stature.[21]

As for a king's subjects, however, rather than changing 'liberty' for 'servitude', they were more likely, on absorbtion into the Roman empire, to exchange one form of servitude for another. For a Roman to take service under a foreign king was, in Republican days, as seen from Rome, to exchange liberty for servitude.[22]

That subjection to an independent king (or prince or chief) was a condition comparable to subjection to Rome is conceded at one point by Tacitus. When Nero sent Polyclitus to Britain in AD 61, the Britons laughed; 'still fired by freedom, they had not learnt the power of freedmen; it amazed them that at the end of a successful war Roman general and army alike should kowtow to slaves'. But among free Germans, in tribes subject to kings, Tacitus admitted, you would find just such powerful freedmen. Otherwise freedmen were inferior; there was still a premium on liberty.[23]

Independent monarchs were sometimes tyrannical monarchs, and it is not to be imagined that the condition of their peoples approached 'freedom' in any sense of the word, or that they were happier or better off than they would have been if subject to Roman rule. But until barbarian tribes were driven by other barbarian tribes across the Rhine and Danube to seek incorporation in the Empire (the earliest case was the application of the Usipites and Tencteri to settle on the west bank of the Rhine, not as yet strictly part of the Roman empire, in 55 BC), the only occasion on which representatives from a vassal kingdom sought admission to the Empire for their country was after Herod's death, when a delegation of Jews asked for provincial status (incorporation of Judaea in the province of Syria) in preference to the continued rule of the house of Herod.[24]

There were barbarian renegades (Arminius himself, until he saw the light) who crossed the frontier to serve in the Roman auxiliary forces and, in the end, achieve Roman citizenship. If they distinguished themselves, they won military decorations which they prized as greatly as Romans themselves – *torquis, corona, hasta*. But what, seen from the other side of the frontier, were these but 'the badges of servitude'?

Freedom for the extreme freedom-fighter must be freedom pure and unalloyed. In AD 47 a delegation of Cherusci sought a king from Rome, the last surviving representative of their own royal family. Arminius' son had died in the course of his Roman upbringing; Arminius' nephew, however, survived, born within the boundaries of the Empire, son of a German who had served loyally in the Roman auxiliary army (Arminius' brother Flavus) and a Roman citizen. Italicus returned to Germany to be king and his behaviour could not be faulted. But there were dissidents. How could Germans take pride in 'liberty' when they had to fetch their king, son of a man who had fought against his compatriots, from Rome? His name, of course, betrayed him – Italicus, a Roman *cognomen*. Or had he already abandoned it in favour of a German name? Anyhow, it came to a fight which Italicus and his supporters won. After which, he gave a less good account of himself; *superbia* intervened.[25]

Client kings played their part in the process of romanisation for, Tacitus wrote, it was a very old Roman tradition to use even kings as instruments in the imposition of slavery, 'ut haberet instrumenta servitutis et reges'.[26]

What better way of doing this than to make Roman citizens of them from the start? This was Augustus' policy and Tiberius', and there was a crop of citizen-princelings – C. Julius Tarcondimotus in Cilicia, C. Julius Iamblichus of Emesa, C. Julius Juba II in Mauretania, Ti. Iulius Aspurgus in the Bosporus.[27] The kings acknowledged their indebtedness in their titulature, 'Friends of Rome', 'Friends of Caesar'.[28] Their subjects, less spirited than Germans or Armenians, did not object.

If Tacitus had been charged with being a fifth-columnist within the Roman empire, his defence could have been that the world was divided between those outside the Roman empire – the free – and those within it. The outsiders, particularly in the North, resolute warriors prepared to sacrifice their lives rather than submit to Roman domination, had many of the qualities which marked the Romans in the days of Rome's expansion, the days of the great wars whose historians he so greatly envied. So in describing the Germans as objectively as he could, Tacitus emphasised their simple and sterling virtues (the sacred bond of marriage, for instance), contrasting these with degenerate contemporary Roman practices (sexual promiscuity). He could have done the same if he had been writing not about the Germans of his own time but of Romans in the age of Cincinnatus.[29]

It could not be denied, of course, that the free barbarians had their weaknesses too – 'ex libertate vitia'. They had little notion of punctuality, and this made public meetings difficult. They were prone to division, squabbling and rivalries, as Caesar had observed in the case of the independent Gauls. They were impetuous, as Seneca pointed out, incapable of intelligent long-term planning. If asked the direct question, Tacitus would have admitted that from the Roman point of view this was fortunate. There was everything to be said for the Germans destroying themselves in internecine conflict rather than fighting the Romans and eroding Roman strength and manpower.[30]

After conquest by Rome, Tacitus considered that there were two stages of subjection. The first was that of obedience (*obsequium*) when the natural good qualities of a people were preserved. In the second, a degeneration deliberately encouraged by romanisation (hot baths and big dinners), the subjects of Rome adopted those very practices which marked the modern Roman in contrast to his simpler ancestor. Good barbarians, in fact, were turned into bad Romans; and this was servitude (*servitium*), which even spread like some kind of infectious disease. Gaul caught it earlier than Britain, Britons of the south of the island before those in the north.[31]

This degeneration was the consequence of the exchange of war for the peaceful and relaxed life (*segnitia* and *otium*) which Rome ensured for her subjects, the *longa pax* in which they had not always to be on the alert to face potential danger.[32]

It is through Tacitus that most of the barbarian talk and thought about 'liberty' has filtered through to us, and it is no doubt generally true that there was a basis of truth in what Tacitus wrote; not everything was invention. To German eyes the very walls of Cologne may well have seemed 'munimenta servitii'. From walls at one extreme to hot baths at the other, all this the foreigner indicated contemptuously by the single word 'toga' (not that the *toga* was a garment which any Roman citizen, newly enfranchised or not, was to be seen wearing if he could possibly help it).[33]

(iii) Material complaints

The average imperial subject, of course, would have laughed at much of Tacitus' ideological nonsense. The real burden of servitude, he would have explained emphatically, lay not in the novel amenities of civilised life but in the price which had to be paid for them, in particular taxation and compulsory military service, the *dilectus*.[34] There was a half-and-half stage, as Civilis pointed out: the condition of the Batavi at the mouth of the Rhine who were not completely inside the empire or completely outside it either. They paid no taxes and the troops which they provided were selected by themselves, not by Roman recruiting officers, and were commanded by their own nationals.[35] Better one of two burdens than both; this in a hard world was as near as you could get to liberty. When in AD 70 the Roman commander Cerealis sent home some freshly levied Gauls, the Gauls were so delighted that they paid their taxes in good heart.[36]

The Frisii, east of the Rhine and technically outside the Empire, had submitted to taxation in the form of ox-hides. This tax, objectionable in itself, was made intolerable under Tiberius when a Roman civil servant with a tidy mind insisted that hides should be of a standard size – far larger than those produced by the local cattle. So, not unnaturally, the Romans found themselves with a rebellion on their hands.[37]

Levy and taxation were disagreeable enough in themselves. Nobody wanted – or wants – to give the government his money; no community wants to say goodbye to its young men, to see them drafted into the army. And the impositions were made worse in far too many cases by the corrupt practices of Roman officials, alive to every unprincipled means of lining their own pockets. The first men to select at the levy were those who could afford to buy themselves out of military service; only then did recruiting officers come down to the sons of the poor who had no such opportunity.[38]

Unless serving in separate units (as they did under Herod), orthodox Jews would obviously have caused great trouble to the Roman authorities in the matter both of diet and of service on the Sabbath and when, after a scandal involving Jews in Rome, Tiberius conscripted Jews to serve in Sardinia in AD 19, they complained that the terms of military service were incompatible with their religion. So, though there is inscriptional and papyrological (as well as literary) evidence of occasional Jews in the legions both in the eastern and the western provinces, it seems that strictly practising Jews were normally exempted from the levy (or allowed to buy themselves out). We know of no general regulation to that effect, however; only that in the province of Asia Jews who were Roman citizens were exempted by the administrative act of Lentulus Crus in the civil war of 49 BC and that later in Asia this act seems to have been held to constitute a valid precedent.[39]

As for tax-collection, the whole of Roman administration is blotted by the cruelty and injustice of the tax-collector.

When Florus and Sacrovir incited Gauls to rebellion in AD 21, taxation was the first of the evils of Roman rule which they stressed – 'the perpetuity of it', continuing unabated year after year. And they protested against the kind of men whom Rome sent out to govern them, monsters of brutality and arrogance.[40]

A further grievance was the heavy interest which had to be paid on borrowed money. Indeed the Roman money-lender had a long and sinister history. The tax-collectors under the Republic lent money to men so as to enable them to pay their taxes; they charged heavy interest and took ample security. When a man defaulted, they impounded most of what he possessed. According to Dio, the virtuous Seneca had large sums of money out on loan in Britain and it was the hardship caused by his sudden calling in of these loans which was a cause of Boudicca's rising under Nero. As the example of Brutus showed, Romans whose integrity was a by-word in Rome were untouched by considerations either of law or humanity when money was to be made by loans to provincial 'allies'.[41]

Provincial subjects, especially if they lived on a main highway, suffered much hardship from the compulsory billeting of Roman troops. This was, no doubt, a heavier burden in the Republic than under the Empire for, with no permanent camps such as were to exist later on the frontiers, any body of troops which was kept under arms during the winter was quartered on civilians, who very rarely received adequate compensation and often received no payment at all. Favoured communities like Termessus in Asia Minor in 71 BC received an undertaking from the government at Rome that no troops were to be billeted on them. Less favoured communities sought exemption by the simple means of bribing the Roman governor; the Cypriots in the late Republic had thought it worth paying as much as two hundred talents. Cicero, who had evidence of this scandal on his own doorstep when he governed Cilicia (and Cyprus) in 51/50 BC, had already spoken of it in Rome as a widespread evil. The vanquished in war were at the mercy of a Roman commander; Sulla showed the utmost vindictiveness when he quartered his troops on householders in Asia.[42]

A little earlier Chaeronea in Boeotia had had a variety of experiences. In winter 87/86 the behaviour of a Thracian unit serving under Sulla and billeted in the city for the winter had been exemplary, and Chaeronea had voted extravagant honours to its Thracian commander in a decree which has survived. In the previous winter the commander of a Roman unit stationed in Chaeronea had, through an unsuccessful attempt to seduce a young man of the city, driven him to retort with force and when the city council, desperately anxious to satisfy the Romans, condemned him to death, he and his companions broke in on the city magistrates and murdered them. When Lucullus arrived on the spot, all he could do was to remove the remainder of the Roman garrison; but by this time the mischief had been done.[43]

Such scandals may have been reduced in the Empire because of permanent camp buildings, but armies were often on the march and, where they marched, they playfully stole and looted. And on leave they demanded accommodation with menaces. We have the complaint of the Scarpetani in Thrace in AD 238 of the intolerable expense to which they were put by Roman officials and soldiers who came to enjoy their hot baths and expected free billets as long as they were enjoying them.[44]

Against some of the charges made against their empire the Romans defended themselves with greater or smaller plausibility. They were, after all, 'standard charges such as were levelled against all great empires'.[45]

Governors and administrators were sometimes harsh and corrupt; granted. But not all Roman administrators were like that. In life you must take the rough with the smooth. *Vitia erunt, donec homines.*[46]

Taxes were heavy, admittedly; but they were unavoidable. Thanks to the armies on the frontiers, the Romans gave protection to the ordinary man in his everyday life. Soldiers required pay, like anybody else. How could they be paid except from taxes?

Slavery, *servitium*. Perhaps not slavery, but admittedly subjection, the opposite of independence. But what did Rome's subjects receive in compensation? Peace, the *pax Romana*, 'wretched slavery misnamed peace', in the language of the secessionist.

The Romans argued differently. If the Gauls thought back to the days of their independence, what had their life been then but a succession of tribal wars, wars among themselves and against the Germans, wars and rumours of war, fears of wars? All that tension was over; instead life held no anxiety and there was the all-extensive Roman peace. So when the Remi summoned the dissident Gauls to conference in early AD 70 with a view to ending the Gallic revolt, the choice presented was a simple one: Independence (*Libertas*) or Peace?[47]

Dio Chrysostom even told the Alexandrians that they were very lucky to have survived independence and to be subject to the rule of Rome.

East of Damascus in Syria, Strabo pointed out, the menace of highwaymen and brigands on the caravan routes was greatly reduced 'under Roman good government and the security resulting from the presence of the Roman army in Syria'.[48]

In Trajan's principate the Nile flood failed one year and the shortfall in the Egyptian harvest was made good by import of grain from Italy. The younger Pliny relished the paradox. If Egypt had been independent and had not the good fortune to be subject to Rome, that would have been the end of Egypt and its inflated population. He adumbrated the advantages to the various – subject – provinces of belonging to a large-scale economic unit, the Roman empire.[49]

When within the Empire city walls fell down, there was no need to rebuild them because peace reigned everywhere, peace or subjection to Rome (or, as Dio Chrysostom, using the stilted language of hyperbole, put it, slavery, *douleia*).[50] There was no apprehension as yet of the barbarians breaking in later and of the walls being desperately needed.

(iv) Roman offensiveness and insensitivity abroad

Many factors contributed to the unpopularity of Romans outside their own country.

In his defence of Fonteius Cicero ascribed the offences of bad Roman governors to sexual incontinence (*libido*) – anybody in the provinces entertaining a certain type of Roman administrator, if he was wise, kept his handsome sons and daughters locked up – impudence (*petulantia*), cruelty (*crudelitas*) and effrontery (*audacia*). Similarly, lust and cruelty disfigured Verres' official life.[51] These two qualities were startlingly illustrated in the scandalous execution of a Gallic prisoner (or deserter) at the dinner-table to entertain a favourite of the drunken Roman consul L. Flamininus in north Italy early in the second century BC.* [52]

That the Romans were cruel by nature is certain; it is not so certain that, in their contemporary world, they were abnormally cruel. Their devotion to gladiatorial fighting is counted against them; yet the gladiatorial games were every bit as popular in the Greek East as they were in Rome.[53] And Roman history shows nothing worse than the tortures which have been practised within the Christian Church at the Inquisition and at the Reformation or the torture of the Jews by Hitler's Nazis. Hirtius' statement that after the fall of Uxellodunum Caesar counted it an act of clemency that, instead of executing the young male prisoners, he ordered the amputation of their right hands, has often been made a charge against Caesar, but wrongly. The men would survive, a living deterrent to others, and this view, which survives in parts of the world today, had long been held by Romans, particularly in the punishment of spies and deserters. There was evidence, in fact, that such punishment achieved its object.[54]

Fronto was right in saying that the Romans lacked warmth; they were a cold people.[55]

The higher a Roman's rank, the worse he suffered from the disease which the Greeks called *hyperêphania*, bossiness, arrogance, the sense of

---

* This combination of vices was not exclusively Roman; witness the close parallel of Herod the tetrarch's murder of John the Baptist.

innate superiority.[56] In Republican times envoys and commanders treated foreigners, particularly in the East, with a certain insensibility, lecturing them on the proper way to behave, Scipio delivering a lecture to Massinissa in Africa on the virtue of sexual continence (Massinissa blushed and wept), Flamininus lecturing Deinocrates of Messenia on drink as the enemy of human dignity, Cicero lecturing Ariobarzanes of Cappadocia on how to be a good king.[57] Indeed at all periods of Roman history client kings, who ruled by Rome's grace and favour, were liable to be addressed by Roman officials in language which they would not have used themselves to their own subjects. On the other hand, the foreigner who spoke his mind to a Roman displayed 'arrogance' or 'contumacy', *adrogantia, contumacia*.

Any request, however unconstitutional or insensitive, was expected to be granted. In its short period of independence under Roman rule the magistrates of the Achaean League were more than once confronted by a Roman envoy's blustering insistence that they should violate the charter of the League by calling an extraordinary assembly for him to address.[58] Late in the second century BC L. Crassus, returning from Asia with no higher rank than that of quaestor, was furious because the Athenians had refused to hold an extraordinary celebration of the Mysteries to suit his convenience.[59] Not content with pilfering Olympia's wealth, Sulla transferred the events of the 80 BC Olympiad (all but the *stadion*) to his new Games, the Ludi Victoriae, in Italy at the end of 81. Emperors were no more considerate, only more successful. Augustus persuaded the Athenians to celebrate the Mysteries out of order and, to honour the idiosyncrasy of Nero, not only were the Olympic games held a year later than the proper date but they included a novel musical competition.[60]

This effrontery was never more evident than when Roman foreign policy was at its most aggressive, as in 58 BC. Why, at a time when Rome's Gallic empire was limited to Provence, should the Helvetii, if they wished, not abandon the mountains of Switzerland to live on the coast of the Atlantic? Why should Ariovistus not settle in central Gaul, if he wished? In both cases, because Caesar said so. And what business was it of Caesar, the Helvetii and Ariovistus not unreasonably asked?

Passing through Athens in AD 18, Cn. Piso, legate of Syria, asked the Athenians to rescind the condemnation of a man for forgery because he was Piso's friend, and was furious when they refused.[61]

Worse than insult, injustice; and the provincial subjects of Rome were frequently victims of harsh injustice, from the governors who were sent out from Rome, from Roman tax-collectors, from Roman and Italian businessmen and from high-ranking Romans travelling on private business but armed with special government papers.

(v) Romans: a liking for loot

Throughout history conquering armies have been armies of vandals and armies of thieves. Cambyses had wantonly destroyed historic monuments in Egypt; in the fourth century BC there was the shameless pillage of Delphi by the Phocians; and the burning of Persepolis had not been Alexander's finest hour. The wild destructiveness of the Roman troops after the capture of Corinth in 146 BC was in the same sinister tradition.[62]

Better, at least, than such wanton destruction was looting, and throughout history imperial governments have pretended that it was in the interest of humanity that prize works of art from conquered territories should find a home in their own cities.

It was in extenuation of Augustus' seizure of an archaic statue of Athena Alea and the teeth of the Caledonian boar from the Arcadians, who had supported Antony, that Pausanias emphasised that the annexation of works of art, including statues of gods in temples, by the conqueror, whether Greek or barbarian, from the conquered was as old as history itself.[63]

On returning from his governorship of Macedonia in 146 BC with his new title 'Macedonicus', Q. Caecilius Metellus built a fine – Velleius Paterculus, moralising, thought a too fine – marble temple to Juppiter Stator next to the temple of Juno Regina in the Circus Flaminius, confronted them with loot from Macedonia, the fine equestrian statues executed for Alexander by Lysippus, and round them built Rome's first art gallery, the Porticus Metelli which, later, Augustus was to pull down and replace by a more splendid complex of buildings, the Porticus Octaviae, in which, among other masterpieces, works of Pheidias and of Praxiteles were on exhibition.[64]

There were the fora in Rome and the temples, particularly the temple of Juppiter on the Capitol, which became museums of world-famous masters, pieces stolen in the main from Greece and later from Egypt. And there were all the rich men's town and country houses, distinguished by the same kind of loot.*

M. Claudius Marcellus had set the fashion, stripping Syracuse of many of its art-treasures after its capture, to exhibit at his ovation when he returned to Rome in 211 BC. Cicero later pictured Marcellus as torn – like Launcelot Gobbo – by conflicting impulses. Victorious Pride told him to transfer these objects which, however unroman, were evidently held in high esteem, to beautify Rome; humanitas, on

---

* How the two masterpieces of the painter Parrhasios (an 'Archigallus' and an Atalanta and Meleager) which, liable evidently to shock the prudish, were hung in the emperor Tiberius' bedroom, reached Rome, we do not know. It is significant that the Roman authors who are our informants (Plin., NH 35, 70; Suet., Tib. 44, 2) stress not their beauty but their cash-value (perhaps a million sesterces each, RE XVIII, 1876f., nos. 17 and 22). The Apoxyomenos of Lysippus which, as emperor, Tiberius annexed (also for his bedroom) and which he was forced by popular clamour to restore to its position before Agrippa's Baths, had been placed there by Agrippa (Plin., NH 34, 62).

the other hand, urged him not to rob the Syracusans of possessions which, in their curious way, they valued so highly. Thanks to this last consideration there were still works of art in Syracuse a century and a half later for Verres to plunder.[65]

For the Roman populace, Marcellus' spoil represented an utterly novel spectacle, and responsible people judged that Fabius Maximus did better when, two years later, he recovered Tarentum and left its temple undisturbed. It was from Tarentum later that the statue of Victory was taken, to stand by the altar of Victory in the imperial Senate-house.[66]

It is not difficult to picture the bitter and lasting resentment of peoples and cities whose artistic masterpieces were stolen.

The conquerors incur not merely jealousy but blazing hatred; for the reminder of one's own downfall encourages a hatred for those responsible for it ... If works of art were left where they were, no jealousy would be incited, and the reputation of the conqueror would be enhanced ... I say this with an eye to those who assume imperial responsibilities; they must not think that by looting cities they give distinction to their own countries from the sufferings of others.

So, at considerable length, Polybius, with reference to Marcellus' stripping of Syracuse. He pictures the art-treasures of the entire world transferred to Rome and imagines the feelings of their former possessors, invited to come and admire them in their new home. Cicero describes envoys from Achaea and Asia, provinces which Verres had plundered, tearfully doing that very thing.* [67]

Works of Greek (and later Egyptian) art, precious metals, even valuable literary works (Aristotle's library) were, after successive Roman victories, there for the taking.[68] But in some potential loot the Romans were uninterested – the contents of the Carthaginian libraries, for instance, when Carthage fell in 146 BC. These were given to 'African princes', except for a practical text-book on farming by Mago, which was handed over for translation into Latin (see p.141).[69] But the younger Africanus, however brutal his conduct during the siege of Carthage, showed some imagination after its fall, for the works of Greek art previously looted by the Carthaginians from Sicily were returned to the Greek cities from which they had been stolen. These cities were lucky (anyhow for the time being, till Verres arrived to govern them), perhaps because Scipio was influenced by the thinking of his friend Polybius, perhaps because, as was to be shown in his subsequent censorial wrangles with his colleague Mummius, he did not think that art gallaries improved the dignity of Rome as an imperial capital.[70]

From Ambracia in 189 BC Fulvius Nobilior brought all the treasures which had once adorned the palace of Pyrrhus – which, admittedly

* It was all the worse if, as Plutarch suggests, numbers of Romans, rather than inspect these looted masterpieces of art, preferred to visit the Bazaar of living human monstrosities in Rome (*De curiosit*. 10, *Mor*. 520C.).

because of senatorial in-fighting, there was an unsuccessful attempt to replace.[71] A year later there was the stuff from Asia Minor, such of it as had not been lost on the way, brought home by Manlius Vulso.[72] After 167 there were the royal treasures from the Macedonian palaces[73] and in 146 BC the great wealth of Corinth, in dealing with which the conqueror Mummius was as zealous as he was maladroit (see p.177).[74] Sulla, whose baneful memory survived for long in Greece, stripped Delphi, Olympia and Epidaurus of numerous works of art, which he gave to his troops, and secured the famous collection of Aristotle and Theophrastus manuscripts at Athens – which, admittedly, had suffered badly from lack of attention already – and brought them to Rome.[75]

These were the high spots, but the process continued as Pompey (with the treasures of Mithridates from his stronghold near Cabeira)[76] and others returned from the East, and the younger Cato set up as Roman state auctioneer in the palace of the Ptolemies in Cyprus.[77] Antony plundered works of art and gave them to 'the Egyptian woman', but many – not all – of these were returned to their original owners by Augustus, though in other cases Augustus was in the tradition, inheriting the true Roman acquisitive itch. In addition to his loot from Arcadia (see p.172), he transferred Myron's statue of Zeus from Samos and Apelles' picture of Aphrodite Anadyomene from Cos, to Rome, in the latter case with some financial compensation.[78]

So far it was with the treasures of Greek art – in the main, sculpture and painting – that Rome had been adorned; now it was Egypt's turn, and engineers and ship-builders were confronted by the novel and daunting task of transporting obelisks from Hierapolis and elsewhere in Egypt down to the sea and across the Mediterranean, and erecting them in their new home in Rome. The first two were brought by Augustus' orders in 10 BC, the first, now in the Piazza di Montecitorio, to be set up in the Campus Martius and made to serve as gnomon in a vast sundial laid out on the ground, the second, now in the Piazza del Popolo, to stand on the *spina* in the Circus Maximus. Other obelisks followed, including the one which now stands in the Piazza delle Trinità dei Monti and that in front of St Peter's, which was brought by the emperor Gaius to stand on the *spina* of his new Circus near where the Vatican is today.[79]

Most of what has so far been described was 'public looting', 'praeda populi Romani', war booty, the acquisition of works of art from defeated enemies for display first in the victor's triumphal procession and after that, in the temples and *fora* of Rome. This was the looting to which Polybius objected and which, according to Cicero, was the looting of the great Roman conquerors, from M. Marcellus down to C. Mummius and even P. Servilius Vatia.[80] Where could people see and admire these works of art better than in Rome, the populous capital of the world? In the case of Lysippus' 'Labours of Hercules', the (unnamed) Roman administrator who transferred the work to Rome could even claim to have found it disregarded in some out of the way spot in Acarnania.[81]

More sinister was private looting, the thefts of works of art by Roman administrators for the embellishment of their private homes or for gifts to their friends. The first and fourth books of Cicero's second speech against Verres describe the extensive depradations of an art-thief masquerading as a Roman administrator.[82] In AD 60 we hear of a freedman of Nero who was infuriated because the authorities of Pergamon were allowed by a Roman proconsul of Asia to prevent him from taking anything that he wanted. Juvenal observed that by his time, greedy as a Roman official might be, there was little of value left anywhere in the Empire for him to take; but the thefts continued.[83]

As early as 149 BC the tendency of Roman senators in responsible administrative positions in the provinces to pilfer and extort money illegally was admitted at Rome and a permanent court was established by law to try such offenders, once their period of administration was at an end; but, despite effort after effort to improve the law, the cards were always stacked in favour of the defendant. He was on his home ground, senators (and there were generally senators, whether or not in a majority, on the juries) were members of the close social class to which he belonged. By the late Republic the bribery of juries was a fine art. The prosecution (individuals or representatives of communities) were hampered from the start by the sitting governor, whose sympathies were all for his predecessor, whose bad example, as likely as not, he was himself already following; they had to make the hazardous and expensive journey to Rome; in Rome they had to find a senator with time on his hands and a willingness to plead their case. Witnesses were reluctant to come to Rome, where the trial was held. The issue of the trial turned, as likely as not, on the political situation of the moment in Rome; in this Rutilius Rufus was unlucky, an innocent man condemned, and so was Verres, an arch-criminal who in a different political climate might without difficulty have bribed successfully enough to secure his own acquittal.[84]

Emperors, of course, were above the law. Gaius took Praxiteles' statue of Eros from Thespiae, but Claudius returned it; however, it was soon taken to Rome again, this time by Nero, and it stood in the Porticus Octaviae until, later, it was destroyed by fire. Nero filched on the grand scale (five hundred statues from Olympia), greatest imperial philhellene before Hadrian and greatest looter in one.[85] And even Hadrian. How many works of art were acquired by him for his villa at Tivoli?

The final mixture of iconoclasm and theft was the exemplary act of

Constantine, hysterically praised by his biographer Eusebius. Gilded statues had the gold ripped off, for gold was valuable, and the poor mistaken pagans were humiliated by the sight of the wood and stuffing which were the core of the idols which they had so mistakenly worshipped. Other works of art – like the statues of the Muses from Italica – were taken to embellish Constantine's new capital, for the amusement and sport of spectators as philistine as Eusebius himself.[86] Under the year 330 Jerome recorded in his *Chronicle*, 'Constantinople was dedicated by the process of stripping nearly every other city bare'.

It would be a mistake to take Juvenal's remark seriously, that there was little left to plunder, for there had not been great change in all places since Strabo wrote (and Pliny the elder), and their accounts, like that of Pausanias, who wrote later, show that an abundance of the classical masterpieces still remained in their original sites.[87]

There was an aspect of Roman looting after conquest far more shattering than the removal of important works of art on which our sources concentrate. There was the removal in their thousands – from Illyricum in 150 BC, 150,000[88] – of men, women and children to slavery in a foreign country, Italy. The treatment of these unfortunates by the big slave contractors until the moment when, with whitened feet, they were sold off the auction platform to Roman purchasers; the intense psychological trauma that they must have suffered and the difficulties which must have confronted them in adapting themselves to their new degradation – all these are among the fundamental features of ancient life about which our sources are completely silent (see p.78).

(vi) The Romans and their ghastly bad taste

The Greeks were capable of obscene public behaviour – to Roman envoys at Tarentum, for instance, early in the third century BC and at Corinth in the second[89] – but they inherited certain standards of culture which Romans at large lacked completely. At Rome the rumour that there were boxers or gladiators to be seen was enough towards the middle of the second century BC to distract the audience which had come to see a play of Terence. The concert of Greek musicians given by L. Anicius as part of his victory-games in 167 BC was turned into a shambles by Anicius himself.[90] Nero and Domitian tried to introduce 'Greek Games' to Rome, but the musical and cultural features of these Festivals had little popular appeal (see p.35).

As for the visual arts, there is little evidence of any genuine aesthetic taste among educated Romans.* Verres, it is true, may have been a

---

* Was Novius Vindex that rare thing, a Roman connoisseur? His guests Martial (9, 43f.) and Statius (*Silv.* 4, 6) were enraptured by the small statue of Hercules which stood on his dining-room table, a signed work of Lysippus. Vindex knew its history; it had belonged in turn to Alexander, Hannibal and Sulla. What would a Sotheby's valuer have made of its credentials?

man of discriminating artistic taste and, given his avidity, this perhaps made him the more dangerous criminal.[91] The elder Piny itemised masterpieces of classical sculpture and painting with the methodical zeal of an auctioneer's clerk. And there is nothing in his private correspondence to suggest that Cicero had any aesthetic taste at all. In public – prosecuting Verres, for instance – he played to the gallery, expressing the worst kind of Roman philistinism. He apologised for knowing the names of the great Greek artists; he only knew them because he had mugged them up for the sake of his brief. Greeks with their art were like children with their toys; Romans were too much men of the world to value such things.[92] The ghost of the younger Scipio might have been standing at his elbow as he spoke.

As for being an artist and producing works of art, that was the last thing that any good Roman would want to do. *Excudent alii spirantia mollius aera;*[93] Romans, on the other hand, had the world to govern. Virgil was no more unorthodox than Cicero in such a matter.

The general view among educated Romans was that what was Greek was good – why, otherwise, should Greek art command such extravagant prices? – and, simply as a status-symbol, a gentleman should have a classical bust or two (a writer or a philosopher) in his library and there should be statues among the trees and on the terraces of his grounds. At the same time every educated man read – or even wrote – in the history books that Romans in the past had been the better for being without such utterly unroman objects.

In art other than Greek art, Celtic art, for instance, the Romans had no interest at all. They took their ideas about art from others, and nobody had suggested to them that Celtic art had any beauty.

The Romans liked things to be big and, though it was, of course, the Greeks who had led the way with colossi, they tended to judge works of art by their size.[94] And, of course, by their price.

More than two centuries after the sack of Corinth in 146 BC, L. Mummius was still remembered in Greece as the typical Roman ignoramus in matters of the aesthetic. He was well cast for the part of Roman bull in the Greek china shop. After Corinth fell in 146 BC such paintings as had not been destroyed through being used by the troops as draughtsboards* were either packed for dispatch to Rome or else they were put up for auction. Mummius told the shippers that, if any of the paintings (classical masterpieces) was damaged in transport, they would be required to replace it by a new one; and when at the auction Attalus bid a high price for the Dionysus of Aristides, Mummius withdrew the picture from the sale; if it was worth all that money, it was evidently a high-class work of art.[95]

The Rhodian habit of using the same dedicatory statue over and over again with a mere alteration of the inscription was severely

* Romans were not the only soldiers in history to behave with such destructive playfulness. The sorry condition of Ribera's *Calvary* is due to the fact that in the Peninsular war French soldiers used it for target practice.

criticised by Dio Chrysostom (see p.207). But no Greek would have taken a valuable artistic masterpiece and modernised it, as Romans had no hesitation in doing. The head of Lysippus' statue of Alexander was replaced by one of Julius Caesar when the statue was looted and set up in Julius Caesar's Forum in Rome; and Claudius arranged for the face of Alexander to be cut out of two pictures of Apelles and replaced by the face of Augustus. Gaius Caligula's ambition to have his own portrait-head replace that carved by Pheidias on the statue of Zeus at Olympia and to have the statue brought to Rome was happily unrealised.[96]

There were other acts of vandalism. A statue of 'Ianus pater' brought by Augustus from Egypt – the work of Scopas or Praxiteles, it was said – was thought to be improved by being gilded. Nero thought that a portrait-statue of Alexander the Great by Lysippus was the better for being gilded and, though the gold was subsequently removed, the statue was seriously damaged.[97]

Not every Greek, of course, was a paragon of aesthetic culture. Plutarch himself nowhere shows great interest in art and, in writing of Lucullus, he gave his view about spending money on buying paintings and sculpture: it was a more puerile extravagance than spending money on building baths.[98]

Still, it was evident to Greeks that there was a considerable affectation in the pretentiously cultured Roman and that the average Greek was born with a 'spiritual' quality which most Romans lacked. 'Should an ass affect the lyre?'[99]

The Greek view of the difference in values between the two peoples is well expressed in a story about Demonax, the Cynic philosopher of the second century AD. When some Greek, a vulgarian devoid of culture, boasted that the Roman emperor had made him a Roman citizen, Demonax retorted caustically, 'A pity he did not make you a Greek.'[100]

(vii) Roman success: all a matter of luck

At moments when the smooth course of Roman expansion was checked, there were widespread hopes on the part of foreign peoples that the tide had turned at last. Philip V of Macedon was fatally encouraged by the sequence of Roman disasters at the start of the second Punic war and hastened to join Hannibal in the expectation of delivering the *coup de grâce*. Likewise in 171 BC Perseus' first successes in fighting the Romans were a great stimulant to Rome's enemies in the Greek world.[101] Yet Rome's advance continued. Why?

The simplest response to the question was to say that the Romans seemed to have the devil's own luck, to attribute their success to this and nothing more; and this view evidently received wide expression, or Polybius and Dionysius of Halicarnassus would not have countered it so strenuously. There was comfort in the thought that luck was fickle. It had favoured the Romans so far; one day it would desert them.

Writers sympathetic with Rome would have none of this nonsense. Polybius, as a rational historian, declared that in Rome's case, as in the case of the Achaean League, to which he owed such great personal devotion, anyone who spoke of 'luck' was scouting the question; success must have a rational cause. In Rome's case he made it his object to teach the educated reading public of the Greek East that Romans succeeded because of an inbuilt superiority, whose causes were to be found in their constitutional stability and in their fighting strength and organisation:

This establishes the thesis with which I started, that it was not by chance, as some Greeks think, nor from some automatic determinism, but as the natural result of their hard training that the Romans boldly aspired to universal dominion and, what is more, achieved what they aimed at.[102]

Dionysius of Halicarnassus trumpeted the message that Roman success was the result of Roman virtues, not of luck. Josephus wrote in the same vein of the Roman army. Agrippa II, trying to dissuade the Jews from revolting in AD 66, assured them that the Romans always won, not in virtue of luck but because of a firmly consistent Fortune, the 'Roman Fortune'. (The Greek word *Tychê* covered both concepts.)[103]

The Roman Fortune, like a King's Fortune, was not just luck; it was a lucky genius, perhaps. It was something which did not just 'favour the bold'; it accompanied their boldness or virtue. As components of the highest success – for the Romans, as for anybody else – they were inseparable. In fostering Rome's early growth, Virtue and Fortune formed an eternal pact, Ammianus Marcellinus wrote.[104]

While the two spectacular successes of the ancient world, of Alexander[105] and of the Romans, were the result of the co-operation of Virtue and Fortune, the question was open for discussion whether *Tychê*, meaning Luck, had been a better friend to the Romans than it had been to Alexander, and on this subject Plutarch wrote a couple of essays.

In the case of Rome, Luck has the lion's share, with a list of all the occasions from the virgin-birth of the Founders down to Augustus when, on critical occasions, Luck tipped the scales in Rome's favour, creating the opportunity for the display of Roman excellence, *Aretê*. It would, of course, have been just as easy to list the critical occasions in Roman history when Luck was against Rome, not on her side. This was what Plutarch did in his essay on Alexander; Luck was never his friend, and he triumphed everywhere in virtue of *Aretê* alone.

There is an obvious connexion between the essays, and Plutarch may well have used a source which stressed the view that Luck was a good friend to Rome and no friend at all to Alexander; this view, if

Roman *Aretê* was undervalued, or indeed passed over in silence, could have been expressed in a form disparaging to Rome by the writer (or type of writer) to whom Dionysius referred as belittling the Roman achievement through over-emphasis on this very factor in her history.[106]

There is nothing, however, in what Plutarch himself wrote which is in the smallest degree disparaging of Rome. Moreover it is possible that his essay on the Romans is incomplete, that we have only one part of the story, the contribution of Fortune to Rome's success and that the balancing contribution of Roman *Aretê* is missing because Plutarch never completed the essay.[107]

(viii) Bricks to throw at the Romans

(a) Skeletons in the Roman historical cupboard

The bitterest of enemies could not have invented a more damaging version of Roman origins than the account handed down by legend which the Romans not only accepted, but accepted with relish.* The founder-twins had no known father; they owed their lives, of all hateful animals, to a she-wolf (a she-goat, such as suckled the baby Zeus would have been better).[108] They murdered their great-uncle, and then one of them killed the other. The first population of Rome consisted of vagabonds and fugitive criminals who sought asylum on the Capitol and, acting in character, these men secured their wives by rape. You could go further and point to some of their kings, base-born, foreign, tyrannical rascals, and you could claim that Rome's hatred of foreign kings was due to the fact that their own history gave them no idea what a decent king was like.

Snide references to Roman kings came best from the mouths of monarchs, from Mithridates for example.[109]

The she-wolf afforded the most obvious point of attack because, in their imperial progress, the Romans, 'children of the sheep-devouring beast', were like wolves, seeking whom they might devour. Mithridates made the point, according to Justin. The Aequi and Volsci were made by Livy to call the Romans demented wolves in 446 BC. In 82, before the battle of the Colline Gate, Pontius Telesinus, the Samnite leader, calling for the destruction of Rome, declared that the only way to get rid of wolves was to fell the forest in which they lurked.[110]

If you rationalised the she-wolf and made her a prostitute (*lupa*), the wife of the shepherd Faustulus, you discredited the story still further.[111]

The Aetolians were made to decry the character of the Founder-Fathers, those who availed themselves of asylum 'between the two groves'; shepherds (not, admittedly, a particularly discreditable race of men), slaves and criminals. Still, the philosophers taught that slaves

* See p.3.

were descended from kings and kings from slaves, and Livy observes amusingly that it is all a matter of words. How different in kind and how much better were the ancestors of people who boasted – like the Athenians – of being 'autochthonous'? Only *internally*, as Juvenal pointed out, such origins threw doubt on the credentials of the so-called 'old Roman families'.[112]

Whether, in fact, Rome's enemies in the critical moments before decisive conflict derived comfort or inspiration from these allegations about the remote beginnings of Rome, we cannot tell. They were part of the rhetorical stock in trade and the anti-Roman speeches and allegations which have come down to us in the history books are, as likely as not, the fictional compositions of rhetorical historians, Greek or Roman.

To their Greek critics the Romans could make a counter-claim which Dionysius of Halicarnassus made on their behalf (see p.161). At least the Roman gods, not being anthropomorphic, had not indulged in the criminal and lustful barbarities attributed to members of the Greek pantheon; they had not eaten their own children. Nor were Roman beginnings made up of the sort of mythological horror-stories which Greek cities recalled without embarrassment, indeed with open delight.[113]

(b) Tu quoque

The Romans soon persuaded themselves that they had gone to war with Philip of Macedon in order to free Greece from his army of occupation and to achieve that 'Freedom of the Greeks' which was so movingly proclaimed at the Isthmian Games of 196 BC. After this, without any clear idea of the real meaning – apart from the nuisance-value – of their claim, they crusaded in the East for the freedom of Greek cities. This was their ultimatum to Antiochus: he must free the Greek cities of his empire. In this they exposed themselves to the damaging charge that they did not themselves practise what they preached.

When Antiochus the Great was told by the Romans that he must concede autonomy to the Greek cities of his empire in Asia Minor in 193 BC, his envoy Minnio had a ready retort. What about Greek cities in Italy? How much independence did the Romans concede to them? 'Are Smyrna and Lampsacus any more Greek than Naples, Rhegium and Tarentum, from whom you exact taxes and demand naval assistance under treaty? Why do *you* send a governor every year to Syracuse and the other Greek cities of Sicily, with the rods and axes, symbols of absolute power?' The Roman answer was disingenuous in the extreme. A single unbroken 'servitude', its terms written large in a charter (*foedus*), was one thing; the 'servitude' of those who had in the past suffered a change of masters – and even intervals of independence – was quite different.[114]

When in 184 BC Appius Claudius sat in harsh judgment on the Achaean treatment of Sparta, the Achaean statesman Lycortas asked, 'And how did *you* treat Capua?' One law for the Romans, another for the rest of mankind.

Ariovistus, too, in Gaul in 58 BC. His answer to Caesar's ultimatum was simple: he did not himself lay down the law as to how the Romans should behave in their own territory; why then should he tolerate Caesar's instruction on what to do in Gaul, which was his, anyhow, and not Caesar's?[115]

(ix) Anti-Roman writings

(a) Historians

It took centuries for the Greek world to reconcile itself to incorporation in the 'barbarian' Roman empire, and the inexorably rising tide of Roman success was naturally viewed with anger and fear by the eastern kingdoms which, in succession, faced submergence. In the end Parthia alone survived unsubmerged and in the period between Mithridates and Augustus conceivably claimed, however incongruously, to be the last stronghold of Hellenism.[116] So, among all these peoples, as the Roman danger threatened, it was described in hostile language by writers in the Greek world who had the anxious Hellenistic kings for their patrons.

At the very first contact of Greece and Rome, when Flamininus laid the basis of a statesmanlike peace-settlement which did not satisfy the greed of the Aetolians, they simply assumed and stated openly that he had been bribed. There were plenty of features of Roman imperialism to criticise, as the most loyal of Romans themselves admitted, Cicero in vehement passages of his public speeches, historians in their writings. Sallust knew what Mithridates felt, Tacitus knew the feelings of the Caledonian Calgacus, and both reproduced these feelings in the bluntest language in their histories. Even Livy, for whom Roman wars were always 'just wars', did not attempt to conceal the fact that Marcius Philippus' trickery of Perseus before the third Macedonian war was unethical by traditional Roman standards: 'nova sapientia.'[117]

Why could nothing be done to stem the Roman advance? Writers sympathetic to Rome like Polybius found the answer in an inbuilt Roman superiority, a superiority of civil and moral discipline and fighting strength. Writers in the Hellenistic courts were bound, whether they believed it or not, to supply a different answer, to encourage their patrons. Roman success, they declared, was simply to be explained as a long run of luck – and luck does not hold good for ever. When Dionysius referred to advocates of this view, 'historians in the service of, and writing to please, barbarian kings', the man he had chiefly in mind was, no doubt, the gifted Metrodorus of Scepsis who served with Mithridates, a man whose tart reflections on Rome evidently received wide currency and were long remembered. He attacked the Roman image (*mores*), Ovid tells us; the elder Pliny, as has been noted, records his nickname, 'Misorhômaios', 'Rome-hater'. There were, without doubt other such writers with Mithridates and in the Hellenistic courts, men known to us by name alone or men not known to us at all.[118]

Livy referred to different, but equally hostile, historians, 'irresponsible Greeks', 'levissimi e Graecis', whose offence – or whose main offence – lay in glorifying Alexander the Great at the expense of the Romans and in 'favouring the glory of the Parthians in opposition to Rome'. In the first case, taking sides in what was evidently an issue debated in the rhetorical schools, they had the impertinence to suggest that if Alexander had lived to campaign in the West, there would have been no Roman empire. Roman growth would have come to an abrupt end at the close of the fourth century BC.[119]

Scholarly erudition in a first flush of enthusiasm has identified two of these historians as being, both of them, contemporaries of Livy, not foreigners outside the Empire but, *trahison des clercs*, writers at the very hub of Roman affairs, the Alexandrian Greek Timagenes,[120] a protégé of Augustus (who wrote, of course, in Greek) and Pompeius Trogus, the Gaul whose grandfather won Roman citizenship for loyal service to Pompey and whose father was Julius Caesar's confidential secretary in Gaul.[121] About Timagenes speculation is easy since only a few fragments of his writing survive; Trogus produced a Latin history of the oriental and Hellenistic kingdoms, a work to be welcomed by any Roman who did not read Greek easily, since all earlier accounts of this subject (the books which Trogus had to read for information) were in Greek. The prologues of Trogus' several books survive, together with a précis of the whole work made in the third century by Justin.

While we know little about Timagenes as a writer, we know a great deal about him as a person. He was an Alexandrian Greek brought as a slave to Rome by Gabinius in the late fifties BC, and in Rome he practised as a teacher of rhetoric until he was taken up by Augustus and commissioned to write an account of Augustus' early life.

As an Alexandrian Greek, he possessed a devastating and poisonous wit, and he had no control over his own tongue. Some of his witticisms were long remembered – his statement, for instance, that the sight of a house on fire in Rome brought tears to his eyes. When asked why, he said because something bigger and better would inevitably be built in its place. So he was 'an enemy of the city's prosperity'. Augustus urged discretion on him, but in vain, and when he heard of some outrageous remark which Timagenes had made about the empress Livia and himself – about his snatching her as a bride when she was in an advanced state of pregnancy? – he expelled Timagenes from Court. Asinius Pollio, however, another caustic wit, remained his friend with Augustus' somewhat reluctant consent, and

Timagenes continued to be lionised in the best society, to write and to give recitations. However in his first fury at Augustus' censure, he burnt the manuscript of his unfinished biography;[122] and this, perhaps, left the way open for Nicolaus of Damascus to write the *Early Life of Augustus*, part of which survives.

From the use made of Timagenes by Strabo and others, it is clear that he was a gifted historian, interested in geography, ethnology and social history in the tradition of Posidonius; and an enigmatic remark of Quintilian suggests that what he wrote was very readable.[123] But what *did* he write? One of his books was called *The Kings* (we do not know what kings); the titles of his other books, of which he wrote a number, are unknown. Two fragments touching on Rome might suggest that he wrote as venomously as he talked: the statement that the sins of the elder Caepio, who incurred disaster in Gaul in 105 BC, were visited on his two daughters, both of whom became prostitutes and an observation about Ptolemy Auletes' departure from Egypt for Rome in 58 BC, lifted from Theophanes, which could be taken to reflect badly on Pompey.[124]

But when did he write his important history? Before he was taken up by Augustus or after Augustus dropped him? In the first case his history cannot possibly have been offensive from a Roman point of view. In the second, Timagenes could not, as an openly anti-Roman historian, have remained the friend of Pollio and have continued to mix in good Roman society.

So that, though his book (or books) may have contained barbed remarks, those remarks were not, perhaps, more offensive than criticisms to be found on almost every page of Sallust.

On the highly implausible assumption that Timagenes' writing was openly hostile to Rome, the first hypothesis was that Trogus had done nothing more than turn what Timagenes wrote into Latin. The simple (and implausible) argument was that since Trogus' book (even judged by Justin's précis) was extremely readable, it must have been based on a book written in Greek; since it showed interest in ethnography and geography, it must have been based on a historian who wrote in the tradition of Posidonius and since its arrangement was dynastic, not annalistic, it must have been based on such a work as *The Kings*.[125]

So a toothcomb was applied to Trogus (Justin) and a gratifying number of snide unfriendly references to Rome and Romans was garnered. In a wild ecstasy of implausibility, West and East were depicted as dipping their pens into the same venomous ink, the Gaul Trogus and the Greeks Metrodorus and Timagenes; it was the union of Sertorius and Mithridates transferred to paper.[126]

This fantasy runs aground on the evidence. According to Justin, Trogus read not one book but a great many (among them, we can be sure, the work of Timagenes); these were chiefly biographies of kings, which in itself could explain the arrangement of his work. And the offending references in Trogus mostly evaporate under close inspection. They are anti-Roman speeches of Rome's enemies (such as are to be found in Sallust and in Tacitus) or they are remarks which do not necessarily reflect bias against Rome at all.[127] Anyhow, what in the world could be more improbable than hostility to Rome on the part of Trogus, a loyal Roman as Justin's account of the introduction to his penultimate book (book 43) on the early history of Rome shows: 'After unravelling the history of Parthia and the East, in fact of practically the whole world, Trogus returns home like some one who has been a long time abroad, thinking that a man would show small patriotism if, after illustrating the history of all other peoples, he wrote nothing about one country alone – his own.'

The suggestion has been made that Livy was not referring to any historian, but to pungent Greek teachers of rhetoric who loaded the dice in favour of Alexander in the hackneyed speculation on what would have happened if he had come into conflict with Rome.[128] But the reference to a particular historian is more likely and it is not inconceivable that that historian was Timagenes.[129] His praise of Alexander may have seemed too extravagant to Livy and, as for 'favouring the glory of Parthia', it must be remembered that Livy's criticism was evidently written before the restoration of the standards by the Parthians in 20 BC.[130] So Livy's *bête noire*, beyond stating the obvious fact* that the Roman and Parthian empires divided the world, may well have given more emphasis than Livy liked to the shattering defeats which Parthia had inflicted on both Crassus and Antony.

So, in general, there was probably an element of (deserved) criticism of Rome both in Timagenes and in Trogus, but this did not make either of them an 'anti-Roman historian'. The same qualities, after all, no doubt marked the earlier history of Posidonius. His account of the slave-rising in Sicily in the late second century BC cannot have made comfortable reading for Romans; on the other hand, he certainly paid generous tribute to the personality and achievement of Pompey.

(b) Lucian

In a kind of hysteria the habit has grown among scholars of finding an anti-Roman under the bed of nearly every Greek whose writings, whether historical, rhetorical or literary, touched on Rome. It is wiser, and safer, to take what was written, suppose it written in Latin by a Roman and to ask whether it would have caused much comment. If Seneca, Martial, Juvenal and Tacitus are not considered to have been moved by hostility to Rome, why should such hostility be assumed in the case of Greeks who criticised the same features of life in the capital (and sometimes outside it) as these Romans criticised: snobbery, social injustice, gross materialism and vice? There were other things

* One stressed by writers whom nobody could accuse of hostility to Rome: Strabo 11, 9, 2, 515; VP 2, 101; CD 40, 14, 3f.

about Rome and its empire than the *dolce vita* of the capital.

Even Lucian has been labelled an enemy of Rome.[131]

After sowing his wild oats in an extremely successful career as a professor of rhetoric, sophist and the author of witty *belles lettres* which happily survive, and after travelling widely in Italy and Gaul – on a lecture-tour[132] – as well as in the Greek East, the Syrian-born Lucian evidently surprised his friends, Roman and Greek alike, and perhaps surprised himself, by becoming an imperial civil servant in Egypt.[133]

A cynic with a devastating wit, a cross between Max Beerbohm and Anatole France, he aimed, in writing, 'through his own laughter to make others laugh'. No holds were barred; nothing was too grave or too sacred for this follower of Menippus to mock: gods, men, philosophers, charlatans, rich, poor (in the *Cock*), indeed Lucian himself. In modern scholarship he has sometimes suffered a fate which he can hardly have anticipated, the fate of being taken seriously by scholars who, for all their brilliance, lack his own most striking quality, a sense of humour.

Rather than live the life of people with money at Rome, men whose culture was scarcely even skin-deep, a sensitive and educated man must prefer the quiet academic atmosphere of a city like Athens. This was the theme of the *Nigrinus*, which admittedly has some of the tedium of a nineteenth-century evangelical pamphlet. There is venom here as there is in Juvenal (whom, whether in the original or in translation, Lucian is likely to have read).[134] In *The Dependent Scholar*, an account of the ignominious status of a Greek tutor in a rich Roman household, there is, of course, sharp satire, and there is great humour too, for instance in the account of an unfortunate Stoic philosopher being forced by a Roman lady, who wished to travel unencumbered with her painted boy-friend, to take charge of her Maltese terrier-bitch on a carriage journey, in the course of which the animal whelped on his coat.[135]

Where Rome was concerned, the target of Lucian's satire, little different from Dio Chrysostom's severe criticism of Rome in his Athenian oration (*Or.* 13), was the sheer materialism and hedonism of the life of a section of the wealthy upper class (in particular, the morning *salutatio* and the dinner parties) and the deplorable social consequences of ostentatious wealth and gross self-indulgence: cattiness, back-biting, sycophancy, contemptuous exploitation of all those who ministered to the pleasures of the wealthy but who were too weak to stand up for their own interests.

There was nothing new in all this. Exactly the same qualities in the life of the rich at Rome had been pilloried by Seneca, deplored by the elder Pliny and criticised by Tacitus. If Romans could write like this about themselves, why should Greeks not follow their example? Indeed Lucian was very generous in accounting for the contempt which so many Romans entertained for Greeks; it was the result, he suggested, of the deplorable type of Greek who, for his own criminal purposes, tried to exploit Roman credulity and superstition.[136]

The Romans in the *Nigrinus* and the *Dependent Scholar*, of course, were not the only Romans; they were the Romans who were good for a laugh, and Lucian's Roman friends delighted in reading what he wrote. Indeed, it is not always noticed that Nigrinus, the man who fled from the gross extravagance of life in Rome to philosophic peace in Athens was himself a Roman property-owner.[137]

The upper-class was no longer divided into sheep and goats, Romans and Greeks. Lucian was a member and a beneficiary of the empire, as were his Roman friends. Though he sometimes writes objectively of the Romans, he is the first Greek to refer to the Roman empire as 'our empire' and to its inhabitants as 'we'. His description of Arrian is significant: 'the pupil of Epictetus, a Roman of prominence'.[138] In a piece like the *Demonax* Lucian is not race-conscious in his mockery; some of his butts are Greek, others are Roman. And praise was given to Romans who merited praise, to good governors, officials and to good emperors.[139]

The theme of *The Apology*, written to his Roman friend Sabinus, is this: how, after my scathing denunciation of the ignominy of a Greek tutor's post in the household of a rich Roman vulgarian, can I defend my own action, when I have one foot in the grave, in becoming a member, a quite well-paid and important member, of the Roman civil service in Egypt? Evidence, the critics declare, of his acute embarrassment.

This view would have surprised Sabinus as much as it would have surprised Lucian himself. How could any man of sense think the status of a private tutor comparable with that of an imperial civil servant? Still, the idea could serve as the basis for a satire on the ridiculous kind of arguments which were devised, pro and con, in an exercise in the rhetorical training schools. This is what the essay was, nothing but a very amusing *jeu d'ésprit*.

What of Lucian's Egyptian appointment? Are we simply to assume, without evidence, that it resulted from nepotism of some kind? Even so, is the post likely to have been given to a man whose writings were thought to show him an enemy of Rome?

(c) Martyr-literature, especially in Alexandria
Highly coloured accounts of martyrdom existed both among Jews (the outspoken courage of those tortured to death for their religious beliefs by Antiochus Epiphanes)[140] and also in Rome (Herennius Senecio's monograph on Helvidius Priscus and Epictetus' account of the confrontation of Helvidius Priscus and Vespasian).[141] And there was evidently a highly coloured account of the contumacious abuse of Vespasian to his face by Epponina, the wife of the Gallic rebel Julius Sabinus, before her execution.[142]

In Alexandria, under the influence of the mime and the novel, accounts of the confrontation, before sentence and execution, of eminent Greeks of the city and Roman emperors, fictional embroidery of actual happenings, were put into circulation.[143] The 'martyrs' faced death with a torrent of noble abuse, boasting of Alexandria and its Greek tradition, proud of their office, if they were magistrates of the city, disdainful of Jews and Romans alike. Any stick would do to beat the Romans, who were accused of injustice and avarice while, for the emperor, abuse was the thing. Claudius was told to his face that he was 'the cast-off son of the Jewess Salome', a 'crazy emperor', Commodus that he was 'tyrannical, dishonest and crude'.[144]

Such are the 'Acts of the Pagan Martyrs', preserved in fragmentary form on a number of papyri. As none survive from the time of Septimius Severus or later, it is plausibly conjectured that the success of the Alexandrian Greeks, after more than two centuries of effort, in securing a local Senate so well satisfied their *amour propre* that this kind of protest-literature came to an end.

Once in Alexandria's royal city there had been the palace and the Court of the Ptolemies. From this to the person and entourage of the Roman Prefect was a sad decline for the upper class of Greek resident, the sort of men who became gymnasiarchs. Of these, some so far overstepped the limits of outspokenness in their contumacy to the Prefect and even, in Rome, to the Emperor himself that they were put to death. The resentment of the rest, it seems, fed on this virulent literature, which circulated and was read privately in Egypt at home or in local clubs and gymnasia.

Underground, resistance literature.

(d) Prophecies of Roman disaster
Not content with ignorance of the past, man perversely desires a knowledge of the future, whether a short-range or a long-range forecast. The credulous believe today that events in our own future are foretold by scratches on the Egyptian pyramids.

In antiquity supernatural powers were not always unhelpful. Through the instrumentality of their professional human agents (oracles and the like) they were capable not only of guiding people out of their existing troubles – telling them, for instance, what to do to end a drought – but also of giving warning of troubles ahead which could still be averted. So in Rome it was the patriot's duty to give public notice of any portentous happening which came to his attention (the divine warning signal), so that the experts – augurs, haruspices or the priests in charge of the Sibylline books – could discover and report what preventive action might yet be taken; and so imminent disaster might be avoided.

Much of the future, however, was predestined and it was a case of what will be, will be. About this, numbers of people, even the greatest, had an inextinguishable curiosity which professional experts claimed the ability to satisfy: oracles, interpreters of dreams, astrologers.

Sceptics like Tacitus were rare. Few emperors or members of the imperial family missed the opportunity of consulting an oracle, following in the footsteps of Alexander the Great, who had gone both to Delphi and to Ammon. So in the East Germanicus consulted the oracle of Clarius Apollo at Colophon and Titus enquired about his future in the temple of Paphian Venus on Cyprus; so at Heliopolis (Baalbeck) did Trajan.

Romans of the highest rank were among those who were deluded in the second century AD by the charlatan Alexander into patronising his bogus oracle at Abonuteichos in Paphlagonia.[145]

The Roman government had concern with public morals and the circulation of ominous 'oracles' might spread gloom and despondency and start a whispering campaign. The harùspices' prophecy of disaster in the twentieth year after the destruction of the Capitol in 83 BC and the tenth year from the absolution of the Vestal Virgins made 63 BC from the start an ominous year. And who, at the same time, was the 'third Cornelius' destined, according to a Sibylline oracle, to be king? Was it Catiline's accomplice Cornelius Lentulus, praetor of the year, a man with a bad reputation already? Lentulus was persuaded to believe that it was.[146]

More whispering in 44 BC by those anxious to discredit Caesar, the rumour of a Sibylline oracle to the effect that Parthia could only be defeated by a king. By King Caesar? The idea suited the conspirators, as Suetonius says.[147] They, perhaps, should have the credit for the oracle's invention.

At Rome the genuine (Roman) Sibylline oracles were under official control, consulted and reported only by an official priesthood of the state, the Decemviri – later Quindecimviri – Sacris Faciundis, themselves ultimately responsible to the Pontifex Maximus. Destroyed when the Capitol was burnt in 83 BC, the Sibylline books were replaced by what were thought to be genuine substitutes, and Augustus as Pontifex Maximus ordered these to be recopied so as to ensure their continuing legibility. He also ordered the destruction of over two thousand prophetic books which were evidently spurious. By this means he might seem to have prevented the future circulation in Rome of literature which could be used to spread alarm and despondency.[148] There were 'oracles', however, which evidently slipped through the net. In AD 19 an oracle was current that 'after thrice three hundred years Rome shall be destroyed by civil war and the folly which once ruined Sybaris', and Tiberius ordered a further destruction of such bogus 'oracles'. Later, in AD 32, he was reasonably incensed by a member of the Quindecemviri who published what he alleged to be a recently discovered Sibylline oracle without first referring the matter to his colleagues in the priestly College. In AD 64, the year of the great fire in Rome, the oracle of AD 19 was in circulation again.[149]

If it was difficult to stop the publication of alarmist prophecies in Rome itself, it was obviously impossible to prevent the circulation at a distance, in the provinces, of oracles which foretold something far more sensational than the imminent demise of a ruling emperor – the imminent destruction of the Roman empire itself. These, circulating among dissident elements in the population, in particular among Jews and, later, Christians, under the Empire, were glad tidings, a welcome assurance of the end of the hateful dominion of Rome, just as, to the Jews, apocalyptic writings had earlier prophesied delivery from the blasphemous tyranny of Antiochus Epiphanes.

Schadenfreude existed before the Germans found a word for it – the Greeks, in fact, had had a word for it far earlier, *epichairekakia* – and disasters suffered by Rome were gloatingly described as portending still worse troubles to come. So in Gaul at the time of Civilis' revolt in AD 69/70 'Druidic verses' circulated which pointed to the destruction by fire of the temple of Capitoline Juppiter at Rome in 69 as presaging success for the revolt; for even during the legendary sack of Rome by the Gauls the Capitol had escaped unscathed.[150]

It was chiefly in the eastern half of the Empire that the forthcoming doom of the Roman empire was, in certain circles, so happily anticipated. The western power of Rome had conquered the East; now in turn the East should conquer the West. A king, perhaps, should come out of the East (at one period, the end of the first century AD, a Nero redivivus). In value of loot the West should suffer three times and in the number of persons enslaved it should suffer ten or twenty times over what it had inflicted on the East.[151]

A Sibylline oracle was in circulation which purported to have prophesied the downfall of Philip V of Macedon,[152] and in the Roman Republic such prophecies were devised and circulated most feverishly at times when the destruction of Rome seemed a real possibility, during the war with Antiochus the Great and later against Perseus, during the domination of Mithridates Eupator and during the catastrophes of the Roman civil wars.

The most insane of such prophecies dates either from one or other of the crises of the first half of the second century BC or from the time of Mithridates. The story, purporting to be the account of historical events, is preserved by Phlegon, who attributes it to the Rhodian historian Antisthenes of the mid-second century BC, a man.whom Polybius criticised but whom he would obviously have lampooned if in fact he had been capable of finding room in his history book for such nonsense as this.[153]

The episode is set in the year 191 BC, immediately after Acilius Glabrio's defeat of Antiochus' army at Thermopylae in Greece. The corpse of general Bouplagos, killed in the battle, returned to life and prophesied the forthcoming invasion of Italy. Delphi, consulted on this prodigious happening, advised the Romans to go home. They moved to the sea at Naupactus and there the Roman 'Publius' – P. Scipio Nasica, Glabrio's consular colleague (who did not in fact go to Greece)? Or P. Scipio Africanus, who came to Greece on his brother's staff a year later? – was inspired with the knowledge of Rome's imminent doom. In his tent he prophesied in verse that Italy would be invaded by a king of Asia with an Epirot ally; then, speaking in prose, he foretold the events of the next two years, the defeat of Antiochus in Asia and the return through Thrace of Manlius Vulso. After this, reverting to verse, he foretold a devastating invasion of Italy.

The pace quickens. 'Publius' climbed into an oak tree from which he announced to the assembled Roman army that a red wolf was on its way to eat him; nobody must interfere. This prodigious event occurred, but it was not the end of the story. From Publius' head, which the wolf had left uneaten, a human voice spoke, forbidding its burial and prophesying once again the relentless invasion of Italy.

From the time of Mithridates, perhaps, dates the publication of the oracle of Hystaspes, which is known to us through Justin and Lactantius; its circulation was later forbidden under pain of death (as being, perhaps, on Augustus' black list). It has been described as 'Zoroastrianism in Greek clothing', and was a prophecy of the end of the world which would be announced by the fall of the Roman empire, a prophecy which purported to date from remote antiquity, from a time before the Trojan wars.[154]

However, our chief, and indeed extensive, knowledge of this kind of literature derives from the surviving Sibylline oracles.

Sibyls sprouted all over the eastern Mediterranean (the chief one at Erythrae, from which the Cumaean Sibyl in Italy derived), as far as Babylon and Persia. Varro counted ten, but there are records of far more.[155] Some of the 'oracles' are recorded by historians of antiquity; eighteen which are Jewish, often with Christian overtones or additions, survive in the original, long, uncouth and mannered hexameter poems, their material thrown together like the unsorted pieces of a jigsaw puzzle, deriving from Syria or Judaea or from Egypt. Such literature had originated, like other Jewish apocalyptic writing – the book of Daniel, for instance[156] – from the time when Antiochus Epiphanes was the arch-enemy. It burst out again – sometimes incorporating earlier non-Jewish 'Sibylline' prophecies – of the Social war, for instance, or of Sulla[157] – when the Jews ceased to be the friends of Rome, as they had been in the time of Julius Caesar and of Augustus, but became, after Vespasian, Trajan and Hadrian, their declared enemies. The Romans were then 'the children of the sheep-eating wolf'.[158] Only on one subject are the 'oracles' curiously silent. One might have expected to find extensive fulminations against the first Roman arch-enemy of the Jews, that second Antiochus Epiphanes, the emperor Gaius Caligula.

Doom and rumours of imminent doom; not demonstrable evidence like a lightning-flash or the prodigious offspring of humans or animals, but a kind of whispering campaign. This was strong in the

East in the early Roman empire: a king or saviour was to come from the East, from Judaea, who would inevitably initiate some kind of revolutionary movement. The first Christians had their own interpretation of this; so, forlornly, had the rebellious Jews in 66 AD; so, with every appearance of justification, had the emperor Vespasian.[159]

In the East there was a very positive anticipation of disaster in AD 195. The letters of the Greek alphabet also did service as figures, and the figures r, ô, m, ê added up to 948. The 948th year from the Foundation of Rome was AD 195.[160] The millennium of Rome, however, in AD 248 occasioned no sinister anticipatory excitement, as far as we know.

In addition to prophecy, abuse was comforting. Of Roman greed for money, of Roman homosexuality and brothels.[161]

Christian apocalyptic followed and grew out of Jewish, and survives in scarcely intelligible form in the book of Revelations, which perhaps dates from the time of Domitian. Rome, the great beast, the harlot, the new Babylon, perpetrator of the blasphemy of emperor-worship, will be overthrown, with horrid economic consequences for those businessmen and merchants all over the world who have traded in Roman luxury-goods. Rome will be overthrown by another beast (the Nero redivivus, perhaps, whose return is featured so strongly in the Sibylline oracles); that beast in its turn will be overthrown, and a Christian millennium will ensue.[162]

The trouble was that it didn't. More than two hundred years later, however, at the time of the great Persecutions, Lactantius was, once again, the trumpeter of Roman doom. The East would throw off its chains and it would be the turn of the West to be enslaved. Sibylline prophecies were remembered, and the oracle of Hystaspes.[163]

At a thoughtful, less ecstatic level sane men, Romans and Greeks alike, had long looked at world history and read in it the simple lesson of a succession of imperial powers, each with a limited span of temporal dominion: Egypt, Assyria, Media, Persia, (Athens and Sparta, if they were worth counting), Macedon. And, after Macedon, Rome. Polybius saw the place of Rome in the series and so, as he destroyed Carthage, did Scipio Aemilianus.[164]

Roma aeterna; here was a claim that the Roman empire would never fall, as other empires had fallen. Simple panegyrists like Melinno had made the same assertion (see p.193). But to anybody who thought, it was evident that Rome was not exempt from the conditions of human existence. She had been young once and was ageing (see p.9). Her empire must come to an end one day, like all other empires. What was prodigious was Rome's resilience, the length of time that she took to sicken and die.

CHAPTER THIRTEEN

A Generally Good Press for Rome[1]

Outside Italy, the romanised world of the West produced no important history of Rome because it evidently asked no questions about Rome which were not already answered in Latin by Roman historians themselves. The only important history in Latin to come from this new world was the oriental and Hellenistic history of the Gaul Pompeius Trogus (see p. 183).

Very different was the case in the Greek-speaking East, which in any case embraced a larger reading public;* for there was a whole succession of Greek historians who were inquisitive about Rome, in particular about the explanation of her phenomenal success as an imperial power and who wrote books to illustrate and explain this success, whether histories of Rome itself or universal histories.

In these writers there is a progression in romanisation itself. Polybius, the first, was a foreign victim of flagrant Roman injustice, for fifteen years on arrest without trial, 'under suspicion'. There followed writers who still were foreign but who (like Polybius) had Roman friends and who moved in good, often the best, Roman social circles. Finally, with Arrian, Appian, and Cassius Dio, we move into a society of mongrels, Greeks who were at the same time Romans, men with significant careers in Roman administration.

None of them was, like the rhetor Aelius Aristides, a simple panegyrist. All of them found a great deal to admire in Rome; none of them denied that features of Roman life were open to criticism. At the same time some of them, Dionysius of Halicarnassus in particular, were anxious to dispel discreditable misconceptions about Rome which were current in the Greek East.

---

* In the period when Rome appeared to the Greek world as a startling new planet, from her withstanding of Pyrrhus to the disillusion which followed first the extinction of free Greece in 146 BC and the outrages of Sulla some half-century after that, there were Greek poets who sang of her as a rising power. Lycophron in Alexandria, perhaps early in the third century was the first (*Alex*. 1226-30). A century or so later in all probability, somewhere in the Hellenistic world Melinno composed the five Sapphic stanzas of her hymn in honour of Rome as a new goddess, daughter of Mars, mother of a race of fine warriors whose power, unlike other ephemeral powers, would endure (Stob., *Ecl*. 3, 7, 12).[2]

The first Greek historian to devote considerable attention to Rome was Timaeus of Tauromenium in Sicily, writing in Athens in the first half of the third century BC, but we know nothing of his attitude to Rome (except for fanciful inferences from the fact that he believed Rome and Carthage to have been founded in the same year, 814 BC).

Polybius was the first, the Achaean man of affairs with practical experience of the things he wrote about – politics, diplomacy, warfare. As one of the Achaeans interned without trial in Italy after the third Macedonian war, he might well have been soured and hostile to Roman imperialism; yet his resentment is shown only in his denigration of A. Postumius Albinus, praetor of 155 BC, who, in Polybius' mistaken opinion, was responsible for preventing the return of himself and his fellow-internees to Greece in that year.[3] His vanity was flattered, of course, by the fact that he was singled out for particularly favoured treatment; while his fellow-suspects languished, often to death, in the Italian country towns, he lived in Rome, a protégé of the Scipios. In such a society it was not difficult for him to shut his eyes and think of himself as an adopted member of the Roman ruling class.

Polybius emphasised the financial integrity of Roman public life and its firm religious basis in the early days of imperial expansion. Roman abstention from bribery in public life was contrasted with the practices of Carthaginians and Greeks, particularly Aetolians. In Rome by the *lex Cornelia Baebia* of 181 BC bribery at elections was made punishable, evidence that its occurrence was no longer outside the bounds of possibility. It was 'a rare thing' for a Roman to lay his hands on public money before the days of overseas expansion. After that, standards declined and complete integrity, as Polybius admits, was no longer the rule, though most men in public life still had high standards and some, like Aemilius Paullus and Scipio Aemilianus, very high standards indeed.

Polybius commended the Romans for their readiness to adopt anything foreign which seemed better than their own product and for their resilience in face of set-backs.[4] At the same time he was prepared to criticise – close-fistedness, for instance, in personal finance; the assumption that resolution and brute force were a guarantee, without nautical expertise, of success in naval warfare[5] – but he was far more ready to condone. His praise, which will have delighted Roman readers, sometimes strikes a jarring note, for he was a choleric man, firmly fixed in his loyalties, seeing people as white men or black. Being tortured and then thrown into the sea to drown, for instance, was far too kind a fate for such an enemy of the Achaean League as the Argive Aristomachus; 'he ought to have been horsewhipped round the Peloponnese';[6] on the other hand, his heroes were all but flawless, Philopoemen and Scipio Aemilianus.

Polybius not only wrote 'pragmatic' history, he thought pragmatically too. He judged political actions by their success rather than by any ethical standard, and Rome during his lifetime was very successful indeed; so, in his judgments, Polybius was sometimes more Roman than many Romans themselves. Success was success was success. From the point of view of Roman interest, Roman methods worked.

The question which every intelligent foreigner asked was why, in virtue of what quality, despite crippling naval disasters in the first Punic war, despite the virtual annihilation of whole Roman armies at Trasimene and at Cannae in the second, despite all the material wealth and resources of the Hellenistic kingdoms pitted against them, Romans always emerged victorious. This was the question which, in the history of Roman development down to the defeat of Macedon in the third Punic war, the period whose history he set out to write, Polybius tried to answer, and in his sixth book he answered it very well. The Roman government, whether he analysed its structure well or badly, had, as he rightly saw, great stability, and nowhere in the world was there any rival to Roman military training, armour and fighting methods on land; in particular the Roman army had an inbuilt advantage in being, unlike the Carthaginian, a citizen and allied, not a mercenary, force. Cynoscephalae had settled once and for all the question whether the phalanx or the legion was the more powerful fighting unit. The legion scored on the strength of flexibility and manoeuvrability.[7]

Polybius changed his mind about finishing his history with the year 167 BC and decided to continue it to 146. Again there were questions to be answered about Roman conduct once Rome had abolished the Macedonian monarchy and become the single unassailable world power. Was the lot of her subjects an acceptable one? (They would not have had to read Polybius, one would have thought, to find out.) And what would be the judgment of posterity on Roman use of supreme power once she had acquired it?[8]

His explicit answers to these vital questions – if he ever answered them – do not survive. His appreciation of the opening up of the Mediterranean world to travel, thanks to Roman dominion, may not be irrelevant.[9] As for the 'period of troubles' with which his history ended, there is nothing to show that he disapproved of Rome's Machiavellian tactics in dealing with Ptolemy VI and Ptolemy VIII of Egypt in 162, of Rome's blatant partiality in arbitrating between Massinissa and Carthage or of the brutal suppression, in the end, of Macedon and Carthage alike. In the case of Carthage – as of Numantia, about 'which he was to write a monograph – one of his 'white men', Scipio Aemilianus, a man in fact as hard-hearted as his father Aemilius Paullus, was involved as Roman hero. As for the overthrow of his own Achaea, the state to which he owed the deepest personal loyalty, he acquiesced on the ground that it was the fault of criminally irresponsible Achaean politicians and that, if it was to be done, it was best done quickly.[10]

Patron of Polybius, Scipio Aemilianus was patron too of Panaetius, the first of the two distinguished Rhodian Stoics to come to Rome and be accepted in the highest social circles. He came round 144 BC, accompanied Scipio on his famous eastern diplomatic tour to Egypt,

Syria, Asia Minor and Greece in 140-138[11] and after that until his death he divided his time between Rome and Athens, where he became head of the Stoa. He evidently acquired fluent knowledge of Latin.[12]

What was it, we should like to know, which brought him to Rome in the first place? He wrote an important book on Moral Duty, of which Cicero later made great use in his *De Officiis* and he is not likely to have been a critic of the Roman governing class or, indeed, of Roman rule; but we have no concrete evidence of his views.[13]

We know what first brought his pupil Posidonius, another brilliant Stoic philosopher in the making, to Rome; he came as an ambassador from Rhodes in the last gruesome weeks of the life of Marius. After that he became a visitor to Rome and travelled into the western Empire, to Gaul and to Spain.[14] He was not, perhaps, as much a friend of Rome as a friend of a number of eminent Romans, the exiled Rutilius Rufus, by whose views he was evidently much influenced, Cicero and Pompey among them.

He decided to write a continuation of Polybius' history and was, indeed, 'the only notable professional philosopher of antiquity to write a monumental account of recent history'.[15] He shared Polybius' deep interest in geography and as a philosopher – a charge which nobody would ever have brought against Polybius – and a believer in the fundamental equality of man, he concerned himself intimately with the social and ethnic life of peoples in the Empire, in writing of which he was an important *Bahnbrecher*. His book, indeed, whether Posidonius was conscious of this or not, supplied an answer to those very questions which, in the second part of his *History* Polybius posed and which, as far as we know, he left unanswered: how good and how bad was life under the Empire for Rome's new provincial subjects?

In his outlook Posidonius was anything but unfair. He castigated the bad features of Roman life, a general degeneration from austerity to indulgence,[16] and of Roman administration, many of them features which Romans themselves had no hesitation in castigating in public: the shortcomings in Roman foreign policy which had allowed the growth of piracy and the slave-trade; the cruel treatment of slaves which led to outbursts such as the Sicilian slave revolts;[17] and the oppression and exploitation of provincials by Italian and Roman businessmen and Roman tax-collectors, one branch of the equestrian order.[18] Which led him to a very one-sided and unfavourable view of Gaius Gracchus (and, perhaps under the influence of his aristocratic Roman friends, of Tiberius Gracchus too).[19]

On the other hand, he recognised Rome's achievement in suppressing brigandage in Spain and generally humanising life in the Iberian peninsula and he recognised the existence of Roman politicians and administrators of far-sightedness and integrity and praised their efforts; in particular it seems that he showed warm

approval of Pompey's act in settling the captured pirates on the land
in the hope that with a change in occupation their characters might be
reformed (a policy long remembered, and sometimes criticised by
Romans themselves[20]). If, as is thought by many, Posidonius' *History*
did not come down as far as this,[21] and he made Pompey the subject of
a special monograph, evidence of his admiration for Pompey is all the
stronger.

Posidonius' book was an extremely good book, and that was why
the compiler Diodorus, who knew a good book when he saw one,
made it his main source in writing about Rome after 146 BC. On the
other hand it may not have been an easy book to read and to use, and
it is significant that Strabo later started his own Roman history from
the point where Polybius finished[22] and not from the end of
Posidonius' work. So, despite its réclame, Posidonius' book survives
only where it has been used or quoted by later writers, in particular by
Diodorus, Strabo and Plutarch.

In view of the fact that what Posidonius wrote is only preserved for us
at second hand and that, on the period when he used him, the history
of Diodorus survives only in a relatively small number of fragments,
and that, in the case of Polybius, we have, after book 6, only a small
part of the last thirty-four of his forty books, it is not particularly
profitable to speculate about the aspects of Rome and Roman history
which may have been neglected by either writer.[23] There is no
evidence, for instance, that Polybius or Posidonius touched on early
Roman creative literature; but, apart from the fact that Polybius
shows no interest at all in culture of any kind,* he – and Posidonius –
if asked the question, would probably have answered, as most Greeks
would have answered, that, by comparison with Greek, there was no
Roman culture worth describing. Polybius shows no understanding of
policy-making, of the in-fighting between conflicting views and
interests in the Senate, nor in any surviving passage does he describe
the structure of Roman administration (*municipia*, colonies, Latins,
socii, brands of *civitas*) outside the central government itself. In this
respect – assuming that he never wrote about such things – Dionysius
of Halicarnassus was to steal a march on him.

Of Dionysius' tediously long twenty books of early Roman history
(the *Antiquitates*), on the other hand, more than half has been fully
preserved.† A profound literary scholar, intimate with the histories of
Herodotus and Thucydides in particular, admiring the first, his
compatriot, at the expense of the second, he knew exactly how history
should be written; the only trouble was that he could not write it. He
lacked the scholarly judgment and instinct of a true historian; his

---

* Except, perhaps, in the case of the musical Arcadians (4, 20f.).

† The first ten books and most of book 11; after that, there are a limited number of fragments.

delight was to strut through the past inserting interminable oratorical masterpieces into the mouths of historical characters. He was the man who declared that nobody could read as bad a stylist as Polybius from cover to cover.[24]

Given the man, his aspiration to be the second small-town boy of Halicarnassus to achieve international fame as a historian, is easy to understand. He went to Rome to teach rhetoric; what was it there that first turned his interest to Rome's past? Whatever that first impulse, he looked and found an – anyhow for a Greek – practically unexplored territory to annex: Roman history down to the point where Polybius started to tell the story. His subject was in the field of Foundation-literature (*Ktiseis*), a *genre* which, for himself, Polybius eschewed, while admitting that it was never without wide popular appeal.[25]

Dionysius went to Rome and was there from 30 BC, when he was, perhaps, rising thirty, until at least 7 BC, when the publication of his history started.[26] He mastered the Latin language (obviously) and with Q. Aelius Tubero, the jurisconsult and historian, father of the consul of 11 BC, as a friend,[27] he was clearly at home in cultured Roman society. Rome was at the time a nest of historical singing-birds. The Sicilian Greek Diodorus was perhaps still there, writing – or patching together from the best books available – a universal Graeco-Roman history to finish with the consulship of Julius Caesar and his conquest of Gaul. Livy was hard at work – did Dionysius know him? – and so was Asinius Pollio; and there was also Valerius Messalla Corvinus.

Dionysius, primarily a stylist, lacked the austere interests of a constitutional historian; at the same time his mistakes show how difficult it was for a foreigner to understand some aspects of Roman life, even if he lived as long in Rome as Dionysius did. He confused senators and patricians, *patrum auctoritas* and *senatus consultum*.[28]

He accepted the view that Roman rule was based on the right of the stronger to govern the weaker.[29] This success was Rome's own achievement, not to be explained in terms of luck,[30] a point underlined by Dionysius as it had been by Polybius before him (see p.195); and, so far from being in any sense barbarians, the Romans were Greeks in origin and were, in fact, in some ways *plus grecs que les Grecs*.[31]

They were better than Greeks in that, so far from nurturing any jealous exclusiveness, they were generous in the extension of their citizenship, even to defeated peoples. This, and the relationship of patron and client, extended from domestic society into their foreign relations, were basic factors of Roman success.[32] In seeing this, Dionysius supplied a gap in Polybius' history, for Polybius had not made this point at all.

Other aspects in which the Romans were better than the Greeks were the achievement of political compromise in early days; their religion (altogether free from the horrific myths which disfigured

Greek religion); the fact that in public life the sins of the fathers were not visited on their children; their impressive funeral orations* (not restricted to the cases of men killed in war); the modesty of their young athletes who wore loin-cloths and did not compete naked like Greeks.[33]

In the period of Roman history of which he wrote, Dionysius found nothing to criticise; since those days, he had to admit, as Polybius had admitted and as all Roman historians admitted, there had been changes which were not changes for the good. Who would prefer the modern type of war-lord to Cincinnatus, a simple ploughman† when he was not in military uniform? And as a Greek viewing the Roman freedman *ab extra* (for there was no Greek counterpart) and approving of the institution of freedmen in general, Dionysius was shocked by the manner in which in the contemporary world slaves of very bad character indeed became Roman citizens overnight at the whim of their often irresponsible masters (see p.87).[34]

Except for its – a Roman would have said, typically Greek – verbosity, Romans can have found little in Dionysius' book to criticise; some young Romans, indeed, may have realised the author's hope that, by reading of their heroic ancestors, they would be inspired to give a better account of themselves in public service.[35]

But this was not the main reason for which Dionysius wrote.[36] He wrote primarily for Greeks, to correct widespread Greek ignorance of Rome and to show Greeks that Romans were like themselves except in as far as, success apart, they were in a number of respects rather better.

While Dionysius spent at least twenty-three years in Rome, Diodorus by his own account had spent thirty. A Greek from Agyrium in Sicily, he had already learnt Latin before he came to Rome, which with its extensive records had the same sort of attraction for him that Athens had once had for Timaeus.[37]

His project was no small one: to write a world-history** from the beginning down to Julius Caesar's conquest of Gaul, a history which would meet a need since no existing world-history came down later than the Hellenistic period and most, indeed, ended with the death of Alexander.[38] A less ambitious man might have made that his starting-point, instead of retracing ground already very fully covered. He had been to Egypt round 60 BC; beyond that there is nothing to bear out his claim (in the Polybian tradition) to have been a great traveller.[39] His book was called 'The Library' because unashamedly, as he moved down from period to period and subject to subject, he found what seemed to him the best book existing and pirated it.

---

* Polybius, too, had laid stress on this (6, 53f.).

† The elder Pliny (*NH* 18, 21) fancifully pictures the saddened soil lamenting that, instead of being ploughed by a Cincinnatus, it is at the mercy of branded slave labourers on great estates.

** In 40 books; 15 are fully preserved (1-5; 11-20) and there are fragments of the others.

Though he was no enemy of Rome, he took no trouble to be sycophantic. Early on he referred to the superiority of Greek over 'barbarian languages' (which presumably included Latin) and of Alexandria he stated baldly that many people considered it the greatest city in the world.[40] Though Polybius was his main source for Roman history before Posidonius, he did not use his account of the first Punic war but instead – as a loyal Sicilian Greek patriot? – used the account of Philinus of Agrigentum; his account of the war is an account, therefore, from the standpoint not of Rome but of her enemy.[41]

And he pulled no punches where Roman failings and degeneration were concerned, contrasting the honesty of Aemilius Paullus with the greed of later Roman administrators, the initial generosity of Romans to the peoples whom they conquered with the terrorism of the mid- and late-second century of which Macedon, Carthage, Corinth and Numantia were the victims; and describing the degeneration of Roman character, the growth of luxury and avarice in relation to 91 BC (though – a surprising remark – some provincial administrators still showed great integrity). This in the spirit of (and perhaps derived from) Posidonius.[42]

We know nothing of Diodorus' life at Rome, not even its exact date, which must have been at the time of the civil wars (a reason, perhaps, why he ended his book where he did). He was an alien, and evidently just as free, in a book published from Rome, to criticise aspects of Roman life as were Romans themselves, Sallust and, every now and then, Livy.

Two Greek historians enjoyed close association with Augustus himself.

With the sharp-tongued Timagenes we have dealt already (p.183).

Nicolaus of Damascus[43] was a man of very different type, according to everything that we know about him (and in one way or another nearly all our knowledge comes ultimately from his own pen), a quite admirable person: a Peripatetic philosopher and distinguished Aristotelian scholar (he wrote a book on plants); a tutor to the best families (to Antony's and Cleopatra's twins in the thirties BC and a sort of companion-tutor and adviser to Herod the Great, a man some ten years older than himself); a most skilful diplomat, as M. Agrippa would have testified.* Augustus sampled his quality when he came to Rome first with Agrippa in 12 BC, then, alone, to defend Herod against charges made by Arabs and finally, after Herod's death, in support of the claims of Archelaus to succeed Herod the Great in 4 BC, and he knew by report of the humane efforts which Nicolaus had

---

* In 14 BC in Ionia Nicolaus persuaded M. Agrippa both to remit a fine which, in ignorance of the true facts, he had imposed on the city of Ilium and, as Herod's mouthpiece, though no Jew himself, to confirm for the Jews of Asia Minor all the special privileges which, though granted already by the Roman government, the Greeks were disregarding.[47]

made, however vainly, to arrest the impetuous anger which led Herod at the end of his life to execute three of his sons in succession. It is possible that from 4 BC until his death, which was later than that of Augustus, he took up permanent residence in Rome (where he was criticised for preferring the company of lower-class people to that of the rich; he said that he met more honest people that way).

More than all this, his output as a historian and writer would not have disgraced a man who played no part at all in public life: a vast world-history coming down to his own time, in 144 books; a book on the individual peculiarities of different peoples (*Ethôn Synagôgê*);[44] an autobiography, written at the end of his life,[45] and, most important for us because quite a lot of it survives, a monograph on the upbringing (very much, in the best Roman tradition, at his mother's apron-strings) and early career of Augustus, through Caesar's death to the assertion of his own claim to be Caesar's successor.[46] This last book, which made full use of Augustus' own account of his early life as well as of other sources, was evidently written in Augustus' lifetime and published after Augustus' death.[48]

As far as prominent Romans of the late Republic were concerned, Nicolaus, in his world-history, could be openly critical; he gave a vivid description, for instance, of the self-indulgence which marked the life of Lucullus in retirement.[49] But in his speech on behalf of the Jews before M. Agrippa, recorded for us by Josephus, he praised the humanity of Roman imperialism – people were better off than they had been under the Hellenistic kings – and in his biography, which is in fact a panegyric, of Augustus he wrote that his youthful decision to accept adoption as Caesar's heir was 'the beginning of good for him and for all men, above all for his country and for the whole Roman people'.[50]

Strabo was a contemporary of Nicolaus – 'Strabo the Cappadocian', though in fact he was born at Amaseia in Pontus, or 'Strabo the philosopher', for he was a Stoic. He came to Rome first round the age of twenty before the death of Julius Caesar and remained there for a long time, nine or ten years perhaps, this being the time, probably, when he studied under Tyrannio. His subsequent travels, from which he returned to Rome from time to time, extended from Tuscany to Armenia and from the Euxine to the Ethiopian border; he never travelled, as Polybius and Posidonius travelled, in the western provinces of the Empire. It is possible that he settled down in old age to live in Naples. He was a geographer and also an historian; his Geography in 17 books survives; his History, written earlier, does not, except for a few fragments.[51]

Coming with good social credentials from the East, he was evidently at home in good society in Rome. He knew Cn. Piso, consul in 7 BC, the man whom Augustus considered a possible successor to himself (and who died, accused of treason, under Tiberius), and he may well have met and spoken to Augustus.[52] He travelled through

Egypt with the Governor (the equestrian Aelius Gallus), and accompanied him also on his unsuccessful Arabian expedition in 24 BC. After which, he spent eleven years in Alexandria, and then returned to Rome.

He was the first of Rome's Greek historians to acquire Roman citizenship, presumably from Aelius Gallus (who may have adopted Sejanus and Strabo's name may have been borrowed from that of Sejanus' natural father, Seius Strabo).[53]

In his History, *Historika Hypomnêmata*, he evidently made Polybius his model. His main subject (history after 146, when Polybius' account ended) in 43 books was prefaced, like Polybius' History, by an introduction (*proparaskeuê*) in four books. He wrote history and geography, just as Polybius wrote, primarily for the guidance of practical men of affairs, for the Roman governing class; indeed he criticised Roman historians (by contrast with their Greek counterparts) for not showing sufficient interest in geography.* [54]

He concluded his Geography with a factual account of the structure of Roman imperial government under Augustus, Roman expansion, of which he had given a summary earlier, being ascribed to military prowess and 'statesmanlike rulership'. In this earlier passage he had attributed Rome's escape from the anarchical conditions of civil war to the strength of the constitution and to the calibre of outstanding Romans.[55]

About one fact he had no doubt at all, that Rome was a civilising power and that the Roman empire brought to a great part of the world far more settled conditions and greater economic prosperity than had existed before, and that the Roman army was a guarantor of internal peace. This was very particularly the case in Spain and in Egypt, the province which – apart, presumably, from his own – he knew best. And it was true elsewhere; the trade routes east of Damascus, for instance, thanks to military surveillance, were more free from brigandage than they had been before.[56] Only once was he critical of Roman administrators; those sent to the north of the Black Sea were negligent in dealing with piracy, less effective than native princes in the area.[57]

He accepted without criticism the fact that the standard type of administration which Rome imposed on her provinces involved the disappearance of the diverse institutions of much of the old free world, the very distinctive social-political life of Crete, for instance.[58]

Once he indulged in special pleading for the Romans, claiming that they were not responsible for the wild prevalence of piracy in the eastern Mediterranean early in the first century BC, because they relied on the Syrian kings who in the event were broken reeds, and they themselves had too many urgent problems nearer home to be

---

* Compare Pliny's criticism (*NH* 5, 12) of Roman administrators for their failure, because of lack of interest, to add to geographical knowledge.

able to interfere. Such an explanation, which takes no account of Rome's deliberate weakening of the Rhodian and the Syrian fleets which might have policed the eastern Mediterranean, cannot carry much conviction.[59]

History, Nicolaus told Herod, was a good thing even for a king to be interested in, and Juba II of Mauretania was to be such a king; 'no monarch ever,' Plutarch wrote, 'was such a historian.'[60] He and his wife Cleopatra Selene (one of the twins born to Cleopatra in 40 BC, over whose earliest education Nicolaus himself had presided) are two of the most fascinating characters in early Roman imperial history; both in childhood had walked ignominiously through the streets of Rome as prisoners, he at the age of about six in Julius Caesar's triumph, she a little older in the triumph of Octavian after Actium. He was brought up in Rome with powerful friends and was with Octavian at Actium. He received Roman citizenship.* In 25 BC he was made king first of Numidia (which had been his father's kingdom) but soon, in exchange, of Mauretania. Round 20 BC he married Cleopatra, who had inherited much of her mother's spirit and in Mauretania was more than a consort; she was a queen. He was king for 48 years until AD 23, when he died (a little before Strabo finished his History),[61] and the Mauretanians in true Mauretanian fashion made him a god.[62] In all these 48 years he had been more than a very good king; he was, in the elder Pliny's words, 'even more memorable on account of the distinction of his studies than as a ruler'.[63]

There was, it seems, no limit to his scholarly interests. He wrote books on the Assyrians, on north Africa and its peoples (a useful source even on elephants for the elder Pliny), on the Theatre, on Painting, and even a monograph on spurge (to which he gave its name, Euphorbia).

We know of these books only from quotations, as is the case with his works which had a direct bearing on Rome: his account of Arabia, written specifically for the young prince C. Caesar, to put him wise about the part of the world which in BC 2/1 he set out to conquer; his *Roman History* in two books† and his 'Similarities', a work of comparative sociology which was a source for Plutarch's *Roman Questions*. All his books were written in Greek, not Latin.[64]

His reputation has come under assault from modern scholarship. He was no better, it seems, than an 'aristocratic dilettante', doing rather amateurishly what Alexander Polyhistor had done professionally; he was, in fact, what Collingwood would have called a 'scissors-and-paste historian', clipping together cuttings from other people's books and contributing nothing original himself. He does not

---

* As we know only from the existence of inscriptions of his freedwomen, who were Iuliae, *CIL* VIII, 21086ff.

† Perhaps on early, legendary Rome, for two quotations in Plutarch on the period of the second Punic war and on Sulla (*FGH* 275, F. 25, 27) may have come from Juba's 'Similarities'.

seem to have read Varro; doubt is even expressed as to whether he knew Latin.[65]

But this is to go too far. It is inconceivable that, brought up from the age of six in Rome, he should not have known Rome and Latin well, even if – influenced, perhaps, by his strong-minded Hellenistic wife – he preferred to write in Greek.* The chorus of praise for his scholarship in antiquity – Pliny, Plutarch, Athenaeus – cannot be disregarded. And though none of the surviving fragments is in praise of Rome, it cannot be believed that he wrote of Rome and of the imperial house, to whom he owed his startlingly successful career, with anything but praise.

For others, Rome, which he visited twice (once in the principate of Vespasian, once in that of Domitian), might be the centre of the world, but not for Plutarch. There were forays to Athens for books and to Delphi to discharge his priestly duties there, but the centre of his quiet, kindly, studious and admirably balanced life was his birthplace, the little town of Chaeronea in Boeotia.

The Romans, whose language he had not had the time to master thoroughly when he visited Italy,[66] gave him no feeling of inferiority. He was, after all, thanks to the consular L. Mestrius Florus,† a Roman citizen himself, Mestrius Plutarchus, though he did nothing to draw attention to the fact.[67] More than this, if the Suda and Eusebius are to be trusted, he received an official appointment (perhaps as procurator) in Achaea towards the end of his life from Trajan, and was honoured with *consularia ornamenta*.

Further, he was on terms of very close friendship with Q. Sosius Senecio, one of the most distinguished Romans alive, an intimate associate of the emperor Trajan and one of his two or three top generals, a man also of the broadest culture. To Sosius Plutarch dedicated his 'Table Talk' (*Quaestiones Conviviales*) and, more important, his *Parallel Lives*.[68]

Plutarch was perfectly ready to criticise Romans where criticism was proper and in the case of the Flavian emperors, now dead, he did not hesitate to criticise. Vespasian had cancelled Nero's gift of Independence to Greece and, by the account of her son, whom Plutarch met at Delphi, he had been singularly cruel to the noble wife of Julius Sabinus, the Gallic rebel. Domitian's expenditure on his vast new imperial palace, the *Domus Augustiana*, was reprehensible.[69]

In general, however, he admired the Roman achievement – it is absurd, as has been seen (p.179), to think that he ascribed it simply to luck – and he respected the Roman administration. Though he may have sighed over the decline of the Greek city-states to a position of

---

* The legends on his coins are in Latin, on hers in Greek.

† Proconsul of Asia in AD 83/4, the man who tried to teach Vespasian how to speak Latin properly (see p.128, n.). Plutarch travelled in north Italy, visiting the battlefield of Bedriacum, in his company on one of his visits to Italy.

political impotence in the world in which he lived, he faced the fact with resignation. In the shadow of the omnipotent Roman governor, the authorities in individual Greek cities were concerned with no more than trifles; yet it was a mistake to toady to Roman governors, most of whom were good men, though it was prudent to be on good terms with them. Greeks should count their blessings, the disappearance of recurrent local warfare and the prevalence of peace.[70]

Plutarch lived at a revolutionary moment in the history of the wealthy upper class in the Greek East, the time when many of them were deserting parochialism in favour of Roman imperial government, entering the Senate, holding magistracies and, at first mainly in the East, governing provinces and commanding armies. This is something to which he never refers. For himself, he had no such ambition, for in his eyes a public career at that level was a rat-race and the careerist, however great his success, was doomed in most cases to end up a disappointed man for he yearned inevitably for greater success still. This was the fate of all those who trod the corridors of power; a king was not satisfied with being a king, he would like to be a god.[71]

Instead Plutarch extolled the quiet life, though at the same time a life of service to a man's city or community, where the highest possible achievement was *homonoia* and the greatest possible disaster civil strife. Instead of dreaming about reviving the great achievements of Greek independence in the past, the local councillor should recognise the unshakeable and unassailable power of the Roman government, making friends of important Romans, as Plutarch himself had been most conspicuously successful in doing (a man's city might always benefit from such a connexion), not calling on proconsuls for the solution of trifling local problems because, as Dio of Prusa also emphasised, the Romans liked their subjects to show independence in the control of their own affairs.[72]

A philosopher, a quidnunc, an antiquarian, a man who questioned the origin and meaning of every belief and practice which came to his notice, he wrote some two hundred essays and dialogues, of which roughly half survive and constitute his *Moralia*. He also embarked on a series of biographies – biographies of Augustus and of the early Roman emperors (of which *Galba* and *Otho* survive) and the *Parallel Lives*, most of which have survived.[73]

Plutarch was a biographer with a number of purposes, the most important being to edify and improve his readers.* The *Lives* were Cautionary Tales, inspirations and deterrents in one. They were character-sketches of great men who had performed on the big historial stage before large audiences; the best of them had a blemish or two, the worst (Demetrius Poliorcetes and Antony, for instance) were not without strong redeeming features. It was in the characters of these men as displayed in the historical drama rather than in the

---

* Dionysius of Halicarnassus had had the same edifying object (see p. 199).

historical drama itself – that is to say, 'history' – that Plutarch was interested; the most trivial facts, if they illustrated character, facts too insignificant for a historian to mention, might for Plutarch's purpose be the most illuminating of all.[74]

He had the further purpose of emphasising that Rome had no monopoly of great men; the days of Freedom had produced Greeks of comparable stature. And so it was Plutarch's plan to present his heroes in pairs, a Greek and a Roman side by side, first the pictured career of one, then the pictured career of the other, like a diptych, with, finally, a short 'Comparison' to frame the two of them together.

Sometimes the pair was a matching pair (Demosthenes and Cicero, for instance); more often, not. The series started, naturally enough, with that great Boeotian hero Epaminondas, matched against the elder Scipio Africanus; these *Lives* are lost, together – probably – with Plutarch's introduction to the whole series.

The amount of research and reading called for (as for some of the *Moralia* essays, like the *Greek* and *Roman Questions*) was obviously large. Plutarch's knowledge of Latin was not perfect, as he admitted in explanation of the fact that he did not feel competent to make any authoritative comparison of the oratorical genius of Demosthenes and Cicero, and it has been conjectured that among those who devilled for him were some whose knowledge of Latin was greater than his and that these men may have supplied him with a great deal of his Roman material (see p.127).

Though the maternal grandfather of Dio Cocceianus (Dio Chrysostom) of Prusa in Bithynia, a friend, perhaps, of the emperor Claudius, was a Roman citizen, as was Dio's mother, he himself, like his affluent father, was not.[75] He was, indeed, a Greek of Greeks, dividing humanity, even when addressing a Roman emperor, into Greeks and barbarians.

He went from his native Prusa to Rome to teach rhetoric and paid the penalty for moving there in the highest court circles, for when, perhaps in AD 84, Domitian executed his cousin Flavius Sabinus and made his widow, his own niece, his mistress, Dio, involved in Sabinus' downfall, was banished by Domitian not only from Rome and Italy but also from his native Bithynia. Exile – more than ten years of it, spent on the Danube – turned him into a philosopher, a Cynic.*

Under gentle Nerva philosophy and the government were reconciled and Dio was recalled. He greeted the birth of the happy new age by addressing Trajan after his accession in four orations on Kingship, a subject on which personal inexperience did not prevent philosophers from posing as experts. Two of these orations were largely concerned with Alexander the Great, a hero in the second (*vis-à-vis* his father), no hero at all in the fourth (but who could be *vis-à-vis* the

---

* Before his exile he had been a pupil of Musonius Rufus.[76]

hard-hitting Diogenes?). The third, in particular, was friendly and laudatory to Trajan, who knew well enough that listening to, or reading, sermons from philosophers on the one hand and panegyrics from well-intentioned sycophants like the younger Pliny on the other was an enforced penalty of rule. It is to be doubted whether he was either influenced or impressed by being told that fish was no food for heroes, that he must aspire to be not a lion but a bull, or that he found anything original in the suggestion that a good ruler needed to surround himself with a number of trustworthy adjutants.

A tedious and verbose itinerant pedagogue with a mawkish sense of humour, Dio was never more eloquent in his public orations than when he was wielding a big stick. Six of the best for Athenians because they enjoyed defiling the theatre of Dionysus with the blood of gladiators; six of the best for Rhodes for devising a system of extensive and costless generosity (re-dedicating one of the island's odd three thousand honorary statues for any Roman whom it chose to honour); six of the best for the citizens of Alexandria for frivolity and the hysterical excitement which they displayed at concerts and horse-races; six of the best for the citizens of Tarsus (which most people would have described as a leading cultural centre of the eastern Mediterranean) for wantonness and snorting; six of the best for the Romans because they were grossly materialistic and needed a better educational system.[77]

Though he moved in court circles in Rome after as before his banishment and had, as Plutarch recommended, a number of important Roman friends, of whom, perhaps, he sometimes spoke a little too loudly,[78] Dio was a Greek of Greeks, looking back to the golden age of Greek achievement, ignorant of – and uninterested in – the history and culture of Rome. As has been seen (p.126), Numa, the philosopher-king, was the only historical Roman whose name he mentioned.

In their attitude to the rule of Rome, particularly as it affected the Greeks, Dio and Plutarch had a lot in common.[79] They saw no point in crying for the moon, indulging in nostalgic dreams of the great past of independent Greek states as if that past could be revived. The Roman empire was there to stay, and there was much to be said in its favour, in particular for the achievement of peace and the end of the once endemic destruction of human life and property in piffling little wars. City walls might now collapse, and there was no need to rebuild them thanks to peace, the object of universal prayer, and subjection to Rome, *douleia* of which there was nothing to be ashamed.[80] The enlarged world was at last one, thanks to the achievement first of Alexander, then of Rome.[81]

Though there had been shocking Romans in high places (Nero and Domitian) and provincial governors were not always as reputable as they should be, the Romans as a people had, by Dio's admission, great qualities of power, fortune, justice and benevolence.[82]

Arrian[83] – Flavius Arrianus, for his father had acquired Roman citizenship – is one of the most attractive figures of the Graeco-Roman world; humanist, huntsman and top-level administrator in one. Nicomedia in Bithynia was his birthplace and here he received his first education; after which Epictetus at Nicopolis was his master and all through his life Xenophon was so much his cultural model that he was called 'the second Xenophon'. Without Arrian's writing we should know next to nothing of Epictetus' teaching; and without his *Anabasis* (not of the Ten Thousand this time, but of Alexander) we should have little idea what Alexander's two main historians, Ptolemy and Aristobulus, wrote about him.

His Boswellian record of Epictetus' improving talk, some half of which survives, was evidently published, whether or not by his contrivance, quite early in his life. For the rest, there are two conflicting opinions, the first that his life was segmented and that it was only after his public career ended – he was consul suffect in 129 or 130, after which for a number of years he governed Cappadocia, where he fought and repelled an invasion of Alani – that he settled down in Athens, a citizen and eponymous archon in 145/6, to produce work after work, the *Anabasis* of Alexander, eight books on his native Bithynia, seventeen on Parthia and a great deal more.[84]

The conflicting and more plausible opinion is that his life was not compartmentalised at all; that it was his general culture, his 'philosophy', which recommended him to Hadrian as having the right qualifications for a public career, and that he was writing and publishing books all through his active public life as well as after his retirement.[85] We can be certain of the date of his *Periplous* of the Euxine, written in Greek and sent to Hadrian to accompany the official report of his voyage of inspection in the south-east of the Black Sea which he submitted in Latin as governor of Cappadocia.

There is one passage in his not particularly original book on *Tactics* in which he expressed his admiration of one particular Roman quality; this was Roman adaptability and readiness to adopt any foreign practice, particularly in armour and tactics, which seemed to them to be better than their own. He even coupled with this Rome's ready acceptance of foreign religious cults[86] (something which later, in the first book of his *Civitas Dei*, St Augustine was to mock).

Rome is the subject of one great, however flaccid, panegyric, the twenty-sixth (Roman) oration of the Mysian hypochondriac Aelius Aristides, delivered in Rome probably in AD 143 during the consulship of his friend Herodes Atticus, quite early in the rule of Antoninus Pius.[87] It has been described as 'a hymn of praise for the ideal state'. There is nothing in it to suggest that Aristides knew anything at all about Roman history or that he was interested in the city of Rome itself.

In this – quite obviously genuine – panegyric the Roman genius is described as a natural flair for ruling such as no other people in history had possessed and which in the contemporary world existed in others only in as far as it had rubbed off on them from Rome.[88]

Of this a constituent element was the Roman conception of citizenship, something which Dionysius of Halicarnassus had stressed.[89]

From the Roman genius followed the Roman achievement – by far the largest empire ever, an empire on which the sun never set – living at peace instead of erupting all over in a lot of silly, wasteful, futile little wars;[90] a world of cities, many of them Roman foundations, all of them adorned with striking modern buildings[91] – the schools and *fora*, of which Tacitus approved, and the gymnasia, of which Tacitus did not approve at all. Over this vast area travel was easy and free from danger, a benefit of Roman rule which Polybius had stressed. You could only feel sorry for people outside the bounds of the Roman empire who were denied this good life.[92]

And what made possible this life of peace and well-being? The Roman army, a standing, professional, not a mercenary, army, remote, out of sight, a wall of iron along the frontiers[93] – a wall which, long after the delivery of this speech but in Aelius Aristides' lifetime, was to be gravely breached.

'Can any good thing come out of Nazareth?' Or out of Alexandria, most emperors and administrators with experience of Egypt would have asked? In the second century AD, in the person of Appian, it did. A friend of Fronto (perhaps from Fronto's student days in Alexandria) he came to Rome and, evidently completely bilingual, practised as a barrister (*causidicus*), received Roman citizenship and, at the solicitation of Fronto, Antoninus Pius gave him a procuratorship in his old age – whether honorary or not, we do not know – and he acquired Roman knighthood.[94]

During perhaps the last ten years of Antoninus Pius' rule, before men's confidence in world-wide peace and stability, the Roman achievement which Aelius Aristides had extolled, was shattered by the first barbarian invasions, Appian was at work on a vast history of Roman expansion from the first beginnings down to the establishment of monarchic government by Augustus and, briefly, the further expansion under the Emperors. So far from shedding a tear over the downfall of the Republic at the end of a century of civil war, he extolled the imperial government which had taken its place, the government which was responsible for the happiness of the time in which he lived.[95]

His method, like that of Diodorus, was to find a succession of good sources and to follow them closely, interspersing from time to time his own, often inept, comments.[96] What is interesting about the structure of his work is that he abandoned the kind of annalistic history which most Romans had written and which Cassius Dio was to write later.

Whether under the influence of Ephorus (who had done something like this) or of Dionysius of Halicarnassus' criticism of the chronological rigidity of Thucydides' narrative, or whether the idea, a highly original one, was his own, he wrote a series of monographs on the peoples and countries whom Rome successively conquered from their first contact with Rome to their absorbtion into the Roman empire, so that his readers could concentrate on one subject at a time instead of having to jump about like fleas from events in one part of the world to events in other parts. The work concluded with five books on Roman history during the civil wars from 133 to 35 BC which survive, and then four more books which are lost, one on Egypt, to conclude with Actium and the end of the Ptolemies, a book called 'The Century' (*Hekatontaetia*), perhaps a sketch of the period from Augustus to Trajan and finally a Dacian and an Arabian history, to incorporate the successes of Trajan.

In his Preface to the whole work Appian ascribed Roman success, as others had done before him, to exceptional moral qualities and consistent good fortune (in Latin, *virtus* and *fortuna*); but he added other qualities: hard work (*phereponia*) and endurance of hardship (*talaiporia*)[97] – in vulgar language, sheer guts.

Pausanias,[98] who came either from Damascus or from western Asia Minor and who had travelled to Rome and south Italy as well as, extensively, in Greece and the eastern Mediterranean, wrote an almost perfect guide book to second-century AD Greece; he wrote in a chatterbox style, punctuating his account of the monuments of the country with vivid, often anything but accurate, digressions into history, with stories of Greek mythology and with aphorisms concerning human nature* and the world at large, with excellent anecdotes and accounts of such things as the natural phenomena which precede an earthquake.

It would, of course, have been easy for him to high-light the widespread poverty and desolation of contemporary mainland Greece and to criticise the Roman government under whose rule the country had sunk so low. Pausanias, however, seems to have felt no such temptation, for it is absurd to give a twist to a passage where the text almost certainly requires emendation and to think that he wrote of 'the misfortune of Roman rule'.[99] Sulla, the only Roman of whom he wrote with repulsion, he described as a most unroman Roman; 'he showed greater brutality than was to be expected from a Roman'; 'he behaved like a madman.' Pausanias reproduced contemporary Greek criticism of the first Roman commanders in Greece, Flamininus included, criticism which was to be found already in the pages of Polybius.[100]

* E.g. 7, 23, 3, 'If it is true that impassioned lovers who bathe in the water of the Selemnos in Achaea forget their passion, then this water is more valuable than a whole fortune in money.' Was Pausanias himself crossed in love? Cf. 7, 26, 8, 'Luck, not looks, secures success in love.'

There were three stages in the decline of Greek fortunes, Pausanias reckoned. There was first the irreparable havoc of the Peloponnesian war; after which there was the Macedonian conquest, and then the Roman.[101]

Pausanias' account of the last fifty years of Greek freedom before the Roman sack of Corinth in 146 BC, was perfectly fair and objective in its description of the lamentable folly of Romans and Greeks alike. Greeks were condemned for their readiness to accept bribes, this, in Pausanias' view, being a Greek failing which was evidenced at all stages of Greek history. The Romans were reasonably criticised for cruelty, disingenuousness bordering on dishonesty and for the transport to Italy of the thousand Achaean 'hostages'.[102] The responsibility for the final disaster was placed on the shoulders of the Greeks themselves; it was not just a misfortune (*Atychia*), which had been Polybius' word for it, it was the consequence of acts of lunacy (*mania*).[103]

There is no great emphasis on Roman looting of works of art, and it is clear that innumerable masterpieces of classical Greek art survived almost everywhere in Greece (see p.176). The thefts of Augustus even are condoned; he was doing no more than was done before him by all the great victors in history, Greek and barbarian alike.[104] As for the most notorious art-thieves, Sulla and Gaius Caligula, Pausanias noted with pious satisfaction that justice caught up with them; they died horrible deaths.[105]

Compared with Nero, however, they were only petty thieves. Nero, the matricide, was a criminal on the grand Platonic scale, a man of exceptional gifts, capable of great acts like the grant of independence to Greece. If only he had had a better education! And Vespasian represented a sad anti-climax, cancelling Nero's gift with the harsh observation that the Greeks had 'unlearnt freedom'.[106]

Pausanias did not in any way belittle the achievements of the Roman empire and there is no reason to think that his warm praise of Hadrian and of Antoninus Pius was anything but sincere. Antoninus Pius 'should, like Cyrus, be called the Father of Mankind'.[107]

With a consular father, the Bithynian Cassius Dio[108] was an established member of the Roman governing class; he himself was a senator under Commodus, was nominated for the praetorship by Pertinax in 193 and was consul under Septimius Severus. After holding the proconsulship of Africa and governing Dalmatia and Upper Pannonia, he was consul for the second time with Severus Alexander for colleague in AD 229. He had a villa near Capua, a good retreat for a writer (from round 196 to round 218 he was researching for and writing his great history of Rome to the death of Septimius Severus),[109] and after 229 he retired to live in Bithynia. He wrote when the calm assurance of imperial security, the background of Arrian, Appian, Aelius Aristides and Pausanias, had been shattered; the iron

wall had been breached and the future of the Empire was a matter of
anxious uncertainty.

He tells us how he came to be a historian. The most superstitious
man alive, believing that every dream and every portent had its
prophetic significance, he found a kindred spirit in Septimius Severus
who evidently communicated to him at his first accession the dreams
and portents which had strengthened his own aspiration to be
emperor. Dio worked the material into a monograph which Septimius
Severus approved and, encouraged by this first success, he wrote a
second monograph on events between the murder of Pertinax and
Septimius Severus' arrival in Rome. This too was a success.
Encouraging, compulsive dreams followed; he must write a full-scale
history of Rome – a work which, in the end, extended to eighty books,
much of which happily survives. And at some time or other, as an act of
pietas, he perhaps wrote a biography of Arrian, his Bithynian
forerunner both as imperial administrator and as writer.[110]

Fifty-one of the eighty books covered the Roman Republic, over
whose demise Dio shed no tears. Then came the new age of prosperity
inaugurated by Augustus. As he started to shape his book, he looked
forward to marking a second age of prosperity inaugurated by the rule
of Septimius Severus, but by the time Septimius Severus had dealt
with Pescennius Niger and Clodius Albinus and their followers, it was
clear that he was not a second Augustus; indeed the age of gold had
ended and an iron age had started at the death of Marcus Aurelius.[111]
There was the horror of Caracalla, the short rule of the Moorish
coward Macrinus and the fantasy of Elagabalus before, under Severus
Alexander, the Senate (and Dio as a prominent senator) saw better
days. But Dio was frightened by the newly enhanced power of the
army and when his own reputation as a harsh disciplinarian in
Dalmatia and Upper Pannonia inflamed the Praetorian Guard at
Rome, who had recently killed their commander Ulpian, Severus
Alexander allowed him to absent himself from Rome during the
tenure of his second consulship and after that to retire to Bithynia.[112]
This (AD 229) was the year to which Dio extended the narrative of his
history. Of the last books, the most valuable part of the work, a
senatorial eye-witness's account of the rule of the succession of
emperors from Commodus to Severus Alexander, little, alas, survives.

Dio's personality and outlook are stamped on what he wrote. There
are, first of all, the portents recorded at all stages of Rome's history
with the fanaticism of the true believer. There is a strong streak of
Stoicism, the belief that the good reputation of a good ruler lives after
him and is his best, indeed his only, memorial; for Dio had no truck at
all with the excesses, indeed with the ordinary trappings, of
'consecration' in ruler-cult.[113]

It has been opined that the long speech which he ascribes to Julius
Caesar when his troops threatened mutiny before the engagement
with Ariovistus at Vesontio in 58 BC is a statement of Dio's own belief,

in the world in which he lived, that aggressive imperialism was the only way of ensuring imperial security; and nobody has any doubt that the lengthy speech of Maecenas in book 52 (29 BC) delineating the kind of monarchy which Octavian should introduce, was Dio's own prescription for the proper stance of a constitutional emperor in his own day, Dio-Maecenas addressing Octavian-Severus Alexander.[114]

If Cassius Dio wrote no fervid panegyric of Rome, that was partly because, even more than Arrian and Appian, he felt himself to be in the direct Roman tradition. His modern biographer writes, 'His identification with Rome is complete and unquestioned and, just as hostility is unthought of, so praise is superfluous'.[115]

The surviving fragments of the end of Dio's work describe, with ominous prodigies and warnings, the birth of the new and menacing power of Persia on the eastern frontier and the breakdown of discipline and the loss of fighting spirit in the Roman army, that army on which the whole empire depended for its survival.[116]

There were other eminent Greeks (apart from Lucian, on whom see p.185) in the second half of the second century AD who had close friends among distinguished Romans or who lived in a Roman *ambiente*. Galen of Pergamon, that most distinguished of doctors and medical writers (nobody, according to Athenaeus had such a vast literary output), was in Rome from AD 162 to 166 and from 169 until his death at the end of the century; sensationally successful in his treatment of the wife of Flavius Boëthus the consular, he was court doctor to Marcus Aurelius (with a special care for Commodus when Marcus Aurelius went off to campaign in the North) and, by his own record, well known to the leading members of Roman society; his only *bêtes noires* were other doctors, Greeks like himself.

Athenaeus from Naucratis in Egypt, a civil servant (*procurator patrimonii*), made a Roman equestrian, P. Livius Larensis, host at the dinner described in the *Deipnosophists*. And in the third century there was Herodian, an imperial freedman perhaps from Antioch in Syria, who has left us an account of the reigns of the emperors from Marcus Aurelius to the accession of Gordian III; he was a born writer but, despite an occasional Thucydidean flourish and the insertion of fictitious speeches in the accepted historial tradition, he did not possess the first instincts of a true historian.[117]

One quality all these Greeks who wrote Roman history had in common – Arrian, Appian, Cassius Dio and Herodian. At one level or another, they knew from personal experience what the business of imperial administration was about. In this respect they have an advantage over their modern critics.

CHAPTER FOURTEEN

Different Peoples: their Looks and Habits[1]

(i) Looks

Though some Romans were taller than others (of early emperors both Tiberius and Gaius were tall, and so was Trajan) and one Roman might be mocked by another for being small, as Dolabella was mocked by his father-in-law Cicero, the average difference in height between Gallic and German soldiers on the one hand and Roman soldiers on the other was probably between two and three inches; so northerners were, from the Roman point of view, a race of giants and from the northerners' point of view the Romans were dwarfs. When Julius Caesar besieged their capital in 57 BC, the Atuatuci laughed at the sight of them: how could such little men handle such great siege-engines? They did not laugh for long.[2]

Britons were thought to be even taller than Gauls; so were Germans. The carrion-crows had never feasted on such gigantic corpses as when Marius defeated the Cimbri.[3]

How without their unrivalled training and discipline should tiny Romans have dared to confront German giants, Vegetius asked?[4]

The Romans saw nothing admirable about being big because size seemed, in Mediterranean conditions, to be the northerner's undoing. Even in the North, he did not know how to husband his strength; in a warm climate he ate too much and, parched by thirst, he drank too much, particularly of that wine which was not easy to obtain in his own country; and so he quickly put on weight. He could not stand the heat or the dust, but ran for shelter to the shade.[5] The Romans themselves, it would seem, adapted better to northern conditions, much as they disliked them.

Of Alpine Gauls Florus wrote that they were 'superhuman in size, with the spirit of wild beasts. At their first attack they are supermen but, after that, like women. With some resemblance to the snow on their own Alps, at the first heat of battle they break into sweat and after slight action they are, as it were, melted by the sun'.[6]

Yet in the case of individuals the Romans were impressed by height. Segestes, whom Germanicus rescued, was a huge man. And Velleius Paterculus, who saw the Parthian king Phraataces, tells us only one thing about him, that he was abnormally tall. And there were the recorded prodigies, men displayed at public shows in Rome, men from the East and taller even than Germans, one a Jew whom Columella saw, another an Arab nearly ten feet high recorded by the elder Pliny. The emperor Maximinus, a northerner, was a huge man.[7]

Northerners were palefaces, pale with fair hair; they were bleached by the cold north wind. The way to make yourself look like a northerner was to smear your face with chalk. The Romans, well sunburnt themselves unless they lived penned up in a large city like Rome, had something of a colour-prejudice against men who were pale. In the case of women, of course, it was a different matter: *femineus pallor*.[8]

Germans were even fairer than Gauls. Arminius' brother, serving as a Roman auxiliary soldier, acquired Roman citizenship. We do not know his name, but he was given the *cognomen* 'Flavus', 'Blondie'. Britons too were fair, but generally less so than Gauls; Boudicca's strikingly fair hair reached down to her waist.[9]

Red hair and fair hair were marks of the northerner; he was *rutilus* or *flavus*. Because so many of the Scotch had red hair, Tacitus inferred their German origin. Thracians, too, were apt to be red-haired, and slaves from this part of the world often had the name Rufus or Rufio; indeed in Roman comedy slaves wore red wigs.[10]

The further south you moved, the darker was people's hair, and it was very unusual to find a red-head in Egypt.[11] By smart Roman women fair hair was much admired and some of them were artificial blondes, having imported from Germany the soap used by German women to improve the tint of their hair.[12]

Like Greeks (who had a variety of coiffures; you could identify a Spartan by his hair-style), northerners wore their hair long, as indeed Romans themselves had done until the third century BC.[13] After that, Romans thought long hair old-fashioned or barbaric. Northern Gaul they called 'Long-haired Gaul', Gallia Comata. Only philosophers – and fancy-boys – wore long hair in Roman households. The proper place for long fair hair was in the servants' quarters, not in the Senate; so Synesius wrote around AD 400 in disparagement of Roman senators from 'Scythia'.[14] Only in the humiliation of awaiting trial on a capital offence or in the squalor of exile would a Roman go to pieces and wear his hair long.

His own short hair evoked no admiration from the long-haired people. For, while Ovid disliked people's long hair at Tomis, Dio Chrysostom described the contempt felt in Olbia on the Black Sea for a townsman who shaved and wore his hair short, ostentatiously aping the Romans.[15] Had he done service as a Roman auxiliary? What, indeed, were Roman army regulations about the length of a soldier's hair?* (Sculpture is rarely informative here, for soldiers in uniform wore helmets or leather caps.)

---

* There certainly were regulations. When a long-haired Gaul joined up, he had to have a hair-cut (Claudian, *In Eutrop.* 1, 383).

When a Roman who lived unostentatiously fetched in a local boy to wait at dinner, his short hair, combed for the occasion, was a contrast to the long curly hair of a Greek slave-boy in a rich household.[16]

Priests of Isis were tonsured; and if you saw a boy with his hair in braids, tied up in a pony tail or bunched over one ear, he was likely to be devoted to the service of Isis, for such coiffure was the 'Horus lock'. According to Lucian, all boys of free birth in Egypt wore their hair in braids.[17]

Romans had once been bearded, but beards went out in the second century BC and, once Romans took to shaving, they talked of their 'bearded ancestors' – 'intonsus Cato' – and in the contemporary world a beard seemed to them to be another mark of the barbarian; except in the late Republic, when a small beard was cultivated by young smarties in Rome, greatly scorned by conservative stalwarts like Cicero. And, of course, philosophers were a legitimate exception, *barbati magistri*. Every respectable philosopher-sophist had a long beard as well as long hair. In the late first and second centuries AD Euphrates' huge white beard was greatly admired, and there was something comic about the fact that Favorinus, from birth an eunuch, had no beard at all. Epictetus for his part declared that if anyone said to him, 'Shave off your beard, or die', he would not hesitate to die.[18]

With these exceptions, for three centuries a beard was the mark of a foreigner (brightly dyed beards – blue, red, purple, green – and dyed hair were a distinctive mark of Indians),[19] until in the second century AD, with Hadrian, the fashion changed again.

On the other hand, smooth-skinned men who had used depilatories – resin, for instance – on their legs and on other parts of their bodies, a practice thought to originate in Greece, were suspect, regarded as catamites. (Except for priests of Isis for whom anything hairy – a sheep for instance – was abomination. So they were under a religious obligation to shave all hair off their bodies. Britons did the same, presumably in order to woad themselves more satisfactorily.)

Northerners were conspicuous because they had blue eyes, '*caerulea pubes*'. Fierce blue eyes at that.[21]

Britons were blue in another sense. They stained their bodies with woad. Martial's friend Claudia Rufina was a prodigy. Sprung from woad-stained ancestors, she had absorbed Roman culture with such facility that Italian women, savage enough critics, no doubt, could mistake her for a Roman.[22]

Arabs had pierced ears, for they wore ear-rings (as, of course, did Roman women); and so did many other people in the near East and in north Africa; the Moorish emperor Macrinus had one ear pierced. Ethiopian women wore a ring through the lip.[23] Jews were circumcised, a practice which Romans thought detestable;* it was,

---

* See p.231 below.

indeed, a bar to complete proselytism, for a number of Romans were attracted by other aspects of Judaism. Dacian and Sarmatian men were tattooed, and so were women in Thrace.[24]

(ii) Colour

There is no sharper contrast than between black and white; so a Roman wishing to say that he had no interest in a person, could say, as Catullus said of Caesar, that he did not want to know whether he was white or black.

In itself 'black' was a sinister epithet. Black bile was a morbid symptom, sign of anger. A backbiter who did not stand up for his friends was 'black'.[25]

Latin words for 'black' or 'dark' like *fuscus* were used variously, sometimes for white people with dark complexions, sometimes for Berbers, Moors, Indians or Ethiopians.

The nearer people were to the sun, the blacker they were, and their features were negroid. Such people were spoken of as Ethiopians, Africans (*Afri*) or Moors (*Mauri*).

'Ethiopians are burnt by the heat of the heavenly body near them and are born with a scorched appearance, and they have curly beards and hair,' the elder Pliny wrote. Also they had flat noses. The Ethiopian woman of the poor peasant in the *Moretum* of the *Appendix Virgiliana* was 'African, every part of her body bearing witness to her origin, woolly-haired, thick-lipped, black, with great pendant breasts, pinched belly, thin legs and huge feet'. At Encolpius' simple suggestion in Petronius' *Satyricon* that he and his fellow-rogue Giton should disguise themselves as negroes by inking their faces, Giton asked, 'How could we make our lips swell to hideous thickness? Or change our hair with curling-tongs? Or walk bow-legged?'[26]

Indians (*Indi*) varied in colour, it was thought, those in the North being similar in colour to Egyptians, less dark than those in the South, who were the colour of Ethiopians; and those nearer the Indus were thought to be darker than those who lived south of the Ganges. Apuleius enjoyed the paradox: 'They face the rising sun and their colour is as black as night.'

But since India was just as sun-baked as Ethiopia (with which it was sometimes confused, imaginatively located on the upper Nile), why did Indians not have woolly hair and flat noses? As concerned their hair, the explanation was simple – the humidity of the Indian climate, the rivers and the floods.[27]

Of the nomadic Moors of Mauretania, Strabo paints a vivid picture: 'They beautify their appearance by braiding their hair, growing beards, wearing golden ornaments, and also by cleaning their teeth and paring their nails. Only rarely can you see them touch one another in walking, for fear that the adornment of their hair may not remain intact.'[28]

Ethiopians were naturally thought to share the common African quality of being over‚sexed and in consequence to have a sinister fascination for women. But for the abortionist, Juvenal declared, a married Roman might find himself fathering a black Ethiopian, 'a coloured heir, whom he would rather not meet by daylight'. According to one version of the story, the young Tarquinius threatened that, if she would not submit to his lust, he would kill Lucretia and leave the corpse of an Ethiopian slave beside her, to establish her utter depravity. And in the course of their fantastic rhetorical training the young were sometimes called on to debate the case of a married woman who gave birth to an Ethiopian baby, the defence being that an Ethiopian-looking child need not necessarily be the son of a black parent.[29]

We cannot say in what circumstances the sight of a black man could be inauspicious. When Brutus' army was marching out to the battle of Philippi, an Ethiopian came face to face with the troops and they ran him through with their swords.[30]

Black boys and girls had their evident attraction, and in Rome, as in the Hellenistic world after Alexander, it was smart to have black boys and girls as slaves – Indians, Ethiopians or Numidians – just as there was a taste for black boys in eighteenth-century English households later. The courtesan Thais in Terence's *Eunuch* wanted a black Ethiopian maid and an eunuch.[31]

The philosopher Favorinus bequeathed to Herodes Atticus, who had been his pupil, a 'blackish' Indian to whom both men were devoted, who had entertained them both in conversation by his admixture of Indian and Attic Greek. Herodes Atticus also had an Ethiopian foster-child, a talented and versatile youth, on whom in life and after death he lavished the affection which he withheld from his own mentally retarded son.[32]

The Moor Lusius Quietus – Mommsen's 'Gaetulian Sheik' – who fought with Moorish cavalry in the Dacian wars, was raised by Trajan to the consulship and in the East commissioned to liquidate Jews until Hadrian recalled him and he was executed for his part in the 'conspiracy of the four consulars', may not have been negroid. He may, like some Moroccan chiefs today, have had a fair complexion and fair hair.[33]

Puteoli, like any other thriving port, had a large mixed population; but it is amazing that there should have been enough Ethiopians there to fill a theatre. Yet, with the curious idea of making the Parthian Tiridates feel at home there, Nero entertained him in the theatre when the audience was exclusively Ethiopian, men, women and children.* [34]

---

* So Dio states. But was it in fact a performance by an all-Ethiopian cast?

A fanciful scholiast on Virgil's *Eclogues* pictures the conflict of Octavian and Antony as a colour-conflict: 'Antony had an army of Egyptians and Ethiopians, Caesar came to war with Romans and Gauls.'[35]

Most Ethiopians doubtless reached Rome as slaves, considerable numbers of them after Petronius' defeat of an Ethiopian army early in Augustus' principate. Some, no doubt, were brought over like other North Africans to hunt wild beasts as a spectacle. A hundred fought at the Games of the aedile Domitius Ahenobarbus in 61 BC, though the record that they fought 'Numidian bears' was far from accurate, as the elder Pliny pointed out; there were no such animals as Numidian bears.[36]

Ethiopians were to be found, no doubt, chiefly in brothels, on the stage and in domestic service. (Trimalchio had a couple of 'Aethiopes capillati'). There is evidence of their employment as actors, dancers, acrobats, boxers, charioteers, bath-attendants, bootblacks, cooks and other domestic servants, divers, hunters and soldiers.[37]

It may well be, and it is very commonly stated, that there was no colour-prejudice against black people in the ancient world; but there is no evidence of the marriage of whites and blacks in the upper levels of Roman society. Indeed the Greeks and Romans thought of black people as suffering an inferiority complex on account of their colour. The elder Pliny declared that the Mesaches in Ethiopia smeared themselves all over with red chalk to efface their natural colour;* and a sentimental poem, twenty lines of iambics, which survives as an epitaph to an Ethiopian slave Epitynchanon from Antinoe in Egypt from, probably, the third century AD, reflects the attitude of the Greek official who was his master: 'his sun-baked skin may have been black, but his spirit was a bower of white blossoms.'[38]

(iii) Clothing

Abroad as at home when formally dressed the Roman wore shoes (*calcei*), red if he was a senator, and a toga, which the Greeks called 'têbenna', a word whose origin even Dionysius of Halicarnassus could not explain.[39] (Its origin was in fact Etruscan, see p.124.) At their first contact with Romans, to judge by what happened at Tarentum in 282 BC (see p.176), the Greeks derived nothing but amusement from the

---

* Pliny could have been right as to the fact, though not as to the motive. On the other hand Dr R. Pankhurst of the Institute of Ethiopian Studies in the University of Addis Ababa writes to me very kindly as follows: 'I suspect that the darker-skinned people were referred to as "black", the paler as "red". This usage is found in a fourth-century inscription of the Aksumite king Ezana who makes a distinction between the "Blacks" and the "Red peoples" to the west of Aksum. The distinction has lasted to this day when Ethiopians speak of themselves in the main as "red", whereas many of the former slaves were "black".'

sight of the Roman toga. Romans, on the other hand, thought the Greek cloak (*chlamys* or *pallium*) and Greek footwear sloppy.

Of Greek cloaks, the *chlaina* was 'the square garment', and the *chlamys* was circular, by contrast with the toga, which was semi-circular in shape.

On holiday in Naples, which was to all intents and purposes a Greek city, it might be excusable for a Roman to adopt Greek dress, a Greek cloak, Greek sandals (*crepidae*) or Greek slippers (*socci*). At Naples Sulla wore *chlamys* and *crepidae* and so, in the Empire, did Claudius and his Court; and men of eminence might hope to get away with it elsewhere. The elder Scipio Africanus wore *pallium* and *crepidae* when off duty and exercising in the gymnasium in Sicily; and Tiberius wore Greek dress – *pallium* and *crepidae* – in the last period of his retirement, which was almost exile, in Rhodes. Criticism of him – or anybody else – on this account was in bad taste in the view of the well-mannered poet Persius.[40]

Games were occasions of relaxation; so when Greek Games were given in Rome by Nero and later by Domitian, performers and a large part of the audience wore Greek dress, but only during the Games themselves.[41]

Men in terror of their lives cannot afford to observe sartorial niceties; so it is not surprising that in 88 BC some Romans in Asia sought to escape detection by wearing Greek clothing when Mithridates had ordered the execution of every Roman in the province.[42]

For a Roman magistrate or official on public service to dress as a Greek was an open offence against Roman *dignitas*. Scipio Africanus' behaviour was therefore criticised; off duty or on duty in Sicily, he was still commander-in-chief. So Cn. Piso was criticised by Cicero for wearing *crepidae* on the way home from his province (Macedonia): 'crepidatus imperator', 'the general in slippers'. Dressing in the Greek fashion was a charge against Verres when governor of Sicily and one against which Rabirius Postumus – forced to wear such dress when he was *dioiketes* for Ptolemy Auletes – had to be defended. In this matter Antony was a prime offender, with Cleopatra in Egypt and even with Octavia in Athens in winter 39/8 BC. Germanicus was criticised by Tiberius for wearing Greek dress in Alexandria in AD 19 – he was supposedly modelling himself on Scipio – and in this Tiberius was not inconsistent, for Germanicus was, after all, on a highly important official commission to the East at the time.[43]

Yet on the Capitol in Rome there was a statue of L. Scipio, the conqueror of Antiochus the Great and brother of Africanus, in *chlamys* and *crepidae* and, according to Cicero, it provoked no criticism. Was it erected in his honour by Greeks, and was that why it was tolerated?[44]

For a Roman it was also discreditable not to wear a belt with his tunic, to be 'discinctus'. Soldiers were punished by being made to parade in tunics without belts and such dress in individuals was thought Bohemian (in the case of the young Julius Caesar, for instance) or, as in Maecenas' case, positively sloppy.[45] (See p.22.)

Northerners – Celts, Germans, Sarmatians – were remarkable for their – generally black – cloaks (*saga, sagi*) of very thick wool, which were also worn commonly in Spain, and their trousers, held up by braces, which were loose and fastened at the ankles; these people were 'sagati', 'bracati', and Provence, later Gallia Narbonensis, was at first called 'Trousered Gaul', *Gallia Bracata*.[46]

The thick cloaks were, obviously, very suitable clothing in cold and wet weather and were already exported in large numbers for sale in Italy by the early Empire.[47] Trousers, which first attracted the Greeks as clothing of the Medes and Persians, and in Roman times continued to be worn by the Parthians,[48] were most sensible clothing. If thick, they kept the legs warm, and they must have been far more comfortable than Roman dress for riding. The northerner, like the eastern warrior, lived on his horse; the Roman did not. Eventually the Romans came to realise the practical good sense of trousers. By Trajan's time many Roman soldiers were wearing long shorts which came down to below their knees, as can be seen from representations on his column; while on the arch of Constantine soldiers wear full-length trousers.

Romans who adopted Gallic dress, no doubt because of its convenience, were criticised. Antony was abused by Cicero for the fact that in Gaul and on his return to Rome in 45 BC he wore Gallic sandals and a Gallic cloak (*lacerna*) and Caecina, who commanded one of the detachments of Vitellius' army of invasion in AD 69, attracted attention in north Italy by the fact that he wore a cloak of many colours and breeks, 'versicolori sagulo bracas indutus'.[49]

In the second century AD the rhetorician Titus Castricius was shocked to find pupils of his who were senators dressed in Gallic cloaks and sandals when they were on holiday.[50]

Barbaric peoples wore coats made of the skins of animals. Germans were clothed in this way and, nearer home, Sardinians; they were 'pelliti', 'mastrucati', and Cicero pilloried them for their sheepskin or goatskin coats. When, on the Rhine at the start of Tiberius' principate, general Germanicus decided to creep round his camp in disguise at night, so as to test the morale of his troops, he threw a skin round his shoulders, assuming that he would be taken for a Gaul or a German.[51]

The Scythian senators to whom Synesius objected round 400 AD only wore the toga when they had to – how could a man draw his sword effectively when so clothed? – and at the first opportunity reverted to wearing their reindeer-skin coats.[52]

Skins in the cold North. At the other extreme, as you approached the

Equator in Ethiopia, you found Ethiopians wearing hardly any clothes at all.[53]

Carthaginians perhaps, Numidians and north Africans generally without doubt, even on horseback, wore long flowing garments like burnouses, without belts. That is to say, they were *discincti*.[54]

As wool was an animal product, it had an objectionable impurity by contrast with the vegetable flax; and so devotees of ritual purity like Apollonius of Tyana and the holy men whom he visited in the far East did not wear woollen clothing, just as they did not eat meat. This in the West was a tradition which was thought to go back to Pythagoras. The practice was observed by priests and initiates of Isis because there was something unclean about wool as there was about human hair and finger nails; also, as Plutarch did not hesitate to point out, linen, unlike wool, did not foster lice.[55]

(iv) Drink, cooking, food, vegetarianism

In antiquity, as today, wine was the staple drink of the Mediterranean peoples, beer of northerners. Latin and Greek writers were therefore much interested in the drinking habits of peoples whose climate was too harsh to permit the cultivation of the vine – in the consumption of beer (from the fermentation of barley or wheat) and of mead (the same, with an admixture of honey) among northern peoples. The Lusitanians in Spain drank beer (*caelia, cerea*); so did the Gauls (*cervesia*) and the Germans; so did the Ligurians in north Italy. In the South beer (*zuthos*) was drunk in Egypt and in Ethiopia; it was a drink which differed from place to place.[56]

Given the opportunity, however, any reasonable person would prefer wine; so even in the days of Gallic independence there was considerable traffic in wine from the Mediterranean to northern Gaul, as there was to Germans living close to the east bank of the Rhine, though Germans in general thought wine-drinking degenerate.[57] There was the legend that the Gauls, like a race of Calibans, originally crossed the Alps into Italy from the excitement of their first taste of wine.[58] Such was Gallic greed for wine that, according to Diodorus, you could secure a slave-boy in exchange for a flask of the stuff. The Nervii were exceptional, Caesar wrote, because they forbad the importation of wine.[59] After the Roman conquest and the extensive planting of vineyards in Provence, Burgundy and on the Rhine, wine-drinking must have increased rapidly in the whole of Gaul and the price of wine must have dropped sharply.

If vines did not grow in the North or in many other places remote from the Mediterranean, nor did olives, which were nature's most resourceful gift to man. Olives were delicious to eat as hors d'oeuvre. You cooked in olive oil. You kept yourself clean and fresh with it, oiling yourself for exercise and in the baths. Expensive oil made you smell nice. In lamps, it supplied you with light.

Some northern people imported oil, though in Gaul, it seems, it was some time before it was properly appreciated.[60]

Where there was no oil, people generally cooked in butter – the Ethiopians, for instance; and as the Lusitanians, to whom olive oil was easily available, also cooked in butter, butter had its evident advantages. Lard was used in Gaul before the introduction of oil. In Egypt there was a vegetable oil, used for lamps, and by the poor for keeping clean. And for lighting, if there was no oil, it was possible to use tallow.[61]

Man is naturally interested in the eating habits of other men, the English, for instance, in the fact that the Chinese eat birds' nests and the French eat frogs and snails.

In the extremities of the earth, north and south, there were nomadic peoples who had not acquired settled agricultural habits and they lived on milk and cheese and on roots. Though of the Scythians, who mostly supported life on a diet of mare's milk, there were some who ate meat.[62]

Whether for religious reasons or from considerations of health, there were birds, fish and animals whose flesh was anathema to one people or another in the ancient world. In the Roman world there was particular interest in the abstention from certain foods by Egyptians and by Jews. Pigs in Judaea could look forward to a tranquil old age; so Juvenal.[63]

When in AD 40, anxious both to establish their conflicting claims, the rival deputations of Jews and Greeks from Alexandria panted round the imperial palace at Rome on the heels of the emperor Gaius and his architect, Gaius suddenly turned and shot the question at the Jews, 'Why do you not eat pork?' After sycophantic laughter by the Alexandrian Greeks, sternly repressed by court officials, when the Jews answered that different people had different eating habits and one of them added, 'Some people do not eat lamb', the Emperor retorted, 'Naturally, because it tastes so horrible.' They were referring to what, except at Lycopolis (because wolves, whom the natives of Lycopolis worshipped, ate sheep), was universal Egyptian practice, refusal to eat mutton or lamb (or, indeed, goat).[64]

The basis of Jewish refusal to eat pork – they did not eat hares either – was probably a belief that it caused leprosy, as we learn from Tacitus and Plutarch (and not, explicitly, from the Bible itself). They were not the only people, they were only the most notorious people, who observed this particular tabu. It was common, evidently, in Cappadocia and elsewhere in Asia Minor, in Syria and among Arabs and Indians, and it appears that in Egypt pork could only be eaten at full moon. It was forbidden food, and pigs were not kept, at the great sanctuary of Comana in Pontus or (because of the belief that Attis was gored by a boar) at Pessinus in Galatia.[65]

There were Jewish tabus also on certain methods of killing animals whose flesh might be consumed; so that Jewish quarters of towns always had their own butchers. A common source of meat in the ancient world, the distribution of flesh after sacrifice, was, of course, shunned by Jews, as it was – unnecessarily, St Paul thought – by certain Christians.[66]

There were practising vegetarians; and to the ordinary man vegetarianism meant Pythagoreanism, adapting one's eating habits to conform with a belief in the transmigration of souls, a doctrine which never failed to intrigue the satirically-minded – Lucian, for instance, whose 'Cockrel', starting off as a Trojan warrior killed by Menelaus in the Trojan war, was subsequently embodied as Pythagoras (introducing vegetarianism for no better reason than to be different from other people and to attract publicity) and, after Pythagoras, Aspasia, mistress of Pericles.

A bird, fish or animal might house the soul of someone who had been your human relative; in piety, therefore, you must not run the risk of eating it. So Pythagoras taught; so did Apollonius of Tyana's Brahmans of India and Sages of Egypt.[67] Pythagoreanism was revived in Rome at the end of the Republic and start of the Empire by Nigidius Figulus, praetor in 58 BC and a friend of Cicero.

Vegetarianism was practised by others (Q. Sextius, for instance, an influential philosopher at the time of Augustus) for less far-fetched reasons. Sextius was in part a neo-Pythagorean, but the reason for which he recommended vegetarianism was that there was plenty of food for man to eat without resorting to bloodshed; that butchery for pleasure induced a habit of cruelty;* that there should be a limit to extravagance; and that the consumption of a variety of foods not suited to our bodies was not good for health.[68]

Or you could appeal to the animal world. Nice, gentle animals like horses, cows and sheep were vegetarian; they ate grass. Wild and ferocious beasts, lions, tigers, bears and wolves, were carnivorous. If those were the beasts on which we really wished to model our lives, why did we not imitate them properly, pouncing on live animals and getting our teeth and claws (admittedly not very well adapted for the purpose) into them, instead of feeding on them when they were corpses, needing all kinds of condiments and flavours to hide their natural taste?[69]

Isis-worshippers did not necessarily practise vegetarianism always, but they refrained from animal flesh for a period before important cult ceremonies.[70]

---

* 'Il est certain que les grands mangeurs de viande sont en général cruels et féroces plus que les autres hommes. Cette observation est de tous les lieux et de tous les tems; la barbarie Angloise est connue', Rousseau, *Emile* book 2.

We could reasonably guess, even without the surviving evidence of Plutarch, that vegetarianism supplied a frequent subject of conversation at dinner-parties when a vegetarian was present.[71]

Seneca, a martyr to indigestion whose road to ineffectiveness was paved with good intentions, was impressed as a young man by the arguments of Sextius as reported to him by Sotion, who had attended Sextius' lectures; so he resolved to become a vegetarian. But this was at a moment (in AD 19) when, after flagrant scandals, the government was taking measures against Jews and Isis-worshippers in Rome (see p.106). Discretion – the voice of his father – advised that this was, therefore, not the right moment to adopt an exotic diet. At the end of his life, however, he drank no wine and was to all intents and purposes a vegetarian, as a result of which – so Tacitus suggests – Nero's design to poison him was frustrated.[72]

Holy men, of course, were vegetarians: Apollonius of Tyana, as a Pythagorean (he did not drink wine either). John the Baptist lived on locusts and wild honey. Josephus does not state that the admirable Essenes were vegetarians; but they took an oath not to eat the food of those who were not Essenes – so that an unfortunate expelled from the Order had no option but to live on grass, a diet which reduced him to such pitiful extremities that he was often forgiven and received back into the Order.[73]

(v) Homosexuality

Homosexuality was one of the paradoxes of ancient life, universally practised and universally reprobated. Such practice could not have originated spontaneously in Rome; it must have been caught like an infection from abroad, from Greece. So Cicero pretended to think. It was part of that luxurious decadence which horrified the elder Cato in the first half of the second century BC, when for the purchase of smoked fish or a good cook whole fortunes were squandered, and also for the purchase of a pretty slave-boy. But already in 226 BC an aedile had been punished for making improper advances to a son of a fellow-aedile, the great Marcellus.[74]

Homosexuality is stigmatised sometimes as a barbarian practice, existing in its crudest form in Gaul, where – we are told – young men of good breeding and devastating charm would go out of their way to invite other men to share their beds and think poorly of those by whom their invitations were declined. But not among the Germans; 'sanctius vivitur ad Oceanum'.[75]

There is reference to homosexuality as a distinctive Roman vice in the third Sibylline oracle (see p.191) and in Boudicca's spirited speech in the pages of Cassius Dio. In the second satire Juvenal reviles homosexuals in Rome: 'magna inter molles concordia'; young Armenians came to Rome and were corrupted. One extremely attractive Arcadian boy, however, sent by his father to Rome to study

law, set his face firmly against all temptation, even from the most
dangerous seducer of all, the emperor Domitian, who threw him into
prison (where he enjoyed the improving company of Apollonius of
Tyana). The boy was prepared to face death to preserve his
innocence, but for once Virtue was rewarded, and he was set free and
allowed to go home. An edifying story, whether or not it contains a
grain of truth.[76]

At slave-sales, the prettier a boy (even without castration, see
p.229), the higher his price. The further he was from adolescence, the
better. So slave-dealers were up to plenty of tricks; one such trick, it is
reported, was to retard the growth of down on boys' faces by the use of
blood from the testicles of castrated lambs.[77]

In an interesting passage at the end of Dio Chrysostom's seventh
(Euboean) oration, in which he urges the abolition of brothels, he
traces a sexual rogue's progress. Bored with harlots, he seduces well-
bred girls and married women and when this too becomes tedious,
because it is too easy, he turns in his last state of degeneracy to
seducing boys.[78]

It is hard to believe that there was not a great deal of homosexuality
in the army. After the sack of a city, boys were in demand as well as
women by the victorious soldiery, and there were stories of gross
behaviour by Roman officers. There was the young officer whom
Marius commended for killing his senior, Marius' own nephew, when
he tried to assault him, a *cause célèbre* which for long featured in the
repertoire of the schools of rhetoric. (Were there any circumstances at
all in which a man could be justified in killing his senior officers?) And
there was the young man at Thespiae who ran amok after desperate
attempts had been made to seduce him by the Roman garrison-
commander in winter 88/7 BC (see p.168). There were other stories in
Roman history of handsome young men at the time of the Samnite wars
who both on military service and at home repelled attempts on their
virtue.[79]

Roman morals being what they were 'in hac licentia temporum',
the importance of a boys' school having a 'good moral tone' and a
schoolmaster's being a man of moral rectitude, the embodiment of
moral *castitas*, was overwhelming; hence the importance of a
trustworthy *paedagogus*, to shield a boy from temptation on his way to
and from school.[80]

Indulgence in unnatural vice in one capacity or another – or both –
according to age – was one of the accusations commonly flung by one
party against another in the courts at Rome, as it had been earlier in
Greece.

And homosexuality was, of course, a weakness of emperors; with
rare exceptions – Augustus, whose relaxation it was to deflower
virgins (supplied him by his dutiful wife) and Claudius, who was an
indiscriminate womaniser – most emperors are pictured as having

homosexuality as one of their numerous weaknesses. Such imputations reach a crescendo in the fantastic accounts of Tiberius' orgies on Capri, stories which do credit to the prurience of Neapolitan imagination.[81]

What of the law? There was a law forbidding male homosexuality, a *lex Scantinia*, on the statute-book, from an uncertain date in the Republic. Condemnation under the law clearly involved undesirable notoriety and, in the case of a man in public life, meant the end of his public career, but the punishment, a fine of the original sum of ten thousand sesterces, was not large enough to worry anybody in the late Republic or early Empire. But we hear next to nothing of such prosecutions; only that in the last mad fantasy of dying Republicanism in 50 BC Cicero's raffish young friend Caelius Rufus, charged under the *lex Scantinia* by a censor Appius Claudius, retorted by indicting the censor under the same law; and that Domitian, no innocent himself, appears to have secured the condemnation of a number of men under the law.[82]

Indeed, it is obvious that it was openly flouted everywhere. There is even, apart from Nero's marriages first to a man called Pythagoras, then to an eunuch (see p.229), a story in Juvenal[83] of a man with a good Roman name, a Gracchus, who was formally married to a young male horn player.*

And Lesbianism? Of this we hear very little. Indeed a woman in Juvenal's second satire is made to assert, as Queen Victoria asserted much later, that homosexuality was a male vice; women could never have practised anything so horrible.[84] More significant is the fact that there is no mention of this in Juvenal's relentless catalogue of the vices and weaknesses of woman, his sixth satire.

(vi) Eunuchs

The Romans encountered eunuchs in great oriental, particularly royal, households and had evidence of their high political importance. There was Pothinus, guardian of the young Ptolemy XIII, who was responsible for the murder of Pompey, whom in due course Caesar executed. The Parthian mission to seek a king from Rome in AD 35 consisted of the distinguished Sinnaces and the eunuch Abdus. 'No stigma attaches to this condition in oriental countries; on the contrary it confers power'; so Tacitus explained to his Roman readers. Cicero had already pointed out that the great heroes of Roman Republican

---

* Extract from an article headed 'Gay GIs?', *Economist*, July 12, 1975, p.63: 'The county clerk of Boulder, California made history in March when she issued the first same-sex marriage licence. Not many homosexual couples have been that lucky. Most have been unable to have a wedding ceremony unless one of the partners feigned to be of the opposite sex or they were prepared to do without the official marriage documents ... Maryland brought in a law in 1973, after several homosexual couples had tried to marry, permitting only heterosexual marriages.'

history could not compete in wealth of material possessions with the eunuchs of Syria and Egypt.[85]

Not that, even in the early Empire, Romans themselves were without experience of the sinister presence of eunuchs at the Roman Court. The freedman-eunuch Posides, a man of prodigious wealth, was on Claudius' staff in Britain and was awarded the *hasta pura* as if he was a knight. Claudius' official 'taster', the eunuch Halotus, who, so far from protecting him against poisoning, was employed by Agrippina to poison him, was a mischievous influence under Nero and, despite popular outcry, was awarded a rich stewardship by Galba. And, when a squadron of troops was sent under a centurion to execute Rubellius Plautus in Asia in AD 62, they were supervised by the eunuch Pelago. Caracalla humiliated the Senate by the favours which he showed to a Spanish eunuch.[86]

Writing in the second half of the fourth century, Ammianus Marcellinus would have smiled – or sighed – at Tacitus' explanation of the political power of eunuchs in oriental courts. For since Diocletian the eastern imperial court of Rome reproduced the accepted features of oriental autocracy, including the all-powerful eunuch, in origin a foreign slave. The corps of eunuchs at court was all-powerful, in particular the Grand Chamberlain, *Praepositus Sacri Cubiculi*, who was an eunuch, closer than anybody to the remote person of the sacred emperor and powerful enough to represent or misrepresent events at will. He controlled (at his own price) admission to the emperor's presence; Eusebius, Chamberlain to Constantius II, Eutropius to Arcadius and Chrysaphius to Theodosius II came near to absolute power, until they met a sticky end.[87]

The inaccessibility of emperors gave the eunuchs their opportunity, but this does not explain their evident ability. Their position and power in the fourth century is reminiscent of the position and power of freedmen in the early Empire. Both insinuated themselves into the higher echelons of society, the senators and the knights, and had greater influence on imperial policy than either.

The penultimate year of the fourth century saw the crowning horror, fit subject of Claudian's vigorous invective: an eunuch (Eutropius) as Roman Consul. The Year of the Eunuch.

People at large were, perhaps, most familiar with castration in the case of the priests of Cybele, the Great Mother, whose cult was introduced to Rome at the end of the second Punic war, and it was the castration of such a Gallus which inspired the Hellenistic poem which survives in Catullus' moving translation. (In the essay on the Syrian goddess falsely ascribed to Lucian there is a hideous account of wild devotees castrating themselves at the great annual festival in Syria and assuming women's clothing.)

The arrival of the goddess in Rome was commemorated annually at the Megalesia on April 4th, when in a cacophony of raucous music the emasculated priests paraded the streets, soliciting alms.[88] They were foreigners, imported from the East for, though the festival was an official festival of the Roman state, Roman citizens were forbidden to serve as the emasculated priests of the goddess. The cult was perhaps reorganised under the emperor Claudius and after that the chief priest (the Archigallus) was a Roman citizen, but was not an eunuch.[89]

There were two sorts of eunuch, the attractively young and the repulsively old. Neither caused surprise; hence the plot of Terence's *Eunuch*. Roman law distinguished between a natural eunuch and a man who had been castrated. The former received a dowry on marriage, the latter did not.[90]

Though a taste for falsetto singing existed (and was criticised by the censorious),[91] the attraction of the castrato voice was, it seems, as yet undiscovered; but there was authority in writing attributed to Aristotle for the view that a boy's voice broke less quickly if at puberty he denied himself a quick taste of sexual indulgence. To facilitate such continence, an operation was performed on adolescents 'for the sake of the voice and for health's sake' which Celsus describes as 'more often superfluous than necessary'. The prepuce was ringed, like a bull's nose, by a *fibula*. The *fibula* described by Martial sounds more like a male chastity-belt; it was worn, it seems, by men playing musical instruments and by tragic and comic actors – also in the baths on one occasion by a man who hoped to conceal the fact that he was circumcised – and is said by Martial to have stimulated the lust of the musicians' female admirers.[92]

In the increasing degeneracy of the private life of the rich at Rome, the pretty boy exercised his fascination on men and women alike, a fascination the greater if he had been castrated and did not quickly lose his youthful charm. In Eumolpus' poem in Petronius' *Satyricon* the castration of boys is numbered among the decadent features of the late Republic and already in the early Empire at all levels of society the rich family possessed its eunuchs. Trimalchio playing ball was accompanied by two, one to score, the other to hold his silver chamber-pot. At a higher level Maecenas in his public appearances was accompanied by a pair of eunuchs, as Seneca records with appropriate horror. One who belonged to Sejanus' household was sold after his death for a fortune.[93]

Indeed, the imperial family led the way. First seduced by Sejanus, the handsome and favourite eunuch of Drusus, his wine-taster, was instrumental in the poisoning of his master; this, at least, was commonly believed. The depth of moral infamy was reached when Nero had Sporus castrated and dressed him up as a girl, married him, gave him the name Sabina and travelled with him as his consort in Greece. After Nero's death, with the name Poppaea, Sporus made a second marriage, to the prefect of the Praetorian Guard, Nymphidius Sabinus. * [94]

With such a market for eunuchs, slave-dealers did a business in arranging for the gelding of handsome slave-boys, until Domitian stopped the practice.

Titus' devotion to eunuchs had been notorious, and this is said to have been Domitian's reason, despite his passion for a favourite eunuch, for forbidding castration throughout the empire, a measure praised by Martial, as by Ammianus Marcellinus later, which with the adaptability of the professional sycophant Statius commended in a poem extolling the rapturous beauty of one of Domitian's own favourite castrated slaves. Nerva confirmed the prohibition and Hadrian imposed the death-penalty on anybody, free or slave, who performed the operation and on anybody responsible for the enforced castration of a slave.[95] Justinian enforced novel penalties; if detected, the castrator was himself castrated.[96] But there was no ban on the importation of slave-boys who had already been castrated outside Roman territory. Presumably, therefore, slave-dealers made the necessary arrangements with their foreign agents and the abuse continued. For, whatever the law might be, in rich families in the fourth century at Rome, eunuchs, old and young, were to be seen in abundance.[97]

The range of speculative interest among the ancients knew few limits. The question was asked whether the fact of an eunuch's being debarred from erotic performance meant that he was by that very fact free from erotic desire. In Philostratus' *Life of Apollonius of Tyana* the question was answered: the sad exposure of an eunuch's lust for a member of the Parthian king's harem. Even without which, the truth was well known.[98]

How often it was the fate of the detected adulterer to be gelded, we cannot say.† [99]

There were, particularly in the Christian Church, some who, not in wild ecstasy like the devotees of the Great Mother but in cold fanaticism, castrated themselves or submitted to castration as a desperate measure to ensure that they should not be led into moral temptation. In Matthew's gospel (19,12) Christ had referred to 'those who had made eunuchs of themselves for the kingdom of Heaven's sake'. In the early third century, according to Eusebius (*HE* 6,8) Origen was such a man.

---

* Cf p. 227 above, n.
† This in the period of slavery was the punishment of a black slave found guilty of the rape of a white woman in the State of Missouri, E.D. Genovese, *Roll, Jordan, Roll*, London 1975, 34.

(vii) Circumcision

Circumcision, in its origin perhaps a symbol of full admission to tribal membership and performed at puberty (as in some parts of Africa today), had once been customary among a number of different peoples in the East. Herodotus declares from his own observation that it was practised in Ethiopia, Egypt and Syria (Palestine) and by Colchians north of the Black Sea, deriving in every case from Egypt. By Roman times, however, though known to be practised in parts of Africa, particularly in Egypt, from which, indeed, the Jews were thought to have derived it, circumcision was popularly associated with the Jews alone.[100]

Among the Jews circumcision, performed on the eighth day after birth, had acquired a deeply religious significance; by the Romans, as by the Greeks and the Arabs, it was held in great contempt; it seemed a gross physical deformity. Hence the dilemma of Izates, king of Adiabene in the time of Claudius and Nero who, as a Jewish proselyte, was anxious to be circumcised but was warned that, while he might practise the Jewish faith, circumcision was something which his people would not tolerate. However, he sent for his doctor and the operation was performed. Trouble followed.[101]

Syllaeus the Arab refused to become a Jew when he was trying to marry Herod's sister Salome. It was, however, an inescapable condition of marriage into the royal family of Judaea. Drusilla, sister of Agrippa II, was to have married C. Julius Antiochus Epiphanes, son of king Antiochus IV of Commagene, but he refused to be circumcised; so she married Azizos, king of Emesa, who was more accommodating. The marriage was short-lived because Drusilla fell in love with Felix, the procurator of Judaea and, breaking with her religious obligations, married him; so he, presumably, escaped circumcision.[102] Polemon of Cilicia, married for a short time to her sister Berenice, had had to be circumcised.[103] Would Titus have had to do the same if he had married her?

The descendants of Alexander, put to death by his father Herod the Great, deserted Judaism from birth; so presumably, they were not circumcised.[104]

While some Roman converts to Judaism went no further than studying the Jewish scriptures and observing the Sabbath, others evidently went the whole way and were circumcised.[105]

When Vespasian imposed a tax on Jews, circumcision was held to be adequate evidence that a man was a Jew; Suetonius saw a man of ninety stripped publicly in Rome, to discover if he was circumcised. Martial tells of a man who tried to conceal the tell-tale evidence in the baths; and there were apostate Jews who regained the uncircumcised state by submitting to epispasm.[106]

Though Domitian was no friend of the Jews, it was probably Hadrian, some time after AD 128, who forbad circumcision, and this fundamental assault on the Jewish religion may have played a part in causing Bar Cochba's revolt in 132. It was not a wise measure, and Antoninus Pius relaxed it to the degree of allowing Jews – and, in all probability, Egyptian priests – to be circumcised, though they were forbidden to follow their traditional practice of circumcising their gentile slaves and servants. If a Roman citizen was found to have been circumcised or to have had a slave circumcised, the doctor was liable to execution, as in the case of castration, and the man himself lost his property and was deported to an island.[107]

A century after the accession of Hadrian, a Roman emperor thought of being castrated, but was circumcised instead – Elagabalus, another of whose exotic qualities was a refusal to eat pork. This before asking his doctor if it was possible to change his sex.[108]

(viii) The seven-day week[109]

In the course of their history the Romans experienced three main calendar changes, the second and, in particular, the third of which altogether changed their life-style. First in 153 BC the civil year altered its starting-point from March 1st to January 1st. Secondly, when Julius Caesar reformed the calendar in 46 BC, the year assumed a regular and dependable length, 365 days with every fourth year a leap year. Before this the year might be 355 days long or 377 or 378 (so as to give an average over four years of $366\frac{1}{4}$ days) according to the annual regulation of the College of Pontiffs, whose carelessness, inefficiency or corruption might throw the times completely out of joint, so that people might be flinching under a midsummer sun when by the calendar it was October.

The third change was the introduction of the seven-day week, for which, unlike the other two changes, there is no certain date. It was something which happened gradually in the early Empire.

The seven-day 'Chaldaean' (astrological) week may not be earlier than the second century BC and one of Cassius Dio's alternative explanations of its basis is probably correct:[110] that for astrologers each hour of the day had its own planet in the accepted order of the planets (Saturn, Juppiter, Mars, the Sun, Venus, Mercury, the Moon), and that the planet which gave each individual day its name was the planet of the first hour of that day (the twenty-fifth hour, counting from the first hour of the previous day). Hence the weekly order Sun, Moon, Mars, Mercury, Juppiter, Venus, Saturn, perpetuated in the names of the days of the week in Italy, France, and Spain and, through Teuton adaptation, in northern Europe today.

From the eighth century BC and even earlier, perhaps, the Jews had observed a seven-day week to the extent of calling every seventh day the Sabbath and making it a rest day.[111]

The astrological and the Jewish weeks dovetailed insofar as the

Sabbath was the day of Saturn. The influence of Saturn was malign; Saturday, therefore, was not a good working day and – very sensibly, as it appeared to some – was made a regular holiday by the Jews (in the way in which Good Friday, an evil day, has been made a holiday by Christians).

The practical advantage of a seven-day week, every day identifiable by name, was infinite – to be able to make an appointment for 'next Thursday' instead of for 'ten days before the Kalends, the fourth day from today' or even, when the days of the week were numbered, not named, as among the Jews,* to make an appointment for 'the first day of next week'.

The Romans acquired the seven-day week in two stages.† There was, first of all, the seven-day week itself, with a different planet giving its name to each of the seven days. This evidently happened in the course of the first century AD. Frescoes from Pompeii indicate the week-day order of the planets. Josephus at the end of the first century speaks with some exaggeration of the use of the Jewish Sabbath all the world over, and little over a century later Cassius Dio said the same of the seven-day week.[112]

The second step was for the Romans to adopt the Jewish practice of a regular day of rest. This at first was one of the features of Jewish religion which invited strong criticism both on moral and on utilitarian grounds.

Morally it was condemned as a blatant encouragement of idleness. People who worked one day short in every seven days idled away a seventh part of their lives and obviously worked less hard than other people. Not every seventh day only but every seventh year was devoted to sloth, 'ignaviae datus' – the Sabbatical year.[113]

Secondly, particularly on the part of troops in war, Sabbath-day-observance was sheer folly. Jews were not, of course, so rabid as to stand up and have their throats cut on the Sabbath; they fought in self-defence, but that was all. Their enemies, in no fear of being attacked on that day, could proceed unhindered in their preparations for mounting an attack. So in 63 BC Pompey made his effective preparations to capture Jerusalem on the Sabbath-day, taking advantage of the absence of any opposition, and Plutarch, in his essay on Superstition, equated this example of superstitious folly with that of Nicias, whose concern about an eclipse of the moon lost Athens an army, a navy and, in the result, an empire.[114]

When Agrippa II attempted to persuade the Jews not to rebel against Rome in AD 66, he asked them how they could expect to succeed if every day in seven they turned their backs on the fighting.

* And in Portugal and Greece today.

† Their previous eight-day week, the *nundinum* was an interval of time rather than a week whose days had individual features, and the regular market-day itself, the *nundinae* was a modified rest-day only for farm-labourers.

If, on the other hand, they fought on the Sabbath (as, in the event, this time they did), how could they pretend that it was Judaism that they were fighting to preserve?[115]

The refusal of the Jews to fight, except in limited circumstances, on the Sabbath was, together with their dietary idiosyncrasies, a reason for excluding them from conscription in the Roman army in the East at the time of the civil wars (just as, because of their refusal to attend courts on the Sabbath, summons might not be served on them for that day). Later, however, there is evidence of Jews serving in units of the Roman army in Egypt and elsewhere. Presumably these men were not strict Jews or, like Tiberius Alexander, the Prefect of Egypt in AD 69, they had turned their backs on the religion in which they had been brought up.[116]

However, just as the majority of those who enjoy the relaxation of Sundays, Christmas and Easter are not practising Christians, so there were Romans who found the regular rest-day an attractive feature of Judaism and who adopted it in their own lives, though they were not prepared to adopt such offensive Jewish practices as circumcision. Juvenal refers to such people. And earlier on it is surmised that the reason why, when Tiberius lived in semi-exile on Rhodes, the grammarian Diogenes lectured only on Saturday (the Sabbath) was that he could attract a larger audience on that day.[117]

The universal adoption of a regular day of rest, not Saturday (the Sabbath) but Sunday, followed the final acceptance of Christianity by Constantine in the fourth century. At the end of that century under Theodosius the seven-day week was adopted for public and official purposes.[118]

(ix) Polygamy

A married Roman could at the same time have one or more concubines, just as today in some countries a man keeps a mistress with the full knowledge of his wife. Juvenal declares that a married woman hated the children born to her husband by a concubine.[119] But this was not a common state of things. Men normally took concubines (as did Vespasian and Marcus Aurelius) after the death or divorce of their wives when for one reason or another they preferred not to marry again.

Polygamy, it was thought, marked a society in which men were over-sexed, and it was incompatible with married or family love; as if a man kept his own private brothel. Africans were notoriously over-sexed; so that polygamy was natural enough among the Numidians and Mauretanians. The Numidian kings Massinissa and Juba I both had numerous wives and concubines.

Of the Mauretanian King Bocchus' readiness to betray his wife's father Jugurtha, Sallust wrote, 'According to their means Numidians and Mauretanians have ten wives, some more, kings more still. Affection is dissipated through number. No woman counts as a helpmeet; they are all of the same trifling account'.[120]

The large female entourage, wives and concubines, of the wealthy easterner, especially of oriental monarchs, was shocking in the eyes of the staid Roman. In a highly coloured passage in Lucan's *Pharsalia* Lentulus attacked Pompey for his desperate plan, after defeat at Pharsalus, to solicit the assistance of the Parthian king. 'What?' he asked, 'and resign your wife, a descendant of the Metelli, to be concubine number one thousand in the Parthian king's harem?'

Ammianus wrote of the Persians later, 'Most of them are extravagantly given to venery and are hardly contented with a multitude of concubines'. Herodotus had told the same story, that they had numerous wives and even more concubines.[121]

In India, too, where, notoriously, when a man died, there was fierce competition between his widows to decide which had been the dead man's favourite and should therefore have the privilege of being burnt with his corpse on the pyre.[122]

Polygamy was permitted under Jewish law but is unlikely to have been common practice, or this would have been an explicit charge against the Jewish religion. Herod the Great was, of course, a notorious polygamist with, at the end, no less than nine wives. Though some were obscure, the jealousy and in-fighting of others created the murderous horror of Herod's Court.[123]

(x) Monotheism and aniconic religion

Roman cities, like Greek, were overpopulated with divinities; Quartilla observed in Petronius' *Satyricon*, 'There are so many gods here that it is easier to find a god than a man'.[124] And the statues of the gods which adorned the temples were in human image; indeed Euhemerus had advanced the view that that was what the Olympian gods and goddesses had been in their origin – men and women.

So that monotheism was at first very unroman, very ungreek.

Equally strange to Greco-Roman ideas was an aniconic religion, a religion whose gods (or god) were not conceived or represented in human form.

There were the Nabatean Arabs, sun-worshippers, who built altars on the tops of their houses and made daily sacrifices on them. There were the Persians, who sacrificed to the sun and the moon, fire, earth, winds and water and who had neither shrines nor altars. And there were the still-primitive Germans who had as yet no temples and who thought it insulting to the majesty of heaven to represent gods in human shape.[125]

And, above all, there were the Jews. Writer after writer stressed the two religious peculiarities of the Jews, that they were monotheist and that they did not worship their god in human image.[126]

Once, of course, before the Romans felt the contaminating touch of Greek culture, the native religion of Rome was aniconic. So, Varro wrote, the Romans continued for a hundred and seventy years, and he thought it a matter of regret that this practice should have changed, supporting his opinion by a reference to the religious beliefs of the Jews.[127] Many educated Romans might have agreed with Varro, without necessarily appealing to the example of the Jews.

To any man of cultivated wit, of course, the idea of gods in human form was idiotically funny: to Plautus (and his Greek predecessor) in the *Amphitryon*; to Seneca when he wrote the *Apokolokyntosis*; to Lucian in the *Dialogues of the Gods* and many of his other pieces.

Trouble arose from the intrusion into genuine religious practice of the cult of rulers. This was not a matter of worship in the accepted religious sense because, while the image of the consecrated ruler was venerated and sacrifice was made as a part of the cult, nobody thought of offering prayer to a consecrated ruler, requesting benefits such as were solicited by prayer from the gods. However, it was the cult of a human being, of a man turned into a god like Heracles, worship of an idol and therefore, for a Jew, unacceptable. And for Christians later.

Educated people, even emperors themselves – the audience which listened to Seneca's *Apokolocyntosis*; Vespasian on his death bed[128] – could mock the institution in private, but not in public. In public it was treated with profound respect.

At the same time it was better that an emperor should not (like Domitian) anticipate the divine status which might or might not be voted to him after death. So the younger Pliny praised Trajan:[129]

If another emperor had even one of these acts to his credit, his radiate image on gold or ivory throne would have been placed between statues of the gods, invoked by the offerings of more splendid victims on more august altars. You, on the other hand, never enter a holy place except as a worshipper and the highest honour that you accept is for your statues to stand guard *outside* a temple; consequently the gods preserve your pre-eminence among men since you do not seek to be pre-eminent among gods. So in the hall of the temple of Juppiter Optimus Maximus we see only one or two statues of you, and those in bronze. Only the other day the entrances, the steps, the whole courtyard gleamed with gold and silver – or rather was defiled when images of the gods were infected by proximity to the statues of an unchaste emperor.

Why, when the whole of the rest of the world accepted, and indeed in its attendant celebrations enjoyed, the imperial cult, should the Jews alone be allowed to indulge their curious idiosyncrasy to the extent of not even paying lip-service to the cult? This was the question for a paranoiac, indeed for a martinet, to ask. Gaius Caligula asked it. There was a simple way of putting an end to the whole nonsense; the Jews should be forced to admit a statue of himself into their temple at Jerusalem. It was a trial of strength which the Jews won.

There was no absurdity about worshipping an invisible god, a god who was not portrayed in human form; far from it. Absurdity entered into religion when people treated animals as gods.

Did the Jews really worship the pig, and was that why they did not eat pork? Did they worship the donkey (and not eat hares because hares look like miniature donkeys)? Both suggestions were made maliciously by anti-semites.[130]

But about the Egyptians there was no doubt at all; they were animal-worshippers, worshippers of crocodiles and cats, of dogs and snakes and, above all, of the bull Apis, a god manifest, on exhibition to tourists.[131] When Augustus was asked whether he would like to see the bull, he declined with the crude remark, 'I worship gods, not cows'.[132]

To most educated pagans it was at first perhaps even more extraordinary to believe in a god who, in the form of man, had been crucified, the official accounts of whose human existence were riddled with contradictions and inconsistencies, whose explicit appeal was primarily to social outcasts and who preached the physical resurrection of the body to life after death.[133] Yet this religion became universal and trampled on polytheistic paganism, only – in a sense – to bring polytheism back in the cult of the saints in the Catholic Church, some of them – Santa Lucia in Syracuse, for instance – closely modelled, as it seemed, on pagan prototypes.

(xi) Religious spread

If Greece was the origin of most of the humane culture of the Roman empire, the source of its religious infection lay further east, in Asia Minor, Syria, Palestine, Egypt and Iran. While the indigenous religions of the western and northern provinces continued to flourish under Roman rule, they did not spread. On the other hand, each of the powerful oriental religions spread into the West through 'carriers', through slaves from the East who cherished the religion of their upbringing as a memory of home and often communicated the infection to rich households in Rome and elsewhere (the empress Poppaea may have acquired her Jewish sympathies from a slave),[134] through sailors (especially Isis-worship), through traders and soldiers who had been born or stationed in the East, whether individuals or whole units. In AD 69 Legion III Gallica, recently returned from Syria to the Danube, saluted the rising sun, 'as is the custom in Syria'.[135]

The novelty and attraction of the various oriental religious imports lay in their concern, greater or smaller as the case might be, with man's moral and spiritual life on earth and in their general belief in some kind of survival after death, questions which by traditional Roman ideas lay in the field not of religion but of philosophy. To many, as to Lucius in Apuleius' *Metamorphoses*, they gave the startling excitement of religious conversion and in some (Isis-worship and

Mithraism) there was a progress in sanctity as the devotee passed by trials and ordeals from neophyte to a place among the holiest of the holy. There were the Mysteries, like the traditional Greek Mysteries at Eleusis, no detail of which must be whispered abroad to the profane, ceremonies which have been compared with the secret rites of Freemasonry in the modern world.[136]

Egyptian cults were established strongly in Nîmes and Arles in south Gaul, but otherwise struck no deep roots in the western provinces. They made a strong impact on Italy (in Rome, the harbour-towns and inland on a main highway at Beneventum, where numerous monuments of Isis-worship are to be seen today), and in Greece Pausanias records the existence of temples and shrines of Isis and/or Serapis at a number of towns on the coast. Plutarch tells us most that we know of the cult, and there is the deeply spiritual account in Apuleius of a conversion. There was the appeal of religious feminism and, though the cult may have provided cover for occasional sexual scandals, as in AD 19 at Rome, a high price was set on chastity and that had its strong (if sometimes irregular) appeal for women.[137]

Syrian cults were spread in the West by merchants and soldiers and flourished particularly in the garrisoned frontier provinces; their golden age in Rome was the half-century from the accession of Septimius Severus to the death of Severus Alexander, thanks to the influence of Julia Domna and her remarkable family.[138]

Asia-Minor cults, in particular the worship of Cybele, seem to have had few soldiers or Roman officials among their devotees, but they were strong at certain points, particularly in Africa and southern Gaul. To this branch of religion. belonged the *taurobolium*, the drenching of a devotee under a grill with the blood of a slaughtered bull and his subsequent cleansing with milk and wool, a deeply emotional rite of purification, a cleansing of the whole congregation whom he represented.[139]

Mithraism was, it seems, to all intents and purposes a religion for men only; and (apart from the vituperations of early Christian writers) epigraphy and archaeology tell us almost all that we know of it. It was a late arrival in the West, and there is no evidence of western observance of the cult earlier than the end of the first century AD. It was a paradoxical religion, a cult of the sun and of light whose ceremonies were held in dark underground chambers. In Rome there were at one time or another up to a hundred Mithraic sanctuaries; but in general it was an eclectic religion without a professional priesthood, a religion for men and, among men, particularly for soldiers. So it is on the frontiers of the Empire where soldiers were stationed, that most of the evidence comes, evidence of devotion in particular by officers, some of them very high-ranking. For, based on Mazdaean dualism, it was a fighting religion, a manly struggle, with Mithras as helper and companion, against Ahriman and the powers of darkness.[140]

In oriental religion there was a penchant towards monotheism and pantheism which from the second century AD onwards infected educated Romans and resulted in a certain syncretism. When Isis appeared to Lucius in Apuleius' *Metamorphoses*, she declared herself to be 'the natural mother of all things, mistress and governess of all the elements ... The Phrygians ... call me the Mother of the gods at Pessinus; the Athenians ... Cecropian Minerva; the Cyprians ... Paphian Venus; the Cretans ... Dictynnian Diana; the Sicilians ... infernal Proserpine; the Eleusinians their ancient goddess Ceres; some Juno, others Bellona, others Hecate, others Rhamnusia. The Ethiopians ... and the Egyptians ... call me by my true name, Queen Isis'.[141]

Such syncretism is evident in a number of inscriptional dedications from the second century onwards in the western empire, nearly all of them by imperial officials, soldiers, in particular by officers, and high-ranking officers at that. This move towards monotheism (and syncretism) was influenced from the East, prominently expressed in the imperial house by Elagabalus' cult of his Baal and Aurelian's imposition, with its vast new temple in Rome, of the worship of the Sun. It was from Rome that this influence emanated through the civil service and the army; there is no evidence that it had any effect on the bourgeois population of the towns in the West or on the peasants.[142]

(xii) Seeing into, even controlling, the future

Where the public life of the State was concerned, Romans had once believed firmly – and, even when scepticism intervened, continued to behave as if they still believed firmly – that the gods, properly approached through those possessing the right kind of expertise, gave reliable tip-offs about future events. The haruspices, with their Etruscan lore, knew what the condition of the inwards of a sacrificed animal signified; so, if in sacrifice before a battle the signs were inauspicious, the wise general knew that was not a day on which to fight. There were warning examples in the history books of commanders who had disregarded such signs, had fought and had been defeated.

Hence, too, in public life, the Roman obsession with publicly reported prodigies (a shower of blood in Tuscany, perhaps, or a calf which spoke with a human voice), for these were warning signs, generously vouchsafed by the gods, that there was trouble brewing. Once such a prodigy was reported (and it was the patriotic duty of a citizen to report it), the experts were called on at once, the augurs or the *decemviri* (later *quindecimviri*) *sacris faciundis* who had charge of the Sibylline books. These priests discovered and told the Senate what apotropaic measures should be taken. So, with luck, disaster was averted; the gods, and their human experts, had enabled the State to extricate itself from what might have been a nasty mess. Livy realised that this was not the kind of thing to be kept out of the history books;

and in the fourth century AD Obsequens, a fervid pagan at a time when paganism was struggling for survival, extracted the reports of prodigies in Livy, to show how truly prophetic they were of disaster (in cases, that is, when apotropaic measures had, for one reason or another, proved ineffective).[143]

But what of the individual?

Man, it was said, is slave to two powerful emotions, hope and fear, both connected with the future. 'Everybody alive is greedy to know what the future has in store for him, and believes such knowledge is to be sought with the greatest accuracy from heaven'; so the elder Pliny.[144]

Pretentious expertise was available in a number of different forms: oracles; dream-interpreters (for few people doubted the prophetic quality of dreams); astrologers. And for those who wished to force the future to suit their own sinister wishes (disaster to a rival charioteer at the games, perhaps, or the death of somebody who stood in the way of a handsome legacy) there was the magician, *magus*.

(a) Oracles

There were no significant oracles in Italy or the West; their home was in the Greek East, the most famous being at Dodona, at Delphi, in Asia Minor at Didyma (Branchidai) near Miletus and in Egypt at Siwa (Ammon), together with the oracle of Clarus (near Colophon in Asia Minor), which achieved prominence in Roman times, and that of Trophonius in Boeotia, where the enquirer was drawn underground, to emerge subsequently, like a mole, often at some other unpredictable spot.[145] Delphi, the greatest of all, had lost standing by the time of the late Republic (presumably through bad business management), as we know from Plutarch's essay on the subject, but it was to enjoy a certain revival later at the time of Septimius Severus;[146] the others were doing very good business when Pausanias, the most credulous of men, was writing in the second century AD[147] and until the middle of the third century.

Indeed, given a good impresario with a business head and a mastery of prestidigitation (if Lucian's *Alexander* or *The Bogus Seer*, our chief evidence, is to be believed) there was room in the credulous world of the second century AD for the establishment of a successful new oracle – by a certain Alexander at Abonuteichos in Pamphylia, which survived its founder for at least a century. According to Lucian, written enquiries, heavily sealed, were opened and skilfully resealed and miraculously apposite answers were given, difficulty arising only in cases where the enquiry was made in a language which none of the staff operating the oracle could understand (see p.137).

The long success of Greek oracles is a remarkable tribute to the genius of their organisers, their skill in a kind of cleverness which Greeks greatly admired, the devising of ambiguous answers to enquiries, answers which could claim to be accurate prophecies, whatever the outcome of events. Hannibal, years after he had left Carthage, was not unduly worried when he was cornered by the arrival of Roman envoys in Bithynia, for Ammon had told him that he would be buried in African soil. He was not to know until it was too late that there was a spot called Africa in Bithynia.[148]

Romans in the East naturally tried their luck at any oracle they passed, from ordinary travellers, business men and common soldiers (a trooper of Sulla, for instance, at the oracle of Trophonius) to great generals, Germanicus (who received no better promise from Apollo Clarius than he did later in Egypt from the bull Apis) and Titus, for whom in the temple of Paphian Venus in Cyprus in AD 69 there was an intimation of good things to come. The younger Cato's refusal to consult the oracle of Zeus Ammon in Libya when the Republicans withdrew to Africa after Pharsalus was predictably idiosyncratic.[149]

The oracle at Abonuteichos had plenty of prominent Romans among its enquirers; Alexander, indeed, married off his daughter (the child, he declared, resulting from his liaison with the Moon) to one of them, a man of prominence called Rutilianus.

And there were the numerous Sibyls, issuing from time to time happy – if forlorn – auguries for the enemies of Rome (see p.191).

(b) Dreams
The whole course of ancient pagan and biblical history is strewn with significant dreams;[150] Thucydides, indeed, may well be the only historian of antiquity who did not anywhere record that somebody or other had a startling (and prophetic) dream. Cassius Dio stands at the opposite extreme, a man whose first published work had to do with dreams which foretold the imperial accession of Septimius Severus (see p.212), who was even more prone to superstitious belief, including belief in the prophetic nature of dreams, than Dio himself.[151]

Sensational dreams (mostly violent nightmares) visited the great (Nebuchadnezzar in the book of Daniel, Astyages, the last king of Media, Xerxes,[152] Caesar's wife and Pilate's) as well as the humble. They were remembered, communicated to others and submitted for interpretation to professional dream-experts. As well as practitioners, there was a large literature on the subject, starting with Aristotle's 'On Dreams' and 'Divination by Dreams' and reaching its climax in Artemidorus' great manual on dreams published in the late second century AD.[153] In these books dreams were classified by type and subject; so that if a man was concerned about the significance of a dream, there was always an informative passage for him to consult.

Interpretations were the matter of a highly mannered sort of rationalisation. To dream of boxing, for instance, was bad for most people because boxing was harmful and involved loss of blood (which signified money), but it was good for those who earned their living by blood–doctors, sacrificial priests and butchers.[154]

In branches of medicine, particularly in the form of treatment at the great hospitals at Epidaurus in the Peloponnese, as in temples of Isis and Serapis where incubation was practised, very considerable importance was attached to the clinical evidence which, it was thought, was supplied by a patient's dreams. In the six books of his *Hieroi Logoi* ('Sacred Teachings') the hypochondriac Aelius Aristides has left a record of prolonged and not markedly successful dream-therapy.

(c) Astrology

For the superstitious masses, belief that human life was influenced, even controlled, by the stars was a natural creed; could anybody deny that growth in nature was influenced by the sun, the tides of the sea by the moon?

All the world over, a number of actions, particularly in agriculture, were determined, sometimes rationally, sometimes irrationally, by the position of the stars, just as today they are controlled by calendar dates.* And there were common superstitions, as there are today, about lucky and unlucky days for particular enterprises, such as getting married or starting a journey. Outside which common conventions, people at large wished to assure themselves of choosing an auspicious moment for any important undertaking, and who could give this assurance better than a man who understood the movements of the heavenly bodies and who was trained to interpret their significance? Who better than an astrologer?

Astrologers were 'mathematici', because of their complicated calculations, 'Chaldaei', because their lore was an eastern lore, even though they themselves more often than not were Greek.

The belief that the whole of an individual's life was conditioned by the position of the stars at the moment of his birth was, like astronomy itself, of great antiquity in Babylon and in Egypt. At Rome its first powerful advocate at the end of the Republic was the 'Pythagorean' Nigidius Figulus, the man who was believed, on the day when the Catilinarian conspiracy was exposed in 63 BC, to have predicted that a child just born to the wife of the senator Octavius would rise to be master of the Roman world.[155]

Professional astrologers covered a wide range, from the scholarly Thrasyllus, court astrologer to the emperor Tiberius on the one hand to unprincipled charlatans at the other. Tacitus was not alone in despising the whole profession as tricksters, faithless to those in power, men who misled their sanguine clients.

They had their advertised successes: Nigidius Figulus' forecast of the future emperor Augustus, the forecast that Nero would become emperor and kill his mother, prognostications that Galba would be an

---

* In my part of England, plant potatoes on Good Friday (irrational); do not sow runner beans before 6 May, and stop cutting asparagus on midsummer day (both rational).

emperor when he reached old age and that Otho would outlive the rule of Nero.[156]

No particular harm was done (except, perhaps, to himself) by the private individual anxious to discover from his horoscope what the remainder of life had in store for him – unless he was a man who could be suspected of imperial ambition. When in AD 16 Libo Drusus, a blood connexion of the imperial family, enquired of an astrologer whether he would ever be rich enough to pave the Appian way the whole length to Brindisi with gold, was this simple insanity, or was it a sign of dangerous ambition?[157] More suspect still was the man who did what the law forbad and asked an astrologer for the emperor's horoscope; for intimation that the ruling emperor's days were numbered was a powerful encouragement to the conspirator. So in the rash of treason cases under the early Empire astrologers were frequently compromised and ostentatiously exiled; yet in no time at all they were back again and up to their old games.

Sceptics who believed the whole thing to be nonsense could make fun of a belief in the truth of horoscopes.[158] In general, however, credulity triumphed. With rare exceptions (Nerva, for instance, and Trajan) emperors kept their own astrologers and consulted them frequently. Society women were fervent astrological addicts and still in the fourth century, as Ammianus Marcellinus records, the rich in Rome were obsessed by their astrological calendars,[159] and general belief in astrology was strong enough to provoke the fulminations of the Christian Church.

Astrology featured in the schoolboy's rhetorical exercises. In one, an astrologer foretold that a man would win glory in war and then kill his father. Having fought with glory, he petitioned the court for leave to commit suicide before the second part of the prediction came true, as he was certain that it would, for, devoted as he was to his father, he was already itching to kill him. He was opposed in his application by his father. It was a nice paradox, the fanatical believer in the truth of astrological prediction seeking to make the prediction false.[160]

(d) Magic

Magical practices were as old as Rome itself, and their employment for the damaging of other people's crops was forbidden by the Twelve Tables.[161] And there was a whole variety of nostrums, carefully researched into by the elder Pliny, which were no more than primitive medicines, cures for toothache or spotty faces with their caveats, for instance that these last would not work in the case of people with freckles.[162] More powerful and sinister were forms of sympathetic and demoniac magic, spells used by witches (who were to be found in great numbers in Thessaly) and devices for the killing and maiming of people which originated in the East, *defixiones*, curses scratched on tablets and buried, invoking the powers of darkness, or the burial of human bones (a device which, it was claimed, helped to ensure the death of Germanicus in the East). And in AD 16 Libo Drusus did more than enquire about gilding the Appian way; he had lists of prominent men of state with sinister marks against their names.[163]

Magi were believed to have the power even to call up the shades of the dead. One of the fantastic cases on which young men who were being educated in rhetoric were called on to sharpen their wits was of a mother in search of a *magus* to recall her dead son; but this was unnecessary because the spirit of her dead son took to appearing spontaneously and regularly to her; so that, on the contrary, a *magus* was employed by her husband to lay the ghost and put an end to the nonsense. For which act he found himself being prosecuted by his wife.[164]

Belief in magic was evidently widespread in north Africa. There it was that Apuleius was prosecuted for magical practices and, however ridiculous the charges are made to appear in his (surviving) defence, he obviously had an interest in the occult and was evidently believed to have acquired a knowledge of magical practices in his journeying in the East. From Africa (Carthage and Hadrumetum) come a great number of *defixiones* which, to judge by the names of the desiderated victims, belong to the life of the lowest dregs of society.[165]

(e) The critics

A number of clever men believed in the prophetic character of dreams, and Stoics opined that dreams could be interpreted by 'wise men'.[166] In the *De divinatione* Cicero made a merciless onslaught on such a view. Dream-interpreters, so far from being the 'wise men' of Stoicism, were the scum of the earth. The idea of a divine dream-purveyor at every bedside was nonsensical and, if heaven had decided to reveal the future through dreams, it would obviously have achieved this in a far more straightforward manner, not making it a matter of chance whether or not on waking people remembered what they had dreamt, not sending dreams which were effective and others which were not effective at all.[167]

We must assume, therefore, that the record of one of the most sensationally prophetic dreams, a dream of Cicero himself, is somebody's invention and not the truth. He is said to have dreamt that a small boy, unknown to him, was taken by the hand by Juppiter and told that he would one day rule and bring an end to civil war. The next day Cicero saw the boy in the flesh, a young Octavius – destined to be Caesar Octavianus and later the emperor Augustus.[168]

Outside the Stoics (with a few exceptions like Panaetius), astrology, anyhow professedly, had few advocates among men of culture, though some, like Tacitus, wavered. Knowledge of the future, if obtainable, would surely cause greater unhappiness than happiness. Astrology was a profit-making business, run by charlatans. If a man was so indiscreet as to open his heart to an astrologer, he might soon find that he was in the hands of a blackmailer.[169]

And what nonsense it was. How explain twins of utterly diverse character and fortune? St Augustine asked the question, as Diogenes the Stoic had asked it earlier. Had heredity no part in the formation of a man's character? Did all the tens of thousands of men killed at Cannae have the same horoscope?[170]

Or astrology was faulted on metaphysical grounds. The events of human life were determined by fate or else they were a matter of pure chance (*tychê*). Tacitus tells us that he had often been tempted to think this; so, of course, had thousands of other people. If the succession of events was determined by random chance, then no prediction of the future was possible. If, on the other hand, events were controlled by fate (or the providence of the gods), the determination of their course would be beyond human knowledge. By such argument the philosopher had persuaded Alexander to enter Babylon in 324, disregarding the prediction of a *magus* that he would die there. He did, of course.[171]

In a world denied the supposed boons of cheap journalism, television and radio, the views of the intelligentsia will not have travelled far outside their own society except when the subject of public orations by orators like Dio Chrysostom in the eastern Mediterranean world. So popular belief in the efficacy of astrology is unlikely to have been affected by rational criticisms. By the law of averages, predictions were sometimes accurate, sometimes uncannily accurate; and such successes were no doubt loudly advertised. For the rest, in the – highly complicated – business of casting horoscopes, mistakes, venial mistakes, could be made; there was no need to ascribe every faulty prediction to corruption and villainy.

Stoics, with their belief in an inexorable Fate, were sympathetic (though where, in a determinist world, was there room for free will?). Epicureans, who did not believe in a determinist Fate, had no truck with astrology at all – or with oracles, as Alexander of Abonuteichos found; the people on whom that charlatan could not impose were the Epicureans and the Christians.

(xiii) Variations on the theme of death

(a) Ritual murder

If questioned, a civilised Roman at the end of the first century AD, would have agreed that human sacrifice, ritual murder, was a barbaric practice, widespread in many countries which the Romans conquered, in particular Carthage, and that its suppression was one of the creditable achievements of Roman imperialism.[172] It had existed in Narbonese Gaul[173] and, further north, there had been the Druids in Gaul and Britain. It had also existed in Spain.

In 97 BC the Roman Senate passed a decree forbidding human sacrifice.[174]

Carthage was the most notorious case. There the sons of prominent families were sacrificed, and regularly, to reinvigorate the god Baal Hammon (whom the Greeks identified with Chronos and who survived in Roman Africa as Saturnus). Diodorus describes how parents cheated the god by purchasing children for sacrifice, so as to avoid the heart-rending surrender of their own. But in 310 BC, shattered by the successes of the Syracusan Agathocles, they were forcibly recalled to a sense of patriotic duty, and five hundred boys of good families were burnt to death. The discovery of urns with the burnt bones of children at Carthage confirms the accounts of our literary sources.[175]

The practice did not end with the destruction of Carthage in 146 BC; it survived, according to Tertullian, until firmly suppressed by the Romans 'in the proconsulship of Tiberius', though even after this it continued surreptitiously. St Augustine states simply that the Romans put an end to such sacrifice. The 'proconsulship of Tiberius' has been variously dated (see p.159) to the rule of the emperor Tiberius which, given Tertullian's language, is improbable, or even to the late second century AD, which is more improbable still. There is much to be said for the speculation that an otherwise unknown Tiberius was proconsul of Africa round 97 BC, and that he enforced the decree which the Senate had recently passed.[176]

In Gaul there were the Druids; and their beastly and barbarous practice of human sacrifice, to which Romans of the Republic referred in shocked horror as if it was a daily event in Gaul, required imperial action for its suppression. Augustus forbad Roman citizens to take part in the cult and Tiberius (by a senatorial decree) and Claudius (by edict) forbad Druidic practices in Gaul. However, there was still Britain, and it was not until AD 60 that Anglesey (Mona), the centre of the cult, was captured. There are reports after this of Druidic seers and wise women, but the cult-practices by whose inhumanity Romans were appalled were evidently brought to an end.[177]

In Spain P. Crassus, consul of 97 BC, armed with the Senate's recent decree, arrested chiefs of the Bletonenses in Further Spain and sent them to Rome, where they explained that they had done no more than follow an established tradition among their own people. On which, they were pardoned, sent home and told not to do it again.[178]

In Italy the murder of the king-priest, always a runaway slave, at Nemi and the succession of his murderer to the priesthood continued at least until the second century AD, the survival, evidently, of some fertility cult. In Iberia in the Caucasus, where temple-slaves wandered round in inspired frenzy, one was caught annually, fed richly for a year and then anointed and slaughtered, prognostications being made about future events from the manner of his dying, just as they were made by the Druids in Gaul. The credulous were even led by enemies of the Jews to believe that a Greek was captured regularly, fed extravagantly in the temple at Jerusalem, and then killed and eaten.[179]

What of the behaviour of the Roman state itself?

Nothing, Livy wrote, could be less Roman: 'minime Romanum sacrum'; and Romans were brought up to believe that human sacrifice had been shunned deliberately or else abolished at an early period of their history. Why, when a thunderbolt fell, did the expiatory sacrifice consist of an onion, a lock of human hair and a sprat? Because when good king Numa haggled with Juppiter over the foundation of Roman cults and Juppiter called for human sacrifice whenever he threw one of his bolts, Numa had been too sharp for him. When Juppiter claimed a head, Numa agreed: an onion. When Juppiter said the offering must be human, Numa agreed: a lock of human hair. When Juppiter insisted on a living sacrifice, Numa agreed: a sprat. At which point Juppiter retired beaten.

There was a widespread belief, however false, that the twenty-seven puppets thrown with great ceremony into the Tiber every year on 14 May had at some early date replaced human beings.[180]

But what of historical facts? Nobody could deny that the punishment of a Vestal Virgin who was judged to have broken her vows was to be buried alive under the Campus Sceleratus at the Colline Gate (her paramour was whipped to death in public), and such punishment had been inflicted in 226 BC (when the Gauls threatened Rome), in 216 after the disaster of Cannae and perhaps in 114-113 at the time of the invasion of the Cimbri and Teutones. Even more horrifying was the burial alive on all these three occasions of four perfectly innocent men and women, two Gauls and two Greeks, this being, as it seems, a part of Rome's Etruscan inheritance, a grim way of averting the threat, sacredly revealed, that Etruscan soil would be occupied by neighbouring peoples to North and South.

So, when Rome boasted of her suppression of human sacrifice in the Empire at large, she invited an obvious retort. It is likely that the point was stressed by Posidonius in his History.[181]

To make this worse, it was not ancient history. The elder Pliny stated that his generation had witnessed the burial alive of Gauls and Greeks. By Gaius Caligula embarking on his German war? Possibly, though the fact is not attested. And, as for the burial of corrupt (or allegedly corrupt) Vestal Virgins, this occurred under Domitian, perhaps in AD 92, and we have the younger Pliny's melodramatic account of the grisly episode; the girl, he declares, was innocent. Again in AD 213 the emperor Caracalla, having managed in a last fling of his failing virility, to debauch a Vestal Virgin, then ordered her burial alive, together with two other members of the little College.

Further there was the story, repeated by Christian writers, that in Rome at the time of the *feriae Latinae* a criminal (*bestiarius*) was sacrificed each year. The story has been dismissed as apocryphal, but about this some scholars have their doubts.[182]

(b) Disposal of the aged and euthanasia

Those who survive to a great age have always constituted a problem for others, in particular in societies living on the verge of starvation: useless mouths. So when Critognatus urged cannibalism on the defenders of Alesia in 52 BC, he suggested that a start should be made on the old, as had been done a generation earlier in Gallic cities beleaguered by the invading Cimbri and Teutones.[183]

Everybody in Rome knew the saying, 'Sexagenarios de ponte', 'Throw the sexagenarians off the bridge'; and while there was complete uncertainty as to its origin, it was easy to believe that at some remote time in the past Romans rid themselves of their sexagenarians by throwing them into the Tiber. Cicero once exploited this belief by claiming that a person whose character he was determined to blacken had thrown a man into the Tiber without even waiting for him to be sixty.

The truth, however, seems different; that the bridge was the bridge to the ballot-boxes at election-times and that once, when generals were being elected (consuls, that is to say, who would command Roman armies), the younger men had shouted for the sexagenarians to be thrown off the bridge and prevented from voting on an issue which, since their own fighting days were long over, did not concern them.[184]

There were places, however, in and outside the empire where there was an age-limit for survival. Among Greeks, the Greek expression 'Sardonic laughter' was fancifully derived from the facial expression of aged Sardinians, whose sons had decided that they had lived long enough, as they sat on the edge of their graves and waited for the clout with which their sons were about to dispatch them, happy – or not so happy? – to die? Hence the mixed expression. And on the small island of Ceos, according to Strabo, they gave hemlock to those who reached the age of sixty, so as to save food.

Strabo does not seem, however, to have got his facts quite right. Not long after his book was published, in about AD 27, another writer, Valerius Maximus, put into Ceos in attendance on his patron Sex. Pompeius, who was on his way to take up the proconsulship of Asia, and he gives an eyewitness's account of the euthanasia of an old lady of ninety. Just as at Massilia a public supply of hemlock was maintained from which anybody could draw a lethal dose if the authorities (the Six Hundred), after hearing the application, gave the necessary permission, so in Ceos, if the citizen body approved, any one might, by a draft of hemlock, take his own life. This old lady, in full possession of her faculties and with a large number of surviving descendants, thought that, with a Roman proconsul on the island, there was the opportunity of dying with suitable panache. Sex. Pompeius, a man of great charm according to Valerius Maximus, tried to deter her but was overcome by the strength of her arguments; and so in the presence of relatives, friends and Roman officials (who broke down and wept), she drank the hemlock and retired from life with all the dignity of Socrates himself.* [185]

According to Pomponius Mela, Scyths who thought that they had lived long enough and feared boredom if they lived longer, jumped, happy and garlanded, into the sea and drowned. [186]

In the East, according to Strabo (who may, of course, be as inaccurate here as he was in the case of Ceos), Caspians locked up their septuagenarians, to die of starvation, while the dervishes of the Caucasus killed and ate men of that age; women they strangled and buried. Until Alexander stopped the practice, the Bactrians were thought by Strabo to have killed anybody enfeebled by age or illness and to have kept what they called 'undertaker-dogs' to eat them; hence the profusion of human bones which were to be seen in the streets of their metropolis. [187]

(c) Suicide

Suicide was often regarded with disapproval and there was a religious, if not a legal, ban on the burial of anyone who hanged himself. A soldier who attempted suicide and failed – 'unless because of pain and grief' – was liable to execution. By the regulations of a funeral club at Lanuvium – and, no doubt, in a number of others too – members who committed suicide were denied burial. Their spirits might be imagined, as by Virgil, sad and repentant in the underworld. And there was a general fear that suicides returned as ghosts. [188]

In certain cases, however, suicide was generally approved: by Lucretia in legend, unwilling to live with the disgrace of having been raped by Tarquin;† by the victims of incurable illness (the younger Pliny records a number of cases); by men who had suffered public disgrace (like Cornelius Gallus in 26 BC, when Augustus renounced his friendship because of the arrogance with which he had advertised his own achievements as first Prefect of Egypt) or by those who took their lives to avoid suffering such disgrace. [189]

Stoics held generally, as Plato had held, that there were circumstances in which suicide was justifiable, an act of *constantia*; when, for instance, whether because of oppressive political conditions or because of the extreme distress of incurable illness, the virtuous man was debarred from living a fully virtuous life. As Marcus Aurelius wrote, borrowing a vivid expression from Epictetus, 'when the chimney smokes, I go out of the room'. Epictetus considered suicide a matter of indifference, available always and justifiable when

---

* *Economist*, 25 October 1975, survey p.27, in a forecast of the future: 'As the death rate drops, mankind will probably have to move towards acceptance of euthanasia and even planned death (with a hell of a going-away party on your eighty-fifth birthday?)'

† St Augustine disagreed (*CD* 1, 19); if a woman was raped against her will, her heart was still pure, whatever the state of her body. If she killed herself, therefore, she murdered an innocent.

suffering was extreme – Epicureans thought the same – or conditions of life were intolerable – 'when god sends a message' – but in general it does not seem to have been a vitally important element in the Stoic creed.[190]

Some expressions of Stoicism go further, as in Cicero's *De finibus*:

When a man's circumstances contain a preponderance of things in accordance with nature, it is appropriate for him to remain alive; when he possesses or sees in prospect a majority of the contrary things, it is appropriate for him to depart from life. This makes it plain that it is on occasion appropriate for the Wise Man to quit life though he is happy and also for the Foolish Man to remain in life though he is miserable ... Very often it is appropriate for the Wise Man to abandon life at a moment when he is enjoying supreme happiness, if an opportunity offers for making a timely exit. For the Stoic view is that happiness, which means life in harmony with nature, is a matter of seizing the right moment ... And since the fool is equally miserable when departing from life and when remaining in it, and the undesirability of his life is not increased by its prolongation, there is good ground for saying that those who are in a position to enjoy a preponderance of things that are natural ought to remain in life.

(*De fin.* 3, 60f., tr. H. Rackham, *LCL*)

Given the aristocratic Roman belief in the *dignitas* and the independence (*libertas*) of the individual, suicide naturally acquired a new publicity with the advent of the dominance of the Caesars. The younger Cato's suicide, correct to the last detail, the only alternative to the ignominy of submission to Caesar's pardon, raised him to the highest pinnacle of uncontested fame. There was much in his life which could be criticised, as Julius Caesar criticised it in writing, but there was nothing at all to criticise in his melodramatic death. When the time came, Marcus Brutus and Cassius (unlike their fellow-conspirator Decimus Brutus) followed Cato's splendid lead.[191] After that came a series of Stoic martyrs, men and women (Thrasea Paetus, for instance, and the elder Arria) and other suicidal martyrs who were not Stoics at all, men who whether from free will or under constraint escaped by death from the tyranny of imperial rule.

So it is not surprising that Seneca (who was in due course to follow in the tradition), living at the time when he did, wrote of suicide differently from other Stoics. It was a subject by which he was all but obsessed: suicide was a free act,* open to all, infinitely ennobling. 'A man could take inspiration even from a slave, and a German slave at that.' Seneca would have committed suicide himself quite early in life, he writes, on account of his recurrent illness, had he not been deterred by fears of the shock which might be felt by his old father.[192]

Wherever you look, there is a way of ending your troubles. Look at that precipice – a descent to freedom; that sea, that river, that well – at the bottom of each there is freedom. That stunted, parched, unfruitful tree; freedom hangs from its branches. You neck, your throat, your heart – escape-routes from slavery, all of them. And if

---

* 'Seneca comes very near to arguing that suicide itself makes one a free man', J.M. Rist, *Stoic Philosophy*, Cambridge 1969, 248.

you think these ways of escape too complicated, in need of courage and strength, then, if you are looking for a way to freedom, any vein in your body will do.[193]

However mentally deranged a man might be at the moment when he committed suicide, he was highly inconsiderate if he did not leave convincing evidence that he had killed himself; for if there was any reason at all to think that he had been murdered by a slave, the whole of his slave-household would face execution. Indeed, it might happen that whatever a slave did was wrong; a case which featured in the rhetoric schools was of a slave who refused his master's order to give him poison – and then, when his master died, the will ordered that he should be crucified. It was one aspect of the nobility of the emperor Otho's suicide that he dismissed his slaves and a confidential freedman before committing the act.[194]

There was in most cases nothing particularly newsworthy about suicide; it was normally a sordid upper-class practice, a bathroom – or a bedroom – act, messy and rarely enlivened by the final witticism of a Valerius Asiaticus – 'Move that pyre; you will ruin the trees where you have put it' – or a Petronius – 'To Nero, with compliments, an attested list of his, as he has so far thought, hidden and unknown delinquencies.'[195] But suicide as a great public spectacle was a different matter, and suicide by burning at that; for by Roman law burning alive ranked with crucifixion as the most terrible of punishments, the fate, for instance, of a soldier who deserted or of a slave who conspired against his master.[196]

This was one of India's innumerable marvels, the public self-immolation of a Brahman Sophist. So far from killing himself first and being burnt afterwards, he climbed, spruce and even smiling, onto the pyre and was burnt on it alive. Like the phoenix. More than this, there was suttee, reports of which had reached the western world. There was a belief, indeed, that in India the elderly and infirm commonly sought a living death on the pyre, fire itself being innobled by consuming the living, polluted by consuming the dead.[197]

The self-immolation of an Indian philosopher on the pyre was an exhibition first staged for a western audience in the presence of Alexander the Great. It was impossible, Arrian stated, to write a history of Alexander without mentioning Calanus, the Indian philosopher who, to the disapproval of his fellow-sophists, joined Alexander's entourage. In Persia he fell ill and, with Alexander's permission, was burnt alive, unflinching, before a gala-parade of the Macedonian troops, with Ptolemy as Master of Ceremonies.[198] The episode was described, no doubt, in Ptolemy's History, as in all other histories of Alexander.

A similar spectacle was offered to an awe-struck audience at Athens, this time during the principate of Augustus. The Indian – called Zarmanochegas, or something like it – had accompanied the embassy sent by the Indian king Poros to Augustus. He committed suicide at Athens, 'leaping onto the pyre with a laugh, his naked body anointed, wearing only a loin cloth', not because he was ill but because he was happy and felt that he might never again enjoy such euphoria; so it was the right moment to die.[199]

The third sensational self-immolation on a pyre, again in the most theatrical fashion, was of Peregrinus of Parium in Mysia at the Olympic Games of AD 165, after four years' advance notice of his intention. This man, whose teaching Aulus Gellius admired, of whom Ammianus Marcellinus was to speak approvingly later and whom Lucian ridiculed as a charlatan, had, after a short stint of Christianity, become a Cynic philosopher. Suicide was approved in certain circumstances by Cynics and in his own fantasy Peregrinus saw himself, in his death, a second Heracles.

The spectacle attracted a large and fascinated audience; the stench – in Lucian's satire on bogus philosophers – drove Zeus from that quarter of heaven to sweet-scented Arabia.[200]

Pausanias mentions a Greek, an Olympic victor, who on retirement kept himself fit by stretching a powerful bow. Forced to leave home for a time, he abandoned this daily exercise and on his return found that it was beyond his strength. So he burnt himself alive on a pyre. 'Whether in the past or the future,' Pausanias wrote, 'such behaviour strikes me not as courage but as simple lunacy.'[201]

(d) Disposal of the dead

There is an extraordinary story in Trogus – it is hardly likely to be true – that early in the fifth century BC when Darius was about to launch the Persian invasion of Greece, Persian envoys arrived in Carthage to solicit assistance, and delivered an edict of Darius by which the Carthaginians were instructed to abolish human sacrifice (see p.245), to stop eating dog-meat and to abandon inhumation in favour of cremation of the dead.[202]

As a general rule corpses were either buried or cremated. The Egyptians in general and the Jews (as, later, the Christians) buried their dead.[203] In early Rome (as in Greece and in Etruria) both methods were practised,[204] but from about 400 BC cremation became the general practice. In the late Republic the burning of Clodius' corpse and Caesar's in the Forum were occasions of sensational disorder. Public figures like emperors were burnt in the Campus Martius at Rome, ordinary people at crematoria (*ustrinae*), at the site of the tomb[205] or (as traditionally in China) at any other convenient place. Valerius Asiaticus' body was burnt on a pyre in his own garden (see p.251).

Even after cremation became common practice there were some families which continued to bury their dead; Sulla, for instance, was the first member of the gens Cornelia to be cremated.[206]

Starting in the time of Hadrian, there was a change of fashion.

Burial became common and by the end of the second century in Rome and Italy it had replaced cremation; the change spread to the western provinces, though in Africa cremation was still normal at the time of Tertullian and in Dacia it remained common practice until the coming of Christianity in the fourth/fifth centuries.[207]

So, starting with Hadrian, there was a fresh field for artistic enterprise, sculpting reliefs on the magnificent stone sarcophagi of the rich; splendid examples have been discovered in the recently excavated cemetery below the Vatican. The sarcophagi of poorer folk were of terra cotta.

What was the reason for this revolutionary change?

There is no evidence that it had anything to do with the spread of oriental and mystery cults in the West and it is too early to have been in response to Christianity.* But the suggestion has been made that in the early centuries of the Empire there was a growing belief in individual survival after death and that 'no pointer to this is more insistent than the superseding of cremation by inhumation during the second and third centuries'. 'The change of rite may well have expressed a vague perhaps but deepening intuition of the human body's meaning and purpose *sub specie aeternitatis* which the Christian doctrines of the Incarnation and the Resurrection of the Body were to clinch and clarify.'[208] No breath of such a view, naturally, comes from Lucian's essay on mourning for the dead (*De luctu*).

Another suggestion made is that the change in origin of the upper class in Rome, which started in Flavian times, may not be irrelevant.[209] The new senators were largely men from the Italian country towns, many from Etruria, where rich Etruscans had once been interred in magnificent sarcophagi.

Materially, a fuel crisis might supply the explanation.[210] We know how the forests disappeared in north Africa. Was it the case that elsewhere, with the great demand for wood for heating all the baths and for the making of pitch, Italy and other places had fears of a wood-shortage? Against this explanation it is argued that the first economic evidence of a fuel shortage would have been a rise in the price of wood and that in that case the poor rather than the rich would have started to change their habits. But in Rome the change seems to have started with the rich, and the rich – worried, as so many Romans were, about the survival of their memory – thought that the new-style carved sarcophagi were a finer and more abiding monument than any fragile urn could be.

Whatever the explanation, the change was a lasting one – still at the start of the fifth century nobody at Rome was cremated[211] – and it must have brought a lot of work and a lot of money to skilled stone-carvers.

---

* In the early Christian Church cremation was evidently held by some to be incompatible with belief in the physical resurrection of the body, Min. Felix, *Octavius* 11, 4 (but cf. 34, 10).

There is archaeological evidence that corpses were sometimes embalmed, and from literary sources we know of the embalming of the empress Poppaea and of Priscilla, wife of Domitian's secretary Abascantus. In the latter case, subject of a poem by Statius, we are told that Abascantus could not bear the thought of cremation. Recently the embalmed corpse of a young girl has been found by the via Cassia in Rome and a small number of embalmed corpses have been found at a variety of places in the western provinces. In such cases Egyptian embalmers were presumably available for families which either had roots in Egypt or who shared the delicate sensibility of Abascantus.[212]

Bodies (or ashes) were interred by the roadside outside the walls of Roman cities; so magnificent funerary monuments flanked the entry to great cities, to Rome on the via Flaminia, the via Latina and the via Appia, where their ruins survive today. Our most vivid knowledge of the construction and decoration of Roman tombs and of the people – generally middle-class, largely of freedman stock – buried in them comes from the excavation of the Isola Sacra and other cemeteries outside Ostia and in Rome below the Vatican of the tombs which once bordered the via Cornelia outside the city.[213]

Mass family burial had been an Etruscan practice, and the remains of a number of people might be buried in a single building. So at Rome later there was, at one extreme, the great mausoleum of Augustus built for himself and for well-behaved members of his family,[214] and the mausoleum of Hadrian and, at the other, the dovecots (*columbaria*)[215] which, in the recesses of their inner walls, housed the ashes of great numbers of the dead, usually humble folk, members of funeral-clubs who had made the necessary preparations, and paid the necessary subscriptions, in their lifetimes. Those which survive are, in large part, of the slaves and freedmen of eminent Roman families, of the empress Livia for instance, and they date from the time (or soon after) of the emperor Augustus,[216] when Maecenas replaced the unseemly collection of paupers' grave-pits (*puticuli*) on the Esquiline with a splendid public garden.[217]

There was also in all cities the family *columbarium*, excellent specimens of which survive at Ostia, built by a man for himself, his wife and their descendants and in due course for the freedmen and freedwomen of the family, with their descendants, the possession of which normally passed to his heir. In the niches were urns, waiting to hold the ashes, and often there was an inscription on the front wall imposing heavy penalties in the way of fines on anybody who should 'sell or give or in any other way alienate the tomb, or if anybody introduces the body or bones of anyone with a name other than is contained in this inscription'.[218] *Columbaria* continued to be built after cremation went out of fashion in the second century AD, with recesses for burial in place of niches in the walls, particularly at floor-level. The corpses of richer folk were contained in sarcophagi of stone or of terra cotta.

Below ground the catacombs* too were places of communal burial in the case of Christians, modelled presumably on Jewish catacombs. These are found outside Italy in Alexandria, at Hadrumetum in Africa and at Kertch in the Crimea, at Syracuse and in Malta and in Italy at Naples (St Januarius) and Albano as well as, most conspicuously, in the suburbs of Rome, particularly on the via Appia, always in places where there was soft rock in which it was not difficult to burrow and cut the recesses (*loculi*), several tiers of them beside the passages, each for the inhumation of from one to four bodies, sealed off by stone slabs. Walls and ceilings, as in the *columbaria*, were ornamented with paintings, those of the catacombs with both Christian and pagan motifs. At Rome the catacomb of St Callixtus, round AD 200, is the earliest public catacomb organised by the Church.[219]

The public burnings of dead emperors in the first centuries of the Empire, occasion – if they had merited it – of a miracle demonstrating metamorphosis into divinity, must have been a great public spectacle. In Augustus' case an eagle flew out of the pyre, evidently carrying his soul to heaven, this being Augustus' own idea, no doubt, since he had left detailed instructions for his funeral.[220] And in those early imperial days, to remove any possibility of doubt, a senator was found to testify to the assembled Fathers that he had witnessed the ascension from earth to heaven of Augustus, Drusilla, and then Claudius.[221] Later it was, seemingly, a different kind of miracle. The dead emperor's body was burnt privately and the private ceremony was followed by a public cremation of his own wax image. When the fire died down and the moment came to collect the ashes, no ashes were found. What further need was there of evidence?[222]

At the other extreme – and there were those who cried out for the emperor Tiberius' body to receive such treatment – the bodies of notorious public criminals (like Sejanus), after exposure on the Gemonian steps, were dragged by a hook and thrown into the Tiber, a barbarous practice which, surely, even Dionysius of Halicarnassus could not have brought himself to condone.[223]

Different people had different habits. Lucian, in an attack on insensate funerary and mourning extravagancies, wrote:

So far, all men are fools alike; but at this point national peculiarities make their

---

* The word, which only appears very late in Latin, is derived from the Greek *kata kumbas*, 'By the Hollows', the name of a locality on the via Appia (near the church of St Sebastian). The catacomb was different from the *hypogeum*, an underground vault, of which many specimens survive in Rome and the provinces and to which Petronius refers as something particularly Greek, *Sat.* 111, 2. On *hypogea*, see Toynbee, *o.c.* (n.1), 199-234.

appearance. The Greeks burn their dead, the Persians bury them; the Indian glazes the body, the Scythian eats it, the Egyptian embalms it. In Egypt, indeed, the corpse, duly dried, is actually placed at table,* I have seen it done; and it is quite a common thing for an Egyptian to relieve himself of pecuniary embarrassment by a timely visit to the pawnbroker with his brother or father deceased.[224]

In the eastern Mediterranean generally corpses were sometimes burnt, sometimes buried, as is evident from another passage of Lucian.[225] The Jews buried their dead, but did not embalm them. The Nabatean Arabs buried their corpses beside dunghills,[226] just as the poor had once been thrown into pits on the Esquiline in Rome. After the full adoption of Zoroastrianism by the Sassanids, Persians followed what was Parthian practice and is Parsee practice today; they placed corpses on 'towers of silence', to be devoured by carrion-birds. They could not burn or bury them for, by so doing, they would defile the sacred elements of fire and earth. Earlier, dead magi had been disposed of in this way; others had been buried with a protective layer of wax to insulate the earth against pollution.[227]

In Egypt the embalmed corpses of rulers from Alexander onwards could be viewed by the privileged. Augustus handled Alexander's corpse and, it is said, broke off the nose by accident. When invited to inspect the embalmed bodies of the Ptolemies, he said in his blunt way that he had wished to see a king and had no desire to look at corpses.[228]

Of the Albanians in the Caucasus (outside the Empire) Strabo records that, showing great respect for the old when alive, they neither thought nor spoke of them once they were dead. But they buried their treasure with them – and, as a result, were themselves, not unnaturally, very poor.[229]

If people at large pictured a life after death, they pictured it in terms of life on earth; hence the burial of food and drink with, or the regular offering of food and drink to, the dead. In the case of the trousered Gauls, belief in survival after death was so unquestioning that, as children today send letters up the chimney to Father Christmas on Christmas Eve, they sent letters to their dead relatives, throwing them onto the blazing pyre at a funeral; they even lent money, we are told, on the understanding that it would be repaid to them after death in the lower world.[230]

There were the traditional accounts in Homer and later in Virgil of the unhappy, shadowy life of the underworld; and there were the stories of the torments of hell which, if Lucretius is to be believed, were responsible for the common man's terror of death. There is, admittedly, little evidence to support Lucretius' claim.

---

* As has been known to happen with the embalmed Jeremy Bentham at University College, London.

Then there were the philosophies. If you were a Pythagorean, you believed in reincarnation, whether as an animal or a human being. Epicureans, with their atomic theory, knew that death meant complete annihilation, of body and spirit alike. And if for Stoics man's spirit was absorbed into the world-spirit after death, this was no survival in human terms. Indeed, in belittling the importance of death, Stoics underlined heavily what death was an escape from, without saying much about what it was an escape to.

From the East in the mystery cults came belief in some kind of spiritual survival after death, culminating in the Christian belief in the full resurrection of the body. The stoic had stressed that, when it came to dying, the poor and insignificant were on a par with the great ones of the world. Christianity suggested that in the life after death they would not be on a par; they would simply change positions.

(e) Consecration and ruler-cult

The monk Bazhakuloff ... gave utterance to what was afterwards known as the First Revelation. It ran to this effect: 'The Man-God is the Man-God and not the God-Man.'

Norman Douglas, *South Wind*, chap. 11.

There was Heracles in legend for a start, son of Zeus and Alcmena, half-man, half-god, who was elevated at death to become not a god but a 'hero', a hero being, by precise definition, not a full god but a near-God.* A hero was honoured not with a temple but with a 'heröon' and he received not divine honours but honours equivalent to those offered to a god, *isotheoi timai*. Next, Alexander the Great, who may even have believed after his visit to Ammon that he had a god for his father. After which, there were Hellenistic kings who received the titles and attributes of gods, the more wilful of them, like Antiochus Epiphanes, demanding cult on a par with that accorded to the gods. In Rome there was the story of Romulus' ascent to Heaven (an alternative to the story that he was murdered by senators and cut up into small pieces), his metamorphosis into the god Quirinus; and then, at Octavian's prompting, Julius Caesar after death was made a god by Act of Parliament, by decree of the Senate. And there were the miraculous events already noticed (p.255) which attended the cremation of Roman sovereigns. Megalomaniac or moon-struck emperors appeared to believe themselves gods incarnate, Gaius Caligula and Elagabalus. And an autocrat like Domitian perverted language when he encouraged the appellation 'our Lord and God'.

The imperial cult became an instrument of rule, a bond of imperial loyalty. Except for Jews and Christians (p.236), people at large accepted the institution. It gave the opportunity of regular public beanos. It was a way of expressing loyalty, genuine or hypocritical, to

---

* Was he, after death, half-dead, half-alive?[233] Labeo had a category of half-gods ('semidei') who ranked above 'heroes' and included Hercules, Romulus and Plato (Aug., *CD* 2, 14).

the government, to the system. What the result of an opinion-poll would have been, with people asked about the nature of their belief in the notion of the godhead of living or dead emperors, we cannot begin to guess.

Sane rulers had never had any illusions: Antigonus Gonatas referring a sycophantic exponent of his godhead to the servant who emptied his close stool; Tiberius Caesar speaking publicly about the nature of a ruler's true immortality, an unsullied record of good conduct; Vespasian observing ironically on his deathbed that the moment of metamorphosis was at hand. And, in his speech, conduct and writing, that humblest of men, Marcus Aurelius.

A ruler, dead or alive, could properly receive god*like* honours, *isotheoi timai*, no more than that. Such was the outlook and language of, for instance, Cassius Dio.

But for anybody with a mischievous sense of humour, the subject had an irresistible attraction: the god Alexander, wounded, bleeding and needing the attention of a doctor; the god Caligula stabbed by a dagger. You had only to picture the Olympian gods, a comfortable conservative club including a few licensed comics like Heracles and Silenus; what did they think of human upstarts, however royal? Must they have such 'new gods' wished on them by mortals? Had they no right of blackball? However vulgarly, Seneca exploited the potential humour of all this to the full in his *Apokolokyntosis*: Romulus, Julius Caesar and Augustus were accepted into membership – but Claudius, no. Julian enjoyed himself with a similar *pastiche* in his *Caesars*: a kind of beauty-competition in which the gods examined the credentials of supposedly good rulers. Marcus Aurelius was the winner, the man whose aim had been, as far as possible, to *imitate* the gods. Lucian naturally mocked the idea of human divinity in many of his *Dialogues of the Dead* with Alexander as the biggest joke of the lot.

Even Pausanias stated baldly that, whatever might have happened in the remote past, modern history afforded no demonstrable instance of a man turning into a god, except in the language of obsequious flattery, any more than of a man turning into a werewolf.[236]

What was disastrous about the imperial cult was the opportunity that it afforded to trouble-makers: 'Whose image and superscription is this?' At Rome in the principate of Tiberius, when accusations of treason were an epidemic, a man went to the lavatory wearing a ring which had the emperor's image on the seal, and found himself accused of treason. Where Greeks and Jews were at one another's throats, as in Alexandria, the Jews could be delated to the authorities for refusal to participate in the imperial cult, and how could the authorities (knowing they were under the eyes of the distant Caesar) refuse to take notice of the delation? And, worse, authority itself used the imperial cult as a kind of litmus test of loyalty. The crimes supposedly inherent in Christianity, cannibalism and incest, could perfectly well have been investigated – as those certainly involved in Bacchic worship had been investigated in early days – and the truth discovered; but how much easier, from the authorities' point of view, to demand recognition of the emperor's divinity, however formal – a mere pinch of incense. *Hinc illae lacrimae.*

ABBREVIATIONS

AG	Aulus Gellius, *Noctes Atticae*
AHR	*American Historical Review*
AJA, AJP	*American Journal of Archaeology, American Journal of Philology*
AM	Ammianus Marcellinus
AP	*Anthologia Palatina*
Aug., *CD, Conf.*	Augustine, *Civitas Dei, Confessions*
BCH	*Bulletin de correspondence hellénique*
BGU	*Berliner griechische Urkunden*
CAI	*Comptes rendus de l'Académie des inscriptions et belles-lettres*
CD	Cassius Dio
CD	See Aug., *CD*
CIL	*Corpus Inscriptionum Latinarum*
CN	Cornelius Nepos
DH, *AR*	Dionysius of Halicarnassus, *Antiquitates Romanae*
Dig.	*Digest*
DL	Diogenes Laertius
EJ²	V. Ehrenberg, A.H.M. Jones, *Documents illustrating the Reigns of Augustus and Tiberius,* 2nd edn.
ESAR	*An Economic Survey of Ancient Rome,* ed. Tenney Frank
FGH	F. Jacoby, *Die Fragmente der griechischen Historiker*
FIRA²	S. Riccobono, *Fontes Iuris Romani Anteiustiniani,* 2nd edn.
HRR	H. Peter, *Historicorum Romanorum Reliquiae*
HSCP	*Harvard Studies in Classical Philology*
HTR	*Harvard Theological Review*
HZ	*Historische Zeitschrift*
IGR	*Inscriptiones Graecae ad res Romanas pertinentes*
ILS	H. Dessau, *Inscriptiones Latinae Selectae*
JC, *BC, BG*	Julius Caesar, *Bellum Civile, Bellum Gallicum*
JHS	*Journal of the Hellenic Society*
Jos., *AJ, C. Ap., BJ*	Josephus, *Antiquitates Judaicae, Contra Apionem, Bellum Judaicum*
JRS	*Journal of Roman Studies*
L.	Livy
L. (CQ), L. (P) etc	Livy, derived from Claudius Quadrigarius, Polybius etc.
LCL	Loeb Classical Library
MRR	T.R.S. Broughton, *The Magistrates of the Roman Republic*
P.	Polybius

PA	S.B. Platner, Th. Ashby, *A Topographical Dictionary of ancient Rome*
PBSR	*Papers of the British School at Rome*
*PIR*²	*Prosopographia Imperii Romani* (2nd. editn., A.L.)
P. Oxy.	*Oxyrhynchus Papyri*
PSI	*Papiri della Società italiana*
Philostr., *VAT, VS*	Philostratus, *Life of Apollonius of Tyana, Lives of the Sophists*
RE	Pauly-Wissowa, *Real-Encyclopädie der classischen Altertumswissenschaft*
REG, REL	*Revue des études grecques, latines*
RGDA	*Res Gestae divi Augusti*
Röm. Mitt.	*Mitteilungen des deutschen archäologischen Instituts, Römische Abteilung*
RRAM	D. Magie, *Roman Rule in Asia Minor*
RSI	*Rivista storica italiana*
Sall., *Cat., BJ*	Sallust, *Catilinae Coniuratio, Bellum Iugurthinum*
*SEHRE*²	M. Rostovtzeff, *Social and Economic History of the Roman Empire*, 2nd. Engl. edn.
SHA	*Scriptores* Historiae Augustae
*SIG*³	W. Dittenberger, *Sylloge Inscriptionum Graecarum*, 3rd. edn.
Suet., *DA, DJ, Tib.* etc	Suetonius, *Lives of divus Augustus, divus Iulius, Tiberius* etc.
TA, TH, etc.	Tacitus, *Annals, Histories* etc.
VM	Valerius Maximus
VP	Velleius Paterculus

NOTES

Chapter One: Romans, the Gods' Own People; Rome, Capital of the World

1. *Bibliography*

F.F. Abbott, *The Common People of Ancient Rome*, London 1912.

P.A. Brunt, *Italian Manpower, 225 BC-AD 14*, Oxford 1971.

G. La Piana, 'Foreign groups in Rome during the first centuries of the Empire', *HTR* 20, 1927, 183-403.

H.J. Leon, *The Jews of Ancient Rome*, Philadelphia 1960.

2. Plin., *NH* 37,201; Strabo 6, 4, 1, 286. There was a second temperate zone, of which nothing was known, between the torrid zone and the frozen South (which corresponded to the frozen North, Cic., *De rep.* 6, 21f.).

3. Plin, *NH* 37, 202; cf. 3, 138 and 33, 78. See *ESAR* 1. 179f., 263f. Prohibition by decree of the Senate of, perhaps, the second century BC, under equestrian pressure, to favour mining in Spain. Iron, however, continued to be mined on Elba.

4. Plin., *NH* 37, 204, tr. D.E. Eichholz (*LCL*). Cf. Stat., *Silv.* 5, 1, 60f. and 210-16.

5. Virgil, *Georg.* 2, 136-76; Prop. 3, 22, 17-42.

6. Plin., *NH* 37, 201f. See Strabo 2, 5, 26, 127 on these as qualities of Europe in general, including scarcity of wild animals. Cf. Pliny's panegyric on Italy, esp. Campania, *NH* 3, 38-42, and Strabo's, 6, 4, 1, 286 and 5, 3, 1, 228; Varro, *RR* 2, 1, 4-7.

7. Plin., *NH* 18, 65; 16, 161; 33, 78.

8. Plin., *NH* 7, 130 and 116; Cic., *De orat.* 1, 197; 1, 15; Plin., *NH* 37, 201.

9. Plin., *NH* 27, 3; 36, 118; 3, 39, 'Italia numine deum delecta quae caelum ipsum clarius faceret'. Cf. Diod. 28, 3, Roman punctilio in treaty observance etc. wins the support of the gods. Cic., *Pro Flac.* 69, disfavour of gods to the Jews shown in their defeat. L. 31, 30, 11, Athenians declare Romans second in power to the gods. Inscription from Teos, 193 BC, *SIG*, 3, 601. Cf. Tertull., *Apol.* 25, 2.

10. Cic., *De har.resp.* 19. Cf. [Quintil.], *Declam.* 3, 14, a closely parallel passage; VM 1, 1, 8. The view that Rome owed her success to divine favour is mocked by Min. Felix, *Octavius* 25.

11. Plin., *Pan.* 51, 1.

12. Auct. ad Herenn. 4, 9, 13.

13. DH 1, 31. Antoninus Pius' benefactions to Pallantion, Paus. 8, 43, 1f.

14. A point emphasised by DH 2, 19, 1f. Cf. Paus. 8, 8, 2f. on the import of such stories in Greek mythology.

15. Juv. 1,100; 8, 56 and 181.

16. Mart. 2, 75, 10; Prop. 4, 1, 55.

17. Justin 28, 2, 4-6.

18. Virg., *Aen.* 8, 626-728.

19. VM 7, 4.

20. *TH* 4, 73. While Florus ascribes great high-mindedness to the Romans at the declaration of the second Punic war, he ascribes the outbreak of the first to simple greed for annexation, 2, 6, 5 (cf. 2, 2, 4). On the bogosity of much orthodox early Roman history, F. Hampl, ' "Stoische Staatsethik" und frühes Rom', *HZ* 184, 1957, 249-71; 'Römische Politik in republikanischer Zeit und das Problem des "Sittenverfalls" ', *HZ* 188, 1959, 497-525.

21. L. 9, 11.

22. L. 9, 11, 7.

23. L. 2, 13, 6.

24. L. 5, 49.

25. L. 1, 22.

26. L. 9, 11, 12.

27. AM 14, 6, 3. Cf. Flor., praef. 2; Cic., *Phil.* 6, 19.

28. Cic., *De rep.* 3, 12, 22; Lact., *Div. inst.* 5, 16, 2-4; 6, 6, 19; 6, 9, 2-4; Tertull., *Apol.* 25.

29. Cic., *Phil.* 3, 15; *TA* 6, 16, 2, 'antiqui et minus corrupti mores'.

30. Plin., *NH* 19, 87. Cf. VM 4, 4.

31. *Asia devicta*, Plin., *NH* 33, 148; 34, 34; 37, 12. Vulso, Plin., *NH* 34, 14 (L. Piso); L. 39, 6, 7. 3rd. Mac. war, P. 31, 25, 6f.; Diod. (P.), 31, 26, 7. 154 BC, Piso ap. Plin., *NH* 17, 244. Destruction of Carthage, Diod. 34/5, 33, 4-6; Sall., *Hist.* 1, 11M; *BJ* 41, 2; *Cat.* 10, 1. See F. Klingner, 'Uber die Einleitung der Historien Sallusts', *Hermes* 63, 1928, 165-92 (Cato on P. Scipio's wish not to destroy Carthage in 201 BC, App., *Lib.* 65, 289-91). VM 9, 1 on the decline.

32. L. 42, 47, 4-9; J. Briscoe, 'Q. Marcius Philippus and *nova sapientia*', *JRS* 54, 1964, 66-77; Hor., *Epod.* 7, 18; Florus 3, 12, 6.

33. Juv. 6, 292f.

34. L. 1, 22. See F. Hampl, *o.c.* (n.20), 1959.

35. Strabo 9, 2, 2, 401. Cf. the diametrically opposite view of DH, *AR* 1, 90.

36. L. 2, 5, 5-8; Cic., *Phil.* 1, 13, 'Ad simile factum stirpem iam prope in quingentesimum annum propagavit'. See my article, 'The Ides of March', *Historia* 7, 1958, 91.

37. Aug., *CD* 5, 18.

38. VM 4, 4, 6; Front., *Strat.* 4, 3, 3; Sen., *Dial.* 12, 12, 5; *De vir. ill.* 40, 2.

39. Cic., *In Pis.* 43; *De offic.* 1, 39; 3, 99f.; Hor., *Carm.* 3, 5; AG 7, 4 etc.; *RE* II, 2086-92, no.51; E.R. Mix, *Marcus Atilius Regulus, Exemplum Historicum*, The Hague, 1970; H.W. Litchfield, 'National *exempla virtutis* in Roman literature', *HSCP* 25, 1914, 1-71; P. 1, 35.

40. Diod. 24, 12, based probably on Philenus.

41. Cic., *De fin.* 5, 64; [Quintil.], *Decl.* 3, 11.

42. Cic., *De dom.* 101; *De rep.* 2, 49; *Phil.* 2, 87 and 114.

43. Cic., *Pro Mil.* 8, 72 and 83.

44. Cic., *De fin.* 2, 62; 5, 64.

45. Cf. Apul., *Apol.* 18.

46. *TA* 15, 13f.

47. DH, *AR* 1, 90; 7, 72, 18 etc.

48. Plin., *Ep.* 1, 16, 8f.; *TA* 2, 88, 4 (Arminius); 3, 55, 6; VP 2, 92, 5.

49. *TA* 4, 33.

50. Sen. Rhetor, F.1 (*HRR* II, pp.91f.); Florus 1, pr. 4-8; AM 14, 6, 3-6. Cf. Stat., *Silv.* 4, 8, 55f., 'Sint qui fessam aevo crebrisque laboribus urbem/voce opibusque iuvent'.

51. Epict., *Diss.* 3, 13, 9. Cf. the Roman oration of Aelius Aristides.

52. Cic., *De rep.* 2, 4, 7, based on translation of C.W. Keyes (LCL). Cf. Plato, *Laws* 704f; Aristotle, *Pol.* 1327a; Strabo 7, 3, 7, 301f.

53. Cic., *De leg. agr.* 2, 95. Cf. *De offic.* 1, 150 for the deception inherent in trading. Also Philostr., *VAT* 3, 23 and 4, 32 for disparagement of ship-captains and sailors.

54. App., *Lib.* 86, 404-89, 422. This at a moment when some critics were saying that Rome's treatment of Carthage was like the final power-mania of Athens and portended for Rome a fate similar to that of Athens, P. 36, 9, 5.

55. Strabo 7, 5, 6, 315; Plut., *Pomp.* 28, 4-7; H. Strasburger, *JRS* 55, 1965, 50f.

56. Cic., *De rep.* 2, 4, 10; *De orat.* 1, 105. Cf. *In Cat.* 3, 1 and 4, 11; *Pro Sulla* 33.

57. L. 5, 51-4.

58. For detailed information on all these historical monuments in Rome, see PA.

59. Suet., *DJ* 79, 4; CD 50, 4, 1; Suet., *C. Cal.* 49, 2; Hor., *Carm.* 3, 3, 57-68; Virg., *Aen.* 12, 826-8.

60. La Piana, *HTR* (n.1 above), 308-18ff.; Apul., *Met.* 11, 26-30.

61. Hor., *Carm.* 4, 3, 13.

62. See F.G. Maier, 'Römische Bevölkerungsgeschichte und Inschriftenstatik', *Historia* 2, 1954, 318-51, esp. 321f., 337, n.8. P.A. Brunt, *o.c.* (n.1), esp. 376-88, 'The urban population of Rome in the Republic', gives Rome a population of *c.*750,000 in the late Republic and early Empire, including between 100,000 and 200,000 slaves.

63. Brunt, *o.c.* (n.1), 383.

64. Sen., *Consol. ad Helv. matr.* 6, 2f.

65. Sall., *Cat.* 37, 4-7; Cic., *De leg. agr.* 2, 71.

66. Juv. 6, 511-626.

67. *Thraliana*, Oxford 1942, 165.

68. Juv. 3, 60-2; Lucan, *Phars.* 7, 535-43.

69. Brunt, *o.c.* (n.1), 378 and 381.

70. Suet., *DJ* 42, 1 (80,000). For the number, see Brunt, *o.c.* (n.1), 257 and 381.

71. Brunt, *o.c.* (n.1), 102.

72. Petron., *Sat.* 57.

73. Cic., *Phil.* 8, 22. Lucian, *De merc. conduct.* 24, implies a far longer period.

74. Tenney Frank, 'Race mixture in the Roman Empire', *AHR* 21, 1916, 689-708, esp. on Greek names (692). The attempt of M.L. Gordon, *JRS* 1924, 93-111, to refute Frank's view that Greek *cognomina* always indicate an eastern origin is itself refuted by H. Thylander, 'Etude sur l'épigraphie latine', *Skrifter utgivna av Svenska Instituet i Rom*, ser. in 8°, Lund 1952, 134-52. See F.G. Maier, *o.c.* (n.62), esp. 341-7, for powerful doubts about the validity of inferences like Frank's from the scanty evidence available.

75. L.R. Taylor, 'Freedmen and freeborn in the epitaphs of Imperial Rome', *AJP* 82, 1961, 113-32; Brunt, *o.c.* (n.1), 387. But see Maier, *o.c.* (n.62), 342f. for criticism.

76. J.Toynbee,J.Ward-Perkins, *The Shrine of St Peter*, London 1956, 107.

77. Cic., *Ad Att.* 1, 19, 4; *Ad Q.f.* 2, 5, 3 etc.

78. Juv. 7, 13-16; Lucan, *Phars.* 7, 541-4; *TA* 4, 27, 3.

79. Juv. 6, 591.

80. VP 2, 4, 4; VM 6, 2, 3; *De vir. ill.* 58, 8.

81. DH, *AR* 4, 24, 8. He could have quoted Julius Caesar's example, because many of Caesar's colonists came from the city of Rome (see n.70 above) and were presumably men whom Dionysius would have regarded as ne'er-do-wells.

82. Hor., *Carm.* 3, 29, 12; Mart. 12, 57.

83. Strabo 5, 3, 7f., 235; 16, 2, 23, 757; Vitruv. 2, 8, 17. Brunt, *o.c.* (n.1), 385, thinks Strabo did not know about the absence of direct water-supply in upper stories of blocks of flats and in the slums.

84. Philo, *Leg. ad Gai.* 23, 155, is wrong in implying that Jews lived exclusively in Trastevere. See La Piana, *o.c.* (n.1) and 'L'immigrazione a Roma', *Ricerche Religiose* II, 1926, 485-547; III, 1927, 36-75; IV, 1928, 193-248, esp. IV, 197ff.; G. Bardy, *La Question des langues dans l'église ancienne*, Paris 1948, 81-3.

85. Mart. 1, 108, 2; 1, 41, 3-5; 6, 93, 4; Juv. 14, 200-5 (with Mayor's notes).

86. Ael. Arist., *Or.* 26, 11ff. Velabrum, Hor., *Sat.* 2, 3, 229; *Epist.* 1, 15, 31; Plaut., *Capt.* 489; *Aul.* 373-5; Varro, *LL* 5, 44. Via Sacra, S. Panciera, *Arch. Class.* 22, 1970, 131-8; T.P. Wiseman, *The Poet Cinna* 24, n.42. Saepta, Mart. 2, 14, 5; 2, 57, 2; 9, 59; 10, 87, 9; *CIL* XV, 7195; Stat., *Silv.* 4, 6, 2. Expense, Apul., *Met.* 11, 28.

87. Strabo 5, 3, 8, 235f.; Front., *De aq.* 1, 16; Calp. Sic. 7, 23f.; Plin., *NH* 36, 102; Paus. 5, 12, 6; 10, 5, 11; AM 16, 10, 14.

88. DioChrys., *Or.* 13, 29 and 34; Lucian, *De Merc. cond.* Cf. AM 14, 6.

89. Ep. 1 Pet. 5, 13.

90. Mart. 12, 57; Juv. 3; Florus, *Virgil Orat.* 1, 7, 'provincialis latebra'; Boswell, *Life of Johnson* (Everyman) II, 131.

Chapter Two: Snobbery Begins at Rome

1. *Bibliography*

A.M. Duff, *Freedmen in the Early Roman Empire*, Oxford 1928.

P. Garnsey, *Social Status and Legal Privilege in the Roman Empire*, Oxford 1970.

W. Kroll, *Die Kultur der ciceronischen Zeit*, Leipzig 1933.

Ramsay MacMullen, *Roman Social Relations 50 BC to AD 284*, Yale U.P., 1974.

E.S. Ramage, *Urbanitas: Ancient Sophistication and Refinement*, Oklahama 1973.

A. Stein, *Der Römische Ritterstand*, Munich 1972.

2. JC, *BC* 1, 8, 3 and 9, 2; Cic., *Ad Att.* 7, 11, 1.

3. L., *Per.* 59.

4. Cic., *De orat.* 2, 274; Plut., *Flam.* 19, 6-8; *Cato mai.* 17, 7.

5. Suet., *DJ* 6, 1; *Galba* 2,

6. Cic., *Post. red. in sen.* 15; *In Pis.* fr. lx; xi; 53, 67. Bambalio, Cic., *Phil.* 3, 16.

7. Cic., *Phil.* 3, 15f.; Suet., *DA* 4, 2; *Vitell.* 2, 1; *TA* 2, 43, 4. Cf, for similar snobbery, *TA* 2, 43, 7; 6, 27, 1.

8. Suet., *C. Cal.* 23, 1. Nobody knew who Agrippa's father was, according to Sen., *De ben.* 3, 32, 4. L. Tarius Rufus, cos.16 BC, another of Augustus' adjutants, was 'infima natalium humilitate', Plin., *NH* 18, 37.

9. Sall., *BJ* 85; Cic., *In Verr.* 2, 4, 81; 2, 5, 180-2; *Pro Planc.* 12; *Pro Mur.* 15-17.

10. VP 2, 34, 3, Cicero 'vir novitatis nobilissimae'; 127f.; VM 6, 9, 7-9 (cf. AG 15, 4); T., *Germ.* 37, 4 (disparagement of Ventidius Bassus). *Mediocritas mea*, VP 2, 104, 3 and 111, 3; cf. *TA* 14, 53, 5; VM praef.; Cic., *Ad Att.* 9, 7A, 1.

11. Two-headed, Varro *ap.* Non. 728L. The 14 rows, Plin., *NH* 7, 117; Mommsen, *Staatsr.* III³, 519-21. Separate seats for senators first in 194 BC, VM 2, 4, 3. The gold ring, Plin., *NH* 33, 8-36; *TH* 4, 3.

12. *TA* 3, 30 (Sallustius Crispus, Maecenas); 16, 17, 3 (Annaeus Mela); *TH* 2, 86 (Cornelius Fuscus).

13. Sen., *Ep.* 114, 4-8.

14. *PIR*,²'C' 1369; CD 53, 23, 5; *ILS* 8995 (EJ² 21).

15. Plin., *Ep.* 7, 29; 8, 6; Sen., *Ep.* 47, 9. Epaphroditus fawning on the emperor's cobbler, a man whom he had himself sold as unsatisfactory, Epict., *Diss.* 1, 19, 19-23 (cf. 4, 1, 150). The proper way to put an officious imperial freedman in his place, Epict., *Diss.* 1, 1, 20.

16. Petron., *Sat.* 34, 7; 41, 5.

17. AM 28, 4, 4.

18. On differentiation in punishment and the privileges and advantages of the upper class and wealthy in the courts, see Garnsey, *o.c.* (n.1).

19. *TA* 4, 3, 4. Cf. VM 6, 2, 8, 'municipali homini servitutem paternam redolenti'; Cic., *Phil.* 3, 15-17.

20. Cic., *Ad Att.* 12, 51, 2 etc.; 7, 7, 6 (Dec. 51 BC); *Pro Balb.* 57; *TA* 6, 18, 5; 12, 60, 5; *RE* VA, 2090-2127 (no.1).

21. *TA* 14, 53, 5; Suet., *DJ* 76, 1 (*semibarbari*); 80, 2; *TA* 11, 23, 4 (*alienigenae*) and 24, 3.

22. *TA* 3, 55, 4. Claudius, *ILS* 212, col.ii, 4 (cf. Cic., *De offic.* 2, 27).

23. Apul., *Apol.* 23; Cic., *Phil.* 8, 9.

24. P. 2, 8, 9-11; 16, 34; 29, 27, 4f. Cf. Plut., *Lucull.* 21, 6-8, Appius Claudius at the Court of king Tigranes of Armenia. This, in the eyes of the foreigner, was Roman: *hyperéphania* (see p.170).

25. Juv. 8, 205f.

26. *TA* 2.37f.

27. E.g. [Quintil.], *Decl.* 269.

28. Cic., *In Pis.* 67.

29. Hor., *Sat.* 2, 8; Sen., *Controv.* 2, 4, 12f.

30. AM 14, 6, 1; 28, 4, 14.

31. Plin., *Ep.* 7, 25, 2-4.

32. Petron., *Sat.* 52, 1-3; 59, 4f.; 68, 4f.

33. Philostr., *VS*, 1, 25, iv.

34. Cic., *De offic.* 1, 150f. (but cf. *De nat. deor.* 2, 150-2 on the advantageous practical use of a man's hands); Dio Chrys., *Or.* 7, 109-37; VM 5, 2, 10; 8, 7, 7 (apology for praising an actor). Occupations mentioned in Petronius' *Satyricon: centonarius* (? old-clothes dealer), 45, 1; barber, auctioneer, attorney, 46, 7; doctor, money-changer, 56, 1; stone-mason, 65, 5. On the great variety of crafts and their practitioners, see G. Kühn, *De Opificum Romanorum Condicione Privata*, Diss. Halle-Wittenberg 1910.

35. Cic., *Ad Att.* 5, 21, 10-13; CD 62, 2, 1; Cato, *De agric.* 1, 1.

36. Cic., *De offic.* 1, 42, 151; Florus, *Virgilius Orator* 3, 2-3.

37. *TA* 6, 2, 2. Snobbery of Horace, *Epod.* 4; *Sat.* 2, 8.

38. AM 14, 6 (14, 6, 22 quoted in text); 28, 4.

39. *Anecdotes of Johnson by Mrs Piozzi*, p.327 note (cf. *Thraliana*, Oxford 1942, 1976).

Chapter Three: The Roman Outlook, 1: Greeks

1. *Bibliography*

F. Altheim, *Rom und der Hellenismus*, Amsterdam 1942.

G. Bardy, *La Question des langues dan l'église ancienne*, I, Paris 1948.

H. Bengtson, 'Das Imperium Romanum in griechischer Sicht', *Gymnasium* 71, 1964, 150-66.

L. Bösing, *Griechen und Römer im Augustusbrief des Horaz (Epist. 2, 1)*, Konstanz 1972.

G.W. Bowersock, *Augustus and the Greek World*, Oxford 1965.

H. Box, 'Roman citizenship in Laconia', *JRS* 21, 1931, 200-14; 22, 1932, 165-83.

W. Capelle, 'Griechische Ethik und römischer Imperialismus', *Klio* 25, 1932, 86-113.

E. Dorsch, *De Civitatis Romanae apud Graecos Propagatione*, Diss. Breslau 1886.

Bettie Forte, *Rome and the Romans as the Greeks saw Them*, American Academy in Rome 1972.

T.J. Haarhoff, *The Stranger at the Gate*,² Oxford 1948.

B. Hardinghaus, *Tacitus und das Griechentum*, Diss. Munster 1932.

A. Hillscher, 'Hominum Litteratorum Graecorum ante Tiberi mortem in urbe Roma commemoratorum Historia Critica', *Jahrb. f. class. Phil.*, Suppl. 18, 1892, 355-44.

C.P. Jones, *Plutarch and Rome*, Oxford 1971.

J. Jüthner, *Hellenen und Barbaren*, Leipzig 1923 (chap. vii, 'Die Römer').

H.I. Marrou, *Histoire de l'éducation dans l'antiquité*, Paris 1965.

A. Momigliano, *Alien Wisdom*, Cambridge 1975.

J. Palm, *Rom, Römertum und Imperium in der griechischen Literatur der Kaiserzeit*, Lund 1959.

H. Strasburger, 'Der "Skipionenkreis" ', *Hermes* 94, 1966, 61-72.

H. Strasburger, 'Posidonios on problems of the Roman Empire,' *JRS* 55, 1965, 40-53.

A.N. Sherwin-White, *Racial Prejudice in Imperial Rome*, Cambridge 1967 (chap. 3).

C.S. Walton, 'Oriental senators in the service of Rome', *JRS* 19, 1929, 38-66.

A. Wardman, *Rome's Debt to Greece*, London 1976.

E. Zeller, *Die Philosophie des Griechen in ihrer geschichtliche Enturcklung*,[5] III, 1, Hildesheim 1963.

2. Plin., *NH* 29, 14 (elder Cato); Plaut., *Trinumm.* 19; *Asin.* 11.

3. DH 1, 5; 1, 89f. (Romans even more Greek than the Greeks); 7, 70-2. See H. Hill, 'Dionysius of Halicarnassus and the origins of Rome', *JRS* 51, 1961, 88-93.

4. *Or.* 26, 63; on which see Palm, *o.c.* (n.1) 60.

5. Plut., *De Fort. Rom.* 11, 324B; cf. C.P. Jones, *o.c.* (n.1), 124f. Cic., *De fin.* 2, 49, 'Non solum Graecia et Italia sed etiam omnis barbaria commota est'.

6. Strabo 1, 4, 9, 66f; Palm, *o.c.* (n.1) 14.

7. Strabo 6, 1, 2, 253; 10, 3, 9, 467; Jos., *AJ* 18, 20; Dio Chrys., *Or.* 1, 14 and 38; 14, 16; 32, 35 and 40; Paus. 1, 14, 2; 8, 25, 13; 8, 46, 4; 10, 32, 3; Galen, *De san. tuend.* 1, 10, 17 (VI, 51 K), a remarkable division of humanity into (a) barbarians, (b) Greeks and people who have adopted Greek ways.

8. Arrian. *Anab.* 1, 12, 4.

9. Liban., *Or.* 15, 25 (to Julian); 48, 28-30.

10. By a Roman, Plut., *Philop.* 1, 7; *Arat.* 24, 2. Cf. Paus. 7, 17, 1-4 on the transitory power of Greek states.

11. Cic., *Pro Flacco* 15-17; Dio Chrys., *Or.* 38, 38.

12. *TH* 3, 47.

13. Plut., *Flam.*, 7-9; *Bell. Alex.* 15, 1.

14. Cic., *Pro Flacco* 9, 24, 31, 36f., 38, 57 (*levitas propria Graecorum*), 61, 71, fr. 2 (*ingenita levitas*). *Graia levitas*, Lucan, *Phars.* 3, 302. Contrast with Roman *gravitas*, *Pro Sest.* 141; Aug. *CD* 2, 14. *Molles*, Mart., *Spect.* 1, 3; *mollitia nominis*, Flor. 4, 2, 24.

15. Cic., *Pro Flacco* 9-12, 'testimonium ludus'; 23, 'natio minime in testimoniis dicendis religiosa'. Cic., *Ad Q.f.* 1, 2, 4; P.6, 56, 13-15 (cf. *Pro Flacco* 44); Lucian, *De merced. conduct.* 40.

16. Cic., *Ad Att.* 6, 2, 5; *Ad fam.* 3, 8, 5; *TA* 2, 54, 2; Plin., *Ep.* 10, 17A. Cf. A.J. Marshall, 'Verres and judicial corruption', *CQ* 17, 1967, 408-13.

17. Plin., *Ep.* 5, 20, 4, 'Est plerisque Graecis pro copia volubilitas'; VM 2, 2, 2; Macrob., *Sat.* 7, 16, 1; 'Graeci loquaces', Phaedrus, App. Perott. 30, 2-5.

18. Strabo 3, 4, 19, 166.

19. Auct. ad Herenn. 1, 1; Cic., *De orat.* 1, 221, 'ineptus et Graeculus'.

20. Cic., *De orat.* 2, 75f.; *TD* 1, 86.

21. Plin., *NH* 3, 42, 'genus in gloriam sui effusissimum'; 5, 4, 'portentosa Graeciae mendacia'; 28, 112 (Democritus' book on the chameleon), 'mendacia Graecae vanitatis'; 37, 31 (amber), 'vanitas Graecorum'; 37, 41, 'intoleranda mendaciorum impunitas'; Cic., *Pro Flacco* fr. 2, 'erudita vanitas'; *TH* 2, 4; Paus. 9, 30, 4; VM 4, 7, 4, 'gentis ad fingendum paratae monstro similia mendacia'.

22. Cic., *Pro Flacco* 31; *Tusc. disp.* 1, 111; 2, 41; Plut., *Q. conviv.* 2, 5, 21; A.N. Sherwin White on Plin., *Ep.* 10, 118f.; Cic., *In Verr.* 2, 4, 134f.

23. L. 42, 47, 7, 'calliditas Graeca'; L. 8, 22, 8, 'Gens lingua magis strenua quam factis'; 'velocitas orationis', Sen., *Controv.* 4, praef. 7. Cf. refs, notes 17 and 18 above.

24. P. 20, 10, 1-7.

25. *TA* 2, 88, 4: a dig at Plutarch? CD only mentions Arminius once, 56, 19, 2. Jos., *BJ* 1, 13-16. *Cf.* Sen., *Controv.* 1, praef. 6; *Suas.* 7, 10 (*insolens Graecia*); VM 3, 2, 22, 'verbosa cantu laudum suarum Graecia'; Macrob., *Sat.* 1, 24, 4, 'Graeci omnia sua in immensum tollunt'. Yet Paus. 9, 36, 5 criticises Greek writers for exaggerating the magnificence of foreign achievements like the pyramids and disregarding such Greek achievements as the walls of Tiryns.

26. Greeks of Magna Graecia, Plato, *Ep.* 7, 326B; Cic., *TD* 5, 100. Sicily, Philostr., *Gymnast.* 44. *Pergraecari*, Plaut., *Most.* 22, 64, 960; *Truc.* 86, 'have a good time'. Festus 235L, 'Pergraecari: epulis et potationibus inservire'. 'Graecos versus agere', Cato ap. Macrob., *Sat.* 3, 14, 9. In Plaut. *Menaech.* prol. 11 'graecissare' is a joke-word like 'atticissare'. Roman decadence an infection from Greece, P. 31, 25.

27. Plut., *Cato mai.* 20, 8.

28. P. 31, 25, 4f.; L. 39, 44, 3; E. Schmähling, *Die Sittenaufsicht der Censoren*, Stuttgart 1938, 77-9. Homosexuality, Cic., *TD* 4, 70; 5, 58, 'more Graeco'; *RE* XI, 905f., s.v. 'Knabenliebe.'

29. L., *Per.* 48; VM 2, 4, 2; VP 1, 15, 3; App., *BC* 1, 28, 125 (misdated); L.R. Taylor, *Roman Voting Assemblies*, Michigan 1966, 29-32. On the Greek habit, Paus. 6, 5, 2.

30. Plin., *NH* 14, 140.

31. Plin., *Ep.*, 10, 40, 2.
32. See my *Life and Leisure in Ancient Rome*, London 1969, 162f.; H.I. Marrou, *o.c.* (n.1), 351f.
33. Hor., *Carm.* 3, 24, 54-7; *Sat.* 2, 2, 9-13; Sen., *Ep.* 15, 2f.; 88, 18; Lucan, *Phars.* 7, 270-2; Plin., *NH* 15, 19; 35, 168; Plin., *Pan.* 13, 5.
34. Plin., *Pan.* 33, 1; DH 7, 72, 2-4; Plin., *Ep.* 4, 22, 1-3; *TA* 14, 20f.
35. P, 2, 12, 8; *BCH* 25, 1901, pp. 365ff., no.19. Tiberius' victory in the four-horse chariot race before AD 4, *SIG,*³ 782. Victory of a Roman senator, time of Pausanias, Paus. 5, 20, 8. Galen, *Script. Min.* (Teubner, 1884), 103-129=1, 1-39K (*Protreptikos epi tas Technas*); V, 806-98 (*Peri iatrikês kai gymnastikês*). Philostr., *Gymnastikos*. See E.N. Gardiner, *Greek Athletic Sports and Festivals*, London 1910, 163-93; *Athletics of the ancient World*, Oxford 1930, 46-52; H.W. Pleket, 'Games, Prizes, Athletes and Ideology', *Arena* 1, 1976, 49-89.
36. Sen., *Ep.* 86, 4.
37. Juv., 6, 184-99.
38. Cic., *TD* 1, 3. 173 BC, Athen. 12, 547A. 161 BC, Suet., *Rhet.* 1; AG 15, 11. 92 BC, Cic., *De orat.* 3, 93-5; Suet., *Rhet.* 1f.; AG 15, 11, 2; T *Dial.* 35, 1; *RE* XXI, 598-601 (on Plotius Gallus). See H.I. Marrou, *o.c.* (n.1), 339-471.
39. Plin., *NH* 29, 12f.
40. Plut., *Cato mai.* 23, 3f.; Plin., *NH* 29, 14-18 and 27; Suet., *Tib.* 68, 4; Petron., *Sat.* 42, 5; A. Gervais, 'Que pensait-on des médecins dans l'ancienne Rome?', *Bull. Ass. Budé* 1964, 197-231.
41. Galen XIV, 599-673K; V. Nutton, 'Galen and medical autobiography', *Proc. Camb. Phil. Soc.* 198, 1972, 50-62.
42. Mart. 1, 30 and 47. Abuse of doctors, Mart. 5, 9; 6, 53; Petron., *Sat.* 42; Juv. 10, 221. (Horace never mocks doctors, Gervais, *o.c.* (n.40), 214f.)
43. *TA* 12, 61 and 67 (Suet., *D.Cl.* 44 does not mention Xenophon by name); Plin., *NH* 29, 7; *SIG*³ 804-6; *RE* IIIA, 2450f., nos. 7 and 8.
44. CD 60, 34, 4; *TA* 12, 53, 5.
45. *Quaestoria* to Narcissus in AD 48, *praetoria* to Pallas in 52, *TA* 11, 38, 5; 12, 53, 2.
46. Pallas, *TA* 12, 53, 3; Felix, Suet., *D.Cl.* 28; Milichus, *TA* 15, 71, 3.
47. Juv. 3, 60-125. J. Mesk, 'Juvenal der Erzfeind des Hellenentums', *Wien. Stud.* 35, 1913, 24. Clever sycophancy, Macrob., *Sat.* 2, 4, 31.
48. 'Graecus' (instead of 'Hellên') offensive to Greeks, Zon. 8, 13, 7. 'Graeculus', Cic., *Phil.* 5, 14; 13, 33, 'In tanta perturbatione rei publicae de duobus nequissimis Graeculis cogitandum fuit?' 'Graeculio', Petron., *Sat.* 76, 10. Cato, Plin., *NH* 29, 14.
49. Cic., *Ad Q.f.* 1, 1, 27; Stat., *Silv.* 3, 3, 59f.
50. Cic., *Pro Flacco* 9.
51. Cic., *De orat.* 3, 197; *TD* 2, 5; cf. Dio Chrys., *Or.* 31, 157-60.
52. Plut., *Sulla* 14, 9; CD 42, 14, 2; Cic., *Ad Q.f.* 1, 1, 27f.; *Pro Flacco* 61f.; Plin., *Ep.*, 8, 24; *TA* 2, 53, 3; 2, 55, 1f.
53. Cic., *Pro Caelio* 40f.
54. Tac., *Dial.* 40, 3.
55. Cic., *Pro Flacco* 15 and 18, 'faex-opificeset tabernarii'. There is a wonderful account of a disorderly assembly in a theatre in Euboea in Dio Chrys., *Or.* 7, 22-64.
56. See A.H.M. Jones, *The Greek City*, Oxford 1940, chap. 11.
57. L. 45, 23, 14-16; *FHG* II, 59, 25, p.260 (and *Geog. Gr. Min.* 1, p.104), a fragment, probably, of Heracleides Criticus (*RE* VIII, 484-6, no.46).
58. Cic., *In Verr.* 2, 2, 7.
59. Paus. 6, 3, 16.
60. Cic., *Ad Q.f.* 1, 1, 23; *Ad fam.* 9, 25, 1; *TD* 2, 62 (Africanus); *De senect.* 59 (elder Cato); Suet., *DJ* 87. See K. Münscher, 'Xenophon in der griech.-röm. Literature', *Philol.*, suppl. 13, 1920, 1-243, esp. 70-106. Of writers, Seneca alone shows no sign of having read Xenophon.
61. Cic., *Brut.* 112.
62. Varro, AG 3, 10; *RE*, Supplb. VI, 1227-9. Cornelius Nepos etc., Schanz-Hosius⁴ I, 356-60; II, 370 and 588-91.
63. CN. praef.; cf. 5, 1, 2; 15, 2, 3.
64. Livius Andronicus, *RE*, Supplb. V, 598-607 (cf. XIII, 892); Ennius, Schanz-Hosius⁴ I, 86-100; Terence, *RE* VA, 598-650.
65. *FGH* 186 and 188; *RE* II, 463f., no.20; VA, 2090-2127.
66. Plin., *NH* 35, 135.
67. Cic., *Brut.* 104; Plut., *Ti. Gr.* 8, 6 and 20, 4-6.
68. Terence, *Andr.* 55-7; Pers. 5, 189-91 (cf. 6, 38); Lucil. XV, 515f. Marx.
69. Sosigenes, Plin., *NH* 18, 211; *RE* IIIA, 1153-7, no.6. Apollodorus (executed by Hadrian), CD 69, 4. Plin., *Ep.* 10, 18, 3; 40, 3 and 62. Of top-ranking architects in Rome, Apollodorus

apart, we know little more than a few bare names; see the index (s.v. 'architects') of A. Boethius, J.B. Ward-Perkins, *Etruscan and Roman Architecture*, London 1970.

70. Stressed strongly by Strasburger in his article (n.1 above) on Panaetius, arguing (p.61) from the failure of Polybius to ascribe any cultural qualities to him (as against Cic., *De rep.* and *Laelius, In Verr.* 2, 4, 98, 'homo doctissimus atque humanissimus' and VP 1, 13, 3, 'tam elegans liberalium studiorum omnisque doctrinae et auctor et admirator'.) See A.E. Astin, *Scipio Aemilianus*, Oxford 1967, 294-306.

71. Plut., *Aem. Paull.* 6, 8-10; Plin., *Ep.* 2, 14, 2; Quintil. 1, 1, 12-14; Cic., *De orat.* 1, 83.

72. VM 2, 2, 2; Quintil. 12, 10, 27-34; 1, 1, 13.

73. Plut., *Flam.* 5, 7; Cic., *Brut.* 79; L. 45, 8, 6; VM 5, 1, 18; Quintil. 11, 2, 50; Cic., *De orat.* 2, 2; 2, 28.

74. Cic., *Brut.* 24; *TD* 5, 102.

75. Petron., *Sat.* 48, 4.

76. Cic., *In Verr.* 2, 4, 5.

77. Cic., *De orat.* 1, 45-7, 82 and 93; 3, 75; *TD* 5, 22.

78. Plut., *Cic.* 4, 5-7; Cic., *De fin.* 5, 1; Suet., *DJ* 4, 1; Sall., *BJ* 95, 3; Plut., *Lucull.* 1, 7f.

79. Suet., *DA* 89, 1 (but he made a speech at Alexandria in Greek, CD 51, 16, 4, and cf Suet. *D.Cl.* 4).

80. Suet., *Tib.* 71; *D.Cl.* 42, 1.

81. Philostr., *VS*, 1, 7, 2; Bardy, *o.c.* (n.1), 1, 124f.

82. Cic., *In Verr.* 2, 4, 147; *TH* 2, 80; L. 45, 29, 3; VM 2, 2, 2.

83. P. Viereck, *Sermo Graecus*, Göttingen 1888, 75ff., on *SIG*^{3} 593, 601, 618, 684 (for date, see *MRR* II, p.644), 768, 780. Letter of Paullus Fabius Maximus (*OGIS* 458, EJ^2 98), see R.K. Sherk, *Roman Documents from the Greek East*, Baltimore 1969, 207ff.

84. P. 39, 1; Plut., *Cato mai.* 12, 6; *Apophtheg.Cat.* 29; AG 11, 8; Macrob., *Sat.* 1, praef. 13-16. Albinus as praetor in 155 BC had presided at the Senate when the release of the Achaean 'hostages' was refused.

85. Cic., *TD* 5, 112; *HRR* I, ccxlf.; Athen. 4, 66, 168d; Plut., *Lucull.* 1, 7f.; Cic., *Ad Att.* 1, 19, 10; 1, 20, 6.

86. Suet., *D. Cl.* 42, 2; *RE* IVA, 625 and 629.

87. Cic., *De nat. deor.* 2, 104 (Germanicus, *RE* X, 458); Columella 12, praef. 7; Plin., *NH* 18, 224; Ovid., *Trist.* 2, 443; Plin., *NH* 25, 7. Cf. Sen., *Suas.* 7, 12.

88. P.G. Walsh, 'The negligent historian; "howlers" in Livy', *G and R* 5, 1958, 83-8. The howler, P. 18, 24, 9; L. 33, 8, 13.

89. Plin., *Ep.* 7, 9, 1f.; Quintil. 10, 5, 2f.; Lucr. 1, 830-3 (cf. Plin., *Ep.* 4, 18); Cic., *De fin.* 3, 3-5 and 15f.; 5, 96; AG 2, 26 (but, in defence of Latin vocabulary, Cic., *De fin.* 1, 3, 10; Sen., *Controv.* 10, 4, 23; AG, 1.c.).

90. Cic., *De fin.* 1, 3, 1-10 (critical).

91. *RE* VIIA, 1611f., no.2; Suet., *Tib.* 70, 2; Plin., *Ep.* 4, 3, 3; 4, 18, 7; 4, 2; 8, 4.

92. Suet., *D. Cl.* 42.

93. Cic., *Phil.* 1, 1 (*?amnestia, homonoia*.).

94. *TA* 3, 65, 3; 4, 52, 6; 6, 20, 3; Macrob., *Sat.* 2, 4, 11 (*hys, hyios*); Suet., *D. Vesp.* 23, 1.

95. Fronto, *Ep. Gr.* 1 and 2 (*LCL* 1, 130ff.; 146ff.); *Ep. Gr.* 3 and 5 (*LCL* 1, 168f., 268ff.).

96. Petron., *Sat.* 40, 1; Mart. 3, 46, 8; Plin., *Ep.* 2, 14, 5; Hor., *Sat.* 1, 10, 20-30; Juv. 6, 184-99; 7, 218; Mart. 10, 68.

97. Cic., *De orat.* 2, 265; Plut., *Cato mai.* 22f.; Plin., *NH* 7, 112; 29, 14; Cic., *De fin.* 5, 89.

98. Sall., *BJ* 85, 32; VM 2, 2, 3; Plut., *Mar.* 2, 2; Cic., *Pro Arch.* 19.

99. Sen., *Controv.* 9, 3, 13f.

100. See H.I. Marrou, *o.c.* (n.1), 380-5.

101. Cic., *Pro Mil.* 28 and 55, 'nugae'.

102. Epicureans, Cic., *TD* 1, 5f.; 2, 7f. (Epicurean Zeno an exception, Cic., *ND* 1, 59). Roman Epicureans, ignorance of Greek, Cic., *TD* 5, 116. Stoics, Cic., *De orat.* 2, 159; *Brut.* 120; *De fin.* 4, 7.

103. On Stoicism at Rome, Zeller, *o.c.* (n.1), 706-91. Stoics mocked by Cicero for inhumanity, Cic., *Pro Mur.* 60-6.

104. On Epicureanism, see Zeller, *o.c.* (n.1), 373-494. Exposition and refutation of Epicurean ethics, Cic., *De fin.* 1 and 2. Cassius, Cic., *Ad fam.* 15, 16 and 19.

105. Cic., *Brut.* 26; CN, *Att.* 4; R.J. Leslie, *The Epicureanism of T. Pomponius Atticus*, Columbia 1950; *TE*, Supplb. VIII, 503-26. His Epicurean friend L. Saufeius was a parallel case, CN, *Att.* 12, 3; *RE* IIA, 256f., no.5.

106. Cic., *Pro Sest.* 110-12; CN, *Att.* 10, 2f.; *RE* VII, 991f., no.1.

107. Lucil. 75-84 Marx; Cic., *Brut.* 131; *De fin.* 1, 8-10; *Orator* 149; *TD* 5, 108; *RE* I, 1330f., no.2.

108. Catull. 10, 9-13; Cic., *Brut.* 247; Lucret. 1, 24-7 and 42; 5, 8; Cic., *Ad fam.* 13, 1; *Ad Att.* 5, 11, 6; *RE* XV, 609-16, no.8.

109. Plut., *Pomp.* 37, 4 (*FGH* 188, F.1).

110. See H. Strasburger, *o.c.* (n.1, *JRS*), 40.

111. Plut., *Ant.* 33, 6; App., *BC* 5, 11, 43f.

- 112. Philostr., *VS* 1, 8; AG passim; Dio Chrys., *Or.* 37 (para 25 quoted in text, *LCL* translation) and 64, both certainly the work of Favorinus; *RE* VI, 2078-84; A. Momigliano, *Quarto Contributo*, Rome 1969, 641f.

113. Paus. 1, 5, 5; 1, 18, 6-9; SHA, *Hadr.* 1, 5; *Epit. de Caes.* 14, 2.

114. See *Hellenica* 8, 95f., *à propos* C. Iulius Hybreas of Mylasa in Caria.

115. On Eurycles, G.W. Bowersock, 'Eurycles of Sparta', *JRS* 51, 1961, 112-18. On Brasidas, H. Box, *o.c.* (n.1), 202 and 205.

116. See G.W. Bowersock, *o.c.* (n.1), chapters 3 and 4 on Augustus' grants.

117. Strabo 13, 2, 3, 618; *TA* 6, 18, 4f.

118. He may have become Praetorian Prefect in Rome, E.G. Turner, *JRS* 44, 1954, 54-64.

119. *PIR²* 'I' 260; 507.

120. *De tranq. an.* 10, *Mor.* 470 Bff. on the ambitious careerist does not refer to Greeks in particular. Cf. *Praec. reip. ger.* 18f., *Mor.* 814C-815B on being friendly with, without kow-towing to, Roman administrators.

121. See S. Mitchell, 'The Plancii in Asia Minor', *JRS* 64, 1974, 27-39.

122. *ILS* 212. Cf. Cic., *De offic.* 2, 27.

Chapter Four: The Roman Outlook, 2: Other Peoples

1. *Bibliography*

F. Altheim, R. Stiehl etc., *Die Araber in der alten Welt*, Berlin 1964-9 (esp. I, chaps. 10, 'Aramäisch als Weltsprache'; 11, 'Geltungsbereich des Griechischen im Orient'; 14, 'Die einheimische Bevölkerung Nordafrikas von den punischen Kriegen bis zum Ausgang des Prinzipats'.

A. Dihle, 'The conception of India in Hellenistic and Roman literature', *Proc. Cambr. Phil. Soc.* 190, 1964, 15-23.

J. Jüthner, *Hellenen und Barbaren*, Leipzig 1923.

J. Palm, *Rom, Römertum und Imperium in der griechischen Literatur der Kaiserzeit*, Lund 1959.

A.N. Sherwin-White, *Racial Prejudice in Imperial Rome*, Cambridge 1967.

E.M. Smallwood, *The Jews under Roman Rule*, Leiden 1976.

F.M. Snowden Jr., 'The Negro in classical Italy', *AJP* 68, 1947, 266-92. *Blacks in Antiquity: Ethiopians in the Greco-Roman Experience*, Cambridge, Mass. 1970 (esp. chap. 8, 'Greco-Roman attitude toward Ethiopians', with large bibliography in the notes).

M. Stern, ed., *Greek and Latin Authors on Jews and Judaism (Herodotus to Plutarch)*, Jerusalem 1974.

K. Trüdinger, *Studien zur Geschichte der griech.-röm. Ethnographie*, Diss. Basle, 1918 (p.175, list of 'topoi').

2. Strabo 1, 1, 8, 5; 2, 5, 5, 112; 2, 5, 9, 116; 2, 5, 18, 121.

3. Varro, *RR* 1, 2, 4f.; Strabo 2, 5, 8, 15 (Ireland); Juv. 2, 161 (short nights); CD 76, 12, 4.

4. Strabo 2, 5, 34, 132. In fact, cinnamon came up from Madagascar, having been brought there from Indonesia; see J.I. Miller, *The Spice Trade of the Roman Empire*, Oxford 1969, 153-72.

5. Plin., *NH* 2, 189f.; Veget. 1, 2; Vitruv. (Posid.) 6, 1, 1-4 and 9-11 (*FGH* 87, 121); Isid., *Orig.* 9, 2, 105.

6. Manil. 4, 729f. (*FGH* 87, 120); Isid., *Orig.* 14, 5, 10 (cf. *RE* XIV, 2349).

7. See Veget., Vitruv., n.5 above.

8. *Phars.* 9, 619-941.

9. JC, *BG*, 2, 30, 3; *Bell. Afr.* 40, 5f.; Jos.; *BJ* 2, 376f.; Vitruv. (Posid.) 6, 1, 3 and 9 (*FGH* 87, 121); Paus. 10, 21, 3; Florus 3, 3, 5; AM 15, 12 (the women as formidable as the men).

10. Philostr., *VAT* 5, 8.

11. Galen, *De tuend. sanit.* 1, 10, 17 (VI, 51K.); Plin., *Ep.* 9, 11, 2; CD 77, 21, 2; AG 19, 9.

12. Fantasies, Strabo 2, 1, 9, 70; 15, 1, 57-66, 711-17; Dio Chrys., *Or.* 35, 18-24; Arrian, *Ind.* 1-17; Apul., *Flor.* 6 and 15. Megasthenes, *RE* XV, 230-326, no.2; *FGH* 715. The book of Daimachos, sent as envoy to Candragupta's successor by Antiochus I, was less widely read, *RE* IV, 2008f., no.2, *FGH* 716. Caste system also in Arabia Felix (Strabo 16, 4, 25, 782f.) and in Egypt (Strabo 17, 1, 3, 787).

13. Macrob., *Sat.* 1, 20, 7; Strabo 17, 1, 33f., 808f. (pyramids); 17, 1, 5, 789-91 (Nile flood); Plin., *NH* 5, 51-9; Lucan, *Phars.* 10, 172-331.

14. *RE*, Suppl. VII, 213f.; JC, *BG* 3, 12, 1; 4, 29, 1; Strabo (Posid.) 7, 2, 1, 292f. (*FGH* 87, 31).

15. Appian, *Praef.* 9, 32f. (no match for the Romans); L. 9, 17, 16; *TA* 6, 34, 6; Lucan, *Phars.* 8, 365-90; *Pan. Lat.* 12, 5, 3 and 24, 1, 'timidi et imbelles'; T, *Germ.* 37 (cf. Sen., *De ira* 1, 11).

16. VM 9, 1, 5.

17. Mart. 10, 65; *TH* 2, 74; 2, 80.

18. Lucan, *Phars.* 8, 362-90; *TH* 4, 17 (Civilis); Hor., *Carm.* 3, 24, 2, 'thesauris Arabum et divitis Indiae'; Stat., *Silv.* 3, 2, 139-41; 5, 1, 60f. and 210-16; Gallic and Spanish cloaks, Mart. 4, 19; 14, 133; Plin., *NH* 37, 30f.; *T. Germ.* 45.

19. Plin., *Ep.* 4, 9. For the law, Sherwin-White on para. 5.

20. Plut., *Tit.* 16, 5-7; Cic., *In Verr.* 2, 2, 51; *Ad Att.* 5, 21, 7; *In Verr.* 2, 2, 52, 114 and 154.

21. *B.M.Pap.* 1912.

22. Dio Chrys., *Or.* 31.

23. Strabo 16, 2, 24, 757; 17, 1, 3, 787. Magic, 'fraudulentissima artium', Plin., *NH* 30, 1-20, brought to Greece in the entourage of Xerxes, to Rome in the entourage of Tiridates at the time of Nero.

24. Cic., *Ad fam.* 1, 1, 27; *Pro Scauro* 36 (Sardinians); *TA* 4, 45, 5 (nearer Spain); *TA* 14, 32, 4 and *Agr.* 11, 1; 16, 4 (Britons).

25. Strabo 4, 4, 5, 197f.

26. VP 2, 117, 3; 118, 1. Germans were 'wild', *feri*, lacking the potential of civilisation which Spaniards and Gauls possessed in the view of Caesar, Strabo and (except in the *Germania*) Tacitus; so Sherwin-White, *o.c.* (n.1), 1-61.

27. Philostr., *VAT* 7, 3.

28. *TA* 14, 23, 2; 15, 9, 1 and 11; App., *Mith.* 104, 488f.; Plut., *Sulla* 5, 10.

29. Cic., *In Verr.* 2, 3, 20; 2, 4, 95; *Brut.* 46; *TD* 1, 15; *Pro Scauro* 24; Quintil. 6, 3, 41.

30. Cic., *Pro Scauro* 42-4; *Ad fam.* 7, 24, 1; *TA* 2, 85, 5; Mart. 4, 60, 6; Florus 2, 6, 35. Cf. Paus. 10, 17, 1-7 on the mixed population of Sardinia (Carthaginians, Spaniards, Greeks) and its wild mountain country.

31. Cic., *Ad fam.* 7, 24, 2; Plut., *QR* 53; G. Sotgiu, 'Sardi nelle legioni e nella flotta romana', *Athenaeum* 39, 1961, 78-97; R.J. Rowland, 'Sardinians in the Roman Empire', *Anc. Soc.* 5, 1974, 223-9.

32. Diod. 5, 14, 3; 5, 13, 5; Strabo 5, 2, 7, 224.

33. Narbonese Gaul, Plin., *NH* 3, 31. Spaniards, Hor., *Carm.* 2, 6, 2; 3, 8, 22; 4, 14, 41; Florus 2, 6, 38; 3, 22, 3; *RE* IXA, 1255f. (Agrippa).

34. Mart. 1, 96, 5; Juv. 12, 41f.; Catull. 37, 18; Plin., *NH* 8, 217; Strabo 3, 2, 6, 144; Varro, *RR* 12, 3, 6f. *Cuniculus* is perhaps a Spanish word.

35. Catull. 37, 20 and 39; Diod. 5, 33, 5; Apul., *Apol.* 6; Strabo 3, 4, 16, 164.

36. Cato, *HRR* I,² p.65, F.34; J. Carcopino, 'Rome et la Gaule', *Points de vue sur l'impérialisme romain*, Paris 1934, 203-56.

37. *RE* XIV, 2132-7.

38. *TA* 12, 23, 1; CD 52, 42, 6f.

39. Strabo 4, 1, 5, 181; *TA* 4, 44, 5; T., *Agr.* 4, 3.

40. Diod. 5, 27, 3 (*FGH* 87, 116); Strabo 4, 4, 5, 197.

41. CD, fr. 50, 2f.

42. CD, fr. 94, 2; Florus 3, 3, 13 (of the Cimbri, in both cases). Justin 24, 7, Brennus' Gauls at Delphi.

43. JC, *BG* 4, 5; Mart. 5, 1, 10; Diod. 5, 31, 1; Strabo 4, 4, 5, 197.

44. Strabo 4, 4, 5, 198; Suet., *D.Cl.* 25, 5.

45. Arrian, *Kyneg.* passim; JC, *BG* 4, 2.

46. 'Barbari', Sen., *Apok.* 8; inhospitable, Hor., *Carm.* 3, 4, 33. Woad etc, Prop. 2, 18, 23; Mart. 11, 53, 1; 14, 99; T., *Agr.* 21, 2. Irish, Pomp. Mela 3, 53. Scotch woman, CD 76, 16; 5.

47. App., praef. 5, 18; Florus 3, 12, 4.

48. Florus 3, 4, 1-3; 4, 12, 10-13; P.27, 12; VP 2, 110, 5.

49. Cic., *Pro Flacco* 65; Lucian, *Epigr.* 43; *Pseudol.* 14. Litter-bearers, Mart. 6, 77, 4; Petron., *Sat.* 63, 5 (British *lecticarii*, *CIL* VI, 8873). Piso, Cic., *Post red. in sen.* 14. Cappadocian slaves, Hor., *Epist.* 1, 6, 39; Mart. 10, 76, 3; Pers., *Sat.* 6, 77.

50. Lucian, *Alex.* 9, and 17.

51. L. 35, 49, 8; 36, 17, 5; Plaut., *Trinumm.* 542; Cic., *D.p.c* 10 W.L. Westermann, *The Slave Systems of Greek and Roman Antiquity*, American Philosophical Society 1955, 97; M. Bang, 'Die Herkunft der röm. Sklaven', *Röm. Mitt.* 25, 1910, 232f., 247.

52. Juv. 6, 351; Mart. 7, 53, 10; 9, 2, 11; 9, 22, 9.

53. See J.B. Mayor on Juv. 1, 104.

54. Rascality, CD 77, 10, 2. Fickle, Herodian 2, 7, 9. Disloyal, SHA, *Aurel.* 31, 1. Shrewd, Herod. 3, 11, 8.

55. A.D. Nock, *CAH* XII, 427. Sailors, Strabo 16, 2, 23f., 757. Traders, V. Pârvan, *Die Nationalität der Kaufleute im röm. Kaiserreiche*, Diss. Breslau 1909, 123, 'the only born traders of antiquity'. Arabs, Strabo 16, 4, 23, 780. 'Nabathaei mercatores', Apul., *Flor.* 6.

56. EJ², 301.

57. SHA, *SA* 28, 7; Lucian, *Adv. indoct.* 19. Palm, o.c. (n.1), 52f. disposes of the curious view of K. Mraas, *Die Hauptwerke des Lukian*, Munich 1954, 511 that Lucian was a 'Syrian nationalist'.

58. 'Superstitiosi', Apul., *Flor.* 6; Strabo 16, 2, 35f., 760f.; Hor., *Sat.* 1, 4, 143; *TH* 5, 5. See Aug., *CD* 6, 11 for Seneca's views of the 'sceleratissima gens'.

59. Diod. 34/5, 1; 40, 3, 4; *TH* 5, 5, 'adversus omnes hostile odium'; Jos, *C. Ap.* 2, 121; Juv. 14, 102-4; Philostr., *VAT* 5, 33.

60. *TH* 5, 1; Babrius 57 (Arabs); Philo, *C. Flac.* and *Leg. ad Gai.*; Jos. *AJ* 16, 45. Antioch, Jos., *BJ* 7, 100-11. Vic., *Pro Flac.* 67, 'barbara superstitio'; *TH* 5, 8, 'taeterrima gens' 5, 13; Florus 3, 5, 30. Jewish monotheism praised, Varro (Aug., *CD* 4, 31), Posidonius (Strabo 16, 2, 35, 761). See M. Stern (ed.), *Greek and Latin Authors on Jews and Judaism (Herodotus to Plutarch)*, Jerusalem 1974.

61. Florus 4, 2, 60; Achilles Tatius 4, 14, 9. Abuse of Egyptians, Stat., *Silv.* 2, 1, 74; 5, 5, 67f., 'convicia Nili'; Plin., *Pan.* 31, 2, 'ventosa et insolens natio'; Plut., *Mor.* 380A and CD 51, 17, 1, 'kouphoi'. Wild abuse of Egyptians by a later writer ('Flavius Vopiscus') and in a fictional letter of Hadrian, *SHA* 29, 7f.

62. Plin., *EH.* 10, 6; CD 51, 17, 1-3; 76, 5, 3-5.

63. *PIR*,² 'A' 918; Mart. 7, 99; 8, 48; Juv. 1, 26-9; 4, 1-33 and 108; *RE* IV, 1720f., no.5; *PIR*,² 'I' 139; Juv. 1, 129-31.

64. Sen., *Consol. ad Helv.* 19, 4-7; Juv. 15, 45; *RE* X, 1042f.; G. Highet, *Juvenal the Satirist*, Oxford 1962, 27-31.

65. There were in fact two other Greek cities in Egypt, Ptolemais and Naucratis.

66. Cic., *Pro Rab. Post.* 35; CD 39, 58, 1f.; 66, 8, 2 (hatred of Vespasian); Dio Chrys., *Or.* 32, 1f.; Sen., *Consol. ad Helv.* 19, 6, 'in contumelias praefectorum ingeniosa provincia'.

67. CD 51, 17, 2f.

68. Dio Chrys., *Or.* 32, esp. paras. 40-3.

69. *Bell. Alex.* 7, 2.

70. Diod. 17, 52; Strabo 17, 1, 13, 798, 'the greatest emporium in the world'; Achilles Tatius 5, 1; Ael. Aristeid., *Or.* 26, 26; Dio Chrys., *Or.* 32, 40.

71. Diod. 1, 83-90; Plut., *De Isid. et Osir., Mor.*, 379E-382C; Lucian, *Deor. concil.* 10; Juv. 15, 1f.

72. Diod. 1, 83, 6-9.

73. Plut., *Mor.* 380Bf.

74. P. 15, 30, 9f.; 15, 33, 5-12. Cf. CD 39, 58, 2.

75. Juv. 7, 148f., 'nutricula causidicorum Africa', with Mayor's note.

76. Cf. Stat., *Silv.* 4, 5, 29-32; 45-8.

77. L. 30, 12, 18, 'gens Numidarum in Venerem praeceps'.

78. Plin., *NH* 8, 42f.; 7, 61; L. 30, 12-15.

79. Justin 32, 4, 11.

80. Col. 3, 8, 1; Plin., *NH* 7, 33.

81. See Schanz-Hosius⁴ II, 652f.; *RE* IV, 757f. (s.v. 'commentarii); JC, *BG* 4, 1-5; 6, 11-24.

82. Cic., *De offic.* 1, 35.

83. T., *Dial.* 36, 5; *TA* 3, 55, 3; Plin., *Ep.* 3, 4, 2-6.

84. Cic., *Pro Balb.* 41, Balbus and Gades.

85. *ILS* 6095-6114; cf. *Lex Malicatana, FIRA²* 1, 24, c.61.

Chapter Five: Romans Abroad

1. *Bibliography*

P.A. Brunt, 'Charges of Provincial maladministration under the early Principate,' *Historia* 10, 1961, 189-227.

L. Hahn, *Rom und Romanismus im griechisch-röm. Osten*, Leipzig 1906.

J. Hatzfeld, *Les trafiquants italiens dans l'Orient hellénique*, Paris 1919.

D. Magie, *Roman Rule in Asia Minor to the end of the third Century after Christ*, Princeton 1950.

V. Pârvan, *Die Nationalität der Kaufleute im röm. Kaiserreiche*, Diss. Breslau 1909.

A.J.N. Wilson, *Emigration from Italy in the Republican Age of Rome*, Manchester U.P. 1966.

2. Cic., *De imp. Cn. Pomp.* 17f. (Asia).

3. CD 60, 19, 2f.; TA 14, 39, 1.

4. Cic., *Pro Flacco* 86.

5. Cic., *In Verr.* 2, 2, 6.
6. App., *Iber.* 38, 153; L. 43, 3.
7. CD 36, 50, 3; Strabo 12, 3, 28, 555; *RE* XVII, 536-8, no.8.
8. CD 54, 8, 1.
9. Cic., *TD* 5, 106; *TA* 2, 62, 4.
10. Cic., *Pro Quinct.* 12; *Pro Font.* 12f.
11. Sall., *BJ* 26; 67, 3; JC, *BG* 7, 3, 1; 42, 5; 55, 5; VP 2, 110, 6; *TA* 3, 42, 1.
12. Heraclea Pontica before Actium, Strabo 12, 3, 6, 543; Armenia, 32/1 BC, CD 51, 16, 2; Cyzicus, 20 BC, CD 54, 7, 6; AD 25, *TA* 4, 36, 2; Lycia, AD 43, CD 60, 17, 3. In general terms, Cic., *De imp. Cn. Pomp.* 11.
13. App., *Mith.* 72f., 85-91; Memnon, *FGH* 434, F. 22, 6-9.
14. CD 68, 32 (see A. Fuks, 'Aspects of the Jewish revolt of AD 115-117', *JRS* 51, 1961, 98-104); 69, 12-14; Fronto, *De bell. Parth.* 2 (LCL II, p.22).
15. *TA* 14, 31f.; *Agr.* 15f.; CD 62, 1-12.
16. P. 2, 8, 6-13; 32, 2f.; App., *Syr.* 46, 240; Cic., *Phil.* 9, 4; Plin., *NH* 34, 23f. (inaccurate).
17. Cic., *In Verr.* 2, 1, 67; 2, 5, 94.
18. L., *Per.* 86; VM 9, 10, 2; Diod. 38/9, 11.
19. *Bell. Alex.* 48-64; *RE* III, 1740-2; no.70; *TA* 4, 45.
20. Cic., *Ad fam.* 5, 10A; 8, 4, 5; *Ad Att.* 4, 21, 10-13; *Ad Q.f.* 1, 2, 11.
21. Cic., *Ad Att.* 7, 1, 6; Catull. 10. A dissatisfied subordinate might give evidence against the governor on whose staff he had served if he was prosecuted; so Verres gave evidence against Cornelius Dolabella under whom he had served in Cilicia, Cic., *In Verr.* 2, 1, 41 etc.
22. JC, *BG* 5, 7, 8.
23. VP 2, 117f.
24. Others (apart from T. Albucius, on whom see p.50): Erucius who, after service with Sulla, married an Athenian woman and settled in Cyzicus, C. Cichorius, *Röm. Stud.*, Berlin 1922, 304-6; Bullatius, Hor., *Ep.* 1, 11; nephew of L. Volcacius Tullus, Prop. 1, 6 and 3, 22. For the names of known Romans on Delos, see J. Hatzfeld, *BCH* 36, 1912, 5-218; Wilson, *o.c.* (n.1), 99-121. Romans in Asia Minor, Wilson, *o.c.* (n.1), 171-93.
25. *EJ²*, 311, i.
26. *TH* 64f.

Chapter Six: Enslavement and the Purchase of Slaves

1. *Bibliography*
M. Bang, 'Die Herkunft der röm. Sklaven', *Röm. Mitt.* 25, 1910, 223-51; 27, 1912, 189-221.
R.H. Barrow, *Slavery in the Roman Empire*, London 1928.
A.M. Duff, *Freedmen in the early Roman Empire*, Oxford 1928.
M.L. Gordon, 'The nationality of slaves under the early Roman Empire', *JRS* 14, 1924, 93-111.
F.G. Maier, 'Römische Bevölkerungsgeschichte und Inschriftenstatistik', *Historia* 2, 1954, 318-51.
J. Vogt, *Sklaverei und Humanität,²* Wiesbaden 1972; English Translation, *Ancient Slavery and the Ideal of Man*, Oxford 1974.
J. Vogt, *Bibliographie zur antiken Sklaverei*, Bochum 1971.
W.L. Westerman, *RE* Supplb. VI, 894-1068, s.v. 'Sklaverei', esp. 1003-14.
W.L. Westerman, *The Slave Systems of Greek and Roman Antiquity*, Am. Philos. Soc. 40, 1955 (with the review of P.A. Brunt, *JRS* 48, 1958, 164-70).
2. Jos., *AJ* 18, 21.
3. Strabo 15, 1, 54, 710 (mistakenly translated, I think, in LCL); Arrian, *Ind.* 10, 8f. Ceylon, Plin., *NH* 6, 89.
4. Strabo 16, 4, 26, 783; L. West, *JRS* 7, 1917, 47.
5. Dio Chrys., *Or.* 14, 13; Epict. *Diss.*, 4, 1, 6-14; Stat., *Silv.* 3, 3, 49-58.
6. Cf. Dio Chrys., *Or.* 15, 14; Sen., *Ep.* 47, 1 and 17.
7. Sen., *Ep.* 47, 10 (reading 'Variana') and 12.
8. Dio Chrys., *Or.* 15, 10-12.
9. Dio Chrys., *Or.* 15, 23; cf. Lucian, *De merced. conduct.*
10. List in Dio Chrys., *Or.* 15-25.
11. On eastern slave trade and pirates, Strabo 14, 5, 2, 668f.
12. If you did, and found you were freeborn, there could be an action for the recovery of your freedom (A.N. Sherwin-White, *The Letters of Pliny*, p.654).
13. Sold by parents, Philostr., *VAT* 8, 7, xii; P.A. Brunt, *JRS* 48, 1958, 167f. Selling yourself, Petron., *Sat.* 57.

14. Plut., *Flamin.* 13, 5-9 (a spontaneous gesture); L.(P.) 34, 50, 3-7, Flamininus' suggestion.
15. Diod. 36, 3, 1-3. CD 27, fr. 93 gives a different account.
16. [Quintil.], *Decl.* 9. Cf. Calp. Flac., *Decl.* 52.
17. AG 6, 4 on the origin of the expression.
18. Ephesus; Byzantium, later Delos; Side in Pamphylia (Strabo 14, 3, 2, 664); Carthage (in the Empire); Alexandria; Syracuse; in Italy, Tarentum, Puteoli, Ostia, Rome. See M. Bang, *o.c.* (n.1), 223-51; H. Wallon, *Histoire de l'esclavage* II, chap.2; M.L. Gordon, *o.c.* (n.1).
19. *Dig.* 21, 1, 31, 21.
20. Cic., *D.p.c.* 10. Syrians, Plaut., *Trinumm.* 542; L. 35, 49, 8 (*servilia ingenia*); 36, 17, 5 (together with Asia-Minor Greeks, 'born to slavery').
21. Bang, *o.c.* (n.1), 247.
22. Bang, *o.c.* (n.1), 248.
23. Bithynians, Catull. 10, 14-20; Cic., *In Verr.* 2, 5, 27. Syrians, Mart. 7, 33, 10; 9, 2, 11; Juv. 6, 351. Cappadocians, Mart. 6, 77, 4. Thracians, Juv. 7, 132. Moesians, Juv. 9, 143. Paphlagonians, *CIL* VI, 6311. Germans, Clem. Alex., *Paid.* 3, 4 (27, 2).
24. Varro, *RR* 2, 10, 4.
25. Noise, Martial 9, 29, 5f. *Catasta, lapis,* Plaut., *Bacch.* 814f.; Cic., *In Pis.* 35; Plin., *NH* 35,200; Mart. 6, 29; Stat., *Silv.* 2, 1, 72 (revolving). White feet (foreign slaves only), Propert. 4, 5, 52; Ovid, *Amores* 1, 8, 64; Plin., *NH* 35, 199; Juv. 1, 111.
26. Pers. 6, 75-7; Propert. 4, 5, 52; Apul., *Apol.* 45; Sen., *Ep.* 80, 9; Claudian, *In Eutrop.* 1, 35f.
27. *Dig.* 21, 1, 31; Cic., *De offic.* 3, 71; Varro, *RR*, 2, 10, 5; Hor., *Sat.* 2, 3, 285f.; Propert. 4, 5, 51; AG 4, 2, 1. *Novicii* were better material for training than old slaves (*veteratores*); it was therefore an offence to represent a *veterator* as a *novicius, Dig.* 21, 1, 31, 37 (Ulpian).
28. Hor., *Ep.* 2, 2, 1-19.
29. Sen., *Dial.* 2, 13, 4
30. Paus. 10, 32, 15.
31. Stat., *Silv.* 2, 1, 74.
32. Col. 3, 3, 8; Plut., *Cato mai.* 4, 5; Hor., *Sat.* 2, 7, 43; Mart. 10, 31; 11, 38; Petron., *Sat.* 68. 100,000HS, Sen., *Ep.* 27, 7; Mart. 1, 58, 1; 3, 62; 11, 70, 1. Greek boys, Mart. 4, 66, 9. Fancy prices, Plin., *NH* 7, 128f: 700,000 HS for a grammarian. 20,000 HS for a deformed joker (*morio*), Mart. 8, 13.
33. Wooden tablets survive with contracts of sale in the second century AD of boys and girls in Transylvania for sums between 820 and 2,400 sesterces, *CIL* III, pp.937ff. Young slaves in the eastern Empire fetched from 700 to 2,400 esterces, older (presumably skilled) slaves from 1,400 to 2,800, Westerman, *o.c.* (n.1, 1955), 100f.
34. Corn. Nep., *Att.* 13, 4.

Chapter Seven: Admission: Becoming a Roman

1. *Bibliography*
G. Alföldy, 'Zur Beurteilung der Militärdiplome der Auxiliarsoldaten', *Historia* 17, 1968, 215-27.
H. Box, 'Roman citizenship in Laconia,' *JRS* 21, 1931, 200-14; 22, 1932, 165-83.
P.A. Brunt, *Italian Manpower 225 BC–AD 14,* Oxford 1971.
E. Dorsch, *De Civitatis Romanae apud Graecos Propagatione,* Diss. Breslau 1886.
A.M. Duff, *Freedmen in the Early Roman Empire,* Oxford 1928.
P. Garnsey, *Social Status and Legal Privilege in the Roman Empire,* Oxford 1970.
C.E. Goodfellow, *Roman Citizenship,* Lancaster, Pa., 1935.
A.H.M. Jones, 'I appeal unto Caesar', *Studies in Roman Government and Law,* Oxford 1960, 53-65.
Chr. Sasse, *Die Constitutio Antoniniana,* Wiesbaden 1958.
A.N. Sherwin-White, *Roman Society and Roman Law in the New Testament,* Oxford 1963.
A.N. Sherwin-White, *The Roman Citizenship,*[2] Oxford 1973.
R. Syme, *Colonial Elites,* London 1958.
S. Treggiari, *Freedmen during the late Republic,* Oxford 1969.
C.S. Walton, 'Oriental senators in the service of Rome,' *JRS* 19, 1929, 38-66.
H. Wolff, *Die Constitutio Antoniniana und Papyrus Gissensis 40.1,* Cologne 1976.
2. Seneca, *Apok.* 3. For opposition, cf. *TA* 11, 23.
3. E.g. Onesimus, the Macedonian who abandoned Perseus when he became actively anti-Roman before the third Macedonian war (enrolment *in formulam sociorum* and grant of 125 acres and a house at Tarentum, L. 44, 16, 4-7). Other foreigners who deserted to the Romans and were rewarded, though not with citizenship, were Himilcon (Phameas), who came over to Scipio with 2,200 cavalry in the third Punic war, App., *Lib.* 109, 518; Archelaus, who deserted

Mithridates and joined Murena in 83 BC, Strabo 12, 3, 34, 558; 17, 1, 11, 796; Monaeses, who deserted to Antony in 36 BC (given three cities, but he returned to Parthia, pardoned by Phraates, CD 49, 23,5-24,5). The three Greek ship-captains Asclepiades, Polystratus and Meniscus, who assisted Rome in the Social war, were enrolled *in formulam amicorum* and exempted from taxation in 78 BC, *FIRA²* 1, 35 (on which see E. Gallet, 'Essai sur le sénatus-consulte "de Asclepiade sociisque" ', *Rev. d. droit fr. et étranger* 16, 1937, 242-93 and 387-425.

4. Sosis and Moericus from Syracuse in 211 BC (each received *civitas* and over 300 acres of land in Sicily), L. 26, 21, 9-12. Myttones, L. 25, 40f.; 26, 21, 14f.; 26, 40; 27, 5, 6f.; Delphic proxenus (with his four sons, Romans too), *SIG*,³ 585, 86ff., 190/89 BC; fought Antiochus, L. (CQ) 38, 41, 12ff.

5. Macrob., *Sat.* 2, 3, 8.

6. Suet., *DA* 74; CD 48, 45, 7; *RE* XV, 896-900, no.1.

7. Cf. the grant of *civitas* to Seleucus of Rhosos in Syria by Octavian, EJ² 301 (letter and edict to the Rhosians).

8. VM 5, 2, 8; Cic., *Pro Balb.* 46.

9. *ILS* 8888.

10. Cic., *Pro Balb.* 48f.

11. Cic., *Pro Arch.* 24.

12. *TA* 6, 37, 4.

13. Cic., *Pro Balbo*.

14. E.M. Smallwood, *Documents of Gaius, Claudius and Nero* 407. On *municipia*, see *RE*, s.v., XVI, 570-638 (E. Kornemann) and, for a list of provincial *municipia* down to AD 14, Brunt, *o.c.* (n.1), 602-7.

15. Maritime Alps, *TA* 15, 32, 1. Spain, R.K. McElderry, 'Vespasian's reconstruction of Spain', *JRS* 8, 1918, 53-102 (esp. 62-4 on Plin., *NH* 3, 30).

16. *Lex Acilia, FIRA²* 1, 7, 78 (85) (cf. *Lex municipii Salpensani, FIRA²* 1, 23, xxi); Gaius 1, 96; O. Hirschfeld, 'Zur Geschichte des Latinischen Rechtes', *Kl. Schr.*, Berlin 1913, 294-309.

17. *Lex Acilia* (n.16 above), 76-8 (83-5).

18. See, for details, *RE*, s.v. *'legio'* (Ritterling), XII, 1381f. (I Adiutrix); 1437-40 (II Adiutrix); 1564f. (V Alaudae).

19. *ILS* 2483 (EJ², 261).

20. On citizenship-grants in relation to length of military service, see the admirable article of G. Alföldy, *o.c.* (n.1), 215-27.

21. Goodfellow, *o.c.* (n.1), 72; 115.

22. *SIG³* 543 (214 BC).

23. App., *BC* 1, 100, 469; 104, 489; *ILS* 871; Ascon., *In Cornelian.* 75C; *RE* IV, 1250.

24. Suet., *DA* 40, 3.

25. DH 4, 24, 6; Gaius 1, 42-6; Paul., *Sent. recep.* 4, 14, 4 etc.; Duff, *o.c.* (n.1), 31f. The younger Pliny freed 100 slaves.

26. Gaius 1, 25-7; 3, 74-6; Ulpian 1, 11; Duff., *o.c.* (n.1), 72-5. The category was abolished by Justinian, *Cod.* 7, 5.

27. As in Petron., *Sat.* 41, 7.

28. *Latini Iuniani*, Duff, *o.c.* (n.1), 75-85; Ulpian 1, 12f. Cf. *ILS* 1985, stressing that a freedman who died at age 31 was 30 when freed by his master's will.

29. Gaius 1, 20.

30. Cf. Plin., *Ep.* 7, 16; 7, 32.

31. Gaius 1, 18-20; Ulpian 1, 13f. For a freedman given full freedom by such a Panel, see *ILS* 1984.

32. Gaius 1, 29 and 31; Ulpian 3, 3.

33. Gaius 1, 32c-34; Ulpian, 3, 5f.

34. Plin., *Ep.* 10, 104f.

35. For the period from Sulla to Caesar (in which Augustus, like Dionysius of Halicarnassus, thought the numbers were excessive), Goodfellow, *o.c.* (n.1), 114 calculates emancipation at the rate of 16,000 a year. P.A. Brunt, *o.c.* (n.1), 549f., challenges the basis of this calculation.

36. Gaius 1, 20; Ulpian 3, 3.

37. Cf. *Dig.* 38, 1, 22, 1.

38. CD 39, 24, 1; DH, *AR* 4, 24, 5.

39. On this issue, see L.R. Taylor, *The Voting Districts of the Roman Republic*, American Academy in Rome, 1960, esp. 132-49.

40. Cic., *Phil.* 3, 10; *Acts* 22, 28; CD 60, 17, 3-8. Cf. *TA* 14, 50, 1.

41. Pliny, *Ep.* 10, 5-7; 106f. Mauretanian chiefs, the *tabula Banasitana*, for whose text (with discussion), see J.H. Oliver, 'Text of the Tabula Banasitana, AD 177', *AJP* 93, 1972, 336-40;

A.N. Sherwin-White, *JRS* 63, 1973, 86-98. Inscriptions showing citizenship granted by emperors: *ILS* 1977 (Augustus); 1978 (Claudius); 1979 and 1981 (Vespasian).

42. Grants to princes by Augustus, Goodfellow, *o.c.* (n.1), 101-8. Nero, Suet., *Nero* 12, 1.

43. Cic., *Ad fam.* 16, 16.

44. See Goodfellow, *o.c.* (n.1), 90-3.

45. *ILS* 8888.

46. Grant extended to parents, wives and children in the case of ex-magistrates in Latin cities and colonies (*FIRA²* 1, 23; *ILS* 6088, xxi, Salpensa) and in some individual cases (e.g. Seleucus of Rhosos under the triumvirs, EJ² 301, ii, 1). No mention of parents, but *conubium* secured citizenship for descendants, in Claudius' grant to Volubilis. Smallwood, *Docts. of Gaius, Claudius, Nero* 407.

47. CD 60, 24, 3; Herodian 3, 8, 5. See P. Meyer, 'Die ägypt. Urkunden u.d. Eherecht d. röm. Soldaten', *Zeitschr. d. Savigny-Stiftung*, 1897, 44-77.

48. *Diplomata, CIL* XVI; a selection in *ILS* 1986-2010 and 9052-60. Such children (and 'wives') were sometimes named on the *diplomata: ILS* 200 (Trajan), name of son; 2002 (Trajan), names of 'wife' and daughter; 2004 (Trajan), names of three sons; 9055 (Hadrian), names of 'wife', son and daughter; 9059 (Domitian), names of son and two daughters (the father an ex-legionary of X Fretensis).

49. E.g. *ILS* 1993 (Vespasian). See G.L. Cheesman, *The Auxilia of the Roman Army*, Oxford 1914, 32-4.

50. *CIL* XVI, p.148 (Nesselhauf); though they were issued to Guardsmen, who were also Roman citizens already. *PSI* IX, 1026, C 30f. seems to prove the point: 'Veterani ex legionibus instrumentum accipere non solent.' See A. Degrassi, 'Il papiro 1026 della Società italiana e i diplomi militari romani', *Aegyptus* 10, 1929, 242-54.

51. Nesselhauf, *CIL* XVI, p.155. See B. Gerov, *Klio* 37, 1959, 199.

52. Suet., *D.Cl.* 25, 1; *TA* 13, 26f. (debate under Nero); Doristh., *Divi Hadriani sent.* 3; *Dig.* 1, 16, 9, 3; 37, 14, 1. Murder of a master, Plin., *Ep.* 8, 14, 12-25. See Duff, *o.c.* (n.1), 36-49.

53. IV, 1, 33-9.

54. *Lex Acilia* of 123 BC, *FIRA²* 1, 7, 78 (85).

55. Paul., *Sent. recep.* 5, 26, 1f.; *Dig.* 48, 6, 7f. (Ulpian).

56. Peter Garnsey in his searching article, 'The *lex Iulia* and appeal under the Empire', *JRS* 56, 1966, 167-89, considers that a provincial governor was not bound, without consideration of the circumstances, to accede automatically to every appeal for the transfer of a trial to Rome.

57. This is the view of A.H.M. Jones, *o.c.* (n.1) and of A.N. Sherwin-White, *o.c.* (n.1); 68-70 and 115; it is rejected by P. Garnsey, *o.c.* (n.56). Plin., *Ep.* 10, 96, 4.

58. On this, see Garnsey, *o.c.* (n.1), esp. 221-80.

59. See n.54 above.

60. Diod. 37, 18.

61. Plin., *Pan.* 37-40.

62. *FIRA,²* 1, 55, ii, 1.

63. CD 77, 9, 5; *P. Giessen* 40. See A. Wilhelm, 'Die Constitutio Antoniniana', *AJA* 38, 1934, 178-80; Sherwin-White, *o.c.* (n.41).

64. Cic., *Pro Caec.* 101; *Pro Balbo* 28; *FIRA²* 1, 55, ii, 3; 1, 56, 5-22; Paul., *Sent. recep.* 1, 1a, 18; *Dig.* 50, 4, 3. The all-important evidence is that of the third Cyrene edict (EJ², 311). On this, F. de Visscher, *Les édits d'Auguste découverts à Cyrène*, Louvain 1940, 87-118; Sherwin-White, *o.c.* (n.41). (n.41).

65. F.F. Abbott, A.C. Johnson, *Municipal Administration in the Roman Empire*, Princeton 1926, no.25, pp. 298f.

66. *P. Oxy.* 7, 1022 (AD 103).

67. E.g. *ILS* 2005 (AD 148).

68. Plin., *Ep.* 10, 7. Imperial archives, see refs. to *Tabula Banasitana*, n.41 above.

69. See F. Schulz, 'Roman registers of births and birth certificates', *JRS* 32, 1942, 78-91 and 33, 1943, 55-64.

70. Cic., *Pro Arch.* 11.

71. So Schulz, *o.c.* (n.69), 63f. (Acts 22, 28).

Chapter Eight: Expulsion from Rome, Italy or your Homeland

1. Bibliography

U. Brasiello, *La repressione penale in diritto romano*, Naples 1937.

F.H. Cramer, 'Expulsion of astrologers from ancient Rome', *Class. et Mediaev.* 12, 1951, 9-50.

A. Giesecke, *De Philosophorum Veterum quae ad exilium spectant Sententiis*, Diss. Leipzig 1891.

Th. Mommsen, *Römisches Strafrecht*, Leipzig 1899.

A.N. Sherwin-White, *The Roman Citizenship*,² Oxford 1973.

2. CN, *Att.* 3, 1.

3. Cic., *Pro Caec.* 99; CD 56, 23, 2.

4. L. 9, 8-11; App., *Iber.* 80, 346-83, 362; Cic., *Pro Caec.* 98; *De orat.* 1, 181f.; 2, 137; *Dig.* 50, 7, 18; *RE* VIII, 2507-11 (Hostilius, no.18).

5. Cic., *In Cat.* 4, 10.

6. CD 60, 17, 4.

7. P. 27, 6; L. 42, 48, 3; App., *Mac.* 11, 9.

8. CD 56, 23, 4; Suet., *DA* 49, 1 (but cf. *TA* 1, 24, 3). The German imperial guard was eventually disbanded by Galba, Suet., *Galb.* 12, 2.

9. DH 8, 72, 5.

10. L. 39, 3, 4-6.

11. L. 41, 8, 6-12; 9, 9-12.

12. L. 42, 10, 3.

13. Cic., *Ad Att.* 4, 18, 4.

14. Cic., *De offic.* 3, 47.

15. App., *BC* 1, 23, 100; Plut., *C.Gr.* 12, 2-4.

16. Cic., *Pro Balb.* 48; E. Badian, *Foreign Clientelae*, Oxford 1958, 212-14.

17. Eldest Perperna, L. 44, 27, 11 and 30, 11; 32, 1-5; VM 3, 4, 5, who confuses *lex Iunia* and *lex Papia*. See *RE* XIX, 893-7, nos. 3-5.

18. CD 37, 9, 5.

19. Suet., *D.Cl.* 15, 2; 25, 3; Epict., *Diss.* 3, 24, 41. Anauni edict, *ILS* 206.

20. Plin., *Ep.* 10, 29f.; Suet., *D.Cl.* 25, 1; Plin., *NH* 33, 32f.; *Cod. Iust.* 7, 20, 2; 9, 21 1 (Diocletian); *Cod. Theod.* 9, 20, 1; *Cod. Iust.* 9, 31, 1 (Valens, Gratian, Valentinian); Mommsen, *Staatsr.* 3,³ 424; 451, n.4; *Strafr.* 856f.

21. *TA* 13, 26, 3 (reading 'centesimum'). Cf. Stat., *Silv.* 3, 3, 162-4; Mommsen, *Staatsr.* 2³, 1076, n.4.

22. P. 6, 14, 8; Cic., *De fin.* 2, 54; Mommsen, *Staatsr.* III,³ 47-53; A.N. Sherwin-White, 'Poena legis repetundarum', *PBSR* 17, 1949, 5-25; 'The extortion procedure again', *JRS* 42, 1952, 43-55; Cic., *Pro Cluent.* 116.

23. Cic., *Pro Caec.* 100.

24. Cic., *Paradox. Stoic.* 30; Suet., *DJ* 42, 3. In the case of murder the whole property was impounded.

25. CD 37, 17, 7; Cic., *Pro Sest.* 29.

26. Provincial governors, Plin., *Ep.* 10, 56f.; *Dig.* 48, 22, 7, 1-14. Prefect of the City, *Dig.* 1, 12, 1, 3 (right of *deportatio* as well as of relegation). See *RE* IA, 564f, s.v. 'Relegatio'. Ovid., *Trist.* 5, 11, 21f., 'ipse (*sc. Caesar*) relegati, non exulis, utitur in me/nomine'.

27. CD 37, 29, 1; *Dig.* 49, 16, 4, 4; Suet., *D.Cl.* 23, 2.

28. *TA* 6, 49. Seven years, CD 76, 5, 5; five, Plin., *Ep.* 3, 9, 17; *Dig.* 1, 6, 2 (a woman, under Hadrian, guilty of maltreating her slave-girls); three, Plin., *Ep.* 10, 56, 2 (by a provincial governor); two, Plin., *Ep.* 3, 9, 18.

29. *PIR*,² 'D' 93. Cf. *TA* 2, 50, 4 (Italy and Africa); 14, 41, 1 (Italy and Spain); Plin., *Ep.* 2, 11, 19 (Italy and Africa).

30. CD 56, 27, 2.

31. *TA* 14, 62, 6.

32. Ovid., *Trist.* 2, 129f.; 5, 2, 56-8; *Dig.* 48, 22, 1; 48, 22, 14, 1; Paul., *Sent. recept.* 2, 26, 14; 5, 25, 8 and 26, 3. CD 56, 27, 3, Augustus' concessions (3 ships, up to 20 slaves or freedmen, property of up to half a million sesterces).

33. CD 57, 22, 5; *Dig.* 48, 22, 6 praef. *Viaticum*, *TA* 12, 22, 3; Sen., *Consol. ad Helv.* 12, 4; Pliny, *Ep.* 4, 11, 13; *Dig.* 48, 22, 16.

34. Philo, *C. Flac.* 162-79. Cf. Thrasea's remarks in the same vein, *TA* 14, 48, 6f.

35. VM 1, 3, 3 refers to an expulsion from Rome in 139 BC.

36. Jos., *AJ* 18, 65-84, who says the 4,000 were all Jews; *TA* 2, 85, 5. CD 60, 6, 6; Suet., *D. Cl.* 25, 4; *Acts* 18, 2.

37. Paul., *Sent. recept.* 5, 21, 1f.

38. Paul., *Sent. recept.* 5, 21, 3f. (In AD 11 Augustus had forbidden — with doubtful effectiveness — any consultation *tête-à-tête* with an astrologer, nobody else being present, or any consultation on the subject of death, CD 56, 25, 5.)

39. VM 1, 3, 3; L., *Per. Oxy.* 54; CD 49, 43, 5; 57, 15, 8; *TA*, 2, 32, 5; 12, 52, 3; *TH* 2, 62; Suet., *Vitell.* 14, 4; CD 66, 9, 2. According to Jerome, *Chron.* and Suidas (s.v. 'Domitianus') there was a further expulsion under Domitian.

40. *TA* 4, 14, 4; CD 57, 21, 3; Suet., *Tib.* 37, 2 (Gaius brought them back, CD 59, 2, 5); *TA* 13, 25, 4 (in AD 56; *pantomimi* back in 60, *TA* 14, 21, 7). See further Friedländer, *Sittengesch. Roms* 9, Leipzig 1919-20, II, 143f.

41. Athen. 12, 547a; Suet., *Rhet.* 1; AG 15, 11, 1 (where 'Latini' is an evident mistake).   ).

42. Suet., *D. Vesp.* 15; CD 66, 12, 2f.; 66, 15, 5; Plin., *Ep.* 3, 11.

43. See for the first formulation of this theory, M. Rostovtzeff, *SEHRE*, 1926, 108-17. Cf. D. Kienast, 'Nerva und das Kaisertum Traians', *Historia* 17, 1968, 51-71, on propaganda that Trajan ruled not as Nerva's adopted son but by the grace of god (Juppiter).

44. Suet., *DA* 42, 3; Oros. 7, 3, 6 (in the 48th year of Augustus' rule); CD 55, 26, 1 (AD 6); AM 14, 6, 19.

45. *Dig.* 48, 19, 4; 48, 19, 28, 13 (edict of Hadrian).

46. Plin., *Ep.* 10, 56f.

47. *TA* 4, 21, 5.

48. *TA* 4, 28-30.

49. *TA* 1, 6; 1, 53, 4-9; 14, 57-9; Philo, *C. Flac.* 185-91; Suet., *D. Vesp.* 15.

50. Suet., *C. Cal.* 28. For a different account of Gaius' mental state in ordering the executions, Philo, *C. Flac.* 183f.; *Leg. ad Gai.* 341f.

51. Wives, *TA* 15, 71, 7; Plin., *Ep.* 7, 19, 4 (Fannia and Helvidius Piscus). Gracchus, *TA* 4, 13, 3-5.

52. *TA* 14, 59, 2; Mart. 7, 44f. (cf. Suet., *Gramm.* 3); 2, 24.

53. Cic., *Pro Balbo* 28; *TA* 4, 43, 7f.

54. *SIG*,[3] 811f. (Smallwood, *Docts. of Gaius, Claudius, Nero* 245); *TA* 15, 71, 7; *PIR*,[2] 'G' 184; *RE*, Supplb. III, 789f., no.2; Philostr., *VAT* 7, 16; Strabo 16, 2, 13, 455.

55. Philo, *C. Flac.* 154 (cf. 161). Archelaus, Jos., *AJ* 17, 344; Strabo 10, 2, 46, 765. Antipas, Jos, *BJ*, 2, 183; *AJ* 18, 252 (*RE*, Supplb. II, 188); Ovid, *Ex Pont.* 4, 13, 37f.

56. *TA* 13, 43, 6; CD 40, 54, 3; L., *Per.* 69; Suet., *Tib.* 11, 3; 32, 2.

57. Cic., *Ad Q.f.* 1, 1, 15; Sen., *Consol. ad Helv.* 6, 5; Stat., *Silv.* 3, 5.

58. *TA* 16, 14, 2; Philo, *C. Flac.* 168; Sen., *Controv.* 2, 5, 13; 10, praef. 10; Plin., *Ep.* 4, 11.

59. Florus, *Virgilius Orator an Poeta*.

60. *Act. Apost.* 18, 3.

61. Philostr. *VS* 1, 7.

62. See A. Giesecke, *o.c.* (n.1); Cic., *In Pis.* 95; Sen., *Consol. ad Helv.*; Plut., *De exilio, Mor.* 599A-607F.

63. Licinian. p.14F, 105 BC; Suet., *DJ* 42, 1 states that Caesar forbad Romans of military age to be out of Italy for more than three years at a stretch.

64. Mommsen, *Staatsr.* III,[3] 912f. Cf. Cic., *Ad Att.* 2, 18, 3; Suet., *D.Cl.* 16, 2; CD 60, 25, 6; *TA* 12, 23, 1; 2, 59, 4.

65. Suet., *DA* 16, 4; *D.Cl.* 23, 2.

Chapter Nine: Communication, 1: Mainly Latin and Greek

1. *Bibliography*

F.F. Abbott, *The Common People of Ancient Rome*, London 1912 (esp. 1-116 on the spoken Latin of the common people).

G. Bardy, *La question des langues dans l'église ancienne* I, Paris 1948.

A. Budinszky, *Die Ausbreitung der lateinischen Sprache über Italien und die Provinzen des römischen Reiches*, Berlin 1881.

A. Cameron, 'Latin words in Greek inscriptions', *AJP* 52, 1931, 232-62.

R. Cavenaile, 'Quelques aspects de l'apport linguistique du grec au latin d'Egypte', *Aegyptus* 32, 1952, 191-203.

S. Daris, 'Il lessico latino nella lingua greca d'Egitto', *Aegyptus* 40, 1960, 117-314.

L. Franck, 'Sources classiques concernant la Cappadoce', *Rev. hitt. et asianique* 24, 1966, 91-4.

G.H. Grandgent, *An Introduction to Vulgar Latin*, Boston 1908.

L. Hahn, *Rom und Romanismus im griechisch-römischen Osten*, Leipzig 1906.

L. Hahn, 'Zum Sprachenkampf im römischen Reich bis auf die Zeit Justinians', *Philol.*, Suppl. 10, 1907, 677-718.

K. Holl, 'Das Fortleben der Volkssprachen in Kleinasien in nachchristlicher Zeit', *Hermes* 43, 1908, 240-54.

K. Jackson, *Language and History in Early Britain*, Edinburgh 1953.

J.G. Kempf, 'Romanorum Sermonis Castrensis ... Reliquiae', *Jahrb. f. class. Phil.*, suppl. 26, 1900/1,342-400.

P. Lambrechts, *De geestelijke Weerstand van de westelijke Provincies tegen Rom*, Brussels 1966.

F. Lot, 'La langue du commandement dans les armées romaines', *Mél. F. Grat*, Paris 1946, 1, 203-9.

Ramsay MacMullen, 'Provincial languages in the Roman Empire', *AJP* 87, 1966, 1-17.

H.I. Marrou, *Histoire de l'éducation dans l'antiquité*,[6] Paris 1965, 374-88; 590-6.

B. Meinersmann, *Die lateinischen Wörter und Namen in den griechischen Papyri*, Leipzig 1927.

L. Mitteis, *Reichsrecht und Volksrecht in den östlichen Provinzen des röm. Kaiserreichs*, Leipzig 1891.

L. Mitteis, U. Wilcken, *Grundzüge und Chrestomathie der Papyruskunde*, Leipzig-Berlin 1912.

A. Momigliano, 'The lonely historian Ammianus Marcellinus', *Annal. Scuol. Normal. Sup. di Pisa* sex. 3, iv, 1974, 1393-1407.

C. Morel, *Archives militaires du Ie siecle à Geneve*, Geneva 1900.

J. Palm, *Rom, Römertum und Imperium in der griechischen Litteratur der Kaiserzeit*, Lund 1959.

O. Rebling, *Versuch einer Charakteristik der römischen Umgangssprache*,[2] Kiel 1883.

J.N. Sevenster, *Do You Know Greek?, Novum Testamentum*, suppl. 19, Leiden 1968.

W.J. Snellman, *De Interpretibus Romanorum deque Linguae Latinae cum aliis nationibus Commercio*, Leipzig, part 1, 1919; part 2, 1914.

J. Sofer, 'Das Hieronymuszeugnis über die Sprachen der Galater und Treverer', *Wien. Stud.* 55, 1937, 148-58.

J. Sofer, 'Die Differenzierung der romanischen Sprachen', *Die Sprache* 2, 1950-2, 23-38.

J. Sofer, 'Reichssprache und Volkssprache im römischen Imperium,' *Wien. Stud.* 65, 1952, 138-155.

A. Thumb, *Die griechische Sprache im Zeitalter des Hellenismus*, Strassburg 1901 (repr. Berlin 1974).

H. Thylander, 'Etude sur l'épigraphie latine', *Skrifter utgivna av svenska Institutet i Rom* in 8°, V, Lund 1952.

P. Viereck, *Sermo Graecus quo S.P.Q.R. magistratusque p.R. usque ad Tiberi Caesaris aetatem ... usi sunt*, Göttingen 1888.

A.J.N. Wilson, *Emigration from Italy in the Republican Age of Rome*, Manchester 1966.

H. Zilliacus, *Zum Kampf der Weltsprachen im oströmischen Reich*, Helsingfors 1935.

2. Festus 31L, s.v. 'Bilingues Bruttaces'; Schol. Hor., *Sat.* 1, 10, 30 (Canusium bilingual); Cic., *De fin.* 1, 7; AG 17, 17, 1; Isid., *Orig.* 15, 1, 63.

3. L. 40, 42, 13. In the first place, of course, Cumae was Greek-speaking.

4. Plin., *NH* 3, 39; P.A. Brunt, *JRS* 55, 1965, 98-101.

5. Cic., *Div. in Caec.* 39. New colonies (Panhormus, Tauromenium, Thermae, Tyndaris, Catana, Syracuse); *ESAR* III, 346. Apul., *Met.* 11, 5, 'Siculi trilingues'.

6. See MacMullen, *o.c.* (n.1) on, in particular, Syriac, Coptic, Punic and Celtic.

7. *TA* 4, 45, 3.

8. See R. MacMullen, 'The Celtic Renaissance', *Historia* 14, 1965, 93-104.

9. Apul., *Apol.* 98; *Epit. de Caes.* 20, 8; Aug., *Conf.* 1, 14, 23.

10. G.L. della Vida, 'Due iscrizioni imperiali neopuniche di Lepcis Magna', *Afr. Ital.* 6, 1935, 1-29; G. Charles-Picard, *La Civilisation de l'Afrique romaine*, Paris 1959, 291-97.

11. Strabo 13, 4, 17, 631; A.H. Sayce, *Anatolian Studies to Sir William Ramsay*, Manchester 1923, 396; Acts 14, 11; Holl, *o.c.* (n.1), with criticism of Thumb, *o.c.* (n.1). Philostr., *VAT* 3, 41 and 4, 19. Galatians, Hieron. on Epistle to the Galatians 2, 3, Migne, *Patr. Lat.* xxvi, 357.

12. Iren., *Adv. heres.*, 1 proem; *Dig.* 32, 11, 1.

13. *TA* 11, 16; 2, 2.

14. *CD* 19, 7. Cf. Plin., *NH* 3, 29 on this achievement of Rome. Plut., *Mor.* 1010D speaks of Latin as the common language of the world.

15. Liban., *Or.* 18, 282.

16. Apul., *Apol.* 18; cf. 66.

17. *TA* 2, 9f. Jugurtha learnt Latin while serving with the Roman army at Numantia, Sall., *BJ* 101, 6; Front., *Strat.* 2, 4, 10.

18. VP 2, 107; *TA* 2, 13, 2.

19. CD 71, 5, 2; *PIR*,[2] 'B' 69. Cf. Rostovtzeff, *SEHRE*,[2] 592, n.36.

20. *TH*2, 37; 2, 74; CD 74, 2, 6 (cf. *TH* 2, 93f. and 99; 3, 33).

21. See Kempf, *o.c.* (n.1); Lot, *o.c.* (n.1).

22. Plin, *NH* 1, praef. 1 (*conterraneus*); AG 10, 9 (a number of *vocabula militaria); AM 17, 13, 9* and Veget. *3, 19 (caput porci)*; *Cod. Just.* 5, 16, 2; *CIL* XI, 39 (*focaria*); Festus 152L (*muger*). *Sesquiplaga* in *TA* 15, 67, 8 may well be a soldier's word.

23. JC, *BG* 7, 73; Suet., *Tib.* 42, 1; Suet., *Galb* 6, 2.

24. Quintil. 1, 5, 57; Arr., *Tact.* 33, 1.

25. Justin 20, 5, 12-14. Greek historians, Philenus, Sosylus (Hannibal's tutor in Greek), Silenus, Chaereas etc. But king Hiempsal II of Numidia in the first century BC wrote the history of his country in Punic, Sallust, *BJ* 17, 7; *RE* VIII, 1394f. Hannibal, CN, *Hann.* 13, 2f.; Cic., *De orat.* 2, 75 (Greek); Zon. 8, 24, 8 (Latin).

26. *RE* XI, 656, against DL 4, 67.

27. Aug., *CD* 1, 14, 23.

28. Apul., *Met.* 1, 1; *Flor.* 17f.; *Apol.* 25, 30 and 82). *ILS* 7761 (AD 229) from Sitifis in Mauretania, 'litterarum studiis utriusque linguae perfecte eruditus'.

29. Plin., *NH* 3, 31; Cic., *Pro Font.* 11-13 (resident Romans). Spread of Latin, Strabo 4, 1, 12, 186; 4, 4, 2, 195. Inscriptions, Snellman, *o.c.* (n.1), 1, 16f.

30. Diod. 5, 36, 3; App., *Iber.* 38, 153; L. 43, 3, 1-4; Strabo 3, 5, 1, 168; Wilson, *o.c.* (n.1), 10f.; 22-5.

31. Noricum, Budinszky, *o.c.* (n.1), 166 (cf. the early second century career of T. Varius Clemens, a native of Celeia in Noricum, *ILS* 1362). Pannonia, VP 2, 110, 5 (cf. SHA, *Aurelian* 24, 3).

32. See András Mócsy, *Gesellschaft und Romanisation in der römischen Provinz Moesia Superior,* Amsterdam 1970, esp. 199-256.

33. See J. Sofer, *o.c.* (n.1, *Die Sprache*), 23-38. It has been suggested that Latin was brought to Dacia by not very well educated Roman colonists and, because of the absence of schools and rhetorical education, Latin speech in Dacia always had a certain crudity.

34. *TA.* 21, 2; Juv. 15, 111; *Ephem. Epig.* III, p.312; H. Dessau, 'Ein Freund Plutarchs in England', *Hermes* 46, 1911, 156-60.

35. Plut., *Sert.* 14, 3f.; *TA* 3, 43, 1; Suet., *C. Cal.* 45, 2; Budinszky, *o.c.* (n.1), 178f.; *CIL* III, 2, p.962, no.2.

36. Strabo 4, 1, 5, 181; *TA* 4, 44, 5; T. *Agr.* 4, 3; JC, *BG* 6, 14, 3; Lucian, *Heracl.* 4.

37. Strabo 3, 2, 15, 151.

38. VP 2, 51, 3, 'non Hispaniensis natus sed Hispanus'.

39. Spaniards, Mart. 1, 61; Gauls, Quintil. 10, 1, 118. Considerably earlier the poet Cornelius Gallus was born at Forum Iulii.

40. Mart 7, 88, 1-4; Plin., *Ep.* 9, 11, 2; Mart. 9, 84; 11, 30; Auson; *Epiced. in Patrem* 9f.; Philostr., *VS* 1, 8; [Dio Chrys.], *Or.* 37, 25.

41. Quintil. 1, 5, 58; Juv. 3, 67f. (mocking); Suet., *Tib.* 71; CD 57, 15, 2.

42. CD 55, 3, 4f.; Hahn, (n.1, 1906) esp. 15, 22, 107, 114ff.; 121-36; 223-68. On words in the New Testament and the Greek Fathers, Bardy, *o.c.* (n.1), 123f., n.4. On Greek papyri, Meinermann, *o.c.* (n.1).

43. M. Holleaux, *Strategos hypatos,* Paris 1918.

44. *SIG,*³ *656* (decree of Abdera, *c*.166 BC).

45. P. 20, 9, 10-12.

46. DH 2, 34, 3; 3, 61, 1; Hahn, *o.c.* (n.1, 1906), 134, n.11; *RE* VIIA, 740.

47. Bardy, *o.c.* (n.1), 52-94 (81f. on Jewish inscriptions); 121.

48. Quintil. 1, 12, 9; CN, *Att.* 13, 4; AG 4, 1, 6. (Affectation, Juv. 11, 148).

49. Suet., *Gramm.* 12 and 8; Plin., *NH* 25, 7; *RE* VIIA, 1819f., no.3.

50. Clodius, Suet., *Rhet.* 5. Cestius, Sen., *Controv.* 3, praef. 14-17; 7, 1, 27 etc.; *RE* III, 2008-11, no.12. Arellius, Sen., *Controv.* 2, 2, 8f. etc; *RE* II, 635-7, no.3. Probus, Suet., *Gramm.* 24; *RE* VIIIA, 195-212, no.315.

51. Educated Greek contempt of Latin literature, AG 19, 9. Translation of Sallust, Suda II, 506 Adler, s.v. 'Zenobios'. Zenobia's knowledge of Roman history was derived from Greek writers, SHA 24, 30, 22.

52. Paus. 3, 11, 4.

53. Plut., *Cato mai.* 22, 5; AG 6, 14, 9; VM 2, 2, 3; CD 60, 8, 2f.; Suet., *D.Cl.* 42.

54. Dio Chrys., *Or.* 47, 22; 49, 6 etc. See Palm, *o.c.* (n.1), 29f.

55. See C.S. Walton, 'Oriental senators in the service of Rome', *JRS* 19, 1929, 38-66; Mason Hammond, 'Composition of the senate, AD 68-235', *JRS* 47, 1957, 74-81, with bibliography.

56. *ILS* 2949. On Claudian, A.D.E. Cameron, *Claudian,* Oxford 1970.

57. Lucian, *De merc. conduct.* 24; Plut., *Dem.* 2f.; C.P. Jones, *Plutarch and Rome,* Oxford 1971, 81-7.

58. *RE* IVA, 81-5 (Strabo's travels); 103-6 (Asinius Pollio and Dellius). Cicero references, Strabo 14, 2, 25, 660 (*Brutus* 315); 17, 1, 13, 798 (from a lost speech). Lucian, *Electr.* 1-5; *Pro lapsu* 13; *Apol.* 12. Lucian in Italy, *Herod.* 5; *Pseudol.* 27; in Rome, *Nigr.* 2; in Gaul, *Bis accusat.* 27; *Herc.* 4. Josephus' Greek, *AJ* 20, 263.

59. Cic., *De offic.* 1, 133; *De orat.* 3, 44; Quintil. 8, 1, 3; Plin., *Ep.* 6, 11, 2 (*os Latinum*); Cic., *Brut.* 108.

60. App., *Hann.* 41, 177; Philostr., *VAT* 5, 36; Arrian, *Peripl. mar. Eux.* 6, 2 and 10, 1, *rhômaïka Grammata,* 'a report in Latin'; cf Luke 23, 38, John 19, 20, Jos., *BJ* 5, 194. Strabo 6, 1, 6, 258; CD 39, 16, 1; 53, 18, 1.

61. Cic., *De orat.* 3, 45; Quintil. 1, 6, 39; Suet., *D. Vesp.* 22.

62. Cic., *Ad fam.* 9, 21, 1; AG 19, 10 (*praeterpropter*); 19, 13 (*nanus*).

63. On this topic, see Rebling, *o.c.* (n.1).

64. Cic., *Orat.* 160; Quintil. 1, 5, 19f.; Aug., *Conf.* 1, 18; Catull. 84, on which see E.S. Ramage, *CP* 54, 1959, 44f. and B. Einarson, *CP* 61, 1966, 187f. as well as Fordyce's very full note.

65. Quintil. 1, 5, 8 and 56ff.; Plin, *NH* praef. 13, 'rustica vocabula aut externa, immo barbara etiam'; Col. 5, 1, 5f.; Macrob. *Sat.* 1, 3, 13; Plaut., *Truc.* 687-91 (*conia* for *ciconia*). Unlike R. Syme, *The Roman Revolution*, Oxford 1939, 485, I see no reason at all for thinking that Quintilian failed to understand what he read in Pollio about Livy.

66. Cic., *Brut.* 171f.

67. Plin., *Ep.* 9, 23, 2.

68. Cic., *Pro Arch.* 26 (cf. Sen., *Suas.* 6, 27); SHA, *Hadr.* 3, 1; AG 19, 9. CF. Messalla's *mot* on the Spanish orator Porcius Latro, 'sua lingua disertus est', Sen., *Controv.* 2, 4, 8. H. Nettleship, J. Conington, *The Satires of A. Persius Flaccus*, Oxford 1874, xxii, 'That Spanish taste for inappropriate and meretricious ornament'.

69. SHA, *SS* 19, 9; 15, 7. Septimius' 'elegant letter' of *Dig.* 1, 16, 6, 3 is no evidence to the contrary; emperors did not always draft their own letters.

70. Apul., *Met.* 1, 1 (cf. *RE* II, 254f.); Macrob., *Sat.* 1, praef. 12.

71. Sen., *Consol. ad Helv. mat.* 7, 9.

72. Hieron., *Ep* 107, 9; Mócsy, *o.c.* (n.32), 199-236.

73. A nice example from Ravenna, 1st century AD (*ILS* 1980): 'C. Iul. Mygdonius generi Parthus, natus ingenuus, capt. pubis aetate, dat. in terra Romana qui, dum factus cives R., iuvente fato colocavi arkam, dum esse annor. L. Peti usque a pubertate senectae meae pervenire; nunc recipe me, saxe, libens; tecum cura solutus ero.' Cf. *ILS* 5795 from Africa, whose blunders must surely be the responsibility of the cutter.

74. *ILS* 2403, Pisidian woman Ba married to soldier of Leg. XII Fulminata.

75. Hahn, *o.c.* (n.1, 1906), 92-6; B. Levick, *Roman Colonies in Southern Asia Minor*, Oxford 1967, esp. 130-44 (on Pisidian Antioch) and 161f.

76. Places with groups of resident Romans listed, D. Magie *RRAM* 1615f.; F. Millar, *A Study of Cassius Dio*, Oxford 1964, 184.

77. AM 15, 13, 1; *RE* IVA, 181f., Strategius no.1.

78. See R.O. Fink, *Roman Military Records on Papyrus*, APA 1971, nos. 1-46 rosters and other lists (cf Veget. 2, 19), 47-57 morning reports, 68-73 pay records; 87ff official correspondence; Lot, *o.c.* (n.1), 203-4; *P. Oxy.* 7, 1022.

79. Mitteis, Wilcken, *o.c.* (n.1), 1, 462f.; *ILS* 2483 (EJ 261), from Coptos, 'castram aedificaverunt'; *Hunt's Pridianum*, *B.M. Pap.* 2851 (see *JRS* 48, 1958, 102-16), AD 99; *P. Geneva* 1 (Woodhead, McCrum 405), AD 81-96.

80. Suet., *Tib.* 71; Apul., *Met.* 9, 39; Lucian, *Onos* 44.

81. *CIL* III, 30, 33f., 36, 42f., 50, 55-60; *CIG* III, 4724, 4750b; *BGU* 2, 423; Smallwood, *Documents, Nerva, Trajan, Hadrian* 307. Cf. inscriptions in verse both in Latin and Greek at shrine of Achilles on island of Leuke off mouth of the Danube, Arrian, *Peripl. mar. Eux.* 21, 2.

82. CD 60, 17, 4.

83. DH 4, 24, 4-8; CD 60, 17, 5-8; Sen., *Apok.* 9; Acts 22, 28.

84. Plin., *NH* 7, 88; Plut., *Ant.* 27, 4f.; SHA 24, 30, 20f.

85. Two of the three surviving texts of the *Res Gestae* found in Asia Minor were published both in Greek and Latin; the third at Pisidian Antioch, a Roman colony, was in Latin alone. Bilingual (Asia Minor), *CIL* III, 6888; *Eph. Epig.* 5, 590, no.1391. Egypt, soldiers' wills, *Gnomon Idiologi, BGU* 5, 1210 (*FIRA²* 1, 99, 34). Fideicommissa, Gaius 2, 281; *Dig.* 32, 1, 11, 1. Greek in wills, *Cod. Just.* 6, 23, 21, 6; 7, 2, 14. Greek (if understood) acceptable also for *stipulation*, Gaius, *Inst.* 3, 93.

86. *Cod. Just.* 7, 45, 12; *FIRA²* III, 174, 176 (Egypt, AD 390-487); *OGIS* 519 (rescript, AD 244-7); W.H.C. Frend, 'A third-century inscription relating to *Angareia* in Phrygia, *JRS* 46, 1956, 46-56; P. Roussel, F. de Visscher, 'Le Procès devant Caracalla', *Syria* 23, 1942/3, 176-94; C.H. Roberts, E.G. Turner, *Catalogue of the Greek and Latin Papyri in the John Rylands Library*, IV, 653f.

87. Liban., *Or.* 62, 21.

88. Liban., *Epp.* 363; 534, 3; 1203; 1539; *Or.* 1, 154 and 214; 62, 21, 24f.; John Chrysostom, *Adv. Oppugnat. Vit. Monast.* 3, 5 (PG 47, 357), on learning Latin and securing a post at Court; J.H.W.G. Liebeschuetz, *Antioch*, Oxford 1972, 251-5.

89. See R. Cavenaile, *Corpus Papyrorum Latinarum*, Wiesbaden 1958; A. Calderini, *Papiri Latini*, Milan 1945; L.P. Jouguet, 'Les papyrus latins d'Egypte', *REL* 3, 1925, 35-50, esp. 43; E.G. Turner, *Studi Calderini Paribeni*, Milan 1957, II, 157-61; A. Bataille, *Studi Calderini Paribeni*, II, 277-83 (writing exercise in Greek and Latin); C.H. Moore, 'Latin Exercises from a Greek Schoolroom', *CP* 19, 1924, 317-28.

90. Cavenaile, *o.c.* (n.89) 14 (Virgil, writing practice); literary, 1-27, 36-40; philosophical, 45-7; historical, 28-35, 41-4; glossaries of Latin words written in Greek, 275, 278; Greek-Latin

dictionary, 280; Greek translation of *Aeneid* 1, 7; model Latin alphabet, 58, etc.
91. See Cavenaile, *o.c.* (n.89).
92. Mitteis, Wilcken, *o.c.* (n.1), I, 85f. (cf. 53f.); *P. Berlin* 10, 582; Cavenaile, *o.c.* (n.89), 281.
93. W. Schubart, 'Ein lateinisch-griechisch-koptisches Gesprächbuch', *Klio* 13, 1913, 27-38.
94. Paus. 4, 27, 11; in Elis, Dio Chrys., *Or.* 1, 54. Boeotian, Paus. 9, 34, 2. Philostr., *VAT* 6, 36 tells of a boy who spoke with a hideous Greek accent and taught his birds to imitate him.
95. Balbilla, *CIG* III, 4725, 4727, 4729f.; Eirenaeus, *RE* V, 2120-4, no.7.
96. Lucian, *Pseudol.* 11; Hahn, *o.c.* (n.1, 1906), 38-52; H. Leclercq, 'Note sur le grec néo-testamentaire et la position du grec en Palestine au premier siècle', *Les Etudes classiques* 42, 1974, 243-55.
97. Lucian, *Pseudol.* 14; Philostr., *VS* 2, 13, p.258; *VAT* 1, 4 and 7; 3, 41; 4, 19 (book on divination); L. Frank, 'Sources classiques concernant la Cappadoce', *Rev. hitt. et asian.* 24, 1966, 91-4.
98. Ovid, *Trist.* 3, 11, 9; 3, 12, 37-40; 4, 1, 89f.; 5, 2, 67f.; 5, 7, 51-4; 5, 12, 55-8; Dio Chrys., *Or.* 36, 9 and 26.
99. Parthia: F. Cumont, 'Une lettre du roi Artabane III à la ville de Suse', *CRAI* 1932, 238-60, esp. 250-2; Plut., *Crass.* 32, 10; 33; Philostr., *VAT* 1, 32. No Latin, Lucan, *Phars.* 8, 348. Indians: Philostr., *VAT* 2, 27; 3, 12 and 36; Strabo 15, 1, 73, 719. Greek spoken far down the west coast of the Red Sea, *Peripl. mar. Eryth.* 5.
100. W.H.C. Frend, *JRS* 46, 1956, 56.
101. Cavernaile, *o.c.* (n.89), 277.
102. *P. Petaus*; H.C. Youtie, 'Pétaus fils de Pétaus ou le scribe qui ne savait pas écrire', *Chron. d'Egypte* 41, 1966, 127-43; '*Agrammatos*: an aspect of Greek society in Egypt', *HSCP* 75, 1971, 161-76.

Chapter Ten: Communication, 2: 'Barbarous Languages' and Interpreters

1. Plut., *De Isid. et Osir.* 47, *Mor.* 370B.
2. Lucian, *Deor. concil.* 9; Seneca, *Apok.* 5.
3. Herod. 4, 10, 5.
4. Lucian, *Alex.* 13 and 51.
5. Heliodor., *Aethiop.* 1, 19, 3.
6. The recently discovered documents from the caves show that Greek was more commonly used in Palestine than had been thought; it was, in fact, second language to Aramaic. See H. Ott, 'Die Muttersprache Jesu; Forschungen seit Gustav Dolman', *Novum Testamentum* 9, 1969, 1-25; J.A. Fitzmyer, 'The languages of Palestine in the first Century AD', *Cath. Bibl. Quart.* 32, 1970, 501-31. For the view that Jesus spoke Greek, Sevenster, *o.c.* (ch.9 n. 1), A.W. Argyle, *Expository Times* 67, 1955/6, 92f.; C.D.F. Moule, *Expository Times* 70, 1958/9, 100-2 (on Hellēnistai and Hebraei of Acts 6, 1). Paul, Acts 21, 37-40.
7. Jos., *AJ* 20, 262-5. Letter of Bar Cochba, Fitzmyer, *o.c.* (n.6), 513f.
8. L. 9, 36.
9. A. Momigliano, *Claudius*, Oxford 1934, 16; Varro, *LL* 5, 55; 7, 29; *RE* VI, 775-7; Suet., *DA* 97, 2; *CD* 56, 29, 4.
20. DH 19, 5.
11. Strabo 14, 1, 25, 642; Plin., *NH* 34, 21; *RE* VIII, 859-61, no.3; Cic., *Pro Balb.* 28; *Dig.* 49, 15, 5, 3; *RE* XXIII, 1902, no.24.
12. L. 45, 29, 3; VM 2, 2, 2 (cf. Lydus, *De Magg.* 2, 12; 3, 42 and 68; Aug., *CD* 19, 7); L. 45, 8, 6; VM 5, 1, 8; Plut., *Cato mai.* 12, 5-7 (cf. Cic., *TD* 2, 35, 'Graeci quorum copiosior lingua quam nostra'); Phaedrus, *App. Perott.* 30, 2-5, 'qui iactant se verborum copia'.
13: P. 15, 6, 3 (L. 30, 30, 1); L. 53, 14, 5-13; App., *Syr.* 10, 38-42.
14. See R.K. Sherk, *Roman Documents from the Greek East*, Baltimore 1969, 13-19; Suet., *DA* 89, 1; G.B. Townend, 'The post of *ab epistulis* in the second century', *Historia* 10, 1961, 375-81.
15. See Hahn, *o.c.* (ch.9 n. 1, 1906), 36-8; R.K. Sherk, *o.c.* (n. 14), 13, 18f.; J. Gagé, *Res Gestae Divi Augusti*, Paris 1955, 9-13; T. Drew Blair, *Historia* 21, 1972, 77-9; M. Hassal, M. Crawford, J. Reynolds, *JRS* 64, 1974, 199f., 210. *SIG*,³ 741, II, letter of proconsul of Asia, 88 BC, is a good example of highly latinised Greek.
16. [Quintil.], *Decl.* 3, 13.
17. *RE* VA, 652f., no.43.
18. Plin., *NH* 18, 22; Varro, *RR* 1, 1, 10; 2, 1, 10; 2, 1, 27; 3, 2, 13 (cf. 2, 5, 18); *RE* X, 1088f., no.160 (Silanus); III, 1722, no.42 (Cassius).
19. App., *BC* 3, 97, 404-7: J. van Burchem, 'La fuite de Decimus Brutus', *Mélanges Carcopino*, Paris 1966, 941-63.

20. Ovid., *Trist.* 5, 7, 51-64; *Ex Pont.* 3, 2, 40; 4, 13, 17-38.

21. L. 39, 42, 11; Plut., *Mar.* 24, 4-7.

22. Sall, *BJ* 109, 4; CD 78, 6, 2.

23. *BG* 1, 19, 3; 1, 47, 4-6; 1, 53, 5-8; *RE* VIIIA, 234f., no. 368. Roman use of negotiating officers as spies, P. 14, 1f. (Scipio Africanus).

24. JC, *BG* 5, 27, 1; 28, 1; 36, 1. Pompeius was certainly not the father of Pompeius Trogus the historian, *RE* XXI, 2300 against *RE* XXI, 2055, no.9.

25. AM 18, 2, 2.

26. *CIL* III, 14507. Cf. III, 10505; VI, 4871; 8481; XIII, 8773.

27. Plin., *Pan.* 56, 6.

28. Jos., *BJ* 6, 327.

29. Florus 4, 10, 4 and 7; Plut., *Ant.* 46, 4f.; Florus 4, 12, 13f.

30. Suet., *Nero* 13, 2.

31. See Bardy, *o.c.* (ch.9, n. 1), 123-54, esp. 139f. with notes.

32. Batnai, AM 14, 3, 3. Sailors to India, Strabo 15, 1, 4, 686; *Peripl. mar. Eryth.*

33. VM 9, 7, ext. 16 (= Plin., *NH* 7, 88; 25, 6; Quintil. 11, 2, 50). AG 17, 17 gives the number of languages as 25, *Vir. ill.* 76, 1 as fifty.

34. Strabo 11, 2, 16, 498; Plin., *NH* 6, 15.

35. Strabo 11, 4, 6, 503. Variety of languages in Asia Minor, Strabo 12, 1, 1f, 533; 12, 3, 25, 553. Disappearance of some languages (?dialects) under Roman domination in N.W. Asia Minor, Strabo 12, 4, 6, 565. Mysian, a cross between Lydian and Phrygian, Strabo 12, 8, 3, 572.

36. Plin., *NH* 6, 84; D. Meredith, 'Annius Plocamus: Two inscriptions from the Berenice road', *JRS* 43, 1953, 38-40.

37. Strabo 2, 3, 4f., 98-101; Strabo is sceptical about the truth of the story.

38. Maës, Ptol., *Geog.* 1, 11, 7 (from Marinus of Tyre); *RE* IIA, 1680. On the site of the Stone Tower, J.I. Miller, *The Spice Trade of the Roman Empire*, Oxford 1969, 126-33. Bardesanes, Euseb., *HE* 6, 10.

39. Miller, *o.c.* (n.38), 90.

40. Augustus, Strabo 15, 1, 4, 686; 15, 1, 73, 719; CD 54, 9, 8-10. Trajan, CD 68, 15, 1. Ceylon, n.36 above and F.F. Schwartz, 'Ein Singhalesischer Prinz in Rom,' *Rh. Mus.* 117, 1974, 166-76. Marcus Aurelius, Frazer on Paus. 6, 26, 6.

41. Philostr., *VAT* 1, 19.

Chapter Eleven: A Problem of Names: The Polyonymous Romans

1. *Bibliography*

General

H.L. Axtell, 'Men's names in the writings of Cicero', *CP* 10, 1915, 386-404.

G.D. Chase, 'The Origin of Roman Praenomina', *HSCP* 8, 1897, 103-84.

Bruno Doer, *Die römische Namengebung*, Stuttgart 1937.

I. Kajanto, *The Latin Cognomina*, Helsinki, 1965 (bibliography, pp. 367-72).

I. Kajanto, 'Women's praenomina reconsidered', *Arctos* 7, 1972, 13-30.

Th. Mommsen, 'Die röm. Eigennamen', *RF* 1, 1-68 and *Röm. Staatsr.* III, 1,³ 200-15.

RE s.v. 'Cognomen', IV, 225-30 (Mau); 'Namenwesen', XVI, 1611-70 (Ernst Fraenkel); 'Spitznamen', IIIA, 1821-40 (Hug).

W. Schulze, 'Zur Geschichte lat. Eigennamen, '*Abh. d. kön. Gesellsch. d. Wiss. zu Göttingen*', phl-hist. Kl., N.F.5, Berlin 1904.

A.N. Sherwin-White, *Roman Society and Roman Law in the New Testament*, Oxford 1963, 151-62.

H. Thylander, 'Etude sur l'épigraphie latine', *Skrifter utgivna av Svenska Institut i Rom in 8°*, V, 1952.

Names of slaves

M. Bang, 'Caesaris Servus', *Hermes* 54, 1919, 174-86.

J. Baumgart, *Die röm. Sklavnnamen*, Diss. Breslau 1936.

A. Oxé, 'Zur älteren Nomenklatur der röm. Sklaven', *Rh. Mus.* 59, 1904, 108-140.

Names of freedmen

A.M. Duff, *Freedmen in the early Roman Empire*, Oxford 1928, 52-8.

M.L. Gordon, 'The Freedman's Son in Municipal Life', *JRS* 21, 1931, 65-77.

Th. Mommsen, *Röm. Staatsr.* III, 1,³ 424-9.

Names of soldiers

R. Dean, *A Study in the Cognomina of Soldiers in the Roman Legions*, Princeton 1916 (with large bibliography).

Adoption of Roman names by foreigners gaining citizenship

R. Herzog, 'Namensübersetzungen und Verwandtes,' *Philol.* 56 (N.F.10), 1897, 33-70, esp. 58-68.

2. *ILS* 1005.

3. Auct. de Praenom. 1, disagreeing with Varro; L. 1, 3, 6-10. See *RE* XVI, 1651.

4. So Festus 107f. L; App., praef. 13; Macrob., *Sat.* 1, 16, 36; Plut., *QR* 102; Ulp. 15 and 16, 1a; Doer, *o.c.* (n.1), 7f. Auct. de Praenom. 3 says the name was given when a boy assumed the *toga virilis*. On Varro, Auct. de Praenom. 3 Mommsen, *Röm. Staatsr.* III, 1,³ 202f.

5. Turranius, see *PIR*, 'T' 137. *Spurii* (bastards), time of Trajan, *ILS* 6675. For this ingenious reconstruction of social history, see W. Kubitschek, 'Spurius, Spurii filius, sine patre filius usw.', *Wein. Stud.* 47, 1929, 130-43.

6. Cic., *Phil.* 1, 32; Suet., *Tib.* 1, 2 (no Lucius Claudius); CD 51, 19, 3; *TA* 3, 17, 8 (*PIR*,² 'C' 293).

7. Fabii, *RE* VI, 1739-41; Plin., *NH* 18, 10. Suillii etc., Plut. (Fenestella), *QR* 41; *Poplic.* 11, 7. For an analysis of the different classes of *gentilicia*, Chase, *o.c.* (n.1), 117-33.

8. Corculum, Cic., *Brut.* 79; *TD* 1, 18; Plin., *NH* 6, 118; *RE* IV, 1497f. Serapio, VM 9, 14, 3; Plin., *NH* 7, 54; 21, 10 (confused); *RE* IV, 1501f., nos. 354f.

9. See *RE* IIIA, 1821-40, s.v. 'Spitnamen'; J. Linderski, *Historia* 23, 1974, 463-80 on 'Lurco' (Glutton) third name of the tribune of 61 BC. 'Gurges', Macrob., *Sat.* 3, 13, 6.

10. Plin., *NH* 7, 62; AG 13, 20, 8; Doer, *o.c.* (n.1), 95-116 with further instances.

11. CD, fr. 44; Mommsen, *Röm Staatsr.* III, 1,³ 213; *RF* 1, 52-4; Doer, *o.c.* (n.1), 68-73.

12. 'Gaetulicus', VP 2, 116, 2; CD 55, 28, 4; *PIR*,² 'C' 1380. 'Britannicus', CD 60, 22, 1f.

13. 'Barbatus', *ILS* 1. Lex Acilia, *FIRA*,² 1, 7, 14.

14. *FIRA*² 1, 13, l. 146; *ILS* 2483 (Coptos).

15. On women's names, see *Doer, o.c.* (n.1), 202-23.

16. *CIL* II, 2582; V, 3045.

17. *RE* XVI, 1670; *CIL* VIII, 169. See Kajanto, *o.c.* (n.1), 17f.; Dean, *o.c.* (n.1), 113.

18. On this see Doer, *o.c.* (n.1), 74-95.

19. Servenia, E. Bosch, *Quellen zur Geschichte der Stadt Ankara im Altertum*, Ankara 1967, no.103; *RE* IIA, 1757.

20. *PIR*,² 'E' 48. Consul of AD 169, Q. Pompeius Senecio etc., *ILS* 1104; *PIR*, 'P' 492; E. Groag, 'Prosopographische Beiträge', *Österr. Jahresh.* XVIII, 1915, Beibl. 265-73; Doer, *o.c.* (n.1), 124-33.

21. Suet., *Galba* 4, 1; *PIR*,² 'L' 305; *FIRA*² 1, 58, 1.

22. *BGU* 423 and 632; *ILS* 2901; 2839; *CIL* X, 3468; 3590; 3590; 3593 (C. Iulius Victor qui et Sola Dini f.); Mommsen, *Hermes* 16, 1881, 466, n.2; Doer, *o.c.* (n.1), 181f.

23. EJ² 261 (*ILS* 2483, from Egypt); Schulze, *o.c.* (n.1), 496.

24. See Dean, *o.c.* (n.1), 108-18.

25. *Eph. Epig.* IX, 1913, p.557.

26. See Dean, *o.c.* (n.1), 99f.

27. *ILS* 2567, 2514.

28. *SIG³* 829A. Cf. *RE* XV, 1292-4, no.3, L. Mestrius Florus.

29. CD 60, 17, 7. See G. Alföldy, 'Notes sur la relation entre le droit de cité et la nomenclature dans l'empire romain', *Latomus* 25, 1966, 37-57.

30. See H. Box, *JRS* 22, 1932, 180.

31. *CILI,*² 2, 1263; 1358; 2046; Plin., *NH* 33, 26; Quintil. 1, 4, 26; Festus, s.v. 'Quintipor'; Mommsen, Röm. Staatsr. III, 1,³ 201, n.3.

32. Varro, *LL* 8, 21; Philostr., *VS* 2, 1, 558; Oxé, *o.c.* (n.1), 108-40; J. Schwab, *Nomina propria Latina oriunda a Participiis*, Leipzig 1898, 637-932; M.L. Gordon, 'The nationality of slaves', *JRS* 14, 1924, 93-111.

33. *CIL* VI, 10730; 8724; 24161. *CIL* X, 1807 (cf. J.H.D'Arms, *JRS* 64, 1974, 110) is a nice example: a freedman, called 'Calf' in Greek (Moschos), gave his son the name 'Vitulus' ('Calf' in Latin).

34. 5, 91.

35. Hor., *Sat.* 2, 5, 32; Pers. 5, 78-82.

36. Suet., *Gramm.* 18; Plin., *NH* 29, 7; Mart. 6, 17; *ILS* 5369; 7812; *PIR*,² 'A' 1183.

37. See A.M. Duff, *o.c.* (n.1), 57f.

38. Stat., *Silv.* 3, 3; *PIR*,² 'C' 860.

39. Cf., e.g., Schulze, *o.c.* (n.1). For important inferences from names, M.L. Gordon, *o.c.* (n.1), 65-77; *RE* IX, 1500f.

40. Dittenberger, *Inschr. v. Olymp.*, p.657, nos. 643f.; Hatzfeld, *Les Trafiquants* 10ff.; E. Badian, *Roman Clientelae*, 256f.; Philostr., *VAT* 4, 5; *Epp.* 71f.; Suet., *D.Cl.* 25, 3. A practice of some Greeks in Sicily, Cic., *In Verr.* 2, 5, 112.

41. Cic., *Ad Att.* 14, 12, 2; *De rep.* 6, 10.

42. *De fin.* 5, 71 and 86.

43. Cic., *Ad Att.* 7, 21; 7, 20, 1; 2, 12, 1; *Ad Q.f.* 3, 4, 6; 3, 6, 2; 3, 1, 6; *Ad Brut.* 4, 6; 5, 6; *Ad Q.f.* 3, 3, 4.

44. Sen., *Controv.* 2, 4, 13 suggests that M. Vipsanius Agrippa called himself M. Agrippa because of the obscurity of the name Vipsanius. But Augustus dropped his *nomen*, 'Iulius'. C. Maecenas is no parallel because Maecenas was a *nomen*.

45. Schulze, *o.c.* (n.1), 491-3.

46. Plin., *Ep.* 4, 9, 3; 6, 31, 3 etc.

47. *TA* 4, 34, 1; 14, 20, 1; Plin., *Ep.* 1, 5. Cf. Strabo 10, 1, 9, 447; 13, 1, 28, 595 (Sulla Cornelius); DH 1, 79, 4. Apuleius' judge was, indifferently, Claudius Maximus or Maximus Claudius.

48. Plin., *NH* 34, 34.

49. Plut., *Tit.* 16, 5-7. Schulze, *o.c.* (n.1), 506-8. Paus. 8, 51, 1 and 4 still referred to 'Titus' (and to 'Manius' of M'. Acilius, cos. 191 BC). Livy refers to him generally in 198 BC as 'the consul' and after that as 'Quinctius'.

50. See G.E. Bean, *JRS* 68, 1948, 53. Mommsen wrote, 'Gentilicia Romana abhorrent a consuetudine Graeca'. Cf. Callimachus, *Dieg.* 5, 25-32, where the Roman war-veteran is simply 'Gaius'; the man of whom Cicero told the same story was named in the proper Roman fashion, 'Spurius Carvilius', *De orat.* 2, 249. See J. Stroux, *Philol.* 89, 1934, 304-10. In the case of a woman known by *nomen* alone similar difficulty can arise. Who was the Antonia who married Pompey's friend Pythodorus of Tralles, the mother of Pythodoris and grandmother of Zeno Artaxias, king of Armenia? Was she the daughter of Mark Antony by his first marriage to his cousin Antonia? Or was she some Greek woman who had adopted a Roman name? See Th. Mommsen, *Eph. Epig.* 1, 270ff.; *RE* XXIV 591, no.13 (R. Hanslik) against H. Dessau, *Eph. Epig.* IX, 691f.; D. Magie, *RRAM* 1130, n.60; *RE* XXIV. 592f., no.13 b. (H.H. Schmitt).

51. A Bauer, 'Posidonios und Plutarch über die römischen Eigennamen', *Philol.* 47 (N.F.1), 1888, 242-73. The discussion by Posidonius evidently came at the start of his 52 books, ib. 258f. Ib.264, mistakes made by Posidonius about Sulla, Maximus, Marcellus.

52. See Jacoby's note on *FGH* 87, F.60. E.g., *QR* 41, from Fenestella, on origin of names like Suillius (= *Poplic.* 11, 6f.; cf. Plin., *NH* 18, 10). Apart from *Coriol.* 11 and *Mar.* 1, Plutarch discusses particular *cognomina* in *Marcell.* 1, 1f. (from Posidonius, *FGH* 87, F.41; Marcellus = Man of War, Claudius Marcellus cos. V first to have the *cognomen*, which is a mistake); *Ti. Gr.* 8, 5f. (Laelius Sapiens); *Pomp.* 13, 7-11 (Pompeius Magnus, and the cognomen 'Maximus'); *Fab. Max.* 1, 2-5 (Fabii Maximus, Ovicula (cf. *Vir. ill.* 43, 1) and Verrucosus; *Cato mai.* 1, 3 (Priscus, Cato); *Sulla* 2, 2 ('Sulla' indicating pale and blushing complexion, with mistaken assumption that it was first introduced for the Dictator; see Macrob., *Sat.* 1, 17, 27 for alternative explanation (shortened form of Sibylla) and *RE* IV, 1513-5); *Poplic.* 1, 1 and 10, 9 (P. Valerius Poplicola); *Cic.* 1, 3-5 (Cicero); *Aem. Paull.* 2, 2 (Aemilius from Greek *Haimulia logou*).

53. Appian, *Praef.* 13; Paus. 7, 7, 8, describing the Roman system of nomenclature in connexion with 'Otilius' (? Villius Tapulus, cos. 199 BC).

Chapter Twelve: A Bad Press for Rome

1. *Bibliography*

E.A. Baumann, *Beiträge zur Beurteilung der Römer in der antiken Literatur*, Diss. Rostock 1930.

L. Castiglioni, 'Motivi antiromani nella tradizione storica antica', *Rend. Ist. Lomb.* Ser. 2, 61, 1928, 625-39.

J. Deininger, *Der politische Widerstand gegen Rom in Griechenland 217-86 v.Chr.*, Berlin/N. York, 1971.

S.L. Dyson, 'Native revolts in the Roman Empire', *Historia* 20, 1971, 239-74.

Bettie Forte, *Rome and the Romans as the Greeks saw them*, American Academy in Rome 1972 (with ample bibliography).

H. Fuchs, *Der geistige Widerstand gegen Rom in der antiken Welt*, Berlin 1938.

J. Geffcken, 'Römische Kaiser im Volksmunde der Provinz', *Gött. Gel. Nachr.* 1901, 183-95.

L. Hahn, *Rom und der Romanismus im griechisch-römischen Osten*, Leipzig 1906.

J. Jüthner, *Hellenen und Barbaren*, Leipzig 1923.

P. Lambrechts, *De geestelijke Weerstand van de westelijke Provincies tegen Rome*, Brussels 1966.
Ramsay MacMullen, *Enemies of the Roman Order*, Harvard U.P., 1967.
A. Momigliano, *Alien Wisdom*, Cambridge 1975.
J. Palm, *Rom, Römertum und Imperium in der griechischen Literatur der Kaiserzeit*, Lund 1959.
H.H. Schmitt, *Hellenen, Römer und Barbaren*, Progr. Aschaffenburg 1958.
J. Schnayder, 'De infenso alienigenarum in Romanos animo I', *Eos* 30, 1927, 113-49.
J. Schnayder, *Quibus Conviciis Alienigenae Romanos Carpserint*, Cracow 1928.
F.W. Walbank, 'Nationality as a factor in Roman history', *HSCP* 76, 1972, 145-68.
C. Wirszubski, *Libertas as a Political Idea at Rome in the late Republic and early Principate*, Cambridge 1950.

Sibylline oracles
ed. J. Geffken, Leipzig 1902; A. Kurfess, Tusculum 1951; A. Rzach, Vienna 1891.
Fr. Cumont, 'Fin du monde selon les mages orientaux', *Rev. de l'hist. des religions* 103, 1931, 29-96 (esp. 64-96 on 'l'apocalypse d'Hystaspe').
H. Diels, *Sibyllinische Blätter*, Berlin 1890.
J. Geffcken, *Komposition und Entstehungszeit der Oracula Sibyllina*, Leipzig 1902.
V. Nikiprowetzky, *La troisième Sibylle*, Paris 1970.
A. Rzach, 'Sibyllen', *RE* IIA, 2073-2103.
A. Rzach, 'Sibyllinische Orakel', *RE* IIA, 2103-2183.
E.M. Sandford, 'Contrasting views of the Roman Empire', *AJP* 58, 1937, 437-56.

Acts of the Pagan Martyrs
H.A. Musurillo, *Acta Alexandrinorum*, Leipzig 1961.
H.A. Musurillo, *The Acts of the Pagan Martyrs*, Oxford 1954.
U. Wilcken, 'Zum alexandrinischen Antisemitismus', *Abh. d. kön. Sächs. Gesellsch. d. Wissensch.*, 27, 1909, 783-839.

Lucian
C. Gallavotti, 'Il Nigrino di Luciano', *Atene e Roma* N.S. 11, 1930, 252-63.
A. Peretti, *Luciano un intellettuale greco contro Roma*, Florence 1946.
J. Schwartz, *Biographie de Lucien de Samosate*, Brussels 1965.

Pompeius Trogus
O. Seel, *Eine römische Weltgeschichte*, Nuremberg 1972.
 2. See p.181.
 3. CD 76, 16, 5.
 4. See p.17.
 5. L. 41, 20, 10-13.
 6. CN, *praef*. Offence caused to a Greek by a request for the presence of his daughter at a male dinner party, Cic., *In Verr*. 2, 1, 66.
 7. Cic., *Phil*. 6, 19; *TA* 14, 13, 3; 15, 59, 6. Cf. 16, 22, 8.
 8. *TA* 3, 60, 6; 13, 49, 2; 13, 50, 3; 14, 12, 2; 14, 49, 1; *TH* 4, 5.
 9. *TA* 3, 65, 3. Cf. 16, 11, 3.
 10. Plin., *Pan*. 66, 4. Cf. 8, 1 (*libertas*, not *servitus*, under Trajan); 55, 2.
 11. *TA* 1, 81, 3.
 12. T. *Agr*. 3, 1; *ILS* 274; Plin., *Pan*. 78, 3; *Ep*. 9, 13, 4. On Vindex, Plin., *NH* 20, 160, 'adsertor a Nerone libertatis'.
 13. JC, *BG* 3, 10, 3. Military discipline in the Roman army is even described as servitude by a mutineer, *TA* 1, 17, 1.
 14. Cf. *TA* 1, 59, 8; 2, 10, 1 and 15, 3; 3, 45, 4; 4, 46, 4 and 48, 5 and, especially, *TH* 4, 73.
 15. CD 54, 7, 6. Florus had no qualms about calling incorporation into the Roman empire 'servitude', 4, 12, 2 and 43.
 16. *TA* 13, 34, 5; 1, 59, 2; *TH* 4, 74; Plut., *Mor*. 824C.
 17. Plut., *Praec. reip. g*. 32, *Mor*. 824C-F; M. Rostovtzeff, *SEHRE*² II, 586f., n.18.
 18. T. *Agr*. 30, 3; *TH* 4, 17 and 64; *TA* 4, 24, 1; 12, 34, 2; CD 62, 3, 1 and 4, 3; JC, *BG* 7, 77, 15f.
 19. *TA* 14, 31, 4.
 20. L. Castiglioni, *o.c.* (n.1).
 21. P. 21, 11 (=L. 37, 25, 4-12); Sall., *Hist*. 4, F. 69) (Mithridates).
 22. Cic., *Pro Rab. Post*. 22-4.
 23. *TA* 11, 39, 3; T. *Germ*. 25, 3.

24. JC, *BG* 4, 7f.; Jos., *AJ* 17, 314.

25. *TA* 11, 16f.

26. T. *Agr.* 14, 2.

27. Tarcondimotus, *RE* IVA, 2297f.; Iamblichus, *PIR*,² I 5; Juba, *RE* IX, 2384-95; Aspurgus, *IGR* 880, cf. 879; *PIR*² 'A' 1265; G.W. Bowersock, *Augustus and the Greek World*, Oxford 1965, 42-61.

28. E.g. EJ² 171f.; *ILS* 8958f.

29. T. *Germ.* 19; *TA* 4, 32. See J.G.C. Anderson, *Tacitus' Germania*, Oxford 1938, xvi-xix.

30. JC, *BG* 6, 12 etc.; Sen., *De ira* 1, 11, 3f.; T. *Germ.* 11, 3; 33.

31. T. *Agr.* 13, 1; 21, 3; 11, 5.

32. T. *Agr.* 11, 4.

33. *TH* 4, 64; A.N. Sherwin-White, *Roman Society and Roman Law in the New Testament*, Oxford 1963, 149f.

34. Levies, *TA* 13, 35, 4 (Galatia, Cappadocia for eastern front, AD 58); 16, 13, 4 (Narbonese Gaul, Africa, Asia for Illyricum, AD 65); *TH* 4, 71 (Gaul for the Rhine, AD 70). Levied soldiers better than volunteers, *TA* 4, 4, 4 (but see *Dig.* 49, 16, 4, 10, replacement of levies by volunteers). The levy normally an anxious occasion, VP 2, 130, 2. Difficult to ensure proper attendance, Cic., *Ad fam.* 15, 1, 5. Provision of substitutes, Plin., *Ep.* 10, 30.

35. *TH* 5; 25; *Germ.* 29, 1f. These were the terms of service in the early Empire generally of auxiliaries from client kingdoms, *TA* 4, 46, 2.

36. *TH* 4, 71.

37. *TA* 4, 72.

38. *TH* 4, 14; T. *Agr.* 31, 1.

39. Jos., *AJ* 14, 223-40; 16, 28; 18, 84; J. Juster, *Les Juifs dans l'empire romain*, Paris 1914, II, 265-79; *P. Oxy.* 4, 735; *CIL* V 8764.

40. *TA* 3, 40, 4; cf. 4, 6, 7.

41. *TA* 3, 40, 4, 'Gravitas faenoris'; CD 62, 2, 1; Cic., *Ad Att.* 5, 21, 10-13; 6, 2, 7-9.

42. *FIRA* 1,² 11, ii, 6f. (cf. 1, 56, 21, exemption granted to individuals); Cic., *Ad Att.* 5, 21, 7; *De imp. Cn. Pomp.* 38f. (Pompey's considerateness was exceptional); Plut., *Sulla* 25, 4f.

43. Plut., *Cimon* 1-2, 1; M. Holleaux, *Etudes d'épigraphie et d'histoire grecques*, Paris 1938, 1, 143-59 (*REG* 32, 1919, 320-37).

44. *Dig.* 19, 2, 13, 7 and 15, 2, 'per lasciviam'; *IGR* 1, 674. Cf. CD 78, 3, 4, hardships caused by Caracalla's billeting of troops in the East, AD 217.

45. *TH* 4, 68.

46. *TH* 4, 74 (Cerealis' speech); Jos., *BJ* 2, 351-4 (speech of Agrippa II).

47. *TH* 4, 73, the Roman point of view (Cerealis); Plin., *NH* 27, 1-3, 'immensa Romanae pacis maiestas'. The opposite view, *TH* 4, 17 (Civilis); T. *Agr.* 30-2 (Calgacus). Remi, *TH* 4, 67 ad fin.; 69, 1.

48. Dio Chrys., *Or.* 32, 69-71; Strabo 16, 2, 20, 756.

49. Plin., *Pan.* 31f.

50. Dio Chrys., *Or.* 31, 125.

51. Cf. Cic., *Pro Font.* 37; 40; *In Verr.* 2, 1, 65-9.

52. L. 39, 42, 7-43; *RE* XXIV, col. 1046.

53. Contrary to generally held views, L. Robert, *Les gladiateurs dans l'Orient grec*, Paris 1940, 239-66. Rhodes alone was an exception, ib. p.248.

54. Hirtius, *BG* 8, 45, 1f. Cf. VM 2, 7, 11, Q. Fabius Maximus in Spain, 145 BC; App., *Num.* 3 (Metellus Numidicus, among far more bestial punishments); Mith. 29, 114 (Bruttius Sura); CD 22, fr. 75 (Popillius Laenas in Spain, 139 BC); 51, 25, 4 (M. Crassus on Danube, 29 BC); 53, 29, 2 (Spain, after Augustus' return to Rome, 24 BC); *Bell. Hisp.* 12, 3; L. 26, 12, 19; Diod. 19, 103, 4f. (Carthaginian practice, cutting off both hands); Florus 3, 4, 7. Cf. [Quintil.], *Decl.* 358, 362 (in rhetorical debate, punishment for striking a father).

55. Fronto, *Ad Ver. imp.* 2, 7, 6 (*LCL* II, p.154).

56. *Hyperêphania*, Popillius Laenas in 168 BC, P. 29, 27, 4; Sulpicius Galus in Greece, in 164, Paus. 7, 11, 1. The word occurs twelve times, applied to Romans, in Diod. 34/5, 2, the account of the 133 BC slave revolt in Sicily.

57. L. 30, 14f.; P. 23, 5, 4-13; Cic., *Ad fam.* 15, 2, 6f.

58. P. 22, 10, 10ff. (Caecilius Metellus, 185 BC); 23, 5, 16ff. (Flamininus, 184 BC). Verres, naturally, cared little for traditions in Sicily, Cic., *In Verr.* 2, 4, 85.

59. Cic., *De orat.* 3, 75.

60. Sulla, App., *BC* 1, 99, 463f.; Augustus, CD 54, 9, 10; Philostr., *VAT* 5, 7.

61. JC, *BG* 1, 7, 34, 44; *TA* 2, 55, 2.

62. Strabo 8, 6, 23, 381; Flor. 2, 16, 6f.

63. Paus. 8, 46. But in 10, 28, 6 he claims, with examples, that sacreligious theft of temple-statues was condemned by the Persians down to the early 5th. cent. BC.

64. VP 1, 11, 3-5; Plin., *NH* 34, 31; 36, 15, 22, 28f., 34f., 42f.: Vitruv. 3, 2, 5; T.P. Wiseman, *PBSR* 42, 1974, 18f.

65. Cic., *In Verr.* 2, 4, 120f. Cf. L. 25, 40, 1-3; 26, 21, 6-8.

66. CD 51, 22, 1f. Criticism of Marcellus, L. 26, 30-2. Comparison of Marcellus and Fabius, L. 27, 16, 8; Plut., *Marcell.* 21, 4-7; Aug., *CD* 1, 6 (ironical).

67. P. 9, 10; Cic., *In Verr.* 2, 1, 59; cf. 2, 4, 132f. Rome the greatest museum in the world, Hahn, *o.c.* (n.1) 192f.

68. After his victory in the 3rd. Macedonian war, Aemilius Paullus gave Perseus' library to his own sons, Plut., *Aem.* 28, 11.

69. Plin., *NH* 18, 22.

70. Cic., *In Verr.* 2, 2, 86f.; 2, 4, 72-93; *De offic.* 2, 76.

71. L. 38, 9, 13; 43f.; 39, 5, 14f.

72. L. 38, 40, 5-41, 10; 46, 6-9; 49, 7-12; 39, 7, 1-5.

73. L. 45, 35, 3; Plut., *Aem.* 28, 10f.; 30, 1-3.

74. Strabo 8, 6, 23, 381f.

75. Strabo 13, 1, 54, 609; Paus. 9, 7, 4-6; 10, 21, 6; Sall., *Cat.* 11, 6.

76. Strabo 12, 3, 31, 557.

77. For refs., see *RE* XXII, cols. 180-2.

78. Strabo 13, 1, 30, 595; 14, 1, 14; 637 (restoration); 14, 2, 19, 657; Plin., *NH* 35, 91.

79. See *PA*, s.v. 'obeliscus'.

80. Cic., *In Verr.* 2, 1, 54-7; 2, 4, 129.

81. Strabo 10, 2, 21, 459.

82. Cic., *In Verr.* 2, 2, 13, 46f.; 83-5; 113; 176; 2, 4, 1; 8; 37ff.; 88; 123 etc. M. Lucullus, Strabo 7, 6, 1, 319; Ap. Claudius, Cic., *De dom.* 111; Piso, cos. 58 BC, *Pro Sest.* 94; *D.p.c.* 7. Governors generally, Cic., *De imp. Cn. Pomp.* 38; 40; Juv. 8, 98-107.

83. *TA* 15, 45, 3; 16, 23, 1; Dio Chrys., *Or.* 31, 149; Juv. 8, 98-124.

84. On the history of the extortion court under the Republic, see my 'Extortion courts at Rome', *PBSR* 1938, 98-114 (=*The Crisis of the Roman Republic*, ed. R. Seager, Cambridge 1969, 132-48); A.N. Sherwin-White, 'Poena legis repetundarum', *PBSR* 1949, 5-25 and 'The extortion procedure again', *JRS* 42, 1952, 43-55; and on maladministration under the Empire, P.A. Brunt, 'Charges of provincial maladministration under the early Principate', *Historia* 10, 1961, 189-227.

85. Gaius, Paus. 9, 27, 3f.; Plin., *NH* 36, 22. Nero, Paus. 5, 25, 8; 26, 3; 10, 7, 1; 10, 19, 2; Dio Chrys., *Or.* 31, 148.

86. Euseb., *Vit. Const.* 3, 54.

87. Surviving works in Asia Minor and the islands, Strabo 13, 1, 41, 601 and 48, 604 (Scopas); 14, 1, 5, 634; 14, 1, 20, 640 (Scopas); 14, 1, 23, 641; Plin., *NH* 35, 13. Samos, Apul., *Flor.* xv. *Rhodes*, sculpture and painting, Dio Chrys., *Or.* 31, 147f.; Strabo 14, 2, 5, 652. Cos, Strabo 14, 2, 19, 657. Greek cities generally, Cic., *In Verr.* 2, 4, 134f. Mainland Greece, *Athens and Attica*, Strabo 9, 1, 15ff., 396; Paus. 1, 1, 3; 1, 2, 4; 1, 20, 1 (Praxiteles); 1, 23, 7 (Myron, Praxiteles); 1, 24, 8 (Pheidias); 1, 28, 2 (Pheidias). *Megara*, 1, 43, 5f. (Praxiteles, Scopas, Lysippus). *Sicyon*, 2, 10, 1 (Scopas). *Argos*, 2, 20, 1 (Polycleitus); 2, 21, 8 and 22, 7 (Polycleitus, Praxiteles, Scopas). *Olympia*, 5, 17, 3 (Praxiteles' Hermes); 6, 25, 1 (Pheidias, – cf Epict., *Diss.* 1, 6, 23 – and Scopas). *City of Elis*, 6, 26, 1 (Praxiteles). *Pellene* in Achaea, 7, 27, 2 (Pheidias). *Mantinea*, 8, 9, 1-3 (Alcamenes, Praxiteles). *Gortys in Arcadia*, 8, 28, 1 (Scopas). *Megalopolis*, 8, 31, 4 (Polycleitus). *Tegea*, 8, 47, 1 (Scopas). *Plataea*, 9, 2, 7 (Praxiteles); 9, 4, 1f. (Pheidias and paintings of Polygnotus). *Thebes*, 9, 10, 2 and 11, 6 (Pheidias, Praxiteles, Scopas). *Thespiae*, 9, 27, 5 (cf. Cic., *In Verr.* 2, 4, 4) (Praxiteles). *Helicon*, 9, 30, 1 (Lysippus, Myron). *Lebadea*, 9, 39, 4 (Praxiteles). *Delphi*, 10, 10, 2 (Pheidias); 10, 15, 1 (Praxiteles); 10, 25, 1 (Polygnotus). *Anticyra*, 10, 37, 1 (Praxiteles). Even if Pausanias' attribution is not always to be trusted, these must all have been impressive works of art.

88. Euseb., *Vit. Const.* 3, 54.

89. DH 19, 5; P. 38, 12, 4; Strabo 8, 6, 23, 381.

90. Terence, *Hec.*, prol. 33-42; P. 30, 22.

91. See F.H. Cowles, *Gaius Verres, an Historical Study*, Cornell Studies in Class. Phil. 20, 1917, 95-135.

92. Cic., *In Verr.* 2, 4, 4; 13, 132, 134.

93. Virg. *Aen.* 6, 847-53.

94. Stat., *Silv.* 1, 1, 1; Plin., *Ep.* 1, 20, 5.

95. VP 1, 13, 4 (with approval), 'tam rudis fuit'; Strabo 8, 6, 23, 381, 'magnanimous rather

than fond of art'; Plin., *NH* 35, 24; Paus. 7, 16, 8; [Dio Chrys.], *Or.* 37, 42, 'a man without education or taste'. Still, Mummius dedicated a bronze statue of Zeus at Olympia, Paus. 5, 24, 4.

96. Stat., *Silv.* 1, 1, 84-8; Plin., *NH* 35, 94; Suet., *C.Cal.* 22, 2.

97. Plin., *NH* 36, 28; 34, 63.

98. Plut., *Lucull.* 39, 2. Criticism of Domitian's extravagant building, *Public.* 15, 3-6.

99. Lucian, *De merced. conduct.* 25.

100. Lucian, *Demonax* 40.

101. P. 27, 9; L. 42, 63, 1f.

102. Achaean League, P. 2, 38, 5 (with Walbank's note). Rome, bk.6; 1, 63, 9 (quoted); 18, 28, 4f.

103. DH 1, 5, 3; 2, 17, 3f.; 18, 1ff.; Jos., *BJ* 3, 70f.; 2, 373.

104. Florus 3, 18, 13; AM 14, 6, 3; *TH* 3, 46, 'fortuna populi Romani'; Cic., *De Rep.* 2, 30; L. 9, 17, 3 (in his discussion of Alexander); Plut., *De fort. Rom.* 316E; AG 17, 21, 33; Fuchs, *o.c.* (n.1) 43, n.41. Cf. Paus. 4, 29, 3 on the Macedonians. In another way, Rome's success could be seen as an act of destiny, P. 1, 4, 4; C.M. Bowra, *JRS* 47, 1957, 25.

105. Apul., *Flor.* vii, 'adeo ut nemo eius audeat virtutem vel sierare, fortunam vel optare'.

106. DH 1, 4, 2f. On the *De fortuna Romanorum*, Palm, *o.c.* (n.1) 33-6 is excellent. See A. Momigliano, 'Livio, Plutarco e Giustino su virtù e fortuna dei Romani', *Terzo Contributo*, Rome 1966, 499-511. He thinks (p.511) that Plutarch was using the source employed by Pompeius Trogus, and that this was the historian against whom Dionysius of Halicarnassus inveighed (and who was not Timagenes). For good criticism, see Fuchs, *o.c.* (n.1), 40, n.36; 42, n.41.

107. Momigliano, *o.c.* (n.106), 501-3.

108. Strabo 8, 7, 387.

109. Justin 38, 6, 7.

110. *r.* Syb. 11, 111; Justin 38, 6, 2f.; L. 3, 66, 4; VP 2, 27, 2. In Hor., *Carm.* 4, 4, 50, resigned and defeated, Hannibal refers to the 'lupi rapaces'.

111. DH 1, 84, 4; Tertull., *Apol.* 25, g. Min. Felix *Octavius* 25, 2f., mocking all the other features of the Roman foundation-legend, omits the *lupa*.

112. Justin 28, 2, 8; Sen., *Ep.* 44, 4 (Plato); L. 1, 8, 5 (cf. DH 3, 10, 4; 7, 70, 1); Juv. 8, 272-5.

113. DH 2, 19, 1f.; Paus. 8, 8, 2f.; Dio Chrys., *Or.* 11, 6-10.

114. L. 35, 16.

115. L. 39, 37, 10-13; JC, *BG* 1, 34; 36, 2; 44, 8.

116. So Schwartz, *RE* IV, 1888.

117. P. 18, 34, 7f.; Cic., *In Verr.* 2, 3, 207; *De imp. Cn. Pomp.* 65; *D.p.c.* 6, 'iustum odium imperi nostri'; Sall., *Hist.* 4, 69M; T. *Agr.* 30-2; L. 42, 47, 9. See J. Briscoe, 'Q. Marcius Philippus and *nova sapientia*', *JRS* 54, 1964, 66-77.

118. DH 1, 4, 2f. Metrodorus, *FGH* 184; *RE* XV, 1481f., no.23; Plin., *NH* 34, 34; Ovid, *Ex P.* 4, 14, 37-40. Other historians,? *FGH* 187, Heracleides of Magnesia;? *FGH* 187a, Aisopos, who wrote a panegyric of Mithridates. See Fuchs, *o.c.* (n.1), 14f. and 43f., n.43.

119. L. 9, 18, 6.

120. *FGH* 88.

121. Justin 43, 5, 11f.

122. Suidas, s.v.; Sen., *Controv.* 10, 5, 22; Sen., *De ira* 3, 23, 4-8; *Ep.* 91, 13.

123. Quintil. 10, 1, 75, 'Intermissam' – since Cleitarchus – 'historias scribendi industriam nova laude reparavit'. (H.E. Butler (*LCL*) translates, 'He revived the credit of history'.)

124. Steph. Byz., s.v. 'Milyai'; Strabo 4, 1, 13, 188; Plut., *Pomp.* 49, 13f.

125. See Jacoby on *FGH* 88 (pp.220f.). The view originated with A. von Gutschmid, 'Trogus und Timagenes', *Rh. Mus.* 37, 1882, 548-55.

126. So J. Schnayder, *o.c.* (n.1; *Eos*), 114, 'Romanorum odium apud Trogum-Iustinum manifestum'.

127. Justin, *praef.* Trogus' supposed anti-Roman passages are 28, 2 (speech of Aetolians); 38, 4-7 (speech of Mithridates); 30, 4, 16, 'Sed Macedonas Romana fortuna vicit' (on the proper interpretation of which, see Fuchs, *o.c.* (n.1), 42f., n.41); 31, 1, 9; 31, 2, 1; 30, 3, 6; 36, 3, 9, 'facile tum Romanis de alieno largientibus' and 41, 1, 'Parthi, penes quos velut divisione orbis cum Romanis nunc orientis imperium est.' See *RE* XXI, 2308 (A. Klotz on Trogus).

128. See *RE* IV, 1889 (Schwartz on Curtius Rufus); R. Laqueur, *RE* VIA, 1066f. (on Timagenes). Auct. ad Herenn. 4, 31 on Alexander in the West as a theme for rhetorical debate.

129. But this is not demonstrable, Fuchs, *o.c.* (n.1) 44, n.44.

130. See *RE* XIII, 818. View that Livy referred to Timagenes held by Jacoby, notes on *FGH* 88, Schanz-Hosius II, 322 and A. Momigliano, *Terzo Contributo*, Rome 1966, 511; rejected by Schwartz, *RE* IV, 1887f.

131. So Baumann, *o.c.* (n.1), 35; S. Schnayder, *o.c.* (n.1, *Eos*), 143f., 'mordacissima quae omnino antiquis in litteris exstat vituperatione affecti sunt Romani a Luciano'; A. Peretti, *Un intellettuale greco contra Roma*, Florence 1946 (criticised, *JHS* 66, 1946, 141-3); B. Baldwin, 'Lucian as Social Satirist', *CQ*, n.s.11, 1961, 199-208. For the contrary (and sensible) view, see C.P. Jones, *Plutarch and Rome*, 128f. and J. Palm, *o.c.* (n.1), 44-56 with full (and critical) bibliography. See a...so *RE* XIII, 1725-77 (Helm); J. Bompaire, *Lucien écrivain*, Paris 1958; J. Schwartz, *o.c.* (n.1).

132. Lucian, *Apol.* 15.

133. *Apol*, passim.

134. J. Mesk, 'Lucians Nigrinus und Juvenal', *Wien. Stud.* 34, 1912, 373-82; 35, 1913, 1-33.

135. *De merc. conduct.* 32-4.

136. *De merc. conduct.* 40.

137. *Nigrinus* 3; 17; 26.

138. *Pseudol.* 8; *De hist. conscrib.* 5; 17; 29; *Alex.* 2.

139. *Domanax* 30; 38; 50; *Peregr.* 14; 18.

140. 2 *Macc.* 16, 18-31 and 7, 1; 4 *Macc.*

141. *T. Agr.* 2, 1; Epict., *Diss.* 1, 2, 19-21.

142. Plut., *Mor.* 771C.

143. Texts: H.A. Musurillo, *Acta Alexandrinorum*, Leipzig 1961; with commentary, H.A. Musurillo, *Acts of the Pagan Martyrs*, Oxford 1954, esp. 273-7 on their composition and, on the general context and background, 236-77; V.A. Tcherikover, A. Fuks, *Corpus Papyrorum Judaicarum*, Harvard 1957, I, 48-93; II, 25-107, papyri nos. 154-9.

144. *P. Cairo* 10448 (*CPJ* – n.143 above – 156d); *P. Oxy.* 33 verso (*CPJ* 159b).

145. *TA* 2, 54, 3-5; *TH* 2, 2-4; Macrob., *Sat.* 1, 23, 14-16; Lucian, *Alexandros*.

146. Cic., *In Cat.* 3, 9; Sall, *Cat.* 47, 2; Quintil. 5, 10, 30; Plut., *Cic.* 17, 5; Florus 2, 12, 80.

147. Suet., *DJ* 79, 4; Plut., *JC* 60, 2; Cic., *De div.* 2, 110f. See my remarks in *Historia* 7, 1958, 85.

148. CD 54, 17, 2; Suet., *DA* 31, 1.

149. CD 57, 18, 5; 62, 18, 3; *TA* 6, 12, 1f.

150. *TH* 4, 54.

151. CD 66, 19, 3b, c (79 AD); Suet., *Nero* 57, 2 (AD 88); *Or. Sib.* 3, 350-5; 5, 137-51; 8, 70f.; 115-32. Cf. Lactant., *Div. inst.* 7, 15, 11, 'imperium in Asiam revertetur et rursus oriens dominabitur atque occidens serviet'.

152. Paus. 7, 8, 8f.

153. *FGH* 257, F.36 III, ascribed to Antisthenes the Peripatetic, evidently the same man as the historian (*RE* I, 2537f., Antisthenes no 9, Schwartz). Jacoby p.846, Schwartz and Forte, *o.c.* (n.1), 41-3 think the date to be the time of Antiochus III; E. Zeller *SB Berl. Akad.* 1883, 1067-73 dates to the time of Mithridates. See Zeller 1070-3 on why Antisthenes cannot be the author. See also J. Mesk, *Philologus* 80, 1925, 307-11 and M. Holleaux, *Rev. de phil.* 56, 305-9 (an important correction of the text). Forte, *o.c.* (n.1), 42-4 thinks the first prophecy originated in Aetolia, the second ('Publius') in Lycia (because of Apollo Lykios, the wolf-god).

154. Justin, *Apol.* 1, 20, 1; 1, 44, 12; Lactant., *Div. inst.* 7, 15, 19; Fr. Cumont, 'Fin du monde selon les images occidentaux', *Rev. de l'hist, des religions* 103, 1931, 29-96, esp. 64-96; *RE*, s.v.; Forte, *o.c.* (n.1), 113, n.52.

155. Varro ap. Lact., *Div. inst.* 1, 6, 8; cf. Paus. 10, 12, 1-9; *RE* IIA, 2075f., 2081-102 (19 listed).

156. See *RE* IIA, 2117-67 (Rzach), esp. 2127f. on Antiochus Epiphanes; 2 *Baruch* 39, 3-5; 4 *Ezra* 12, 11f., with R.H. Charles' notes.

157. *Or. Sib.* 3, 46-49 (Social war); 470-3 (Sulla).

158. *Or. Sib.* 5, 11; 11, 111; 12, 11.

159. Euseb., *HE* 3, 8, 10f.; Suet., *D. Vesp.* 4, 5; *TH* 5, 13; Oros. 7, 9, 2; Jos., *BJ* 6, 5, 4, 312f.

160. *Or. Sib.* 8, 148-50.

161. *Or. Sib.* 3, 184-9 (cf. P. 31, 25, 4).

162. Esp. *Rev.* 17-20, 3, with notes in Peake's commentary.

163. Lact., *Div. inst.* 7, 15, 19.

164. P. 29, 21, 1-6 (Diod. 31, 10); 38, 22; Lact., *Div. inst.* 7, 15, 13. This is also a theme in Sibylline oracles.

Chapter Thirteen: A Generally Good Press for Rome

1. *Bibliography*
General
G.W. Bowersock, *Augustus and the Greek World*, Oxford 1965.
G.W. Bowersock, *Greek Sophists in the Roman Empire*, Oxford 1969.
W. Capelle, 'Griechische Ethik und römischer Imperialismus', *Klio* 25, 1932, 86-113.
E. Gabba, 'Storici Greci dell'impero romano da Augusto ai Severi', *RSI* 71, 1959, 361-81.
A. Momigliano, *Alien Wisdom: the Limits of Hellenisation*, Cambridge 1975.
J. Palm, *Rom, Römertum und Imperium in der griechischen Literatur der Kaiserzeit*, Lund 1959.
RE articles, esp. on Plutarch (XXI, 636-962, K. Ziegler).

Polybius
P. Pédech, *La Méthode historique de Polybe*, Paris 1964.
F.W. Walbank, *A Historical Commentary on Polybius*, Oxford 1957.
F.W. Walbank, *Polybius*, California, 1972.

Panaetius
H. Strasburger, 'Der "Scipionenkreis" ', *Hermes* 94, 1966, 60-72.

Posidonius
H. Strasburger, 'Poseidonios on Problems of the Roman Empire', *JRS* 55, 1965, 40-53.

Plutarch
R.H. Barrow, *Plutarch and his Times*, Indiana 1967.
C.P. Jones, *Plutarch and Rome*, Oxford 1971.
D.A. Russell, *Plutarch*, London 1973.
K. Ziegler, *RE* XXI, 636-962, s.v. 'Plutarchos'.

Dio Chrysostom
H. von Arnim, *Leben und Werke des Dio von Prusa*, Berlin 1898.

Arrian
A.B. Bosworth, 'Arrian's literary development', *CQ* 22, 1972, 163-85.
F. Reuss, 'Arrian und Appian', *Rh. Mus.* 54, 1899, 446-65.

Aelius Aristides
J.H. Oliver, 'The ruling power', *TAPh.S* 43, 1953, 871-1003.

Appian
E. Gabba, *Appiano e la storia delle guerre civili*, Florence 1956.
E. Gabba, *Appiani Bellorum Civilium liber primus*, Florence 1958.

Cassius Dio
E. Gabba, 'Sulla storia romana di Cassio Dione', *RSI* 67, 1955, 289-333.
F. Millar, *A Study of Cassius Dio*, Oxford 1964.
    2. Dating of *Alexandra* of Lycophron to soon after the defeat of Pyrrhus (274 BC), A. Momigliano, *JRS* 32, 1942, 57-62; *CQ* 39, 1945, 49-53; to *c.* 196 BC, W.W. Tarn, *Alexander the Great*, Cambridge 1948, II, 28f.; F.W. Walbank, *CQ* 36, 1942, 145n. 3. On Melinno, C.M. Bowra, *JRS* 47, 1957, 21-8.
    3. P. 33, 1, 3-8; 39, 1, 1-12.
    4. Financial integrity, P. 6, 56, 4 and 15; 18, 34, 7 and 35; 31, 22-30. Adaptability and resilience, 6, 25, 10f. (cf. Arrian, *Tact.* 33); 6, 52.
    5. P. 31, 27, 10f.; 1, 37, 7-10.
    6. P. 2, 59f. Cf. 2, 38f., praise of the Achaean League.
    7. P. 6, 52, 5-11; 18, 28-32.
    8. P. 3, 4. For this distinction between ability to conquer and ability to rule, cf. Ael. Aristides, *Or.* 26, 51: the Athenians, like the Romans, were able to conquer; unlike the Romans, they were unable to rule.
    9. H. Strasburger, *o.c.* (n.1, *JRS*), 46; P. 3, 58f.
    10. P. 31, 10, 7; 31, 21, 5-8; 36, 9 (on which see F.W. Walbank, *Entretiens Hardt* 20, *Polybe*,

1974, 13-18); P. 36, 17, 8-12; 38, 18, 8-12.

11. VP 1, 13, 3; Cic., *De rep.* 1, 34; *FGH* 87, F. 30 (cf. F. 6, T. 10, where Athenaeus confuses Panaetius and Posidonius).

12. Cic., *TD* 4, 4.

13. A point strongly emphasised by Strasburger, *o.c.* (n.1, *Hermes*); but W. Capelle, *o.c.* (n.1), thinks it can be inferred from passages in Cic., *De rep.* (e.g. 3, 37) that Panaetius believed it to be to the interest of the weaker to be ruled by the stronger, and therefore thought the Roman empire a good thing.

14. Plut., *Mar.* 45, 7; Strabo 3, 1, 5; 3, 2, 5; *FGH* 87, F. 56, 63, 73, 88.

15. A.D. Nock, 'Posidonius', *JRS* 49, 1959, 4.

16. Diod. 37, 3.

17. Diod. 34/5, 2 (F. 108).

18. Diod. 5, 26, 3 (F. 116); 5, 36, 3 (F. 117); 37, 5. There is a good word, however, for one Eques, resident in Sicily, who helped Asellio, Diod. 37, 8, 1-3.

19. Diod. 34/5, 25 (F. 111b); 34/5, 7, 2f. (F. 109 e, f); 34/5, 33, 7 (F. 112).

20. Scipio Nasica Corculum and Scipio Nasica, cos. 111 BC, Diod. 34/5, 33 (F. 112); L. Sempronius Asellio, governor of Sicily, Diod. 37, 8; Q. Mucius Scaevola, cos. 95 BC, governor of Asia, Diod. 37, 5; Scipio Aemilianus and his fellow-diplomats in the East, Diod. 33, 28b. Piracy and Pompey, Plut., *Pomp.* 28, 4-7; VP 2, 32, 5 (criticism); Lucan, *Phars.* 1, 346; 3, 244; see Strasburger, *o.c.* (n.1, *JRS*), 49-51.

21. Strasburger thinks that it did, *o.c.* (n.1, *JRS*), 42-4.

22. *FGH* 91, T. 2. It is hard to believe – so *RE* IVA, 87 – that Strabo did not know of the existence of Posidonius' book.

23. For such speculation, see A. Momigliano, 'Polibio, Posidonio e l'imperialismo romano', *Att. dell. Accad. d. Scienze di Torino* 1973, 693-707.

24. DH, *De comp. verb.* 4, 30.

25. P. 9, 1f.

26. DH, *AR* 1, 3, 4; 1, 7, 2; *RE* V, 934-71, no. 113.

27. Latin, DH 1, 7, 2; Tubero, *De Thuc.* 1, 810.

28. See *RE* V, 939-42.

29. DH, *AR* 1, 5, 2. Whether Panaetius had voiced this opinion in Rome is uncertain, Strasburger, *o.c.* (n.1, *Hermes*).

30. DH, *AR* 1, 5, 2; 2, 17, 3f.; 2, 18, 1. Cf. P. 1, 63, 9.

31. DH, *AR* 1, 89, 2 and 90; 2, 9, 2; 12, 3; 13, 4; 18, 2; 7, 70-2.

32. DH, *AR* 2, 10f. See my 'Dionysius on Romulus: a political Pamphlet?', *JRS* 61, 1971, 18-27.

33. DH, *AR* 7, 66, 4f.; 2, 19f.; 8, 80; 5, 17; 7, 72, 2-4.

34. DH, *AR* 10, 17, 6; 4, 24. Cf. P. 6, 57.

35. DH, *AR* 1, 6, 4.

36. See E.A. Baumann, *Beiträge zur Beurteilung der Romer in der antiken Literatur*, Diss. Rostock 1930. For the claim that DH's book was addressed primarily to a Roman reading public; Palm, *o.c.* (n.1), 10f.; Bowersock, *o.c.* (n.1), 130-2.

37. Diod. 1, 4.

38. Diod. 1, 3, 3. It is absurd, on the strength of 1, 5, 1, to think that Diodorus' book ended in 46/5 BC.

39. Diod. 1, 44, 1; 1, 83, 9; 3, 11, 3; 17, 52, 6.

40. Diod. 1, 2, 5f.; 17, 52, 5.

41. Diod. 23, 8, 1 and (?)17. The discreditable story of Regulus' widow (24, 12) is not likely to have featured in any Roman history book; see p.6f above.

42. Diod. 32, 4, 4f.; 37, 3.

43. See *FGH* 90, with Jacoby's notes; *RE* XVII, 362-424, no.20 (R. Laqueur).

44. *FGH* 90, *History*, F. 1-102; *Ethôn Synagôgê*, 103-24. Aristotle had written a book on a similar subject, *Nomima barbarika. FGH* 90, F. 138, on the company he kept in Rome.

45. *FGH* 90, F. 131-9.

46. *FGH* 90, F. 125-30.

47. *FGH* 90, F. 134; Jos., *AJ* 16, 30-57, 'eine rhetorische Meisterstück' (*RE* XVII, 370).

48. *FGH* 90, F. 125f., Augustus' achievement in the past tense. In this dating I follow *RE* XVII, 405f. (Laqueur) against Jacoby (on *FGH* 90, p.263f.) and Bowersock, *o.c.* (n.1), 137.

49. *FGH* 90, F. 77.

50. Jos., *AJ* 16, 40f., 49; *FGH* 90, F. 130, 55. Cf. the panegyric of Augustus at the start of the biography, *FGH* 90, 125f.

51. *RE* IVA, 76-155, no.3 (see 76-85 for an account of his life); *FGH* 91.

52. Strabo 2, 5, 33, 130; *PIR*,² 'C' 287; Macrob., *Sat.* 2, 4, 18.
53. See Bowersock, *o.c.* (n.1), 128f.
54. *FGH* 91, T.2, F.1; Strabo 1, 1, 22f., 13f. (*FGH* 91, F.2); 3, 4, 19, 166.
55. Strabo 17, 3, 24f., 839f.; 6, 4, 2, 286-8.
56. Strabo 2, 5, 26, 127. The West (probably from Posidonius), 3, 2, 5, 144; 3, 2, 15, 151; 3, 3, 5, 154; 3, 3, 8, 156; 3, 4, 20, 166f.; 4, 1, 5, 180f. Synnada in Asia Minor, 12, 8, 14, 577. Egypt, 17, 1, 12f., 797f. Caravan route, 16, 2, 20, 756.
57. Strabo 11, 2, 12, 496. In 12, 8, 9, 574 he criticised Augustus' generosity to Kleon (*RE* XI, 718, no.6), a turncoat from Antony, whom he made High Priest of Comana.
58. Strabo 10, 4, 22, 484.
59. Strabo 14, 5, 2 ad fin., 669 (a passage which may be derived from Posidonius, Strasburger, *o.c.* (n.1, *JRS*), 43).
60. *FGH* 90, F. 135; Plut., *Sert.* 9, 10. For accounts of Juba's career and writings, both by F. Jacoby, see *RE* IX, 2384-95 and the notes on *FGH* 275.
61. Strabo 17, 3, 7, 828.
62. Tertull., *Apol.* 24, 7; Min. Felix., *Oct.* 21, 9.
63. Plin., *NH* 5, 16.
64. For details of all these books, see *RE* IX, 2389-95.
65. See Jacoby on *FGH* 275, esp. 318f.
66. Plut., *Demosth.* 2f.
67. 'Mestrius Plutarchus' only in one surviving dedication, a statue of Hadrian at Delphi. *SIG*,³ 829A. On Mestrius Florus, see *RE* XV, 1292-4, no.3. His criticism of Vespasian's speech, Suet., *Vesp.* 22. With Plutarch at Bedriacum, Plut., *Otho* 14.
68. Sosius Senecio, cos. AD 99, cos. II, 107, *RE* IIIA, 1180-93, no.11.
69. Plut., *Amat.* 25, *Mor.* 770D-771C; *Poplic.* 15, 5f. Criticism of Gaius and Nero, Plut., *Ant.* 87, 8f.; *De garrul.* 7, *Mor.* 505Cf.
70. *Praec.r.p.g.* 19 and 32, *Mor.* 814E-815B, 924C-E.
71. *De tranq. an.* 10, *Mor.* 470B-D.
72. *Praec.r.p.g.* 17f., *Mor.* 814A-E. Cf. Dio Chrys., *Or.* 31, 111; C.P. Jones, *o.c.* (n.1), 110-21.
73. On the works which have not survived, see *RE* XXI, 696-702, 895-7.
74. Plut., *Alex.* 1.
75. Dio, *Or.* 41, 6.
76. Fronto, *Ad M. Ver.* 1, 1, 4 (*LCL* II, p.50).
77. Athens, *Or.* 31, 121f. (cf. Philostr., *VAT* 4, 22). Rhodes, *Or.* 31 (cf. Plin., *NH* 34, 36). Alexandria, *Or.* 32. Tarsus, *Or.* 33 (*rhegkein*). Romans, *Or.* 13, 29-37.
78. *Or.* 47, 22.
79. Palm, *o.c.* (n.1), 43, 'Anhänger der röm. Weltherrschaft sind sie auch beide'.
80. Palm. *o.c.* (n.1), 25; Plut., *De Pyth. or.* 29, *Mor.* 408Bf.; *Praec.r.p.g.* 17, *Mor.* 814A; 32, *Mor.* 824C; *De tranq. an.* 9, *Mor.* 469E; Dio, *Or.* 31, 125 and 165.
81. Plut., *De fort. Rom.* 2, *Mor.* 317C.
82. Dio, *Or.* 41, 9 (delivered at Apamea). Romans preferred a measure of independence in their subjects, Dio, *Or.* 31, 111; Plut., *Praec.r.p.g.* 19, *Mor.* 814Ef.
83. *PIR*,² 'F' 219; *FGH* 156.
84. *RE* II, 1230-47, no.9 (Schwartz).
85. So A.B. Bosworth, *o.c.* (n.1), following F. Reuss. 'Arrian und Appian', *Rh. Mus.* 54, 1899, 446-65.
86. *Tact.* 33.
87. For a close study of this oration, with text, translation and notes, J.H. Oliver, *o.c.* (n.1). See also Palm, *o.c.* (n.1), 56-62.
88. Paras. 51, 58, 91.
89. Paras. 59, 63.
90. Paras. 10, 69f.
91. Paras. 92-8.
92. Para. 99.
93. Paras. 72a-89.
94. *RE* IV, 1313; Fronto, *Ad A.P.* 9, 2 (*LCL* I, p.262); *Ep. Graec.* 4f. (*LCL* I, p.264); J. Hering, *Lateinisches bei Appian*, Diss. Leipzig 1935.
95. Praef. 7, 24; *BC* 2, 299; 4, 61 and 64.
96. Gabba, *o.c.* (n.1, 1958), xvi-xix. *Mith.* 110f. is a good specimen of his 'asides' (disparagement of philosophers).
97. Praef. 11, 43. Cf. *BC* 1, 24.
98. Palm, *o.c.* (n.1), 63-74; *RE*, Supplb. VIII, 1008-1097, no.17.

99. Paus. 8, 27, 1. See Palm, *o.c.* (n.1), 72-4 (insert *epi* before *archēs*). Nor, unlike *RE*, Supplb. VIII, 1070, should I attach great significance to the statement in 8, 30, 9 that Scipio Aemilianus only succeeded on the occasions when he followed Polybius' advice.

100. Sulla 1, 20, 7; 9, 33, 6; Flamininus 7, 8, 2. Slight criticism of Q. Metellus (185 BC), 7, 9, 1; of Appius Claudius (184 BC), 7, 9, 4.

101. Paus. 3, 7, 11. Cf. 1, 4, 1; 1, 25, 3; 7, 17, 1.

102. Paus. 7, 7-16.

103. Paus. 7, 14, 6. Cf. P. 38, 1, 2; Strabo 8, 6, 23, 381.

104. Paus. 8, 46.

105. Paus. 9, 27, 3f.; 9, 33, 6.

106. Paus. 7, 17, 3f.

107. Roman reduction of Thrace, 1, 9, 5. Hadrian, 1, 5, 5; 1, 36, 3; 8, 10, 2; 10, 35, 2-4 and 6. Antoninus Pius, 8, 43, 3-6.

108. *PIR*,[2] 'C' 492; *RE* III, 1684-1722, no.40 (Schwartz); Millar, *o.c.* (n.1).

109. CD 76, 2, 1; 72, 23, 5; *RE* III, 1686; Gabba, *o.c.* (n.1, 1955), 298.

110. CD 72, 23. *Life of Arrian* (mentioned by the Suda) doubted by Millar, *o.c.* (n.1), 70.

111. CD 71, 36, 4. Cf. 72, 15, 6.

112. CD 80, 1, 2-2, 1; 4, 2-5, 3.

113. CD 52, 35, 3-6; Gabba, *o.c.* (n.1, 1955); D.M. Pippidi, *Autour de Tibère*, Bucharest 1944, 135-178.

114. CD 38, 36-46; 52, 14-40. See Gabba, *o.c.* (n.1, 1955).

115. Millar, *o.c.* (n.1), 190.

116. CD 78, 26, 1; 28-30, 1; 80, 3f.

117. Galen II, 215K; VIII, 144; XIV, 599f., 641ff, 647; XIX, 15-19; 22f.; Athen., *Deipn.* 1, 1ef.

Chapter Fourteen: Different Peoples, their Looks and Habits

1. *Bibliography*

G. Becatti, *Enciclopedia dell'arte antica V*, Rome 1963, s.v. 'Negro', 393-400.

F.H. Colson, *The Week*, Cambridge 1926.

F.H. Cramer, *Astrology in Roman Law and Politics*, Amer. Philos. Soc., Philadelphia 1954.

F. Cumont, *Les Religions orientales dans le paganisme romain*,[4] Paris 1929.

K.J. Dover, *Greek Homosexuality*, London 1977.

J. Ferguson, *The Religions of the Roman Empire*, London 1960.

J. Geffcken, *Der Ausgang des griechisch-römischen Heidentums*, Heidelberg 1929-34.

M.K. Hopkins, 'Eunuchs in politics in the later Roman Empire', *Proc. Cambr. Phil. Soc.* 1963, 62-80.

J. Juster, *Les Juifs dans l'empire romain*, Paris 1914.

A.D. Nock, *Conversion*, Oxford 1933.

E. Schürer, *A History of the Jewish People in the Age of Jesus Christ, 175 BC-AD 135*, I, rev. G. Vermes, F. Millar, Edinburgh 1973.

A.M. Smallwood, 'Domitian's attitude towards the Jews and Judaism', *CP* 51, 1956, 1-13.

A.M. Smallwood, 'The legislation of Hadrian and Antoninus Pius against circumcision', *Latomus* 18, 1959, 334-47.

A.M. Smallwood, *The Jews under Roman Rule*, Leiden 1976.

F.M. Snowden Jr., *Blacks in Antiquity: Aethiopians in the Greco-Roman Experience*, Cambridge, Mass. 1970.

F.M. Snowden Jr., 'The Negro in classical Italy', *AJP* 68, 1947, 266-92.

J. Toutain, *Les Cultes païens dans l'empire romain*, Paris 1907-20.

J.M.C. Toynbee, *Death and Burial in the Roman World*, London 1971.

K. Trüdinger, *Studien zur Geschichte der griechisch-römischen Ethnographie*, Basle 1918.

M.J. Vermaseren, *Mithras the Secret God*, London 1963 (translated from the Dutch).

R.E. Witt, *Isis in the Graeco-Roman World*, London 1971.

Z. Znigryder-Konopka, 'Les Romains et la circoncision des Juifs', *Eos* 33, 1930/1, 334-50.

2. Suet., *Tib.* 68, 1; *C. Cal.* 50, 1; Plin., *Pan.* 22, 2; Macrob., *Sat.* 2, 3, 3; J.G.C. Anderson, *Tacitus, Germania*, Oxford 1938, p.55; JC, *BG* 2, 30, 3. On the size of northerners, Germans, *TA* 1, 64, 3; *Germ.* 4, 2, [Quintil.], *Decl.* 3, 13; Florus, 1, 45, 12; Gauls, L. 5, 44, 4; 38, 17, 3; Strabo 4, 4, 2f., 195f.; Diod. 5, 28, 1; Mart. 8, 75; Paus. 10, 20, 7 etc.

3. Strabo 4, 5, 2, 200; 7, 1, 2, 290; Juv. 8, 252.

4. Veg. 1, 1.

5. Germans, T. *Germ.* 4, 3; 23, 3; *TH* 2, 32; Gauls, L. 10, 28, 3f.; 27, 48, 16f.; 34, 47, 5; 38, 17, 7.

6. Florus 1, 20, 2.

7. *TA* 1, 57, 6; VP 2, 101, 1; Col. 3, 8, 2; Plin., *NH* 7, 74 (referring, perhaps, to the same man); SHA, *Maximin. II*, 2, 2.

8. Plin., *NH* 2, 189; Florus, *Virgil. Orat.* 2, 3; Petron., *Sat.* 102, 14; Ovid, *AA* 1, 513; Mart. 1, 55, 14; 10, 12. *Femineus pallor*, Plin., *Pan.* 48, 4 (cf. Mart. 4, 42, 5, the pale pretty boy).

9. Flavus was a rare name for slaves, M.L. Gordon, *JRS* 14, 1924, 96. Boudicca, CD 62, 2, 4 (but cf. Strabo 4, 5, 2, 200). 'Flavi Britanni,' Lucan, *Phars.* 3, 78.

10. *Flavus*, Mart. 6, 61, 3 (Usipites); Juv. 13, 164; Manil. 4, 715f. (Germans); L. 38, 17, 3; AM 15, 12, 1 (Gauls); cf. Strabo 4, 5, 2, 200; Diod. 5, 28, 1 (Gauls). *Rufus, rutilus*, T. *Agr.* 11, 2 (Scotch); Sen., *De ira* 3, 26, 3 (Germans).

11. Diod. 1, 88, 5.

12. Prop. 2, 18C; Mart. 5, 68. Cf. my *Roman Women*,[2] London 1974, 258-60.

13. Romans, Juv. 5, 30; Spartans, Paus. 7, 14, 2; Philostr., *VAT* 8, 7, vi. Greeks, Philostr., *Ep.* 8. Germans, T., *Germ.* 31, 1. Gauls, Strabo 4, 4, 3, 196. Getae, Ovid, *Trist.* 5, 7, 50. Persians, Liban., *Or.* 18, 282.

14. Dio Chrys., *Or.* 35, 11; Plin., *Ep* 1, 10, 6 and Epictet., *Diss.* 4, 8 (philosophers); Mart. 11, 78, 4; Petron., *Sat.* 58, 5; 63, 3; 70, 8; Synes., *De regno* 15, Migne 66, 1092f.

15. Dio Chrys., *Or.* 36, 17.

16. Juv. 11, 149.

17. Apul., *Met.* 11, 30; Plut., *De Isid. et Osir. Mor.* 352C; Lucian, *Navig.* 2f.; V. von Gonzenbach, *Untersuchung en zu den Knabenweihen im Isiskult der röm. Kaiserzeit*, Bonn, 1957.

18. Cic., *De fin.* 4, 62; Hor., *Carm.* 2, 15, 11; L. 5, 41, 9; Juv. 16, 31; Cic., *Ad Att.* 1, 14, 5; 1, 6, 11; *In Cat.* 2, 22. Philosophers, Hor., *Sat.* 1, 3, 133; 2, 3, 17 and 35; Pers. 1, 133. Euphrates, Plin., *Ep.* 1, 10, 6. Favorinus, Lucian, *Demonax* 13. Epict., *Diss.* 1, 2, 29.

19. Strabo 15, 1, 30, 699; Arrian. *Ind.* 16, 4f.

20. Juv. 8, 114f.; Epict., *Diss.* 3, 1, 27-35 (a very interesting passage); Lucian, *Demonax* 50 (a proconsul); Dio Chrys., *Or.* 33, 63f.; Plut., *De Isid. et Osir. Mor,* 352Df.; JC, *BG* 5, 14, 3.

21. Hor., *Epod.* 16, 7; T., *Germ.* 4, 2; Juv. 13, 164; Vitruv. 6, 1, 3.

22. JC, *BG* 5, 14, 3; Prop. 2, 18, 23; Mart. 11, 53, 1; Pomp. Mela, *Geog.* 3, 51, 'incertum ob decorem an quid aliud'. Cf. Sil. Ital. 17, 416.

23. Petron., *Sat.* 102, 14; Arrian, *Parth.* F.46 (son of king Abgar of Osroene); Macrob., *Sat.* 7, 3, 7. See Mayor on Juv. 1, 104. Roman women, Juv. 6, 459. Moors, CD 78, 11, 1. Ethiopians, Strabo 17, 2, 3, 822.

24. Plin., *NH* 22, 2; Dio Chrys., *Or.* 14, 19f.; Pomp. Mela, *Geog.* 2, 1, 10 (Scythians); Claudian, *In Rufin.* 1, 313.

25. Catull. 93 (cf. Apul., *Apol.* 16); Hor., *Sat.* 1, 4, 85, 91 and 100.

26. Plin., *NH* 2, 189 (cf. Mart., *Spect.* 3, 10); Manil. 4, 723-30; Strabo 15, 1, 14, 695; PLM II, pp. 179-85, 11, 31-5 (cf. Juv. 13, 163, great breasts); Petron., *Sat.* 102, 15. For Negroes in ancient art, see Becatti, *o.c.* (n.1), Snowden, *o.c.* (n.1, 1970) and G.H. Beardsley, *The Negro in Greek and Roman Civilisation*, Baltimore 1929.

27. Plin., *NH* 6, 70; Strabo 15, 1, 13, 690; 15, 1, 24, 695f.; Arrian. *Ind.* 6, 9; Apul., *Flor.* 6; Florus 4, 12, 62; Lucan, *Phars.* 4, 678f., 'concolor Indo Maurus'. India-Ethiopia confusion, Virg., *Georg.* 4, 293; Lucan, *Phars.* 9, 528; Indians 'burnt by the sun', Tibull. 2, 3, 55f.

28. Strabo 17, 3, 7, 828, tr. H.L. Jones, LCL.

29. Juv. 6, 598-601; Serv. ad *Aen.* 8, 646; Calp. Flac., *Decl.* 2; ([Quintil.], *Decl.*, fr.8); Ithyphallic negroes in art, Snowden, *o.c.* (n.1, 1970), 272f. On inherited colour, Plin., *NH* 7, 51 (white-w nan, fruit of her mother's adultery with an Ethiopian; her son was black); Mart. 6, 39, 6f., illegitimate child by a black cook, evidently negroid in appearance. (In the days of slavery in America, it was believed that the negro possessed outstanding sexual potency.)

30. App., *BC* 4, 566 etc.

31. Theophr., *Char.* 21, 4; Ter., *Eun.* 165-71; Auct. ad Herenn. 4, 50, 63; Juv. 5, 53f. Hor., *Sat.* 2, 8, 14, 'fuscus Hydaspes'; Tibull. 2, 3, 55f.

32. Philostr., *VS* 1, 8, 207; 2, 1, x, 240f.; *VAT* 3, 11.

33. See *RE* XIII, 1875.

34. CD 63, 3, 1.

35. Schol. Virg., *Ecl.* 2, 16.

36. Strabo 17, 1, 54, 820f.; Plin., *NH* 8, 131. W.L. Westerman, *The Slave Systems of Greek and Roman Antiquity*, Philadelphia 1955, 97, thinks the number of negro slaves to have been comparatively small.

37. Suet., *C. Cal.* 57, 4; Petron., *Sat.* 34, 4; F.M. Snowden, *o.c.* (n.1, *AJP*) 286.

38. Plin., *NH* 6, 190 (cf. Stat., *Theb.* 5, 427f. on such redskins); F.M. Snowden, *o.c.* (n.1, 1970), 3; C. Schmidt, 'Eine griechische Grabinschrift aus Arsinoe', *Festschrift G. Ebers*, Leipzig 1897,

99-106. Cf. Juv. 2, 23, 'derideat Aethiopem albus'

39. DH 3, 61, 1.

40. Naples, Strabo 5, 4, 7, 246; *TA* 15, 33, 2. Scipio, L. 29, 19, 11f.; VM 3, 6, 1; *TA* 2, 59, 2f. Sulla, Cic., *Pro Rab. Post.* 26f.; VM 3, 6, 3. Claudius, CD 60, 6, 1f. Tiberius, Suet., *Tib.* 13, 1; Pers., *Sat.* 1, 127.

41. *TA* 14, 21, 8; Suet., *Domit.* 4, 4. Agrippina wore a *chlamys* at the naval display for the draining of the Fucine lake, *TA* 12, 56, 5. Cf. CD 60, 6, 1f.

42. *FGH* 87, F. 36, 50 (Posidonius); Cic., *Pro Rab. Post.* 27.

43. Cic., *In Pis.* 92f.; *In Verr.* 2, 5, 31, 40, 86 and 137; *Pro Rab. Post.* 25-8. Antony, App., *BC* 5, 11, 43; 5, 76, 322. Germanicus, *TA* 2, 59, 2f. (The idea of his imitating Scipio may have been Tacitus', D.G. Weingärten, *Die Ägyptenreise des Germanicus*, Bonn, 1969, 99-108.)

44. Cic., *Pro Rab. Post.* 27; VM 3, 6, 2.

45. L. 27, 13, 9; Suet., *DA* 24, 2; VM 2, 7, 9; Frontin., *Strat.* 4, 1, 43; Suet., *DJ* 45, 3; Sen., *Ep.* 114, 6.

46. Cloaks, Diod. 5, 33, 2 (Spanish); P. 2, 28, 7 and 2, 30, 1 (Gallic); Cic., *Pro Font.* 33 (Gallic); Strabo 3, 3, 7, 155 (Lusitania); 4, 4, 3, 196; Mart. 14, 128 (Gaul.) *Sagos* probably a Gallic word adopted in turn by Latin and Greek, L. Hahn, *o.c.* (ch.12, n. 1), 49, 'The Scottish plaid and Spanish cloak are its survivals,' J.G.C. Anderson on T, *Germ.* 17, 1.

Trousers/breeks, P. 2, 28, 7; 2, 30, 1; Cic., *Pro Font.* 33.; Diod. 5, 30, 1; Strabo 4, 4, 3, 196f. (tight); 11, 13, 9, 526 (good for cold climates); Plin., *NH* 3, 31; Juv. 8, 234; *RE* on 'anaxurides'. Illustrations on Trajan's column.

47. Strabo 4, 4, 3, 197. Cf. Suet., *DA* 40, 5.

48. Herod. 1, 71, 2 (leather); 5, 49, 3; 7, 61, 1; Strabo 11, 13, 9, 26; Juv. 2, 169 (Armenians); Pers. 3, 53, 'bracati Medi'; Strabo 15, 3, 19, 734. In art, Parthian hostage on the grand cameo of Paris (illustrated, *JRS* 26, 1936, pl.X).

49. Roman cavalry breeks, Arrian, *Tact.* 34, 7. Gallic dress, Cic., *Phil.* 2, 76; *TH* 2, 20.

50. AG 13, 22.

51. T., *Germ.* 17, 2; L. 23, 40, 3; Cic., *Pro Scauro* 45n.; *D.p.c.* 15; Quintil. 1, 5, 8; *TA* 2, 13, 1. Cf. Synes., *De regno* 5, Migne 66, 1092f.

52. Synes., *o.c.* (n.51).

53. Strabo 17, 2, 1f., 821f.

54. L. 35, 11, 7; Sil. Ital. 3, 235f.; Virg., *Aen.* 8, 734; Plaut., *Poen.* 1008.

55. Apul., *Apol.* 56; Plut., *De Isid et Osir., Mor.* 352C-F; *Or. Sib.* 5, 492.

56. Plin., *NH* 22, 164; Strabo 3, 3, 7, 115. British mead, Strabo 4, 5, 5, 201. Beer and mead in Gaul, Posidon., *FGH* 87, F. 15, 4; DH 13, 10; Diod. 5, 26, 2. Germany, T., *Germ.* 23, 1; *AP* 9, 368. Ligurians, Strabo 4, 6, 2, 202. *Zuthos*, Plin., *NH* 2, 164; Strabo 17, 1, 14, 799; 17, 2, 2, 821; 17, 2, 5, 824.

57. Posidon., *FGH* 87, F. 15, 4; JC, *BG* 4, 2, 6; T., *Germ.* 23, 1.

58. L. 5, 33, 2-4; Plut., *Camill.* 15; DH 13, 10f. (in pursuit also of oil and figs).

59. Diod. 5, 26, 3; JC, *BG* 2, 15, 4. I have little sympathy with the suggestion of M. Rambaud *L'Art de déformation historique dans les commentaires de César*, Paris 1966, 269f., that Caesar expected applause (and electoral support) from Italian wine-exporters for this revelation to them of a large potential new export market.

60. Posidon., *FGH* 87, F. 15, 2.

61. Butter, Strabo 3, 3, 7, 155; 16, 4, 24, 781; 17, 2, 2, 821. Lard, DH 13, 11. Vegetable oil, Strabo 16, 4, 26, 783 (Nabataean Arabs); 17, 2, 5, 824. Tallow, Strabo 17, 2, 2, 821. Today Mediterranean people generally cook with oil, northern European peoples with butter, margarine or other fat.

62. Strabo 17, 3, 15, 833; 11, 2, 2, 493.

63. Juv. 6, 160; cf. 14, 98.

64. Philo, *Leg. ad Gai.* 361f.; Plut., *De Isid. et Osir.* 72, *Mor.* 380B; Juv. 15, 11f.

65. Jews, no hare, Plut., *Quaest. conviv.* 4, 2, *Mor.* 670E. Leprosy, Plut., *Quaest. conviv.* 4, 5, *Mor.* 670F; *TH* 5, 4. Non-Jewish abstention from pork, Plut., *De Isid. et Osir.* 8, 354A; Epict., *Diss.* 1, 11, 12; Strabo 12, 8, 9, 575; Paus. 7, 17, 10; K. Holl, *Hermes* 43, 1908, 254. See Mayor on Juv. 14, 98.

66. Cf. Lucian, *Peregr.* 16; *Act. Apost.* 15, 20; 1 *Corinth.* 10, 23-9.

67. Philostr., *VAT* 8, 7, iv.

68. Sen., *Ep.* 108, 18.

69. Ovid., *Met.* 15, 85-90; Plut., *De esu carn., Mor.* 994f.

70. Apul., *Met.* 11, 28 and 30; Plut., *De Isid. et Osir.* 4, *Mor* 352D.

71. Plut., *De esu carn., Mor.* 993-9; *Quaest. conviv.* 2, 3, 1, *Mor.* 635E; 8, 7, *Mor.* 727B; 8, 8, *Mor.* 728D-730F.

72. Sen., *Ep.* 108, 22; *TA* 15, 45, 6.

73. Philostr., *VAT* 1, 8 and 32; 8, 7, iv; Jos., *BJ* 2, 143f.

74. Cic., *TD* 4, 70; 5, 58; P. 31, 25, 5f.; L. 39, 6, 9. 226 BC, see *MRR* on the aediles; VM 6, 1, 7; Plut., *Marcell.* 2, 5-8.

75. Diod. 5, 32, 7; Strabo 4, 4, 6, 199; [Quintil.], *Declam.* 3, 16.

76. *Or. Sib.* 3, 185; CD 62, 6, 4; Juv. 2, esp. 44-50; Philostr., *VAT* 7, 42.

77. Plin., *NH* 30, 41.

78. Dio Chrys., *Or.* 7, 133-52. The rival attractions of homosexuality and heterosexuality are compared in pseudo-Lucian's *Amores* and at the end of the second book of Achilles Tatius' novel.

79. Plut., *Mar.* 14, 3-9; VM 6, 1, 7-12; [Quintil.], *Decl.* 3; Plut., *Cimon* 1; DH 16, 4f.

80. Plin., *Ep.* 3, 3, 3f., with Sherwin-White's note.

81. Suet., *Tib.* 43f.

82. Quintil., 4, 2, 69 (size of fine); Cic., *Ad fam.* 8, 12, 3; 8, 14, 4; Suet., *Domit.* 8, 3.

83. *TA* 15, 37, 8f.; Juv. 2, 117-42; cf. Mart. 12, 42, a similar all-male marriage.

84. Juv. 2, 47-9. Lesbianism discussed, [Lucian], *Amores* 28.

85. JC, *BC* 3, 108; 112, 12; Seneca, *Suas.* 6, 6; *RE* XXII, 1176f.; *TA* 6, 31, 3; Cic., *Orat.* 232.

86. Suet., *D.Cl.* 28, 1; Juv. 14, 91 (with schol.); *RE* XXII, 829; *TA* 12, 66, 5; Suet., *Galba* 15, 2 (cf. Jos., *AJ* 16, 230, Herod's three handsome eunuchs, wine-pourer, butler and chamberlain); *TA* 14, 59, 3; CD 77, 17, 2.

87. AM 18, 4, 3-6; Claudian, *In Eutrop.* 1, 412-99; *RE* VI, 1367 (no.5); VI, 1520f. (no.6); III, 2485f.; M.K. Hopkins, *o.c.* (n.1).

88. Catull. 63 (cf. Lucr. 2, 614-28); DH, *AR* 2, 19, 3-5; VM 7, 7, 6; Juv. 6, 512-6; Mart. 3, 91; Ovid., *Fast.* 4, 179-372; [Lucian], *De dea Syria.*

89. G. Wissowa, *RK,* 319f.; J. Carcopino, 'Attideia', *Mél. d'arch. et d'hist.* 40, 1923, 135-59.

90. Hor., *Epod.* 9, 13f., 'spadonibus rugosis'; *Dig.* 1, 7, 2, 1; 1, 7, 40, 2; 23, 3, 39, 1; 28, 2, 6; 40, 2, 14, 1; 50, 16, 128. 'Inter pueterumque senemque/nil medium', Claudian, *In Eutrop.* 1, 469f.

91. *TA* 14, 20, 7; Quintil. 1, 10, 31; Plin., *Pan.* 54, 1.

92. Aristotle, *Hist. an.* 7, 1, 581a; Celsus 7, 25, 3; Mart. 7, 82; 11, 27; 11, 75; 14, 215. See E.J. Dingwell, *Male Infibulation,* London 1925; *RE* IX, 2543-8, s.v. 'Infibulatio'. I am grateful to Professor Waldo E. Sweet of the University of Michigan for information on this subject.

93. Phaedrus 4, 5, 22; Mart. 6, 39, 20f.; Sen., *Controv.* 10, 4, 17; Petron., *Sat.* 119, 19-27; 27, 3; Sen., *Ep.* 114, 6; Plin., *NH* 7, 129 (but the figure in the text cannot be right).

94. *TA* 4, 10; Suet., *Nero* 28; CD 63, 13, 1f.; Plut., *Galba* 9; *RE* IIIA, 1886-8.

95. Suet., *Domit.* 7, 1; CD 67, 2, 3; 68, 2, 4; Philostr., *VAT* 6, 42; Mart. 2, 60; 6, 2, 9, 5 (6) and 7, (8); Stat., *Silv.* 3, 4, 68-77; 4, 3, 13-15 (cf. 2, 6, 38-40); AM 18, 4, 5. Nerva and Hadrian, CD 68, 2, 4; *Dig.* 48, 8, 4, 1.

96. *Cod.* 4, 42, 1f.; *Nov.* 142.

97. AM 14, 6, 17.

98. Philostr., *VAT* 1, 33 and 36; Terence, *Eun.* 665; Epict., *Diss.* 2, 20, 19; Dio Chrys., *Or.* 4, 35f.

99. VM 6, 1, 13; Mart. 2, 60.

100. Herod. 2, 36, 3; 2, 104; Strabo 16, 4, 17, 776 (Ethiopia and Egypt); 17, 2, 5, 824 (Egyptians and Jews, men and women).

101. Strabo (Posidon.) 16, 2, 37, 761; Jos., *AJ,* 20, 38-48 and 75-91; *PIR*² 'I', 891. Zmigryder-Konopka, *o.c.* (n.1) denies that the practice was universally derided by non-Jews.

102. Jos., *AJ* 16, 220-5; 20, 139-43.

103. Jos., *AJ* 20, 145.

104. Jos., *AJ* 18, 141.

105. Juv., 14, 96-106, with Mayor's notes.

106. Suet., *Domit.* 12, 2. Epispasm, Smallwood, *o.c.* (n.1, *Latomus*).

107. Juv. 14, 99. (A cause of the revolt in SHA, *Hadr.* 14, 2, but not in CD 69, 12, 1f.); Paulus, *Sent. Recept.* 5, 22, 3f.; *Dig.* 48, 8, 11 pr. (Modestinus). Egyptian priests, Jos., *C.Ap.* 2, 141.

108. CD 79, 11, 1 and 16, 7.

109. On this subject see Colson, *o.c.* (n.1) and my *Life and Leisure in Ancient Rome,* London 1969, 61-5.

110. CD 37, 19. (In 37, 18, 1 he states that the general adoption of the seven-day week, originally Egyptian, is comparatively modern, since it was not known in classical Greece.)

111. *Exodus* 16, 22-30 etc.; CD 37, 17, 3.

112. See my *Life and Leisure in Ancient Rome* (n.109 above), 61-5; Philostr., *VAT* 3, 41; Jos., *C.Ap.* 2, 282; CD 37, 18, 2.

113. Juv. 14, 105f., 'lux ignava'; *TH* 5, 4.

114. CD 37, 16, 1-4; Jos., *BJ* 1, 146f. (cf. *AJ* 14, 63ff.); Plut., *De superstit.* 8, *Mor.* 169A-C.

115. Jos., *BJ* 2, 391-4. Cf. Front., *Strat.* 2, 1, 17, Vespasian successful against Jews on a Sabbath.
116. *P. Oxy.* 4, 735 (205 AD); *CIL* V, 8764; Philo, *Leg. ad Gai.* 158; Juster, *o.c.* (n.1), II, 265-79.
117. Juv. 14, 96-106; Suet., *Tib.* 32, 2; Tertull., *Apol.* 16, 11. Familiarity with Sabbath in Augustan Rome, Hor., *Sat.* 1, 9, 69; Ovid, *AA* 1, 415f.; *RA* 219f. Josephus' statement, *C. Ap.* 2, 282, that the Sabbath was universally observed in his contemporary world is an obvious exaggeration.
118. See my *Life and Leisure in Ancient Rome* (n.109 above), 64.
119. Juv., 6, 627.
120. Juba, *Bell. Afr.* 91, 1 and 3; Bocchus, Sall., *BJ* 80, 6f.
121. Lucan, *Phars.* 8, 398-416; AM 23, 6, 76 (tr. J.C. Rolfe, *LCL*); Herod. 1, 135.
122. Cic., *TD* 5, 78. Cf. Strabo 15, 1, 30, 699f.
123. Jos., *AJ* 17, 14; A.H.M. Jones, *The Herods of Judaea*, Oxford 1938, chap. 4.
124. Petron., *Sat.* 17, 5.
125. Strabo 16, 4, 26, 784; 15, 3, 13, 732; T., *Germ.* 9, 43, 4.
126. Diod. 40, 3, 4; Strabo (Posidonius) 16, 2, 35, 760f. (*FGH* 87, F. 70); Juv. 14, 97; *TH* 2, 78; 5, 5; CD 37, 17, 2.
127. Aug., *CD* 4, 31.
128. Suet., *D. Vesp.* 23, 4.
129. Plin., *Pan.* 52.
130. Pig: Plut., *Quaest. Conviv.* 4, 5, *Mor.* 670Dff. Ass: Plut., l.c.; Jos., *C.Ap.* 2, 80; *TH* 5, 4; Tertull., *Apol.* 16.
131. Plut., l.c. (n.130); Cic., *TD* 5, 78; Stat., *Silv.* 3, 2, 113; Strabo 16, 2, 35, 760; 17, 1, 31, 807 (Apis); 17, 1, 44, 814 (crocodiles, except at Tentyra); Plin., *NH* 8, 184-6 (Apis); *TH* 5, 5. On the wide variety of animals, fish etc. worshipped in Egypt, Strabo 17, 1, 40, 812f.
132. CD 51, 16, 5.
133. See, for pagan views of Christianity, the collection of texts, *Scriptorum Paganorum I-IV Saec. de Christianis Testimonia*, ed. W. den Boer, Leiden 1948.
134. Jos., *AJ* 20, 195; cf. *RE* XXII, 87f.
135. *TH* 3, 24.
136. See Witt, *o.c.* (n.1), 152-64.
137. Prop. 2, 33A; 4, 5, 34; Ovid, *Am.* 1, 8, 24; 3, 9, 34f.; Juv. 6, 526-41; Jos., *AJ* 18, 65-80; Toutain, *o.c.* (n.1), II, 5-34; Witt, *o.c.* (n.1).
138. Toutain, *o.c.* (n.1), II, 35-72.
139. Toutain, *o.c.* (n.1), II, 102-19.
140. Toutain, *o.c.* (n.1), II, 144-77; Vermaseren, *o.c.* (n.1); F. Cumont, *Les mystères de Mithra*,³ Brussels 1913; A.D. Nock, 'The genius of Mithraism', *JRS* 27, 1937, 108-13.
141. Apul., *Met.* 11, 5, tr. W. Adlington (LCL).
142. Toutain, *o.c.* (n.1), II, 227-57. Vermaseren, *o.c.* (n.1), 187, 'The search for a monotheistic cult, stimulated by the philosophical doctrines of the time, led inevitably to the all-embracing cult of the unvanquished Sun-god.'
143. Sometimes because of supernatural conflict. Juppiter warned Pompey by prodigies not to fight Caesar, but *invictae leges necessitudinis* blinded him to their significance, VM 1, 6, 12.
144. Lucian, *Alex.* 8; *Demonax* 20; Plin., *NH* 30, 2.
145. Paus. 9, 39, 5-14; Philostr., *VAT* 8, 19f.; *RE* VIIA, 684.
146. Lucan, *Phars.* 5, 111-3; Juv. 6, 555; Geffcken, *J.c.* (n.1), 6.
147. Including oracles at Patrai (for the sick, Paus. 7, 21, 12); Pharai in Achaea (Paus. 7, 22, 3); and north of river Bouraïkos (Paus. 7, 25, 10).
148. Paus. 8, 11, 10f.
149. Plut., *Sulla* 17, 1-4; *TA* 2, 54, 4f; Plin., *NH* 8, 185; *TH* 2, 3f. Cato, Lucan, *Phars.* 9, 564-85.
150. Notable Greek and Roman dreams, Cic., *De div.* 1, 39-59.
151. CD 72, 23, 1f.; 80, 5, 2.
152. Herod. 7, 12-18, with Artabanus, a sceptic of the divine origin of dreams, converted by his experience.
153. On the multitude of such writings, *RE* VIA, 2236-41.
154. Artemid. 1, 61. See D.del Corno, *Graecorum de re onirocritica scriptorum reliquiae*, Milan 1969; *RE* VIA, 2233-45, s.v. 'Traumdeutung'. On athletes' dreams, H.A. Harris, *Sport in Greece and Rome*, London 1972, 244-61.
155. Suet., *DA* 94, 5; *RE* XVII, 200-12. There is nothing in Cicero's *De divinatione* (45/4 BC) to suggest that astrology had as yet any widespread vogue in Rome (but cf. *TD* 1, 95, people who die before 'Chaldaeorum promissa'). On astrology and magic, see Toutain, *o.c.* (n.1), II, 179-226.

156. *TA* 14, 9, 5; *TH* 1, 22. Galba, CD 57, 19, 4.

157. *TA* 2, 30, 1.

158. See n.170 below.

159. AM 28, 4, 24. Emperors etc, *RE* II, 1819f.; 1823f. Women, Juv. 6, 553-81.

160. [Quintil.], *Decl.* 4.

161. 'Qui malum carmen incantassit,' tab. viii, *FIRA*,² 1, p.52.

162. Plin., *NH* 30, 1ff, 'magicae vanitates'.

163. *RE*, s.v. 'defixio', 'devotio'; A. Audollent, *Defixionum Tabellae*, Paris 1904; *TA* 2, 69, 5; 2, 30, 2.

164. [Quintil.], *Decl.* 10, esp. 4, 7f., 13, 15.

165. Audollent, *o.c.* (n.163), e.g. 216f., 232-45, 246f., 252f.; Toutain, *o.c.* (n.1), II, 217.

166. Just as Stoics believed in oracles, Epict., *Diss.* 3, 1, 16-18.

167. Cic., *De div.* 2, 119-48.

168. Plut., *Cic.* 44, 2-7.

169. Panaetius, Cic., *De div.* 2, 97. Stoics, *RE* II, 1813f.; *TA* 6, 22; Lucian, *Alex.* 8; 32; Apul., *Apol.* 97.

170. Aug., *CD* 5, 1-4; Cic., *De div.* 2, 90; 94; 97.

171. *TA* 6, 22; Sen., *Suas.* 3, 3 (Cestius); [Quintil.], *Decl.* 4, 13; Justin 12, 13, 5.

172. Plin., *NH* 30, 13.

173. Cic., *Pro Font.* 31.

174. Plin., *NH* 30, 12.

175. Diod. 20, 14; B.M. Warmington, *Carthage*, London 1960, 130-3. Cf. Cic., *De rep.* 3, 15.

176. Tertull., *Apol.* 9; Aug., *CD* 7, 26; Toutain, *o.c.* (n.1), III, 78-80.

177. JC, *BG* 6, 16; Pomp. Mela 3, 18; Plin., *NH* 30, 13; Suet., *D.Cl.* 25, 5; *TH* 4, 54; *RE* V, 1733-5. The absence of any mention of Druidism in Tacitus' *Agricola* is significant.

178. Plut., *QR* 83, on which see C. Cichorius, *Röm. Studien*, Berlin 1922, 7-21.

179. Nemi, Strabo 5, 3, 12, 239; Paus. 2, 27, 4; Frazer on Ovid, *Fast.* 3, 271. Iberia, Strabo 11, 4, 7, 503. Druids, Diod. 5, 31, 3. Jews, Jos., *C.Ap.* 2, 89-96. Cf. Dio Chrys., *Or.* 4, 67 (Persia).

180. L. 22, 57, 6; Plut., *Numa* 15, 7-10; Ovid, *Fast.* 3, 333-44. Argei, Ovid, *Fast.* 5, 621-2 with Frazer's note; DH 1, 38, 3; Varro, *LL* 7, 44; Plut., *QR* 32; G. Wissowa, *RE* II, 689-700 and *Gesammelte Abhandlungen*, Munich 1904, 211-29 (who believes that 27 Greeks were in fact sacrificed in the third century BC).

181. Oros. 4, 13, 3; CD fr. 47; Plut., *Marcell.* 3, 6; L. 22, 57, 6; Plut., *QR* 83 with Rose's note; Cichorius, *o.c.* (n.178), 10f.; G. Wissowa, *RK*,² 420f.

182. Plin., *NH* 28, 12; Suet., *Domit.* 8, 3f.; CD 67, 3, 4; Pliny, *Ep.* 4, 11; CD 77, 16, 1-3. See my *Roman Women*² London 1974, 238-42. *Feriae Latinae*, Tertull., *Apol.* 9, 5; Min. Felix 30, 4, etc. Wissowa, *RK*² 124, n.8 rejects; *RE* VI, 2215 (Samter) keeps an open mind.

183. JC, *BG* 7, 77; Cic., *Pro Rosc. Am.* 100. In Mysia, Lucian alleged, Peregrinus killed his father on the ground that at sixty he had lived long enough, *De mort. Peregr.* 10.

184. So Ovid, *Fast.* 5, 633f. See my *Life and Leisure in Ancient Rome*, London 1969, 169, 392f., n.2.

185. Sardinia, *FGH* 566, F. 64 (Timaeus); Ceos, Strabo 10, 5, 6, 486; VM 2, 6, 7f.

186. Pomp. Mela 3, 37.

187. Strabo 11, 11, 3 and 8, 517, 520.

188. Serv. on Virg., *Aen.* 12, 603; *Dig.* 48, 19, 38, 12; *ILS* 7212, II, 5f.; Virg., *Aen.* 6, 434-9; [Quintil.], *Decl.* 10, 16.

189. Plin., *Ep.* 1, 12; 1, 22; 3, 7, 1; 3, 9, 5; 6, 24; CD 78, 23, 6 (Julia Domna, because of cancer on the breast). Cf. Plut., *Aem.* 35 (Paullus' indication to the defeated Perseus that there was an easy way out of his troubles, if he liked to take it).

190. Plato, *Laws* 873c,d; Cic., *Ad fam.* 3, 60; MA, *Med.* 5, 29; 8, 47; 10, 8 and 32; 11, 3; Aug., *CD* 1, 16-27; Epict. 1, 9, 10-17; 1, 24, 20; 1, 25, 20; 1, 29, 29; 2, 1, 19f.; 2, 6, 22; 3, 13, 14f. Epicureans, Cic., *De fin.* 1, 49 and 52. See J.M. Rist, *Stoic Philosophy*, Cambridge 1969, 233-55; R. Hirzel, 'Der Selbstmord', *Archiv f. Religionswiss.* 11, 1908, 75-104, 243-84, 417-76, esp. 433-76 on the Romans.

191. Augustine, however, thought Regulus' death a far better example than Cato's, *CD* 1, 24 (cf. 1, 15). D. Brutus, Sen., *Ep.* 82, 12f.

192. Sen., *Ep.* 12, 10; 26, 10; 70; 77; 104, 21.

193. Sen., *De ira* 3, 15, 4.

194. [Quintil.], *Decl.* 380 (Sen., *Controv.* 3, 9); Sen., *Ep.* 77, 7; Plut., *Otho* 17.

195. *TA* 11, 3; 16, 19, 5.

196. *Dig.* 48, 19, 28 praef. and 11; 48, 19, 38, 1.

197. VM 2, 6, 14; Quint. Curt. 8, 9, 32; Lucan, *Phars.* 3, 240-3.

198. Arr., *Anab.* 7, 3; Strabo 15, 1, 68, 717f.; *RE* X, 1544-6.

199. Strabo 15, 1, 73, 720; CD 54, 9, 8-10.

200. AG 12, 11; AM 29, 1, 39; Lucian, *De mort. Peregr.; Fugitivi* 1; *RE* XIX, 656-63.

201. Paus. 6, 8, 4.

202. Justin 19, 1, 10-12.

203. *TH* 5, 5.

204. Cic., *De legg.* 2, 58 (quoting XII Tables); Toynbee, *o.c.* (n.1) 39f.; Plin., *NH* 7, 187, who says inhumation was earlier.

205. Festus, s.v. 'bustum', 29L.

206. Plin., *NH* 7, 187 (cf. App., *BC* 1, 105f., 493-500 for a vivid account of Sulla's funeral). *ILS* 6087, 73 shows both cremation and inhumation practised in a Roman colony at the time of Julius Caesar.

207. See A.D. Nock, 'Cremation and burial in the Roman Empire', *HTR* 25, 1932, 321-59; J. Toynbee, J. Ward Perkins, *The Shrine of St Peter*, London 1956, 109-117; Toynbee, *o.c.* (n.1), 40f.

208. Toynbee, Ward Perkins, *o.c.* (n.207), 112f.

209. Nock, *o.c.* (n.207), 358f.

210. Nock, *o.c.* (n.207), 357.

211. Macrob., *Sat.* 7, 7, 5.

212. *TA* 16, 6, 2; Stat., *Silv.* 5, 1, 208-46, esp. 226f.; Toynbee, *o.c.* (n.1), 41f.

213. See R. Meiggs, *Ostia*,² Oxford 1973, 455-70; Toynbee, Ward Perkins, *o.c.* (n.207).

214. His will forbad interment in his mausoleum of his daughter and granddaughter, Suet., *DA* 101, 3.

215. On *columbaria* in general and at Ostia in particular, R. Meiggs, *o.c.* (n.213), 458-63.

216. *CIL* VI, 2, nos. 3926-8397.

217. Hor., *Sat.* 1, 8, 8-16; PA, s.v. 'Horti Maecenatis'.

218. H. Thylander, *Inscr. du port d'Ostie*, Lund 1952, A19.

219. See I.A. Richmond, J.C.M. Toynbee, *OCD*,² s.v. 'Catacombs'; Toynbee, *o.c.* (n.1), 234-44.

220. Suet., *DA* 101, 4; CD 56, 42, 3. The 'miracle' repeated in the case of Pertinax, CD 74, 5, 5.

221. Suet., *DA* 100, 4; CD 56, 46, 2; 59, 11, 4; Sen., *Apok.* 1.

222. See on all this E. Bickermann, 'Die römische Kaiserapotheose', *Archiv. f. Religionswiss.* 17, 1929, 1-34. On the burning of the image of Pertinax, CD 74, 4f.

223. See PA, s.v. 'Scalae Gemoniae'; Suet., *Tib.* 75, 1. Some Ethiopians threw their dead into a river, Strabo 17, 2, 3, 822.

224. *De luctu* 21 (inaccurate in some of its statements), tr. F.G. Fowler. Cf. Strabo 17, 2, 3, 822, a variety of practices in Ethiopia.

225. *De luctu* 18.

226. Strabo 16, 4, 26, 784.

227. Strabo 15, 3, 18, 734 and 20, 735; 16, 1, 20, 746 (cf. Herod. 1, 140); Cic., *TD* 1, 108; Justin 41, 3, 5.

228. Strabo 16, 2, 45, 764; Suet., *DA* 18, 1; CD 51, 16, 5.

229. Strabo 11, 4, 8, 503.

230. VM 2, 6, 10; Diod. 5, 28, 6.

231. DH, *AR* 2, 56.

232. Suet., *Domit.* 13, 2.

233. Lucian, *Dial. mort.* 3, 2.

234. Plut., *Mor.* 360Cf.; *TA* 4, 38; Suet., *Vesp.* 23, 4.

235. See F. Täger, 'Zum Kampf gegen den antiken Herrscherkult', *Arch. f. Religionswiss.* 32, 1935, 282-92 for references to Cassius Dio's language about consecration and ruler-cult; also D.M. Pippidi, *Autour de Tibère*, Bucharest 1944, 135-45.

236. Lucian, *Dial. mort.* 3; 12-14; 16. Paus. 8, 2, 5-7; cf. 8, 9, 7f. (Mantineans regarded Antinous as a god); 9, 27, 6-8 (on Heracles).

INDEX